The Antebellum Origins of the Modern Constitution

This book argues that conflicts over slavery and abolition in the early American Republic generated a mode of constitutional interpretation that remains powerful today: the belief that the historical spirit of founding holds authority over the current moment. Simon J. Gilhooley traces how debates around the existence of slavery in the District of Columbia gave rise to the articulation of this constitutional interpretation, which constrained the radical potential of the constitutional text. To reconstruct the origins of this interpretation, Gilhooley draws on rich sources that include historical newspapers, pamphlets, and congressional debates. Examining free black activism in the North, abolitionism in the 1830s, and the evolution of proslavery thought, this book shows how in navigating the existence of slavery in the District and the fundamental constitutional issue of the enslaved's personhood, antebellum opponents of abolition came to promote an enduring but constraining constitutional imaginary.

Simon J. Gilhooley is Assistant Professor of Political Studies and American Studies, Bard College. He has been the recipient of fellowships from the American Council of Learned Societies, the McNeil Center for Early American Studies, the Andrew W. Mellon Foundation, and the Gilder Lehrman Institute of American History, among others.

Cambridge Studies on the American Constitution

Series Editors

Maeva Marcus, The George Washington University
Melvin I. Urofsky, Virginia Commonwealth University
Mark Tushnet, Georgetown University Law Center
Keith Whittington, Princeton University

Cambridge Studies on the American Constitution seeks to publish works that embrace constitutional history, politics, law, and legal and political theory to better explain constitutional politics outside the courts, the determinants of constitutional change, the relationship between constitutional lawmaking and conventional politics, the nature of constitutional regimes, comparative approaches to constitutional systems, and the criteria for evaluating constitutional success and failure. Books in the series will explore these and similar issues within a variety of theoretical and methodological traditions, with special emphasis given to research using interdisciplinary approaches in innovative ways.

Titles in the Series

The Antebellum Origins of the Modern Constitution

Slavery and the Spirit of the American Founding

SIMON J. GILHOOLEY

Bard College, New York

CAMBRIDGE
UNIVERSITY PRESS

CAMBRIDGE
UNIVERSITY PRESS

University Printing House, Cambridge CB2 8BS, United Kingdom

One Liberty Plaza, 20th Floor, New York, NY 10006, USA

477 Williamstown Road, Port Melbourne, VIC 3207, Australia

314-321, 3rd Floor, Plot 3, Splendor Forum, Jasola District Centre, New Delhi - 110025, India

103 Penang Road, #05-06/07, Visioncrest Commercial, Singapore 238467

Cambridge University Press is part of the University of Cambridge.

It furthers the University's mission by disseminating knowledge in the pursuit of education, learning and research at the highest international levels of excellence.

www.cambridge.org
Information on this title: www.cambridge.org/9781108791458
DOI: 10.1017/9781108866125

First published 2020
First paperback edition 2022

A catalogue record for this publication is available from the British Library

Library of Congress Cataloging in Publication data
NAMES: Gilhooley, Simon J., author.
TITLE: The antebellum origins of the modern Constitution : slavery and the spirit of the
American founding / Simon J. Gilhooley.
DESCRIPTION: Cambridge, United Kingdom ; New York, NY : Cambridge University Press,
2021. | Series: Cambridge studies on the American Constitution | Includes bibliographical
references and index.
IDENTIFIERS: LCCN 2020024247 (print) | LCCN 2020024248 (ebook) | ISBN 9781108496124
(hardback) | ISBN 9781108866125 (ebook)
SUBJECTS: LCSH: Constitutional history – United States. | Slavery – Law and legislation –
United States – History. | Antislavery movements – United States – History. | United States –
Politics and government – History.
CLASSIFICATION: LCC KF4541 .G548 2021 (print) | LCC KF4541 (ebook) | DDC 342.7308/7–
dc23
LC record available at https://lccn.loc.gov/2020024247
LC ebook record available at https://lccn.loc.gov/2020024248

ISBN 978-1-108-49612-4 Hardback
ISBN 978-1-108-79145-8 Paperback

For Pınar.
And S., N., & L.

All new laws, though penned with the greatest technical skill and passed on the fullest and most mature deliberation, are considered as more or less obscure and equivocal, until their meaning be liquidated and ascertained by a series of particular discussions and adjudications.

James Madison
"Federalist No. 37" (1787)

Base of heart! They vilely barter
   Honor's wealth for party's place;
Step by step on Freedom's charter
   Leaving footprints of disgrace;

John Greenleaf Whittier
"At Washington" (1845)

Contents

Acknowledgments

No book is the work of a single author alone, and this book is no different. I owe a debt of gratitude to more people and in more ways than I will be able to do justice to here. But in the hope of doing some justice to that task, I would like to thank the following people and institutions for their help and support.

Two institutions – the McNeil Center for Early American Studies and the American Council of Learned Societies – provided yearlong support at different junctures of this project. Without that support this book would not exist. Additionally, I would like to thank the Library Company of Philadelphia, the Historical Society of Pennsylvania, the Gilder Lehrman Institute of American History, and the Institute for Political History for supporting research for this project at different points.

At the McNeil Center I was surrounded by a group of generous and inspiring scholars. They pushed me to think more about slavery and race, and so this project owes much to them. My thanks go to Daniel K. Richter and Laura Keenan Spero for the opportunity and to Cheryl Collins, Rob Gamble, Kate Gaudet, Alea Henle, Nicole Ivy, Matt Karp, Whitney Martinko, Jayne Ptolemy, Joseph Rezek, Caitlin Fitz, and Christopher Bilodeau. In particular, Felicity Donohoe and Michael Goode were great companions throughout the year.

The Humanities Institute at the University of South Florida provided a home for me during a sabbatical that enabled much of the writing to be carried out. I remain deeply grateful to Elizabeth Kicak and Mallory Danley for making this possible and for their support during that year.

At my permanent academic home, Bard College, I have been supported in so many ways by so many people that I hesitate to pick anyone out for particular thanks lest I forget others or suggest that their support was not appreciated. But with this risk in mind, I point to a few. Special thanks are due to Christian Crouch, who has been a kind and available mentor for a fellow early Americanist. Bard College students in two seminars, "The Individual and American Democracy" and "Ideology in America," have allowed me to discuss the themes of this book and sharpen my ideas in conversation with theirs. My colleagues in Political Studies have allowed me the intellectual space to pursue my interests beyond the confines of the common American Politics curriculum and so to them, and to the culture of Bard, I am thankful. I arrived at Bard as part of a cohort of young scholars who have proven stimulating and exciting colleagues and great friends and it is through them that we have found a home in the Hudson Valley – thank you.

This project emerged from a dissertation at Cornell University. The help and advice I received from my committee then and since have shaped this book and myself as an academic. Without Jason Frank, M. Elizabeth Sanders, Richard Bensel, and Aziz Rana, this book would not exist. Their encouragement to think more about constitutional text and spirit prompted the transformation of the dissertation into something almost wholly new. All have been great mentors to a young scholar in the years since. Alex Livingstone came to Cornell as I had one foot out of the door. He has nevertheless been an outstanding source of guidance and support, modeling a generous member of the academy.

The chair of my committee, Isaac Kramnick, sadly passed away before this book reached publication. I could not have wished for a more formidable example of how to be a scholar, teacher, and citizen than Isaac. He was without equal.

A group of friends made the years at Cornell University an enjoyable experience despite the winters – as they have made life since. Thanks to Ulaş Ince, Sinja Graf, Benjamin Brake, Julia Ajinkya, Phillip Ayoub, Jaimie Bleck, Idrissa Sidibe, Simon Cotton, Igor Logvinenko, Don Leonard, Berk Esen, Janice Gallagher, Desmond Jagmohan, Pablo Yanguas, Nolan Bennett, Kyong-Min Son, Alison McQueen, Kevin Duong, Vijay Phulwani, Aaron Gavin, Michelle Smith, and Michael Gorup.

At Cambridge University Press, Sara Doskow, Cameron Daddis, Padmapriya Ranganathan, and Gayathri Tamilselvan have overseen this project's transition through to completion. Thanks to them and to the series editors for making this possible and enjoyable.

The final round of thanks comes closer to home. My grandparents believed in education when it would perhaps have been easier to not have. I would not be where I am today without that commitment, made years before I was born. My parents maintained that commitment and have supported me at every turn, as well as in a myriad number of ways. The author of this book, and the achievement of this career, is much more "Gilhooley" (and "Morgan") than it is "Simon." Neşe, Lale, and Pınar have given me time for this project when I'm sure they would have rather I be doing something with them. None of this would be possible without Pınar. She has read every word, edited every chapter, talked me down, encouraged me to move forward, taken on childcare, let me work on weekends, and indulged more conversations on Antebellum constitutionalism than any individual desires. Thank you for agreeing to a second date after a disastrous first one. And thank you for building a life with me. It's your turn now.

Introduction

[I]n a Democracy, where all Men are equal, Slavery is contrary to the Spirit of the Constitution.[1]

Montesquieu (1748)

In early 1840, William Slade rose from his seat in the House of Representatives and began a wide-ranging speech on the right of petition, slavery, and the slave trade in the District of Columbia. Slade's speech came in the midst of an eight-year battle over the gag rule in the House of Representatives. The gag rule sought to ensure that the House did not discuss the issue of slavery by automatically laying any petitions relating to slavery "on the table" – which meant putting them on the agenda for later, but with the firm – indeed, clearly stated – intention of never getting around to them. The gag rule had been initiated in 1836 and lasted until 1844 and during that time, William Slade was a key figure in resistance to it.[2]

The crux of Slade's speech in 1840 was that Congress had the constitutional right to abolish slavery and the slave trade in the District of Columbia. In taking this position, he echoed many of his colleagues who had opposed the gag rule since its establishment in 1836. But the way in which he made this argument is worthy of note. In 1840, to establish that Congress had the power to abolish slavery in the District of Columbia, Slade examined a mass of evidence from the early Republic, including the opinions of James Madison in the *Federalist*

---

[1] Montesquieu's *Spirit of the Laws*, quoted as an epigram on the title page of St. George Tucker's *A Dissertation on Slavery*. St. George Tucker, *A Dissertation on Slavery: With a Proposal for the Gradual Abolition of It, in the State of Virginia* (Philadelphia: Mathew Carey, 1795).

[2] In 1837 his attempts to speak on the issue of slavery had resulted in Southern delegations walking out of the Chamber. Following his 1840 attempt to break the gag, the House of Representatives made the gag rule a standing rule of the House, and subsequently reaffirmed it each year until its defeat in 1844.

Papers, the ratification debates in Virginia, the 1789 and 1791 acts of cession that created the District of Columbia, and the practices of Congress since then. He took issue with what he labeled *"the compromise which lies at the basis of our federal compact"* – the possibility that the adoption of the Constitution contained within it an "implied faith" that Congress would not legislate upon slavery in the District of Columbia. Further evidence, including a common sense reading of the Constitution, the 1787 Northwest ordinance, Benjamin Franklin's petitioning, and once again the testimony of Madison, "the very father of the Constitution," was deployed to deny that *"this Union* was formed *to perpetuate slavery."*[3]

But then Slade changed tack. Thus far, he suggested, he had occupied a defensive ground, seeking only to show that claims that abolition in the District was unconstitutional were incorrect. He now intended to advance his argument in a positive direction. He would show:

Whoever will look into the history of the period when the Constitution was formed, will find that it was the universal expectation – an expectation excited by the slave States themselves, especially by Virginia and Maryland – that slavery would, at no distant day, be abolished by their own legislation. Abolition, as I have already intimated, and will now show, was emphatically the spirit of those times.

Slade then produced a litany of quotations from eminent figures from the founding era to show that antislavery "pervaded the Convention that formed the Constitution," that it "was the prevalent feeling of the Revolution," that a belief that slavery was destined for a *"speedy death"* was "the *public opinion* of that day." Slade ransacked the history of the founding period to show that opinion at that time was in favor of abolition, that *"Abolition ... was emphatically the spirit of those times."* Which is to say that in 1840, Slade believed a – perhaps, the – key to showing that Congress had the power to abolish slavery in the District of Columbia was to show that the spirit of the period in which the Constitution was being drafted and ratified had been in favor of abolition.[4]

William Slade's speech was the culmination of the series of developments in the 1830s that had made argumentation about the spirit of the founding period a crucial component of debates over slavery in the District of Columbia and indeed over slavery more broadly. Over the process of that decade abolitionists,

[3] *Speech of Mr. Slade, of Vermont, on the Right of Petition: The Power of Congress to Abolish Slavery and the Slave Trade in the District of Columbia; The Implied Faith of the North and the South to Each Other in Forming the Constitution* (Washington, DC: Gales and Seaton, 1840), 7–10, 17–22. Quotes at 17, 19, 20. Original emphasis. (Here and throughout the remainder of the book, pamphlet titles in excess of 200 characters have been pared down so as to be manageable while attempting to keep title clauses intact.)

[4] *Speech of Mr. Slade, of Vermont, on the Right of Petition: The Power of Congress to Abolish Slavery and the Slave Trade in the District of Columbia; The Implied Faith of the North and the South to Each Other in Forming the Constitution*, 23, 23, 25, 23. Emphasis added in last quote.

defenders of slavery, and a vast population that located itself between those two groups faced an unrolling of a constitutional issue to which neither the constitutional text nor their then established practices of navigating the issue of slavery could provide a solution. In the process of first articulating and then addressing this issue these Americans developed an understanding of the US Constitution that transcended the debates over expressed and implied powers that had animated constitutional debate in the early Republic. By the time Slade made his speech in 1840, abolitionists were attempting to occupy ground that opponents of abolition had been variously occupying since the mid-1830s. In arguing that Americans should understand the *spirit* of the 1780s as a basis for legitimating or restricting action in terms of constitutionality, Slade was acquiescing with a mode of constitutional construction developed by anti-abolitionists over the 1830s. Slade was appropriating and mobilizing the claim that a spirit of 1787 could define what was constitutional even if he sought to reach his own conclusions as to what that spirit actually was.

This book traces those developments to show how the spirit of the 1780s came to hold constitutional authority by the 1840s. It shows how the invocation of the concept of spirit was tied to the necessity of defending the institution of slavery from an abolitionist campaign that initially relied upon textual authority in order to seek abolition in the nation's capital. In doing so, I highlight the way in which a mode of appealing to the spirit of the founding arose in a particular historical context, and through a contentious dialogue between abolitionists and defenders of slavery. Rather than being an inevitable or natural way of thinking about constitutional authority, this account suggests that recourse to a spirit of 1787–88 was prompted in the 1830s by the requirements of slavery. Facing an abolitionist challenge that pressed directly upon the Constitution's equivocations as to the personhood of slaves, defenders of slavery sought to step outside the boundaries of the constitutional text while also retaining the rhetorical and political power of a constitutional argument against abolition. By invoking a spirit of the Constitution, and more precisely, a spirit of the time of the Constitution's creation, defenders of slavery read the Constitution's three-fifths clause as the entrenchment, in 1787, of a compromise to the institution of slavery.[5] In response to the pressure from abolitionists to acknowledge the humanity of slaves and to read the constitutional text as neutral with regard to slavery, defenders of slavery instead imbued it with historical significance. They refused the abolitionist proposition that the Constitution was an abstracted text and instead rendered it a record of a specific historical moment. It was, in short, to defend slavery and ensure its continuation that actors in the 1830s embraced the concept of a "spirit" of the founding.

---

[5] The Fugitive Slave and the Slave Trade clauses would also be offered as similar evidence.

SLAVERY AND THE CONSTITUTION

Recent scholarship has done much to enhance our understanding of the relationship between slavery and the Constitution. Scholars have shown how the creation and development of the US Constitution can only be fully understood against the backdrop of the "peculiar" institution.[6] Alongside these studies, other scholarly work has challenged the view of slavery as a premodern institution within the antebellum United States, such that contemporary assessments highlight the forward-looking vision of advocates of slavery.[7] Taken together, they present slavery as a robust institution in the mid-Antebellum period that shaped the politics surrounding it and which bent the Constitution to its own benefit. Comparatively, the study of the constitutional thought of abolitionists has been largely stable following the seminal work of William M. Wiecek in the 1970s.[8] Nonetheless, scholarship on the abolitionists as a body has remained constant, often joining the studies of slavery in presenting abolitionist constitutional thought within broader

---

[6] David Waldstreicher, *Slavery's Constitution: From Revolution to Ratification* (New York: Hill and Wang, 2009); Matthew Mason, *Slavery & Politics in the Early American Republic* (Chapel Hill: The University of North Carolina Press, 2006); Martha S. Jones, *Birthright Citizens: A History of Race and Rights in Antebellum America* (Cambridge, UK: Cambridge University Press, 2018); Don E. Fehrenbacher and Ward M. McAfee, *The Slaveholding Republic: An Account of the United States Government's Relations to Slavery* (Oxford: Oxford University Press, 2001); George William Van Cleve, *A Slaveholders' Union: Slavery, Politics, and the Constitution in the Early American Republic* (Chicago: University of Chicago Press, 2010).

[7] Edward E. Baptist, *The Half Has Never Been Told: Slavery and the Making of American Capitalism* (New York: Basic Books, 2014); Matthew Karp, *This Vast Southern Empire: Slaveholders at the Helm of American Foreign Policy* (Cambridge, MA: Harvard University Press, 2016); James Oakes, *Slavery and Freedom: An Interpretation of the Old South* (New York: Alfred A. Knopf, 1990); Seth Rockman, *Scraping By: Wage Labor, Slavery, and Survival in Early Baltimore* (Baltimore: The Johns Hopkins University Press, 2009); Sven Beckert and Seth Rockman, "Introduction: Slavery's Capitalism," in *Slavery's Capitalism: A New History of American Economic Development*, ed. Sven Beckert and Seth Rockman (Philadelphia: University of Pennsylvania Press, 2016), 1–27. For the sophistication of Southern thought in this period, see Michael O'Brien, *Conjectures of Order: Intellectual Life and the American South, 1810–1860* (Chapel Hill: The University of North Carolina Press, 2004). For a discussion of the attempts of proslavery thinkers to grapple with progress, see Eugene D. Genovese, *The Slaveholders' Dilemma: Freedom and Progress in Southern Conservative Thought, 1820–1860* (Columbia: University of South Carolina, 1992). For an account of proslavery thought as rhetoric, see Patricia Roberts-Miller, *Fanatical Schemes: Proslavery Rhetoric and the Tragedy of Consensus* (Tuscaloosa: The University of Alabama Press, 2009). For an account of proslavery thought as a mode of modern counterrevolution, see Manisha Sinha, *The Counterrevolution of Slavery: Politics and Ideology in Antebellum South Carolina* (Chapel Hill: The University of North Carolina Press, 2000).

[8] William M. Wiecek, *The Sources of Antislavery Constitutionalism in America, 1760–1848* (Ithaca: Cornell University Press, 1977). Two notable recent exceptions are Randy E. Barnett, "Whence Comes Section One? The Abolitionist Origins of the Fourteenth Amendment," *Journal of Legal Analysis* 3, no. 1 (2011): 165–263; Helen J. Knowles, "The Constitution and Slavery: A Special Relationship," *Slavery & Abolition* 28, no. 3 (2007): 309–28.

histories.[9] The result has been a greatly enhanced understanding of the Constitution and its relationship with the politics of slavery.

However, this burgeoning literature tends to be pulled in two directions at the expense of deeper understandings of the context in which a spirit of the Constitution arose in the 1830s. Positioned between the two historical landmarks of the founding era and the Civil War, studies of slavery and the Constitution often tend toward treating mid-Antebellum constitutional debates over slavery as legacies of the founding or precursors to the Civil War, or both. With respect to the legacy of the founding, the constitutional politics of slavery is presented as an unfolding of the ideological tensions, agreements, and institutional arrangements forged in the 1770s and 1780s. Slavery is a constitutional constant and the potentiality of division over it is always present until a decisive constitutional reordering becomes possible.[10] Here, the founding often becomes a moment of "original sin," and slavery's constitutionality is the consequence of a failure of the founding generation to adequately address it.[11] In the second instance of mid-Antebellum constitutionalism as precursor to the Civil War, which is not mutually exclusive with the first approach, the 1830s debates over slavery are positioned on a path to the 1860s, as further steps toward the sectional disunion that marks the beginning of the end of formal slavery in the United States.[12] Particularly with regard to the constitutional thought of the abolitionists, this approach seeks to understand the constitutional debates of the 1830s to 1850s as developments toward the constitutional amendments that followed the Civil War. Reading back into history, such approaches look for continuity and the endurance of ideas, placing actors and concepts in a narrative

---

[9] For a flavor of the broader work on abolitionism, see Manisha Sinha, *The Slave's Cause: A History of Abolition* (New Haven: Yale University Press, 2016); Lawrence J. Friedman, *Gregarious Saints: Self and Community in American Abolitionism, 1830–1870* (Cambridge, UK: Cambridge University Press, 1982); Benjamin Quarles, *Black Abolitionists*, (New York: Oxford University, 1969); Richard S. Newman, *The Transformation of American Abolitionism: Fighting Slavery in the Early Republic* (Chapel Hill: The University of North Carolina Press, 2002); Robert Fanuzzi, *Abolition's Public Sphere* (Minneapolis: University of Minnesota, 2003); Benjamin Lamb-Books, *Angry Abolitionists and the Rhetoric of Slavery: Moral Emotions in Social Movements* (New York: Palgrave MacMillan, 2016); W. Caleb McDaniel, *The Problem of Democracy in the Age of Slavery: Garrisonian Abolitionists & Transatlantic Reform* (Baton Rouge: Louisiana State University Press, 2013).

[10] Van Cleve, *A Slaveholders' Union: Slavery, Politics, and the Constitution in the Early American Republic*; Padraig Riley, *Slavery and the Democratic Conscience: Political Life in Jeffersonian America* (Philadelphia: University of Pennsylvania Press, 2016); Paul Finkelman, *Slavery and the Founders: Race and Liberty in the Age of Jefferson* (New York: Routledge, 2015); For a more polemical account, see Lawrence Goldstone, *Dark Bargain: Slavery, Profits, and the Struggle for the Constitution* (New York: Walker & Company, 2005).

[11] For a critique of this approach, see Matthew Mason, "A Missed Opportunity? The Founding, Postcolonial Realities, and the Abolition of Slavery," *Slavery & Abolition* 35, no. 2 (2014): 199–213.

[12] For example William Lee Miller, *Arguing About Slavery: John Quincy Adams and the Great Battle in the United States Congress* (New York: Alfred A. Knopf, 1996).

that could only be understood after the event.[13] In a parallel manner, both approaches inhibit recognition of the agency of actors in the 1830s, in terms of developing approaches to the Constitution within their own historical moment or informed by their own pressing contemporary concerns. For instance, such approaches often treat discussion over slavery in the District of Columbia in the 1830s as one among many concerns, despite being the very issue over which Congress ground to a halt in 1836 and in response to which the gag rules were initiated. Within the broad scope of 1787–1861, the District of Columbia may be one of a series of issues, but in the 1830s it is *the* issue around which innovative constitutional thought develops and petitioning of Congress mobilizes. Treating the 1830s as only part of a broader story obscures the theoretical and historical importance of that decade.

In treating the 1830s as the culmination of the founding, the beginnings of the Civil War, or a stop on the journey between them, the discursive and dialectical developments of abolitionist and proslavery constitutionalism in that decade are marginalized. As my analysis here will show, the understanding of the Constitution offered by William Slade in 1840 emerged from a rich and swirling brew of what might be labeled mezzo-constitutional thought. I borrow and adapt the concept of "mezzo" as applied by Daniel Carpenter in his study of bureaucratic innovation in between 1862 and 1928. Carpenter uses mezzo to identify administers positioned between executive level and subordinate administers who possessed "the ability to learn and the authority to innovate."[14] Here, I use the prefix to denote actors who possess those similar traits within the field of intellectual production. Such actors – for example, newspaper editors, activists, pamphleteers, and, crucially for this study, politicians – occupy a space close enough to popular debate to respond to resonances and through reprints and quotations legitimate and organize embryonic ideas and concepts. At the same time, they are in a position to diffuse and popularize ideas offered in elite texts and debates through selective editing, translation, and the authoritative framing of reprints of debates and public events.[15] The notion of a constitutional spirit that tied

---

[13] See, for example, Randy Barnett's attempt to "rehabilitate [the] memory" of the abolitionists by "expos[ing] the marked continuity" between abolitionist constitutionalism and that of the authors of the Fourteenth Amendment. Barnett, "Whence Comes Section One? The Abolitionist Origins of the Fourteenth Amendment," 169, 172. Identifying the origins of the Fourteenth Amendment is a characteristic of these approaches. Jacobus tenBroek, *Equal Under Law* (New York: First Collier Books, 1965). Knowles is notable for addressing abolitionist constitutionalism largely within its immediate historical context. Knowles, "The Constitution and Slavery."

[14] Daniel P. Carpenter, *The Forging of Bureaucratic Autonomy: Reputations, Networks, and Policy Innovation in Executive Agencies, 1862–1928* (Princeton: Princeton University Press, 2001), 21.

[15] On the role of newspaper editors as "nodal points" within the political system of the early nineteenth century, cf. Jeffrey L. Pasley, *"The Tyranny of Printers": Newspaper Politics in the Early American Republic* (Charlottesville: University Press of Virginia, 2002), 13.

actors back to the creation of the Constitution emerged from the interaction of disparate attitudes toward the Constitution, few of which reach the high levels of systematic constitutional thought contained within legal treatises.[16] Pamphlets, newspaper articles, debates between activists, and petitions provided spaces in which ideas could be developed, tested, and given coherence before percolating up into national debates and dispersing down into popular consciousness.

Seeing a constitutionalism centered on the historical moment of 1787–88 as emerging from a dialectical process centered on the 1830s has connotations for our understandings of constitutional development. At a first pass, the history traced here points to the contingency of constitutional development. As the structure of the book highlights (see below), the development of this constitutionalism was the result of a series of responses to the challenges and arguments being offered by actors within a political field. Black abolitionists responded to the challenges of the American Colonization Society (ACS), Southern supporters of slavery responded to the abolitionist pressures on the District of Columbia, and political abolitionists responded to the invocations of a founding spirit by the defenders of slavery. Each response was both a mobilization of political rhetoric to address a proximate goal and a further evolution of the political field itself, creating new frames of constitutional understanding and generating new challenges and options for responding to them. As a result of this complex process, it is difficult to maintain notions of constitutional development as the blossoming of seeds planted at the founding or even as the inevitable unraveling of institutions in the face of inherent tensions. The development of the constitutionalism traced here is, if not haphazard, then certainly incidental and somewhat self-generating.

This observation has implications for recent work on constitutional development and the relationship between slavery and the Constitution. Sean Wilentz's recent account of the evolution of constitutional thought regarding slavery during the Antebellum period suggests that the absence of the words

---

[16] In this regard, the book draws upon recent work to dedicated to tracing the ways in which constitutional development in the United States has occurred through interactions between a multiplicity of constitutional authorities, not least of which are individuals acting in "irregular" or extralegal ways. As H. Robert Baker reminds us, "the process of making constitutional law is more complicated than merely citing a line of cases." H. Robert Baker, "The Fugitive Slave Clause and the Antebellum Constitution," *Law and History Review* 30, no. 4 (2012): 1174. For other examples of approaches to constitutional law that move beyond legal opinions, see Christian G. Fritz, *American Sovereigns: The People and America's Constitutional Tradition before the Civil War* (New York: Cambridge University Press, 2008); Larry D. Kramer, *The People Themselves: Popular Constitutionalism and Judicial Review* (Oxford: Oxford University Press, 2004); Jones, *Birthright Citizens: A History of Race and Rights in Antebellum America*; H. Robert Baker, *Prigg v. Pennsylvania: Slavery, the Supreme Court, and the Ambivalent Constitution* (Lawrence: University of Kansas Press, 2012); Barry Friedman, *The Will of the People: How Public Opinion Has Influenced the Supreme Court and Shaped the Meaning of the Constitution* (New York: Farrar, Straus and Giroux, 2010).

"slavery" or "slave" in the Constitution provided a basis for the ultimate excising of slavery from the constitutional order.[17] In this telling, Abraham Lincoln's efforts at emancipation took hold of the potential of the Constitution of 1787, rendering the textual possibilities for antislavery real in the actualization of (some of) the framers' refusal to fully countenance slavery.[18] Placing much emphasis on the constitutional text, Wilentz suggests that to "dismiss the delegates' refusal to recognize the legitimacy of slavery as a linguistic technicality is to trivialize an important part of the convention's work."[19] In Wilentz's history, the Constitution always then held a kernel of antislavery, which though waylaid and shrouded by the ambiguity of the Constitution's relationship with slavery, ultimately came to fruition in the ending of slavery during the Civil War. But in light of the contingency of constitutional development over the decades of the mid-Antebellum period explored in this book, such a teleological account is hard to sustain. Where Wilentz argues that it is only "by evaluating the events of 1787 [that it is] possible to understand the struggles over the Constitution's meaning that unfolded over succeeding decades," the account offered here suggests that it is only through the struggles over the Constitution's meaning for slavery in those decades that the heightened significance of 1787 within those very debates came to be.[20]

Wilentz is not alone in viewing the textual product of 1787 as setting up a subsequent constitutional history that privileged that historical moment. Offering a very different argument in his *The Second Creation*, Jonathan Gienapp has argued that in navigating the ambiguities of the constitutional text, early American leaders came to "imagine the Constitution as *fixed* rigidly in place ... as an authoritative text circumscribed in historical time."[21] Gienapp shows convincingly that political actors in the 1790s grappled with a project of constitutional construction that gave rise to a novel way of seeing the constitutional text. Attempting to wrest from the text answers to questions not directly engaged by it, these actors came to see themselves as recovering meanings from the Constitution as "an archival object," an "untouchable historical artifact lodged in the archives."[22] As actors in the 1790s sought to "fix" the uncertainties and gaps in the text, they moved toward a project of "excavation" in which the reconstructed judgments of the original creators of the Constitution held greater authority than any contemporary actor.[23] Merging conceptions of the "textual constitution, the archival constitution, and the contingently authored Constitution," these actors unwittingly worked

[17] Sean Wilentz, *No Property in Man: Slavery and Antislavery at the Nation's Founding* (Cambridge, MA: Harvard University Press, 2018).
[18] Wilentz, *No Property in Man*, 241–42.   [19] Wilentz, *No Property in Man*, 11.
[20] Wilentz, *No Property in Man*, 20.
[21] Jonathan Gienapp, *The Second Creation: Fixing the American Constitution in the Founding Era* (Cambridge, MA: The Belknap Press of Harvard University Press, 2018), 4.
[22] Gienapp, *The Second Creation*, 168, 189.   [23] Gienapp, *The Second Creation*, 245.

to circumscribe the Constitution in time, gradually replacing "contemporary discretion" with "fixed historical meaning," and "[t]he "people's" Constitution" with the "framers' Constitution."[24]

The account of constitutional development in this book resonates in important ways with Gienapp's account. In foregrounding the contingent nature of constitutional development, contextualizing that development within a frame of actors navigating immediate political challenges, and in seeing a turn to the founding as motivated by a desire to bring stability to ambiguities contained within the Constitution, my own account and Gienapp's contain theoretical overlaps. And in seeing the legacy of those developments in contemporary constitutionalism and as a weakening of democratic modes of constitutionalism, we share, I think, political concerns. But there is also a significant departure in the conception of how 1787 came to be privileged within the American constitutional tradition. For Gienapp, it was the desire to "fix" the textual constitution that drove actors in the 1790s to turn to the project of excavation and to a privileging of the intentions of the actors of 1787. The argument in *The Second Creation* takes as its basis, and as a structuring assumption, a desire to bring fixedness to an ambiguous text. In that account, as with Wilentz, the historical turn to the framers is motivated by an attempt to bring specific meaning to the constitutional text. But I suggest that the turn to 1787–88 was not in support of the text but despite it.[25] As is discussed in the pages ahead, the congressional authority over slavery within the District of Columbia was not a question of textual ambiguity. Until the 1830s, few actors regarded that authority as in question. Indeed, during the Missouri Crisis those opposing the restriction of slavery asked why, if restrictionists really opposed slavery, they did not act against it in the District of Columbia where "the power of providing for their emancipation rests with Congress alone."[26] As I argue subsequently, the appeal to a spirit of the founding came not from a need to fix the constitutional text, but rather in an attempt to circumnavigate it. In the debates of the 1830s, it was not that the history of 1787 was holding as to the meaning of the textual constitution, it rather came to be the case that the history of 1787–88 illustrated a spirit that itself became holding *as* the Constitution.

This history also points to the centrality of slavery for constitutional development, but also for American political development more broadly. While the ideological tension between liberalism and republicanism has been presented in the past as the orientating battle within the early United States (and, indeed, in some cases across the entirety of its history), the centrality of

---

[24] Gienapp, *The Second Creation*, 290, 322.
[25] I use "1787–88" advisedly: the constitutional *text* arose from actions which took place in the summer 1787, but a constitutional *spirit* of that founding must stretch beyond that summer and Philadelphia and to the process of Ratification across the future States.
[26] *Annals of Congress, 16th Congress, 1st Session* (Senate, 1819), 351.

slavery and antislavery to the evolving understanding of the US Constitution suggests Rogers Smith is correct in calling for greater attention to the "ascriptive Americanist" tradition within the United States.[27] However, the historical story depicted in this book points to a centrality for slavery that belies its containment to particular moments or even extended periods – compromise over slavery was central to the initial formation of the US Constitution in the late eighteenth century, but its influence over American constitutionalism did not end there or even in 1865–68.[28] Slavery shaped both the text of the Constitution and the subsequent understanding of it in popular and elite political culture. The very constitutionalism that we navigate today is inflected by the historical intertwining of slavery and the Constitution that left an imprimatur on the latter, which remained long after the legal ending of slavery. This legacy is all the more striking as it implicates a facet of American political life that is often closely associated with liberalism and republicanism. The American conception of constitutional government, understood as an attempt to place constraint on democratic excess and to act as a guarantor of individual liberty through the tying of politics back to an initial moment of heightened political agreement, has its roots in the societal institution of slavery that operated to deny individual liberty and political agency to millions of black men and women. Even after the constitutional text was altered to forbid slavery, the constitutional grammar of the United States has remained modulated by its engagement with slavery.

THE RISE OF CONSTITUTIONAL SPIRIT

The argument of the book unfolds in several parts. The first part traces the various developments over the course of the 1820s and 1830s that formed the components of an emergence of a constitutional spirit of 1787–88. I begin by examining the manner in which the Missouri Crisis highlighted different concepts within competing constitutional imaginaries that would be important for the constitutional developments of the 1830s. As they debated Missouri's admission to the Union, "restrictionists" and "antirestrictionists" offered ideas about constitutional time, the role of a founding spirit in constitution construction, and the constitutional value of "compromise" that were echoed in the debates of the 1830s and then 1840s. Although they would not consolidate into the robust appeal to a constitutional spirit that developed in the mid-1830s, the Missouri debates provided a context for those later developments, signaling their centrality to constitutional thought regarding slavery and the potentiality of the latter as a site for a reconfiguration of constitutional construction.

[27] Rogers M. Smith, "Beyond Tocqueville, Myrdal, and Hartz: The Multiple Traditions in America," *American Political Science Review* 87, no. 3 (1993): 549–66.
[28] For discussion of the role of slavery in the Constitution's formation, see Waldstreicher, *Slavery's Constitution*; Finkelman, *Slavery and the Founders*.

In the second and third chapters, attention is turned to the ways in which claims of black citizenship led to invocations of a constitutional spirit, drawn from the Declaration of Independence and utilized to enable an expansive reading of the constitutional text. Beginning in the constitutional theories being developed in free black communities in Northern cities during the 1820s, the Declaration of Independence was read into the Constitution to create a constitutional obligation of equality under law. These arguments were taken up by the broader interracial abolitionist movement of the 1830s that grew out of free black opposition to the ACS and the white supporters converted to that opposition. The third chapter explores the expansion of those ideas in the wider movement of the 1830s and the complications they created for abolitionists' understandings of their relationship with the founding fathers and the generation of the Revolution.

The fourth chapter turns to the ways in which proslavery advocates defended the institution during and after the Virginia Debates in 1831–32. Just as shifts within antislavery circles in the 1820s and 1830s altered thinking about the Constitution, so too did the reaction to Nat Turner's Rebellion have repercussions for proslavery attitudes toward the Constitution. These developments produced less apologetic and future-oriented defenses of slavery, and foregrounded an understanding of slavery as a form of property relationship supported by constitutional principles. The result was the articulation of a defense of slavery reliant upon a constitutional interpretation that was subsequently shown to be vulnerable to abolitionist challenge.

The second part of the book turns its attention to the particular case of slavery in the District of Columbia and the constitutional implications of the abolitionist and proslavery clashes over the District in the early and mid-1830s. Chapter 6 explores the ways in which slavery and the slave trade in the District of Columbia became increasingly significant to both abolitionists and the defenders of slavery in the 1830s. Home to between 4,500 and 6,200 slaves during most of this period, tens of thousands more slaves likely passed through the District during forced migrations to the South and West. As a result of the developments discussed in the previous chapters, as well as the changing international attitude toward slavery, the symbolism of slavery within the capital took on heightened significance in the 1830s, raising the political and constitutional stakes of abolition within the ten miles square. Chapter 7 details the consequences of this rising symbolism in terms of the heated congressional debates of 1836 and the pressures brought to bear on the District by the abolitionist petition campaigns. It shows how the congressional debate became an opportunity for elite articulations of a constitutional theory of "return to the founding" as a mechanism for addressing the abolitionist claims of an express textual constitutional power of abolition in the District.

Chapter 8 offers a theoretical account of the constitutional theory of "the Compact" developed in parallel to the congressional debates over the course of the 1836 presidential election. The culmination of these trends and debates was Martin Van Buren's articulation of a constitutional theory that bound him – and the United States – back to 1787. The analysis highlights the ways in which the latter theory both departed from the theory of constitutional compact offered in 1798–99 and, at the same time, reinterpreted the notion of constitutional spirit so as to apply it to a specific historical moment.

In the final chapter, the book assesses the longer-term impact of these developments through an examination of the manner in which the abolitionists themselves adopted the theory of a constitutional spirit after the publication of Madison's *Notes*. It then traces the transformation of constitutional spirit as developed in 1836 into the notion that 1787–88 marked a constitutional "recognition" of slavery that subsequent Americans were obliged to honor. Such recognition was central to Chief Justice Taney's *Dred Scott* opinion in which Taney returned to the founding in order to resolve debates over the personhood of slaves by definitively rejecting their claims to citizenship. In conclusion, the book provides an overview of the development of constitutional spirit during the mid-Antebellum period, and considers what possibilities there might be for a constitutional politics that breaks free from the dead hand of the founding.

CONSTITUTIONAL SPIRIT IN THE NINETEENTH AND TWENTY-FIRST CENTURIES

In 2010, in the middle of his Dissent in the case of *McDonald* v. *Chicago*, Justice Stevens deviated from the immediate subject at hand (the Second Amendment's right to bear arms) to offer criticism of Justice Scalia's approach to the study of history. Justice Scalia, wrote Stevens, remained oblivious to the "malleability and elusiveness" of history and Scalia's "defense of his method" was "unsatisfying on its own terms."[29] Explaining the difficulties of historical research, Stevens offered:

Even when historical analysis is focused on a discrete proposition, such as the original public meaning of the Second Amendment, the evidence often points in different directions. The historian must choose which pieces to credit and which to discount, and then must try to assemble them into a coherent whole.

In place of Scalia's historical approach, Stevens offered his own method, which "focused more closely on sources contemporaneous with the [Second] Amendment's drafting and ratification," and which consciously acknowledged

---

[29] *McDonald* v. *Chicago* (2010). *McDonald* v. *Chicago* concerned the selective incorporation of the Second Amendment's right to bear arms (i.e., whether the individual right to bear arms recognized in the earlier *District of Columbia* v. *Heller* (2008) applied to the States as well as to the federal government). Quotations in remainder of the paragraph are taken from *McDonald* v. *Chicago*.

the subjectivity of the judge's use of history and thus allied it with a "transparency" that invited critique. Responding in his Concurrence, Scalia conceded, "Historical analysis can be difficult." But he argued that despite such difficulties his "historically focused method" was "less subjective [than Stevens'] because it depends upon a body of evidence susceptible of reasoned analysis rather than a variety of vague ethico-political First Principles whose combined conclusion can be found to point in any direction the judges favor." Stevens, wrote Scalia, sought not to "*replace* history with moral philosophy, but would have the courts consider *both*."

This episode, on its face, should strike the observer as extremely odd. Why would two Justices of the Supreme Court, legal practitioners at the apex of their professional field, in the middle of a landmark case, interrupt their examination of the legal precedents and points of law to engage in a squabble over historical methodology? But anyone who has paid attention to constitutional debates in the United States in recent years might regard this exchange as wholly unexceptional.[30] For as Stevens noted in his Dissent, "When answering a constitutional question to which the text provides no clear answer, there is always some amount of discretion; our constitutional system has always depended on judges' filling in the document's vast open spaces" – and, as both Stevens and Scalia concede, judges have, in turn, depended upon history to help them fill in those "vast open spaces."[31] To a significant extent, the modern Supreme Court Justice is expected to be an amateur historian, piecing together evidence to discern the underlying historical meaning of the Constitution.[32]

The judicial reliance upon history reflects a broader societal willingness to turn to history, and particularly to the history of the founding period, as a guide to resolving constitutional disputes. Appeals to the attitudes present at the Constitution's founding litter contemporary political discourse in the United States. Arguments for the constitutionality or unconstitutionality of particular policies that rest on a notion of what was intended or understood at the time of the Constitution's creation are regularly heard in the modern United States. As a society we follow our Justices in looking to historical endeavors to fill in the "vast open spaces" of our constitutional life. In such a way, we today retread the steps taken by the political moderates of the 1830s, aping their attempts to settle the controversial but unavoidable constitutional issues "to which the text provides no clear answer," by making recourse to the authority of a group of

---

[30] See, for instance, Saul Cornell, "Meaning and Understanding in the History of Constitutional Ideas: The Intellectual History Alternative to Originalism," *Fordham Law Review* 82 (2013): 721–55; Jonathan Gienapp, "Historicism and Holism: Failures of Originalist Translation," *Fordham Law Review* 84 (2015): 935–56.

[31] *McDonald* v. *Chicago*, 561 U.S.

[32] Whether they can do so effectively, or have taken advantage of those who can, is a point of contention. See, for example, Martin S. Flaherty, "History 'Lite' in Modern American Constitutionalism," *Columbia Law Review* 95, no. 3 (1995): 523–90.

historical actors dubbed "founders."[33] On issues as broad as freedom of
religion, reproductive rights, and control of firearms, we take our unconscious
lead from the debates over slavery in the 1830s and seek to tap the founding for
constitutional guidance. But rarely, if at all, is the historical context that gives
rise to such an approach to questions of constitutionality considered.
Examining the emergence in the 1830s of the claim that the spirit of the
founding provides the boundaries of legitimate politics can help us to think
about what such practices entail.

In striking ways, the recourse to the founding for meaning emerged in that
decade in a similar environment to the one that gave rise to originalism in the
late twentieth century. In both instances, a broad societal turn to the history of
the revolutionary period and questions concerning the position of the current
generation in the history of the nation provided a receptive environment for
a turn to the founding. Within such an environment, the emergence of issues to
which the constitutional text provided no direct answer, but which progressive
political forces sought to resolve constitutionally, spurred conservatives to
pursue the development of a mode of constitutional interpretation that made
recourse to the values of a founding generation. In the late twentieth century,
the bicentennial of the Revolution drew Americans' attention to an apparently
simpler time when political debates were more starkly black and white – both
metaphorically and literally. A seductive alternative to the "malaise" of the
1970s and the complex constitutional debates arising around racial equality
and reproductive rights for which the constitutional text apparently provided
no clear answers, the founding came to loom larger in constitutional theorizing
than it had in the 1950s and 1960s. One dimension of this shift was the growth
and success of constitutional originalism.[34]

---

[33] Indeed looking back to "The Founding" for guidance as to the parameters of contemporary
politics has become so accepted that a subgenre of literature has emerged which documents and
analyzes the phenomena. See, for example, Andrew M. Schocket, *Fighting over the Founders:
How We Remember the American Revolution* (New York: New York University Press, 2015);
David Sehat, *The Jefferson Rule: How the Founding Fathers Became Infallible and Our Politics
Inflexible* (New York: Simon & Schuster, 2015).

[34] In 1999, Randy Barnett declared, "Originalism is now the prevailing approach to constitutional
interpretation," a declaration that seems equally plausible twenty years later. Since Attorney
General Edwin Meese III's attempts to make a "jurisprudence of Original Intention," the
conventional approach to questions of constitutionality in the 1980s, some form of "originalism," be it original intent, original understanding, original meaning, or more recently public
meaning originalism, has been a locus of constitutional debate. For discussions of this approach
as a coherent approach to constitutional interpretation, cf. Keith E. Whittington, *Constitutional
Interpretation: Textual Meaning, Original Intent, and Judicial Review* (Lawrence: University of
Kansas Press, 1999); Antonin Scalia, *A Matter of Interpretation: Federal Courts and the Law*
(Princeton: Princeton University Press, 1997). On the changing construction of originalism, see
Keith E. Whittington, "The New Originalism," *Georgetown Journal of Law & Public Policy* 22
(2004): 599–613; Martin S. Flaherty, "Historians and the New Originalism: Contextualism,
Historicism, and Constitutional Meaning," *Fordham Law Review* 84, no. 3 (2015): 905–14. For

The constitutional thought of the 1830s, like the 1970s and 1980s, came on the back of a bout of nostalgia for the purity of a founding moment. For the generation that followed the revolutionaries of 1776 and the founders of 1787–88, history and historical memory proved a vital tool for navigating the pressures that their political inheritance bestowed upon them.[35] As François Furstenberg has noted, a political culture that prioritized "consent" could not embrace a historical legacy without some accommodation for autonomy. The result was an embrace of civic texts, and the veneration of them which saw "Americans ... continually recur to the moment of founding, and *choose* to grant their consent, if only tacitly, to the nation."[36] Through such recurrence, and in the development of a shared public memory of that moment, the second generation of Americans forged for themselves a role as the preservers of the social and political institutions that had secured liberty. At the same time, the political elites of the early Republic were highly conscious of the history of their Revolution and founding and the uses to which such a history could be put. Facing the release of a popular energy that risked destabilizing social order, they saw, and addressed, history as a theater within which the meaning of the Revolution could be shaped and contested.[37] Elites sought to preserve and

criticisms of originalism as a historical endeavor, see the essays of the *Fordham Law Review* to which Flaherty's article serves as an introduction. Randy E. Barnett, "Originalism for Nonoriginalists," *Loyola Law Review* 45, no. 4 (1999): 611–54; Edwin III Meese, "The Attorney General's View of the Supreme Court: Toward a Jurisprudence of Original Intention," *Public Administration Review* 45 (1985): 701–4; Edwin Meese III, "Address of the Honorable Edwin Meese III Attorney General of the United States before the D.C. Chapter of the Federalist Society Lawyers Division, November 15, 1985" (Washington, DC, 1985), www .justice.gov/sites/default/files/ag/legacy/2011/08/23/11-15-1985.pdf.

[35] I identify this generation as the second generation of Americans to emphasize their coming of age in the period after the Revolution and founding. In doing so, I depart from their usual designation as "the rising generation" within the literature of the 1820s for the purposes of clarity (there was always a "rising generation" within the literature and speeches of Antebellum America). By contrast, Joyce Appleby has identified this generation in her works as the first generation of Americans. Joyce Appleby, *Inheriting the Revolution: The First Generation of Americans* (Boston: The Belknap Press of Harvard University Press, 2000).

[36] François Furstenberg, *In the Name of the Father: Washington's Legacy, Slavery, and the Making of a Nation* (New York: Penguin Books, 2007), 22.

[37] On the uses of history and memory to shape the politics of the early Republic, see, for example, David Waldstreicher, *In the Midst of Perpetual Fetes: The Making of American Nationalism, 1776–1820* (Chapel Hill: The University of North Carolina Press, 1997); Peter C. Messer, *Stories of Independence: Identity, Ideology, and History in Eighteenth-Century America* (DeKalb: Northern Illinois University Press, 2005); Catherine L. Albanese, *Sons of the Fathers: The Civil Religion of the American Revolution* (Philadelphia: Temple University Press, 1976); Joyce Appleby, "The American Heritage: The Heirs and the Disinherited," in *A Restless Past: History and the American Public* (Lanham: Rowman & Littlefield Publishers, Inc., 2005), 71–90. On the popular pressures released by the Revolution and their threat to elites, see Woody Holton, *Unruly Americans and the Origins of the Constitution* (New York: Hill and Wang, 2007); Terry Bouton, *Taming Democracy: "The People," the Founders, and the Troubled Ending of the American Revolution* (New York: Oxford University Press, 2007).

spread a history that enhanced their own reputations and which aggrandized the roles they had played in the founding of the nation.[38] Making use of history as a didactic tool, political and social elites offered a history of the Revolution and founding that focused on the stories of high-status individuals and which linked republican virtue to submission to established governmental institutions.[39] The history of the Constitution itself was both colored by, and served as, an important site for this project. The early history of the Constitution "place[d] particular emphasis on the role played by the educated part of society" and tempered any democratic narrative through the use of Whiggish and classical modes of historical writing.[40] Motivated by a desire to unify the nation and secure reputations, such a practice of history left to the second generation of Americans a historiographical framework of great events undertaken by a great generation.[41] But in reality, the historical legacy of the founders did not leave their hands as a sacred and untouchable inheritance

---

John Adams famously predicted, "The History of our Revolution will be one continued Lye from one end to the other." His concern was that it would overly focus on Washington and Franklin. John Adams, "John Adams to Benjamin Rush, April 4, 1790," in *Old Family Letters, Series A*, ed. Alexander Biddle (Philadelphia: J. B. Lippincott Company, 1892), 55.

[38] Douglass Adair, "Fame and the Founding Fathers," in *Fame and the Founding Fathers: Essays by Douglass Adair*, ed. Trevor Colbourn (New York: W. W. Norton & Company, 1974), 3–26; Michael Warner, *The Letters of the Republic: Publication and the Public Sphere in Eighteenth-Century America* (Cambridge, MA: Harvard University Press, 1990); Paul K. Longmore, *The Invention of George Washington* (Berkeley: University of California Press, 1988); David D. Van Tassel, *Recording America's Past: An Interpretation of the Development of Historical Studies in America, 1607–1884* (Chicago: The University of Chicago Press, 1960); Robert E. McGlone, "Deciphering Memory: John Adams and the Authorship of the Declaration of Independence," *Journal of American History* 85, no. 2 (1998): 411–38. On the tensions that this gave rise to, see Albanese, *Sons of the Fathers: The Civil Religion of the American Revolution*, 209; Appleby, "The American Heritage," 79; Messer, *Stories of Independence*, 159.

[39] Messer, *Stories of Independence*.

[40] Messer, *Stories of Independence*, 146; Sydney G. Fisher, "The Legendary and Myth-Making Process in Histories of the American Revolution," *Proceedings of the American Philosophical Society* 51, no. 204 (1912): 53–75; Eran Shalev, *Rome Reborn on Western Shores: Historical Imagination and the Creation of the American Republic* (Charlottesville: University of Virginia Press, 2009). On the efforts of historians of the early Republic to aggrandize the founders, see R. B. Bernstein, *The Founding Fathers Reconsidered* (Oxford: Oxford University Press, 2009), chap. 4. On the self-fashioning of the founders, see Gordon S. Wood, *Revolutionary Characters: What Made the Founders Different* (New York: The Penguin Press, 2006), 23. Young Federalists grappled with the tendency to aggrandize the individual within Whiggish histories, but even they occasionally succumbed to a history of great men. Marshall Foletta, *Coming to Terms with Democracy: Federalist Intellectuals and the Shaping of an American Culture* (Charlottesville: University Press of Virginia, 2001), 205.

[41] This historiographical legacy was passed on to the second generation in the midst of a transition to historicism and Romantic conceptions of history. Dorothy Ross defines historicism as "the doctrine that all historical phenomena can be understood historically, that all events in historical time can be explained by prior events in historical time." Dorothy Ross, "Historical Consciousness in Nineteenth-Century America," *The American Historical Review* 89, no. 4 (1984): 910; On Romantic history in the United States, see Arthur H. Shaffer, *The Politics of*

but was negotiated and reconceived through the interactions between generations.[42] Only with time and incrementally did the Revolution and the founding take on the mantle of a historical Golden Age and were its figures and exploits deemed worthy of veneration.[43]

A crucial moment within this negotiated transition from founding to second generation came in the 1820s, and particularly 1826, as something of a symbolic changing of the generational guard took place. The deaths of Thomas Jefferson and John Adams, within hours of each other and fifty years to the day after the adoption of the Declaration of Independence, impressed heightened significance on the semicentennial.[44] Following Lafayette's tour of the United States (1824–25), which had prompted American attention to the history and legacy of the founding era, the deaths in 1826 served to underline the distance between the contemporary generation and the events of the founding era and the need to come to terms with them.[45] Although the second generation's efforts to understand their political inheritance did not begin in 1826, it marked a high point within an era of pointed and self-conscious consideration of history. It was this environment in which the developments within abolitionist and proslavery thought detailed in later chapters would evolve and take root. This history made the possibility of recourse to a spirit

History: Writing the History of the American Revolution 1783–1815 (Chicago: Precedent Publishing, 1975), 177.

[42] As indeed all history continues to be. Cf. Lowenthal's discussion of the later twentieth century's boom in "heritage" which seeks to "clarif[y] pasts so as to infuse them with present purposes." David Lowenthal, *The Heritage Crusade and the Spoils of History* (Cambridge, UK: Cambridge University Press, 1998), xv. See also Daniel Levin, "Federalists in the Attic: Original Intent, the Heritage Movement, and Democratic Theory," *Law & Social Inquiry* 29, no. 1 (2004): 105–26. On the intergenerational production of a collective memory of the Revolution, see Edward Tang, "Writing the American Revolution: War Veterans in the Nineteenth-Century Cultural Memory," *Journal of American Studies* 32, no. 1 (1988): 64.

[43] Sacvan Bercovitch suggests it took a "generation or so," while Michael Kamman dates constitutional veneration to the significantly later period of the 1850s. Albanese places it within "a 'winding down' of patriotism" following the founding. Sacvan Bercovitch, *The Rites of Assent: Transformations in the Symbolic Construction of America* (New York: Routledge, 1993), 165; Michael Kammen, *A Machine That Would Go of Itself: The Constitution in American Culture* (New York: First Vintage Books, 1987), 22, 94; Albanese, *Sons of the Fathers*, 9. By contrast, Edward Corwin believed that such veneration had been and gone by the Civil War. Edward Corwin, "The Worship of the Constitution," in *Corwin on the Constitution: Volume One, The Foundations of American Constitutional and Political Thought, the Powers of Congress, and the President's Power of Removal*, ed. Richard Loss (Ithaca: Cornell University Press, 1981), 55.

[44] For Jennifer Mercieca the event marked the second generation's arrival. Jennifer R. Mercieca, *Founding Fictions* (Tuscaloosa: The University of Alabama Press, 2010); Also, Andrew Burstein, *Sentimental Democracy: The Evolution of America's Romantic Self-Image* (New York, NY: Hill and Wang, 1999), 271–72.

[45] On Lafayette's visit, cf. Andrew Burstein, *America's Jubilee* (New York: Alfred A. Knopf, 2011), chap. 1.

of the 1780s ideologically available to the actors of the 1830s. But it also made the preservation of that spirit a normatively significant commitment.

The parallels between the 1830s and today's constitutional debates encourage us to think more critically about the alternatives to originalism offered in the current era. An appeal to an animating constitutional spirit is often a pivotal mechanism in constitutional theories that seek to break away from originalism and a commitment to interpreting the constitutional text in accordance with late eighteenth-century intentions, meanings, or expectations. Such theories often suggest that principles, rather than the text alone, allow for a constitutional interpretation that is forward-looking and broadly progressive. "Principle" is often offered in constitutional accounts as an alternative or addendum to text, often within a broader frame of "fidelity" to a constitutional settlement. While perhaps lacking the visceral and emotional attachment of "spirit," to the extent that "principle" invariably seems to come down to being some constellation of values its supporters attach to the Constitution, I suggest here its function resembles that of the idea of spirit.[46] In 1985, Justice Brennan sketched an alternative to a jurisprudence of "fidelity to ... 'the intentions of the Framers.'"[47] In this alternative, Brennan argued for judges to oversee the application of the "fundamental principles" of the Constitution to contemporary situations so as to further the "ideals of human dignity" entrenched in the Constitution.[48] This "Living Constitutionalism," with its concern for the unfolding of the principles of liberty and human dignity contained within the Constitution, was exemplified in Justice Kennedy's opinion for the Court in *Obergefell* v. *Hodges* (2015), upholding a constitutional right to same-sex marriage.[49] Reviewing the changing historical understandings of marriage, Kennedy said:

These new insights have strengthened, not weakened, the institution of marriage. Indeed, changed understandings of marriage are characteristic of a Nation where new dimensions of freedom become apparent to new generations, often through perspectives that

---

[46] For Justice Brennan, "principle" denotes those "certain values" declared "transcendent" by the Constitution. For Balkin, the principles "underlie the text." Liu, Karlan, and Schroeder talk of the "Framers memorialize[ing] our basic principles of government with broad language whose application to future cases and controversies would be determined ... by an ongoing process of interpretation." William J. Brennan, "The Constitution of the United States: Contemporary Ratification (Presentation to Text and Teaching Symposium, Georgetown University, October 12th 1985)" (Washington, DC, 1985), http://3197d6d14b5f19f2f440-5e13d29c4c016cf96cbbfd197c579b45.r81.cf1.rackcdn.com/collection/papers/1980/1985_1012_ConstitutionBrennan.pdf; Jack M. Balkin, *Living Originalism* (Cambridge, MA: The Belknap Press of Harvard University Press, 2011), 3; Goodwin Liu, Pamela S. Karlan, and Christopher H. Schroeder, *Keeping Faith with the Constitution* (Oxford, UK: Oxford University Press, 2010), xviii.

[47] Brennan, "The Constitution of the United States: Contemporary Ratification, (Presentation to Text and Teaching Symposium, Georgetown University, October 12th 1985)."

[48] Brennan, "The Constitution of the United States."   [49] *Obergefell* v. *Hodges* (2015).

begin in pleas or protests and then are considered in the political sphere and the judicial process.[50]

Under this view of Living Constitutionalism, the Constitution evolves with society, updated to reflect new technologies or societal norms, but always in accordance to the fundamental values that had inspirited it.[51] As an approach to moving away from the rigidity of a constitutional text written in the late eighteenth century, the notion of a constitution that evolves with society has much to be said for it. However, the Living Constitution approach has been subject to the persistent critique that it gives to judges an unlimited power to idiosyncratically define those fundamental principles and apply them at will to the country at large.[52]

Recent contemporary opponents of originalism have sought to mitigate the criticisms of the Living Constitution as overly empowering the judiciary by suggesting that an approach of "text-and-principle" offers a more anchored counter to the excesses of originalism. Critics of constitutional conservatism, including the American Constitutional Society in their 2009 *Keeping Faith with the Constitution*, have looked to "constitutional fidelity" and the principles of the Constitution to argue for more expansive constitutional interpretation than that allowed by the original expected applications or strict constructions of the constitutional text.[53] These constitutional theorists seek to guard the Constitution from devolving into "whatever a sufficient number of people think it ought to mean," by paying due attention to the "fixed and enduring character of its text and principles."[54] Balkin's *Living Originalism*, which the authors of *Keeping Faith with the Constitution* draw upon, spells this idea out in terms of *"framework originalism,"* which requires fidelity to the "rules, standards and principles stated by the Constitution's text," but also that Americans remain "faithful to the principles that underlie the text."[55] This approach seeks to empower not the judiciary but the people, offering space, in Balkin's words, for each "generation [to] do its part to keep the plan going and to ensure that it remains adequate to the needs and values of the American people."[56] Or as Liu, Karlan, and Schroeder put it, "the American people have

---

[50] *Obergefell v. Hodges*, 576 U.S. Quote at p. 7 Kennedy's opinion. (Page numbers refer to the slip opinion, available in pdf at www.supremecourt.gov/opinions/14pdf/14-556_3204.pdf.)

[51] Other approaches to Living Constitutionalism include common-law Living Constitutionalism (Strauss) and the Moral Reading (Dworkin). David A. Strauss, *The Living Constitution* (Oxford: Oxford University Press, 2010); Ronald Dworkin, *Freedom's Law: The Moral Reading of the American Constitution* (Cambridge, MA: Harvard University Press, 1997). See also Bernadette Meyler, "Towards a Common Law Originalism," *Stanford Law Review* 59, no. 3 (2006): 551–600.

[52] This is the very critique that Chief Justice Roberts and Justice Scalia offered in their dissents to Kennedy's opinion in *Obergefell v. Hodges*. *Obergefell v. Hodges*, 576 U.S.

[53] Liu, Karlan, and Schroeder, *Keeping Faith with the Constitution*.

[54] Liu, Karlan, and Schroeder, *Keeping Faith with the Constitution* 31.

[55] Balkin, *Living Originalism*, 3.   [56] Balkin, *Living Originalism*, 4.

kept faith with the Constitution because its text and principles have been interpreted in ways that keep faith with the needs and understandings of the American people."[57]

As positive as this "third way" between originalism and the Living Constitution sounds, the experience of the 1830s suggests that we ought to be wary of appeals to principle or reinterpretations of the latter to meet contemporary needs and understandings. One indicator that might induce concern for the critics of originalism is the extent to which erstwhile originalists seem to be willing to embrace the concept of principle.[58] Indeed, even the authors of *Keeping Faith with the Constitution* concede, "our view of constitutional fidelity is not at odds with originalism if originalism is understood to mean a commitment to the underlying principles that the Framers' words were publicly understood to convey."[59] As the debates of the 1830s discussed in this book illustrate, there is nothing inherently progressive or constitutionally expansive in the invocation of principle or spirit. Advocates of slavery and their anti-abolitionist allies saw in the spirit or principles of the Constitution a conceptual mechanism for foreclosing the emancipatory constitutional interpretation pushed by the abolitionists. Where abolitionists understood the Constitution's grant of exclusive jurisdiction over the District of Columbia to be an opportunity, or even duty, to emancipate and acknowledge the citizenship of the District's thousands of slaves, their opponents offered the spirit of the Constitution as a justification for rejecting that opportunity and reaffirming the constitutional politics that reduced the black population held in bondage to property rather than people. In the longer term, the development of this mode of constitutional thought would provide a basis for a *Dred Scott* decision that had broader territorial reach and which sought to collapse ascribed proslavery constitutional principles with an ambiguous text. We should be wary of a belief that spirit or principle offers the prospect of an easy or automatic corrective to any perceived excesses of originalism.

But if the history studied here pours some cold water on the progressive hopes of constitutional spirit, it should also prompt us to question whether the real issue is not, in fact, the broader willingness to turn to foundings per se. Despite Anne Norton's warnings of the "temporal imperialism" of a founding generation whose "dead hand of the past ... may weigh so heavily (or give so much assistance) to the living," the view that the origin of constitutional legitimacy lies with the initial authority of the people is shared across different

---

[57] Liu, Karlan, and Schroeder, *Keeping Faith with the Constitution*, 51.

[58] For example, see Randy E. Barnett, *Restoring the Lost Constitution: The Presumption of Liberty* (Princeton: Princeton University Press, 2003). Although some would debate the extent to which Barnett's embrace of principle is originalist. Paul O. Carrese, "Restoring The Lost Constitution: The Presumption of Liberty," *First Things*, August 2004.

[59] Liu, Karlan, and Schroeder, *Keeping Faith with the Constitution*, 40.

shades of political belief.[60] In the case of the United States, the process of drafting and then ratifying a constitution has become the moment in which the people themselves assent to a constitutional order and grant it democratic legitimacy.[61] Located during a moment of exceptional sovereign presence, much work on the democratizing of constitutional theory is concerned primarily with recapturing or reanimating that moment in subsequent chronological time.[62] Such is the reach of this framework, that David Singh Grewal and Jedediah Purdy have persuasively argued that neither originalism nor Living Constitutionalism have escaped from its grip, with each, albeit in different ways, laboring under the inability to reanimate the initial moment of sovereign power.[63] The experiences of the 1830s urge us to think in creative ways about the possibilities for a democratic constitutional politics that is not tied back to a moment of origin.[64] Indeed, this book seeks to guide us toward such an approach by turning at the end to Thomas Jefferson and Thomas Paine and examining the loose threads of a constitutional history not taken up. In the conclusion, I pick up some of those threads in the pursuit of a constitutional politics that offers a separation of chronology and authority. In place of the

[60] Anne Norton, "Transubstantiation: The Dialectic of Constitutional Authority," *The University of Chicago Law Review* 55, no. 2 (1988): 460. For example, Whittington, *Constitutional Interpretation*; Balkin, *Living Originalism*; Jason Frank, *Constituent Moments: Enacting the People in Postrevolutionary America* (Durham: Duke University Press, 2010); Kramer, *The People Themselves*; Scalia, *A Matter of Interpretation*. Norton nonetheless notes that through such "imperialism" founders, as "figures of history and public myth . . . will become the creation of their posterity." Norton, "Transubstantiation," 460.

[61] On the ratification, cf. Pauline Maier, *Ratification: The People Debate the Constitution, 1787–1788* (New York: Simon & Schuster, 2011).

[62] The seminal theorization of a "returning" popular sovereign remains. Bruce Ackerman, *We The People: Foundations* (London: The Belknap Press of Harvard University Press, 1991). On attempts to "tap" the founding moment in subsequent politics, cf. Jürgen Habermas and William Regh, "Constitutional Democracy: A Paradoxical Union of Contradictory Principles?" *Political Theory* 29, no. 6 (2001): 766–81; Cf. also Frank, *Constituent Moments*. On one hand, Stephen Holmes sees constitutions through the lens of a self-binding process that "can make it easier for the living to govern themselves." On the other hand, Norton has noted the ability of the present to constrain and shape the past in a dialectical process. In a somewhat similar vein, Bonnie Honig has urged democratic theorists to embrace the "paradox of politics" in which the people can navigate and contest their own historical understanding of their constitutional origin. Stephen Holmes, *Passions and Constraint: On the Theory of Liberal Democracy* (Chicago: The University of Chicago Press, 1995), 177; Norton, "Transubstantiation"; Bonnie Honig, "Between Decision and Deliberation: Political Paradox in Democratic Theory," *American Political Science Review* 101, no. 01: 1–17.

[63] David Singh Grewal and Jedediah Purdy, "The Original Theory of Constitutionalism," *Yale Law Journal* 127, no. 3 (2018): 664–705. On the historic prevalence of this viewpoint in the modern Anglo-American political thought, cf. Richard Tuck, *The Sleeping Sovereign: The Invention of Modern Democracy* (Cambridge, UK: Cambridge University Press, 2016).

[64] For an effort to similarly complicate the association of founding to an originary moment in time, see Angélica Maria Bernal, *Beyond Origins: Rethinking Founding in a Time of Constitutional Democracy* (New York: Oxford University Press, 2017).

responses offered by contemporary political theory of subsequent tapping of a founding, or later contestation over the founding, Paine and Jefferson instead conceive of a popular sovereign unmoored to a particular moment in secular time.[65] In a polity in which policies regarding the regulation of weapons, the provision of healthcare, and reproductive rights are beholden to a constitution originally authored over 225 years ago and well before the creation of the technologies governed by these policies, the discussion of a constitutional politics rooted in the present seems, at the very least, a timely endeavor.[66] If we are to create a truly democratic polity, it is perhaps time for us to leave 1787–88 behind. But first I turn to the story of constitutional spirit that begins in the late 1810s.

---

[65] For an example of each approach, cf. Habermas and Regh, "Constitutional Democracy"; Honig, "Between Decision and Deliberation."

[66] *District of Columbia* v. *Heller* (2008); *National Federation of Independent Business* v. *Sebelius* (2012); *Roe* v. *Wade* (1973).

I

The Constitutional Imaginaries of the Missouri Crisis

> The time has arrived which brings to the test the theory of the Constitution.
>
> Senator James Barbour (1820)[1]

Missouri's application for statehood was immediately and universally recognized as a moment of crisis for the Union.[2] The significance of the moment for the nation was signaled through references to it as the most pivotal debate since the adoption of the Constitution itself.[3] The sectional dimension of the conflict meant that the "Missouri question must necessarily excite warm feelings," reasoned the editor of *The American*, but the nature of the conflict meant more than that was at stake.[4] From the start of these debates, the important subtext of Missouri's admission as a conflict over slavery's place within the United States was widely recognized. A report of the congressional debates unusually editorialized in parenthesis "[*Here the SLAVE question will*

---

[1] *Annals of Congress, 16th Congress, 1st Session* (Senate, 1819), 107.

[2] Following the admission of Alabama as a slave State in 1819 and Illinois as a free State in 1818, the Union comprised twenty-two States, eleven free and eleven slaveholding. Debates regarding the admission of Missouri began in 1819 but became contentious when James Tallmadge attached an amendment to the needed bill in the House of Representatives requiring the manumission of children born to slaves after statehood upon reaching the age of twenty-five. In the following session, the Senate joined bills concerning the admission of Maine and Missouri, keeping the balance of free and slave States, and on February 17, 1820, agreed to forbid slavery north of 36° 30′ (the Thomas Amendment). The House of Representatives acceded to the compromise dividing the territory into free and slave at the 36° 30′ line, and after parliamentary maneuvering an Act admitting Missouri was signed by President Monroe in March 1820. For a summary of the events see William W. Freehling, *The Road to Disunion: Volume 1, Secessionists at Bay 1776–1854* (New York: Oxford University Press, 1990), 144–54.

[3] For example, cf. "Missouri Question," *The Genius of Liberty*, February 8, 1820; "The Missouri Question No. 1," *Boston Weekly Messenger*, December 2, 1819.

[4] *The American*, December 15, 1819.

23

come up]" after reporting the introduction of a bill to accord Missouri statehood.[5] A Virginian newspaper offered a poetic account of the debate's importance:

> This knotty point e'er long must be decided,
> On which the country is at large divided,
> Whether Missouri is, or ought to be,
> Like other states, entitled to be free –[6]

Of course, both sides of the ensuing debate agreed that the question raised was one of Missouri's freedom, but they held radically opposing views as to what that entailed. Those opposed to slavery's western expansion sought to marshal arguments inside and outside Congress to effect the admission of Missouri as a free rather than slave state. Against such "restrictionists" stood those who rejected any such restrictions upon the movement of enslaved persons, and so slavery, into the Western territories. The debate exposed sectional tensions over western expansion hitherto suppressed, revealing stark disagreements over the envisioned future of the country and prompting rhetorical feints toward disunion.[7] The resolution of the crisis would come in the form of a compromise that came to structure antebellum responses to intersectional conflict over slavery until its collapse in the Civil War.[8] In moving toward this compromise, the congressional debates would furnish debates over slavery and abolition with important components of a constitutional imaginary that would be invoked to navigate these issues in the following decades.

Three elements are evident in the congressional debates over Missouri's admission that provided building blocks for future constitutional development: the notion of a chronological gap between an authoritative founding and the contemporary moment, the idea of compromise, and the deployment of a founding spirit as a basis for deriving constitutional meaning. These elements were deployed within congressional debates, but in ways that did not reflect their subsequent importance. Glimpses of an embryotic idea of a historically binding spirit of compromise are present within this debate, but in a form short of its incarnation during the 1830s debates over slavery in the District of Columbia, or the broad concensus on the authority of the founding spirit that developed from the 1840s onward. Crucially, both restrictionists and antirestrictionists in

---

[5] "U.S. Congress," *Massachusetts Spy, or Worcester Gazette*, December 22, 1819.

[6] "Missouri Question," February 8, 1820.

[7] Robert E. Bonner, *Mastering America: Southern Slaveholders and the Crisis of American Nationhood* (New York, NY: Cambridge University Press, 2009), 12. On the rhetorical use of "disunion" in the debates, see Elizabeth R. Varon, *Disunion! The Coming of the American Civil War, 1789–1859* (Chapel Hill: The University of North Carolina Press, 2008), 42–45.

[8] Peter B. Knupfer, *The Union As It Is: Constitutional Unionism and Sectional Compromise, 1787–1861* (Chapel Hill: The University of North Carolina Press, 1991); John R. Van Atta, *Wolf by the Ears: The Missouri Crisis, 1819–1821* (Baltimore: Johns Hopkins University Press, 2015), 2.

1819–21 conceded that there had been a constitutional compromise over – and therefore recognition of – slavery in 1787–88. But both positioned such recognition within a chronological frame that pointed toward, respectively, historical aberration or a continuous process of compacting rather than teleology. Restrictionists saw a misalignment between the founding period and the present moment, while antirestrictionists urged a correspondence but not necessarily the playing out of a teleological spirit. Through appeals to the Declaration of Independence and the depiction of 1787–88 as a moment of exception, restrictionists largely distanced themselves from the Philadelphia convention and ratification. At the other extreme, proslavery antirestrictionists sought to deny any historical distance between 1787–88 and 1819–21 lest the federal compact be regarded as a historical artifact and thus not applicable to the novel challenges presented by Missouri's admission. The complex interactions of temporal frameworks, invocations of founding spirit, and appeals to conciliation rendered unlikely their consolidation into a singular constitutional imaginary. Nevertheless, the debates over Missouri's admission evince the presence and potential of these strands, and mark them as the context within which the history discussed in the following chapters unfolded.

1.1 MISSOURI'S ADMISSION AND THE CONSTITUTION

The Missouri Crisis marked a moment in which the national divisions over slavery and western expansion were brought into relief.[9] It was, in Robert Pierce Forbes's words, "a flash of lightning that illuminated the realities of sectional power in the United States and ignited a fire that smoldered for a generation."[10] It was also a crisis in which the constitutional status of slavery was a central feature.[11] For the most part, opponents of restriction

---

[9] Matthew Mason, *Slavery & Politics in the Early American Republic* (Chapel Hill: The University of North Carolina Press, 2006), 211; George William Van Cleve, *A Slaveholders' Union: Slavery, Politics, and the Constitution in the Early American Republic* (Chicago: University of Chicago Press, 2010), 256; Christopher Childers, *The Failure of Popular Sovereignty: Slavery, Manifest Destiny, and the Radicalization of Southern Politics* (Lawrence: University of Kansas Press, 2012), 40–41.

[10] Robert Pierce Forbes, *The Missouri Compromise and Its Aftermath: Slavery and the Meaning of America* (Chapel Hill: The University of North Carolina Press, 2007), 5.

[11] Gerald Leonard and Saul Cornell, *The Partisan Republic: Democracy, Exclusion, and the Fall of the Founder's Constitution, 1780s–1830s* (Cambridge, UK: Cambridge University Press, 2019), 157. While some accounts posited the conflict as a manufactured controversy on the part of a dying Federalist party, more recent accounts tend to suggest genuine ideological as well as moral issues gave rise to a conflict within the broad Republican coalition. Joshua Michael Zeitz, "The Missouri Compromise Reconsidered: Antislavery Rhetoric and the Emergence of the Free Labor Synthesis," *Journal of the Early Republic* 20, no. 3 (2000): 447–85; Sean Wilentz, "Jeffersonian Democracy and the Origins of Political Antislavery in the United States: The Missouri Crisis Revisited," *The Journal of the Historical Society* 4, no. 4 (2004): 375–401. However, for a recent account that foregrounds political motivations, see Varon, *Disunion! The Coming of the American Civil War, 1789–1859*, 39–49. Nonetheless, the complex manifestation

sought to avoid a discussion of whether slavery could be justified in itself and instead foregrounded arguments as to why any interference with it would be inexpedient or, preferably, unconstitutional.[12] Similarly, advocates of Missouri's admission with a restriction on slavery made recourse to the Constitution a pillar of their position and turned to the constitutional text for support. The debate came to hinge on what restrictions, if any, Congress could place upon a State's admission to the Union under its congressional power. As such, the Constitution and its meaning with regard to slavery was a focal point of the debate.

The constitutional debate over Missouri's admission focused on three elements of the Constitution that gave rise to duties on the part of Congress. Beginning with Congress's powers over the territories and the latter's admission as States, opponents of slavery urged restrictions on slavery on the basis of the constitutional provisions that "New States may be admitted by the Congress into this Union" and that "Congress shall have Power to dispose of, and make all needful Rules and Regulations respecting the territory and other Property of the United States."[13] By stating that new States "may" be admitted and by giving Congress power over the territories, advocates of restriction argued that Congress had the authority to attach conditions to statehood, including restrictions on slavery. As articulated by Senator Rufus King in two speeches of late 1819, it was the case that "every regulation upon this subject, belongs to the power whose consent is necessary to the formation and admission of such a state."[14] As Congress was that power, it could "therefore make it a condition of the admission of a new state, that slavery shall be forever prohibited within the same."[15]

With this reading of the Constitution in favor of qualified admission of new States as a basis, restrictionists sought to mobilize other constitutional clauses. The first was Article IV, Section 4's guarantee of a "Republican Form of Government" to every State in the Union, which some restrictionists argued precluded slavery from new States. A second important constitutional clause for the restrictionist argument concerned the potential for regulation of the slave trade after 1808. The advocates of restriction looked to the Constitution's

---

of these commitments in different regions and political contexts should not be discounted. For example, see Matthew Mason, "The Maine and Missouri Crisis: Competing Priorities and Northern Slavery Politics in the Early Republic," *Journal of the Early Republic* 33, Winter (2013): 675–700.

[12] Forbes, *The Missouri Compromise and Its Aftermath*, 40; Padraig Riley, *Slavery and the Democratic Conscience: Political Life in Jeffersonian America* (Philadelphia: University of Pennsylvania Press, 2016), 232–33; Mason, *Slavery & Politics in the Early American Republic*, 196.

[13] Article IV, Section 3, US Constitution.

[14] Rufus King, *The Substance of Two Speeches, Delivered in the Senate of the United States, on the Subject of the Missouri Bill* (Philadelphia: Clark & Raser, 1819), 2.

[15] King, *The Substance of Two Speeches*, 2.

provision that "the Migration or Importation of such Persons as any of the States now existing shall think proper to admit, shall not be prohibited by the Congress prior to the year eighteen hundred and eight," in order to show that the Constitution granted Congress regulatory powers over the movement of slaves.[16] Crucial to this argument was the use of the terms "migration" and "importation" in the clause. Laying out this argument in his *Free Remarks on the Spirit of the Federal Constitution* (1819), Robert Walsh Jr. argued that

the federal government is recognized to have the power of prohibiting at once and for ever, not only the *importation* of slaves from abroad, into the territories and new states, but their *migration*, or removal from the old states into the new or into the territories.[17]

Assuming that there was no excessive wording in the Constitution, opponents of slavery argued that "migration" must denote movement distinct from "importation." Walsh argued again:

We are entitled to imagine, that the lettered men and distinguished writers who framed the constitution would, where precision was so important, have confounded terms correctly and commonly understood to be of distinct import; or, in the hypothesis that this was not notoriously the case, have fallen into sheer tautology.[18]

Writing in the *Baltimore Patriot*, "W.W.H." outlined similar claims: "it is a rule of construction, that a statute (and the Constitution is a statute) ought upon the whole to be so construed, that if it be possible, no clause, sentence or word shall be superfluous, void, or insignificant."[19] Given to understand the text in this manner, W.W.H. concluded that "migration is not a mere expletive to round a period; but a substantive term, signifying a distinct idea." As such the clause ought to be read as giving Congress the power to regulate the importation *and* migration of slaves after 1808. As Missouri could only be populated with slaves through their migration into that territory or State, W.W.H. argued that the congressional restriction of slavery was implicitly constitutional.[20]

Opponents of restriction countered these constitutional interpretations by offering a reading of the Constitution in which the broader sense of the document was prioritized. For many antirestrictionists, the forensic reading of the Constitution offered by restrictionists seemed to be at the expense of its commonsense meaning. Representative Robert R. Reid of Georgia rejected the restrictionists' constructions of the Constitution as "in direct hostility with the letter as well as the spirit of the Constitution" and urged his colleagues to

---

[16] Article I, Section 9, US Constitution.

[17] Robert Jr. Walsh, *Free Remarks on The Spirit of the Federal Constitution, the Practice of the Federal Government, and the Obligations of the Union, Respecting the Exclusion of Slavery from the Territories and New States* (Philadelphia: A. Finley, 1819), 18.

[18] Walsh, *Free Remarks on The Spirit of the Federal Constitution*, 18–19.

[19] "Missouri Question," *Baltimore Patriot & Mercantile Advertiser*, January 26, 1820.

[20] For further discussion of this point of debate, cf. William M. Wiecek, *The Sources of Antislavery Constitutionalism in America, 1760–1848* (Ithaca: Cornell University Press, 1977), 118.

"receive words according to the intention of those who utter them."[21] As the framers of the Constitution were themselves the owners of enslaved people and recognized slavery in the Constitution, opponents of restriction rejected the premise that the former had envisioned a prohibition on the admission of slave-holding States. Appealing to the notion that the Constitution had been a compact between free and slave states, antirestrictionists emphasized the importance of not prizing the abstracted constitutional text over the principles informing it. As expressed by a writer in the *Rhode-Island American*, this view held that the "only safeguard of our liberty is a scrupulous fidelity to the principles of our Constitution."[22] Worried about the dangers arising "whenever attempts are made to impose new constructions upon the Constitution," this writer voiced an opinion that allowing questions over the meaning of precepts invited "sophistical construction[s]" and struck a blow to "that feeling of reverence, which is the safeguard of all institutions."[23] In his extended articulation and defense of States' rights, John Taylor warned that in the Missouri debates, "the pure and invigorating spirit of the constitution has been assailed by the science of construction; and its words are turned into worms for eating up its vitals."[24] Merging a fidelity to "strict construction" with a resistance to the dilution of States' rights, antirestrictionists called on their opponents to administer the Constitution in the same "spirit of concession" that allowed for its creation – that is, to respect the interests of the slave-holding States in their "five hundred millions of dollars" of slave property.[25]

1.2　CONSTITUTIONAL COMPROMISE

Peter B. Knupfer has convincingly shown the importance of "compromise" for the constitutional politics of the Antebellum period.[26] In Knupfer's telling, the debates over the admission of Missouri present an important site in which the "ritual" of compromise and the associated "politics of conciliation" were both enacted and enshrined as responses to the constitutional politics of slavery and sectional tensions it gave rise to.[27] It is certainly the case that appeals to compromise, conciliation, and amity punctuated the congressional debates

---

[21] *Annals of Congress, 16th Congress, 1st Session*, 1028.

[22] "The Constitution," *Rhode-Island American, and General Advertiser*, January 14, 1820.

[23] "The Constitution."

[24] John Taylor, *Construction Construed, and Constitutions Vindicated* (Richmond: Shepherd & Pollard, 1820), 303.

[25] *Annals of Congress*, 1013, 1014. On the revival of States' rights during the Missouri Crisis, cf. Christopher Childers, "The Old Republican Constitutional Primer: States Rights After the Missouri Controversy and the Onset of the Politics of Slavery," in *The Enigmatic South: Toward Civil War and Its Legacies*, ed. Samuel C. Hyde (Baton Rouge: Louisiana State University Press, 2014), 15–16.

[26] Knupfer, *The Union As It Is*. See also Michael F. Conlin, *The Constitutional Origins of the American Civil War* (Cambridge, UK: Cambridge University Press, 2019), 134–82.

[27] Knupfer, *The Union As It Is*, 90–102.

over Missouri, and that the idea of compromise offered a framework for resolution of the Crisis. But it was also the case that "compromise" became itself a site of contestation within the debates. For opponents of restriction and those who prized Union over addressing slavery, constitutional compromise offered a template, drawn from the past founding of 1787–88, for statesmanlike responses to the impasse of 1819–20. However, for restrictionists, the idea of constitutional compromise only served to highlight the very distance of 1819–21 from the actions of 1787–88.

The intertwining of opposition to restriction and the preservation of enduring constitutional compromises was a mainstay of the South and its supporters during the Missouri debates. Perhaps Mathew Carey stated the obvious when he wrote in 1820 that compromise was "not a new feature of our political history."[28] But in the context of the Missouri Crisis it was – and was meant to be – politically significant when he stated:

> That the union of these states derived its existence from a spirit of compromise; that our present admirable constitution was built upon the basis of compromise; that its spirit has pervaded our whole legislation; and that nothing but an adherence to that original and vital spirit can preserve us from discord and disunion.[29]

Carey's view, that a singular strand of compromise enabled the creation of the Constitution, animated its subsequent history and provided the template for contemporary political action, chimed with the claims of antirestrictionists in Congress. At one level, the idea of compromise was used to attempt to shut down debate over slavery in the territories. Mobilizing calls for a return to "moderation" in the service of opposing restriction and depicting the Missouri debates as a significant departure from established norms, antirestrictionist Members of Congress articulated nostalgic regret for the loss of "that spirit of conciliation which produced this great Confederacy," "the spirit of concession and brotherly love in the formation of the Constitution," and the "spirit of concession" that formed the Constitution.[30] Conjuring a norm of conciliation and grounding it in the authority of the Constitution, antirestrictionists hoped to preclude robust discussion of slavery. In such a vein, Representative Alexander Smyth of Virginia opined that restriction was deemed a serious wrong to the South and that this alone ought to be a sufficient objection to its implementation.[31] In a more moderate incarnation, Representative Henry Meigs of New York reminded the House, "Our free Constitution was made by men who were wise enough to know the dangers of sectional divisions."[32]

---

[28] *Considerations on the Impropriety and Inexpediency of Renewing the Missouri Question. By A Pennsylvanian* (Philadelphia: M. Carey & Son, 1820), 36.
[29] *Considerations on the Impropriety and Inexpediency of Renewing the Missouri Question*, 13.
[30] *Annals of Congress*, 190, 335, 1013. [31] *Annals of Congress*, 1013.
[32] *Annals of Congress*, 946.

The notion of compromise was invoked in a directed fashion with the claim that the question of the constitutionality of slavery had already been settled in the compromises of 1787–88. The constitutional recognition of slavery, itself ascribed to a need for compromise in 1787, was offered as proof that there could be no constitutional restriction on slavery. In arguing against any interference with slavery in the territories, Representative John Holmes of Massachusetts reminded the House of Representatives that the "Constitution as every one knows, is the effect of compromise."[33] That compromise was over slavery and, Holmes stated, "we are bound by it."[34] Emphasizing that it was compromise that had enabled the constitutional recognition of slavery, Senator Nathaniel Macon of North Carolina informed his colleagues, "The Constitution tolerates [slavery]; and that was not adopted from necessity, but through choice."[35] The constitutional compromise over slavery made restriction in Missouri a new and illegitimate form of congressional power. Alexander Smyth argued that the "whole nation sanctioned the right of slavery, by adopting the Constitution," while Representative Benjamin Hardin of Kentucky claimed the "right to slave property is unequivocally recognised by the Constitution."[36] Representative John Tyler of Virginia goaded the restrictionists, suggesting that they might rail against slavery as much as they pleased, but "I point you to the Constitution, and say to you, that you have not only acknowledged our right to this species of property, but that you have gone much further, and have bound yourselves to rivet the chains of the slave."[37] In their willingness to compromise with slavery in 1787–88, antirestrictionists argued the North had willingly recognized the constitutionality of slavery.

The response of restrictionists to these claims regarding the sanctity of compromises over slavery was striking. Rather than rejecting the claim of compromise with slavery in 1787–88, they embraced it but argued that the very fact that it represented a compromise made the constitutional recognition of slavery a restricted one. As such, antirestrictionists in the Senate were reminded by restrictionist Senator David Morril of New Hampshire of their "solemn compact – our mutual agreement." [38] Sketching the history of the founding, he noted of the founders, "to obtain a Constitution, they came to

---

[33] Annals of Congress, 987. Holmes, as a Representative of Maine within Massachusetts's delegation, pursued such arguments with an eye to ensuring Maine's admission as a State. Mason, "The Maine and Missouri Crisis: Competing Priorities and Northern Slavery Politics in the Early Republic."

[34] Annals of Congress, 987.

[35] Annals of Congress, 228–29. Beyond Congress, Mathew Carey described the Constitution in terms of a "compromising act [that was] to all purposes a treaty between two sections of the Union," which the South having honored the North had "no alternative left" but to observe. Considerations on the Impropriety and Inexpediency of Renewing the Missouri Question, 41–42.

[36] Annals of Congress, 1005–6, 1076.　　[37] Annals of Congress, 1388.

[38] Annals of Congress, 136.

a compromise", which was now "binding on the whole."[39] That compromise involved the recognition of slavery in the existing States who "may retain their slaves as long as they please."[40] Others shared his view that "framers of the Constitution have settled those principles in the spirit of compromise" and that the compromise was "sacred, and must be carried into effect."[41] Representative John Taylor (New York) disclaimed "any wish to alter the basis of the compromise on which the Federal Constitution was founded" while emphasizing the importance of a "spirit of amity and mutual concession" to the preservation of the Constitution.[42]

But turning the tables on the antirestrictionists, the restrictionists offered the argument that this "solemn compact" forestalled the extension of slavery into the territories. Conceding that a compromise had been reached in 1787, they argued that its very nature as a compromise limited the reach of its authority. Pro-restrictionist memorialists in Hartford, Connecticut, acknowledged the constitutional recognition of slavery yet saw its existence as a compromise as necessarily qualifying that recognition: "*But* this was done in the spirit of compromise."[43] The compromise, and its spirit, was here understood as the product of a moment of urgency, as the offspring of a specific historical juncture. The Constitution, stated Representative Thomas Forrest (Pennsylvania), "was a compromise to prevent disunion ... It was a compromise for the sake of peace."[44] Recognition of slavery had been the price of that peace, but it ought not to be understood to extend beyond the scope of that historical compromise. Representative Charles Rich (Vermont) conceded that "when the Constitution was adopted, there was a necessity for slavery," but he "utterly and absolutely" denied that this created a precedent for the extension of slavery without limits.[45] Representative John Taylor (New York) echoed him in suggesting, "The extent of this concession was supposed to be seen and clearly understood."[46] For Senator Jonathan Roberts (Pennsylvania) the compromises of the Constitution, "made in the dark days of peril and calamity," would be "given to the winds" by an expansion of slavery into the new States.[47] For these restrictionists, the Constitution was indeed the result of a compromise over slavery, but to the extent that compromise denoted a departure from enduring principles or interests in a moment of mutual sacrifice, it could not itself have meaning beyond the scope of the precise historic compromise. Summarized by the Hartford memorialists, this view saw the constitutional compromise over slavery as "a bargain made between distinct and independent contracting parties," which in "good faith ... ought

---

[39] *Annals of Congress*, 138.   [40] *Annals of Congress*, 139.
[41] *Annals of Congress*, 279–80; *Annals of Congress*, 1040.   [42] *Annals of Congress*, 952.
[43] "Prohibition of Slavery in Missouri," in *Annals of Congress, 16th Congress, First Session*, 1819, 2460. Emphasis added.
[44] *Annals of Congress*, 1560.   [45] *Annals of Congress*, 1398.   [46] *Annals of Congress*, 965.
[47] *Annals of Congress*, 124–25.

not to be stretched in its application to any new parties, without the consent of all those who originally made it."[48] There had indeed been a compromise over slavery and it should be honored. But in the minds of restrictionists, the compromise amounted to a constitutional acknowledgment that slavery had existed in some States who were direct parties to the constitutional compact of 1787 and that its regulation therein was a matter for them.

1.3   CONSTITUTIONAL TIME AND THE FOUNDING SPIRIT

Constraining the compromise to a distinct bargain made by discrete actors in a precise historical moment resulted in a need to articulate what if any legacy that compromise held for the navigation of slavery as a constitutional issue in 1819–21. Put another way, the identification of the constitutional compromise over slavery with the particular historical moment of 1787–88 gave rise to the question of how that moment fit within the narrative of American history. Responding to this challenge pushed each side of the restriction debate toward their own theory of how constitutional authority operated in time. For restrictionists this resulted in a theory of the constitutional compromise as historical exception, a deviation from the broader arch of US history, in which the Constitution was both a historical event and to some extent an aberration from the broader American commitment to liberty. Developing their own theory of constitutional time, antirestrictionists offered a view of the constitutional compact as essentially timeless, without a precise anchor in chronological time. In this constitutional imaginary, the compromise was a somewhat mechanistic contract between the States, subjected to constant renewal with the admission of each new State. Far from being the legacy of 1787, such an understanding was suggestive of "the compromise" as being in a constant state of redemption.

Restrictionists' concession that there had been a compromise over slavery in 1787–88 was not taken by them to indicate an obligation to tolerate slavery in the new States. In arguing against the geographical expansion of slavery, they emphasized a division between the original States that were parties to constitutional compromise and the "new" States that were subsequently admitted to the Union. Within this framework, the chronological separation of 1819–21 from the compromises forged in 1787–88 placed actors during the Missouri Crisis in a distinct constitutional position, facing a different constitutional role. If the actors of 1787–88 had to negotiate the diverse interests of the emerging Union, then the restrictionists of 1819–21 saw themselves, instead, as the guardians of a Union already in place.[49] Representative Clifton Clagett characterized that difference by stating the convention of 1787 "had a compromise to make: we find it already made,

---

[48] "Prohibition of Slavery in Missouri," 2461.
[49] For a discussion of the historical worldview of this generation, see the introduction to this book.

they had a Constitution to form: we find one already formed."[50] For Representative Joshua Cushman of Massachusetts, this foreclosed from the actors of 1819–21 the possibility of compromise – they were not "negotiators, but legislators. It is our office, not to make bargains, but to enact laws."[51] The members of the Sixteenth Congress were "not the architects, but the superintendents of the civil edifice which the Convention erected."[52] As such, it fell to them to guard the Union against the admission of those who would "sap its foundations, impair its strength, or deface its ornaments" through the practice of slavery.[53]

This divergent responsibility arose from an understanding of the new States as holding a distinct position from that of the original States. The original States had met as equals and striven for unity through a series of compromises. By contrast, the new States faced a union of States already in place, equipped with a Constitution that outlined a process of admission for the former. For restrictionists, this meant a new State was "the creature of the Constitution; deriving from the Constitution its existence and all its rights, and possessing no power but what is imparted to it by the Constitution."[54] If the Constitution was itself a compact between thirteen original States, then each new State entered into a compact with the United States as a whole, with Congress acting as the representative of that whole. It could not then be the case, argued Senator Roberts, that the new States were entitled to the same compromises over slavery as those granted to the original States.[55] As the new compact comprised of new parties (the United States and the new State), it was not the case that the new State was a participant to the compromise struck in 1787.[56]

Absent the authority of the original compromise, the admission of new States opened up a series of constitutional issues without clear resolution. Key among these was the distinction between recognizing slavery in existing States and creating new territories for slavery. Restrictionists in Congress argued that absent the authority of the compromise, a space for congressional regulation of slavery in new territories and States was opened up. Senator Benjamin Ruggles of Ohio acknowledged the original compromise and conceded that "all parties to Federal compact are bound to it," but denied that this provided guidance for issues associated with the admission of new States – as to the latter, he suggested "Congress may exercise a sound discretion."[57] Highlighting the passage of time, Senator Prentiss Mellen of Massachusetts contended that the "vast wilderness beyond the Mississippi formed no part of the country for whom the great men of our nation were preparing a Constitution."[58] Its acquisition marked a "new event" that rendered to Congress a "question

---

[50] *Annals of Congress*, 1033. [51] *Annals of Congress*, 1304. [52] *Annals of Congress*, 1304.
[53] *Annals of Congress*, 1304. [54] *Annals of Congress*, 1188. [55] *Annals of Congress*, 125.
[56] For an example of this argument, see Representative Thomas Forrest: *Annals of Congress*, 1819, 1560–61.
[57] *Annals of Congress*, 280. [58] *Annals of Congress*, 180.

about which [they] are at liberty to legislate as they think just and proper."[59]
Within this new era, it was suggested, the constraints of the compromise of
1787–88 had limited application. Indeed, even the text of the Constitution
ought to be understood in new ways. Some restrictionists suggested that the
constitutional text itself reflected a determination that the compromise of 1787
should not extend beyond its immediate scope. Where the Constitution's
elusion of the words "slave" and "slavery" had hitherto been viewed as an act
of discretion, one restrictionist now deemed it an "expressive silence,"
connoting a condemnation of slavery "of which no one could mistake or
misunderstand the meaning."[60] Following a similar line of logic while
implicating the framers themselves in the view of the Constitution's
compromise as a historically situated bargain, Senator Roberts argued that
the absence of the word "slave" in the Constitution indicated a hope that the
Constitution would "survive a state of things where the word could be
applicable."[61] Pushing these suggestions to the outer limits of their credibility,
Representative Taylor even went as far as to suggest that the Fugitive Slave
clause of the Constitution was not concerned with slavery.[62]

If the compromise of 1787–88 belonged to a different era and held little in
terms of guidance regarding admission of new States then the onus was on the
restrictionists to supply something in its place to anchor the momentous
adjudications they sought to undertake. In line with the view of the
Constitution's compromise over slavery as an aberration, they offered in its
place a vision of a broader American commitment to liberty as expressed in the
Preamble to the Declaration of Independence.[63] Restrictionists turned to the
"first truth declared by this nation," that "all men are created equal," in order to
ground their opposition to slavery in a founding spirit of the nation and to
present the compromise over slavery as an anomaly.[64] Positing the commitment
to universal liberty that they saw in the Declaration as the foundational
principle of the Revolution and the institutions that emerged from it, the
restrictionists called for Americans to "refer to our original charter [the
Declaration]," to return to "the principles upon which ... independence was
proclaimed and established," and to come to see emancipation of the enslaved
as "a righteous consummation of the promise of the Revolution."[65] Positioning
slavery as "repugnant to the great and essential rights contained in the
Declaration of Independence," such restrictionists could only interpret the

[59] *Annals of Congress*, 180.   [60] *Annals of Congress*, 1190; See also *Annals of Congress*, 211.
[61] *Annals of Congress*, 340.
[62] *Annals of Congress*, 960; See also Walsh, *Free Remarks on The Spirit of the Federal
Constitution*, 58.
[63] On the use of the Declaration of Independence by restrictionists, see Mason, *Slavery & Politics in
the Early American Republic*, 200; Riley, *Slavery and the Democratic Conscience*, 239–40;
Philip F. Detweiler, "Congressional Debate on Slavery and the Declaration of Independence,
1819–1821," *The American Historical Review* 63, no. 3 (1958): 598–616.
[64] *Annals of Congress*, 957.   [65] *Annals of Congress*, 1396, 1252; *Annals of Congress*, 340.

compromise with slavery in 1787–88 as a necessary concession to the pressures of that historical moment – the broader, indeed truer, spirit of the United States was in direct opposition to such a compromise.[66] Reading that spirit back into the text of the Constitution, these restrictionists saw a document pregnant with emancipatory potential beyond the narrow, historicized compromises made between the original States.

In response to the restrictionist arguments that the compromises of the Constitution and the spirit of concession that facilitated them were a specific historical pivot away from the universal liberty of the Declaration, antirestrictionists pushed back on several points. They denied that the compromises of Constitution represented deviation from an American spirit. They rebutted the notion that those compromises were historically specific. And they conspicuously rejected the authority of the Declaration of Independence in the questions at hand.

The antirestrictionist rejection of the authority of the Declaration of Independence was robust and recurrent. Drawing a sharp distinction between the Declaration and the Constitution, Senator Macon declared, "the words of the Declaration of Independence ... are no part of [the Constitution]."[67] Senator Nicholas Van Dyke of Delaware followed him in expressing shock that "the Declaration of Independence would be resorted to, as furnishing a key to the construction of the Constitution of 1787."[68] The Declaration, "a recital of abstract theoretical principles, in a national manifesto in 1776," ought not, he suggested, be equated with the authority of the Constitution.[69] At other points, antirestrictionists went further, rejecting the claim that "all men are created equal" held any meaning for slaves or indeed black Americans more broadly. Senator Barbour sardonically asked who were the parties to the Declaration – "the slaves? No." – while denying its applicability to slavery.[70] Senator Johnson of Kentucky disputed the universality of the Declaration's claim; "the meaning of this sentence is defined in its application ... that Americans are equal with Englishmen."[71] Maryland's recently arrived Senator William Pinkney likewise explained that the "self-evident truths announced in the Declaration of Independence are not truths at all, if taken literally ... [and] were never designed to be so received."[72] Reflecting on the intentions of the Declaration's author, Senator Macon noted, "[Jefferson's] democracy ... appears to be of the white family."[73] Similar sentiments in the House of Representatives saw Representative John Holmes denounce "this strange and ridiculous vision, that the Declaration of Independence was a decree of universal emancipation," while Representative Alexander Smyth argued that the Declaration held the "same force and effect, as a declaration of the like opinion by any other equal number of persons of the same ability and

---

[66] *Annals of Congress*, 279. [67] *Annals of Congress*, 227. [68] *Annals of Congress*, 301.
[69] *Annals of Congress*, 301. [70] *Annals of Congress*, 325. [71] *Annals of Congress*, 350.
[72] *Annals of Congress*, 405. [73] *Annals of Congress*, 229.

intelligence, having no political power."[74] Representative Hardin stated "the Declaration of Independence cuts no figure in this question," and suggested that the view that the Declaration emancipated slaves was "certainly a very late discovery," given that the document was "nothing but a manifesto to world" justifying independence.[75]

The push back against the Declaration was necessary if antirestrictionists were to avoid conceding a spirit had animated the founding whose teleology lay in emancipation. By instead suggesting that the spirit of conciliation which gave rise to the compromises over slavery was a better template for constitutional politics in 1819–21, antirestrictionists could offer a stronger case for regarding the expansion of slavery into the territories as constitutionally sanctioned, or at least not prohibited. In the place of a spirit that traveled down the ages from the Revolution, antirestrictionists offered the spirit of compromise as a model for administering a constitutional compact aimed at reconciling distinct sectional interests.[76] The Constitution here was timeless rather than teleological, a guide to harmonizing contending interests with a spirit that, instead of competing with the text, directed attention to the latter as the framework for achieving such harmonization. In this way, Representative McLane could look to the Fugitive Slave clause as the embodiment of the "whole spirit of the Constitution," in its acknowledgment of the ability of "each State to make its own regulations upon this species of property."[77] Other antirestrictionists, reflecting the period's broader commitment to strict construction, more decisively collapsed the spirit of the Constitution with its text. In such matters, the "Constitution must be construed strictly" warned Representative Robert Reid, lest conclusions be reached that were "in direct hostility with the letter as well as the spirit of the Constitution."[78] Representative John Holmes questioned why, when the "language is explicit and positive," notions of spirit were even invoked.[79] Such recourse to the text was useful for the antirestrictionists as it provided them with what they argued was a documented constitutional recognition of slavery. Working from there, rather than an overarching ethos of the founding period, gave them a surer footing for the claim that this constitutional issue of slavery had been settled.

However, showing that the constitutional text recognized slavery did not in itself undermine the restrictionists' case. As we have seen, the latter generally admitted that a compromise over slavery had taken place in 1787–88 but argued that it extended only to the original thirteen States. For the antirestrictionists' arguments to be convincing, they had to explain why that original compromise held for newly admitted States as well. Superficially, the

---

[74] *Annals of Congress*, 969, 1004. [75] *Annals of Congress*, 1074, 1071.

[76] Or as Representative Henry Meigs put it, "This Constitution is no more than a profoundly wise agreement to differ." *Annals of Congress*, 946.

[77] *Annals of Congress*, 1154. [78] *Annals of Congress*, 1026, 1028.

[79] *Annals of Congress*, 987.

explanation came in the form of an argument that contained no small degree of circularity. It suggested that new States could not differ in sovereignty from the original States without forming in effect a new union. A new union was unacceptable, as it would mean that new States were not really equal parties to *the Union*. Conceding any difference between the original and new States would mean, according to Representative Hardin, that the new States were not a "joint partner in the original agreement ... [and so effectively] not a member of the Union."[80] Missouri's representative echoed this argument with the claim that if Missouri was admitted with conditions that were not a applied to the original States, it would not be "'into the Union' that Missouri was admitted, but into a new union."[81]

The desire to ensure admission to the existing Union reflected States' rights-antirestrictionists' concerns that acknowledgment of a new union would enhance federal authority at the expense of the States. The creation of a new union would mean Congress spoke for the existing Union as a whole during the admission process and could use that power to accrue further power; any form of admission that placed Missouri in a subservient position to the then-existing States would introduce the precedent of a diluted form of State sovereignty for the new States and thus potentially open the door to congressional acts of emancipation. For Representative Philip P. Barbour, the ability to apply conditions to a State's admission was the grant of a right to Congress to "increase their capital stock of power."[82] Alexander Smyth argued that granting Congress a distinct power over the new States would render them equivalent to the District of Columbia, which was wholly under the Legislative authority of Congress.[83] Always on the guard against a growth of federal power, Southern antirestrictionists and their allies were wary of such an empowered Congress.[84] Emphasizing the constitutional similarity between the original and new States offered an elegant response to such pressures. If the new States were the same as the original States then the sovereignty of both was equal and so Congress held no "extra" authority over new States, either as a result of its acting as a representative of the whole Union or vis-à-vis any individual new State. Bolstering the sovereignty of the States while boxing in the discretion of Congress in matters of admission, the claim that new States navigating the constitutional process of admission were identical to the original States who had formed the Union became a lynchpin of the antirestrictionist case.

The fear that restriction would in effect mean a new union reflected the central antirestrictionist desire to view any compact formed in 1819–21 as not

---

[80] *Annals of Congress*, 1080–81.   [81] *Annals of Congress*, 1504.

[82] *Annals of Congress*, 1235.   [83] *Annals of Congress*, 992.

[84] On the Southern suspicion of federal power at this historical juncture, cf. Forbes, *The Missouri Compromise and Its Aftermath*, 6–7, 164; Mason, *Slavery & Politics in the Early American Republic*, 161–63; Childers, "The Old Republican Constitutional Primer," 15–16.

new or revised but simply an extension of the compromise of 1787. Without such continuity it would be difficult to justify the extension into new territory of an institution of slavery that many antirestrictionist speakers readily conceded was evil "in the abstract."[85] The argument for continuity of the compromise across chronological time was supported by the constitutional imaginary in which that chronological gap was denied, and Missouri was not entering a preexisting Union but joining the Union as an equal to the "original" States that formed the Union of 1787–88. Underlining the contemporariness of the Constitution, Senator Macon argued that the "Constitution is now as much an experiment as it was in the year 1789."[86] Representative Tyler rejected the notion that there was a difference between the original States and the new States with regard to constitutional creation: the new States were not the creatures of the Constitution but rather "the Constitution is the creature also of the new States."[87] Drawing a parallel between States and generations, Tyler insisted, "Government ... receives from each succeeding generation of men a new being. ... If it remains unaltered, it is owing to the implied assent which is given to it by the community in whom it operates."[88] Extending that observation to the admission of States and the compromise, this suggested that each new organization of the Union represented a contemporaneous assent to the compromise said to have made the Union possible. Representative Louis McLane of Delaware agreed, arguing that new States and their populations enjoy their federal rights "not in consequence of any new compact, but in virtue of the old compact in the Constitution of the United States, to which ... [they] become parties when they are admitted into the Union."[89] The extension of the compromise across (non-)time operated to secure slavery in the face of restrictionist pressure. The new States were parties to the ongoing compromise over slavery, as to treat them otherwise would be to render them distinct and thus not parties to the 1787–88 constitutional compact.

In tracing these different components in the debate over Missouri's admission, two competing visions of American constitutional development can thus be seen to emerge. Restrictionists looked to the Declaration of Independence as containing the principles upon which the American state was founded. Ascribing to that document a commitment to universal liberty, they saw emancipation as the ultimate end of the United States. Within that framework the compromises over slavery that informed the 1787–88 Constitution were identified as anomalies produced by the specific pressures of that historical moment. The result was – from the viewpoint of those opposing slavery – an understanding of the Constitution as merely a product

---

[85] Freehling notes that it was only in South Carolina that prominent voices called for perpetual slavery. Freehling, *The Road to Disunion: Volume 1, Secessionists at Bay 1776–1854*, 150.

[86] *Annals of Congress*, 220.   [87] *Annals of Congress*, 1385.   [88] *Annals of Congress*, 1385.

[89] *Annals of Congress*, 1150.

of its time: At best, its wording denoted a hope of transcending the recognition of slavery it had been necessary to undertake, and at worst, it was a corrupt bargain which could only hold for the territories over which agreement was struck in 1787–88.

Antirestrictionists rejected such a view of the Constitution. Instead, they depicted the US Constitution, at least at the theoretical level, as not beholden to any specific historical moment. In this framework, 1787–88 represented one incarnation of a compact that was always in the process of being struck between an ever-expanding number of States. Denying a constitutional distinction between "original" and "new" States, antirestrictionists saw each admission of a State as the ascension of an equal partner to the Union of States. Such a view broke any association between the compromises struck over slavery in the Constitution and the historical moment of 1787–88. Shorn of its attachment to the "original" States or 1787–88, compromise over slavery bypassed any question of historically specific necessity, and instead was offered as an instance of the politics of conciliation that enabled constitutional politics. Most crucially, the relation between the constitutional compromise over slavery and a wider American spirit was rendered mute.

1.4 THE CONSTITUTION AFTER MISSOURI

The constitutional debate prompted by the Missouri Crisis incorporated many of the conceptual building blocks of the constitutional politics of slavery that developed across the 1820s and 1830s. But the appearance of these concepts was – from the perspective of the constitutional politics of the 1830s – disordered and raw, protean but lacking the associations that would give durable structure to them in the hands of abolitionists and their opponents. Scattered across the Missouri debates, the notions of a founding spirit, compromise, and a chronological gap between the Constitution's creation and the contemporary moment offered the materials for the theories of the Constitution subsequently developed. But in 1820 their arrangement did not reflect what they would become.

While restrictionists drew upon the idea of a commitment to universal liberty, emergent from the Revolution and articulated in the Declaration of Independence, they saw it as having only limited value in navigating the Constitution. As has been shown, the Constitution – and specifically its compromise over slavery – was seen as a deviation from the broad principles that had informed the Revolution. Adhering to this founding spirit required one to adopt a pose of skepticism toward the compromises of the Constitution and to firmly reject their expansion. Such an argument placed the Declaration and the Constitution in potential tension with one another, presenting the Constitution as a historical moment of deviation from the path of the United States toward greater liberty.

For antirestrictionists, the Constitution's formation through a process of compromise and a spirit of conciliation provided a template for resolving the conflict over slavery. Treating the Constitution as an apparatus by which to reconcile competing interests, antirestrictionists called upon the spirit of compromise they ascribed to the convention of 1787 as a guide for responding to the sectional pressures of 1819–21. But that model had validity precisely because the Constitution and the compact that it signified remained an ongoing project. To the extent that the Constitution had "settled" the question over slavery in 1787–88, it did so only because such a settlement was reaffirmed by the continuous participation in and acknowledgment of that settlement by the States. The authority of 1787–88 was that of a model for addressing constitutional tensions, rather than that of an origin from which subsequent political actors drew their own authority. To be sure, appeals to a spirit of compromise punctuated the Missouri debates, but it was not conceived as the founding spirit. Indeed, given the overwhelming restrictionist recurrence to the founding spirit as defined by the Declaration, compromise was mobilized as counterpoint to the authority of a founding spirit.

Finally, and intertwined with those two concepts, was the idea of a chronological separation of the present and the past of 1787–88. Antirestrictionists, advocating for the continued relevance of the compromise struck during 1787–88 and sensitive to any distinction between old and new States, played down the theoretical significance of the passage of chronological time. Reaffirming the idea of 1787–88 as template, they stressed the continued contemporariness of the Constitution. For restrictionists, whose position rendered them more responsive to a progressive view of constitutional time, the gap between 1787–88 and 1819–21 was important. But its importance came in the form of a justification for moving away from the principles of 1787–88, rather than in conveying a particular obligation to 1787–88. A gap was there, but it denoted distance, not legacy or inheritance.

Matthew Mason suggests, "[T]he Missouri Crisis was at once a culmination and a new beginning."[90] The Crisis and its resolution marked the initial steps toward a new party system and the generation of "a durably sectional constitutional politics" to underwrite it.[91] In this crucible, old ideas were refined and sharpened and others "new and unalloyed" were put to the test.[92] Ideas about the Constitution and the nature of constitutional authority were among these, including notions of constitutional time, the role of compromise, and the concept of a founding spirit. But just as the new political alignments that emerged from 1819 to 1821 took time to settle, so too did the novel

---

[90] Mason, *Slavery & Politics in the Early American Republic*, 179.
[91] Leonard and Cornell, *The Partisan Republic*, 176; Forbes, *The Missouri Compromise and Its Aftermath*; Van Cleve, *A Slaveholders' Union*, 259–64; Mason, *Slavery & Politics in the Early American Republic*, 211–12.
[92] Mason, *Slavery & Politics in the Early American Republic*, 204.

constitutional responses to the Crisis need time to unfurl. And just as the ideas in the congressional debates over Missouri's admission developed through their interaction with one another, so too would ideas about the Constitution develop through broader interactions across the 1820s, 1830s, and 1840s.

The invocation of a founding spirit during the congressional debates over Missouri saw that spirit positioned in tension with the Constitution. However, in a different pocket of the American political landscape, the relationship between the founding principles as expressed in the Declaration of Independence and the Constitution was being theorized in other terms. The next chapter turns to that intellectual space and traces the ways in which free black communities in the early Republic theorized the Declaration and its relationship to the US Constitution.

The Declaration of Independence and Black Citizenship in the 1820s

Declare how freemen can a world create,
And slaves and masters ruin every state.

Joel Barlow, *The Columbiad* (1807)[1]

Pauline Maier, in her seminal account of the Declaration of Independence, pointed to an evolution in the document's place in American national culture in the 1820s.[2] As the United States entered the "Era of Good Feeling" following the Treaty of Ghent, "the Declaration of Independence became the subject of massive public attention ... and began to assume a certain holy quality."[3] Encouraged by figures including Thomas Jefferson, a return to the history of the revolutionary period and the sanctification of the symbols and relics of that era was seen as a salve to the fissures developing around the role of slavery in western expansion. The fear that the divisions drawn over the entry of Missouri into the Union reflected disagreements that would come to risk the Union itself induced Jefferson and others to mobilize revolutionary history in order to "strengthen [America's] determination to honor and preserve the accomplishments of the Revolution, including the federal union."[4] Alongside this mobilization – and as we have seen as itself part of the debates over Missouri's admission – came an understanding of the Declaration of Independence as an expression of a national ideology, in place of its earlier understanding as a justification of revolt. Maier has suggested a shifting textual focus in the post-1815 period from the final paragraph of the Declaration – the claim to be "free and independent states" – and toward the second paragraph – "all men are created equal" – reflected this change.[5]

---

[1] Quoted in Julius Rubens Ames, *Liberty* (New York: American Anti-Slavery Society, 1837), 25.
[2] Pauline Maier, *American Scripture: Making the Declaration of Independence* (New York: Alfred A. Knopf, 1997), 175–89.
[3] Maier, *American Scripture*, 175. [4] Maier, *American Scripture*, 187.
[5] Maier, *American Scripture*, 160, 191.

This transformation of the Declaration's symbolism progressed on two axes that proved useful for those advancing claims on behalf of black Americans. In the first instance, with the shift in focus from the final to the second paragraph came the association of the Declaration with a commitment to equality and liberty at the individual or group level. Although less useful within judicial proceedings than the States' Bills of Rights due to its lack of legal standing, an equality-inflected reading of the Declaration of Independence nonetheless offered important rhetorical ammunition for groups pursuing claims of equality.[6] In the second instance, the project of unifying the nation around the sacred text of the Declaration of Independence had the effect of providing a written expression of American nationalism as a value-laden concept. While the federal Constitution had provided an institutional basis for national governance and initiated a legal framework for "being an American," it contained little philosophical material from which to articulate what was substantially contained within a claim to be a member of the national community.

Free black writers sought to exploit both opportunities in the early Republic and through the 1820s, ultimately generating an understanding of American citizenship that would inform the wider immediate abolitionist movement of the 1830s. These efforts, which intensified in the face of the founding and growth of the American Colonization Society (ACS), saw free black writers advance claims upon American citizenship with pamphlets, including David Walker's *Appeal*, and the first African American owned and operated newspaper in the United States, *Freedom's Journal*. Alongside the enactments of citizenship seen in public meetings, these writings advanced a black claim upon American citizenship that rested upon a substantive understanding of American nationalism associated with the Declaration of Independence. Read into the US Constitution, this national citizenship provided an external framework for understanding the Constitution as committed to an expansive notion of the people and provided an important orientating concept for the abolitionist movement as it evolved into the 1830s.

2.1 THE DECLARATION OF INDEPENDENCE IN FREE BLACK THOUGHT

Of the two developments noted earlier, the association of the Declaration of Independence with equality was easier to grasp and certainly easier to utilize in rhetorical attacks on slavery and discriminatory practices, but the two were closely related. The germs of both ideas could also be seen in the period before

---

[6] Maier, *American Scripture*, 197. Martha S. Jones has documented the ways in which black men and women enacted and claimed their citizenship in interactions with the court system. Martha S. Jones, *Birthright Citizens: A History of Race and Rights in Antebellum America* (Cambridge, UK: Cambridge University Press, 2018).

the canonization of the Declaration of Independence. The essence of the first argument – the connection between the Declaration's promise and the conditions of American society – certainly predated the Declaration itself and was contained within Samuel Johnson's 1775 quip, "how is it that we hear the loudest yelps for liberty among the drivers of negroes?"[7] Nevertheless, the Declaration afforded a direct opportunity to highlight apparently hypocritical behavior by comparison between its textual promise of equality and the practices found within what would become the United States.[8] Lemuel Haynes, a mulatto minuteman in the Revolutionary War, did so in his "Liberty Further Extended" in 1776.[9] So too did James Forten in his "Letters by a Man of Colour" (1813) when he described the self-evident truth that "GOD created all men equal" as "one of the most prominent features in the Declaration of Independence," linked it to the Pennsylvanian constitution, and then asked:

Has the God who made the white man and the black, left any record declaring us a different species. Are we not sustained by the same power, supported by the same food, hurt by the same wounds, pleased with the same delights, and propagated by the same means. And should we not then enjoy the same liberty, and be protected by the same laws.[10]

---

[7] Samuel Johnson, *Taxation No Tyranny: An Answer to the Resolutions and Address of the American Congress* (London: T. Cadell, 1775), 89.

[8] Apparent hypocrisy, as one was only a hypocrite if one accepted that the Declaration was committed to equality and that it bound Americans to a similar commitment. Some proslavery thinkers would come to reject the latter premise. See Maier, *American Scripture*, 199; Alexander H. Stephens, "Cornerstone Speech" (Savannah, GA, March 21, 1861).

[9] Mia Bay, "See Your Declaration Americans!!! Abolitionism, Americanism, and the Revolutionary Tradition in Free Black Politics," in *Americanism: New Perspectives on the History of an Ideal*, ed. Michael Kazin and Joseph A. McCartin (Chapel Hill: The University of North Carolina Press, 2006), 25.

[10] James Forten, "Series of Letters by a Man of Colour," in *Pamphlets of Protest: An Anthology of Early African-American Protest Literature, 1790–1860*, ed. Richard Newman, Patrick Rael, and Philip Lapsansky (New York: Routledge, 2001), 67–68. On Forten's writing of "Letters by a Man of Colour," see Julie Winch, "The Making and Meaning of James Forten's 'Letters from a Man of Colour,'" *William & Mary Quarterly* 64, no. 1 (2007): 129–38. Forten's essays represent just one of the many arguments for racial equality offered during the early Republic. As Paul Goodman notes, by the 1820s "forty years of freedom had reshaped the African American communities north of Baltimore." The results were a black public sphere that saw the use of "the printed word and the public meeting to formulate the defining doctrines of immediatism" and "an American identity crafted through decades of struggle and made confident" by the securing of emancipation in northern states. Andrew K. Diemer, *The Politics of Black Citizenship: Free African Americans in the Mid-Atlantic Borderland, 1817–1863* (Athens, GA: The University of Georgia Press, 2016), 5–6; Paul Goodman, *Of One Blood: Abolitionism and the Origins of Racial Equality* (Berkeley: University of California Press, 1998), 9; Elizabeth R. Varon, *Disunion! The Coming of the American Civil War, 1789–1859* (Chapel Hill: The University of North Carolina Press, 2008), 62; Bay, "See Your Declaration Americans!!!," 36.

The link between the promise of the Declaration and the condition of free blacks in Pennsylvania was further advanced when Forten substantiated the black population's claim to equal treatment through participation – including his own – in the revolutionary struggle; "many of our fathers, many of ourselves, have fought and bled for the independence of our country."[11] In doing so – and elsewhere in calling for the protection of "our privileges, as citizens" – Forten also moved to ally the natural right claims of the Declaration with specifically American claims of citizenship. Supporting the call for equal treatment with a claim on American citizenship brought the two elements of the Declaration's transformation together, suggesting that to be an American was to be entitled to equal treatment.[12]

Later reprinted in *Freedom's Journal* in 1827, Forten's use of the Declaration of Independence's commitment to equality in "Letters" was reflected in the sentiments of the community associated with that newspaper. As with Forten, *Freedom's Journal* and the community around it advanced the claims that the black population of the United States should be rightly regarded as American citizens and that the United States was founded alongside a commitment to equality. Crucial for the broader movement toward black emancipation, *Freedom's Journal* operated between 1827 and 1828 as the first African American owned and operated newspaper in the United States.[13] Some readings of *Freedom's Journal* suggest it "indicated a new independence and militancy in Black struggle," which sought to "international[ize] the Black struggle," or that it looked to the example of Haiti instead of the legacy of the revolutionary-era documents.[14] However, the use of the Declaration of

---

[11] Forten, "Series of Letters by a Man of Colour," 68. The premising of black citizenship claims in military service and the memory of it were important elements of this literature. Cf. Bay, "See Your Declaration Americans!!!," 39.

[12] Diemer suggests Forten's use of the Declaration emphasized its universality rather than American-ness, but Forten also directly linked the Declaration to the constitution and politics of Pennsylvania. Forten's use of the Declaration of Independence was echoed by other black writers of the time. For other examples see Diemer, *The Politics of Black Citizenship*, 16–17; Richard S. Newman, *The Transformation of American Abolitionism: Fighting Slavery in the Early Republic* (Chapel Hill: The University of North Carolina Press, 2002), 93; Peter P. Hinks, *To Awaken My Afflicted Brethren: David Walker and the Problem of Antebellum Slave Resistance* (University Park: The Pennsylvania State University Press, 1997), 176–78; Bay, "See Your Declaration Americans!!!." By the time of their reprinting in *Freedom's Journal*, Forten's essays were situated in the context of other abolitionists making particular American claims upon the Declaration, for example, Vigornius, "Slavery No. IV," in *Essays on Slavery: Re-Published from the Boston Recorder & Telegraph, for 1825. By Vigornius, and Others* (Amherst: Mark H. Newman, 1826), 16; Hieronymus, "Slavery No. 1," in *Essays on Slavery*, 39.

[13] On the history of *Freedom's Journal*, see Jacqueline Bacon, *Freedom's Journal: The First African-American Newspaper* (Lanham: Lexington Books, 2007); Jacqueline Bacon, "The History of Freedom's Journal: A Study in Empowerment and Community," *The Journal of African American History* 88, no. 1 (2003): 1–20.

[14] Gayle T. Tate, "Free Black Resistance in the Antebellum Era, 1830 to 1860," *Journal of Black Studies* 28, no. 6 (1998): 764–82; Charlton W. Yingling, "No One Who Reads the History of

Independence and claims on American identity carried within the newspaper suggest that Elizabeth McHenry is correct to say that free blacks in the 1820s "maintained faith in the nation's founding documents ... [and] were intent on asserting their right to citizenship according to these texts."[15] Indeed, references to the Declaration of Independence within *Freedom's Journal* and David Walker's *Appeal* suggest that it was a vital resource for free black reflections on and claims to American citizenship.[16]

Setting out to be a "voice ... in defence of the *five-hundred thousand free people of colour*" in the United States and primarily concerned with the "uplift" of Northern free blacks, *Freedom's Journal* was comprised of a variety of materials more often aimed at moral and educational improvement than political claims making.[17] Indeed, insofar as the newspaper had a consistent response to racial inequities it was one grounded in the belief, detailed by McHenry, that the "daily behavior and activities of black Americans, would sway public opinion and dispel negative attitudes toward free blacks."[18] Seeking to prove "the sublimity of the black mind by demonstrating literary abilities and a propensity for developing 'literary character,'" while also informing readers of the moral standards that would ensure respectability, the newspaper echoed the faith of earlier reformers in educational uplift as a bridge to full citizenship.[19] In line with this commitment, the newspaper set out with an intention to include materials selected with the aim of cultivating "moral and religious improvement," and "whatever concerns us as a people ... interwoven with all the principal news of the day," resulting in articles on a wide variety of subjects.[20] Nevertheless, although "better understood as a journal designed to serve a developing black community than as a paper of protest," the materials within *Freedom's Journal* contained a variety of approaches to critiquing the

Hayti Can Doubt the Capacity of Colored Men: Racial Formation and Atlantic Rehabilitation in New York City's Early Black Press, 1827–1841," *Early American Studies* 11, no. 2 (2013): 317–18.

[15] Elizabeth McHenry, *Forgotten Readers: Recovering the Lost History of African American Literacy Societies* (Durham: Duke University Press, 2002), 29.

[16] David Walker was an agent for the newspaper and his *Appeal* – further discussed subsequently – can be seen as emerging from the same intellectual community as *Freedom's Journal*. Cf. Hinks, *To Awaken My Afflicted Brethren*, 109; Melvin L. Rogers, "David Walker and the Political Power of the Appeal," *Political Theory* 43, no. 2 (2015): 216; Timothy Patrick McCarthy, "'To Plead Our Own Cause': Black Print Culture and the Origins of American Abolitionism," in *Prophets of Protest: Reconsidering the History of American Abolitionism*, ed. Timothy Patrick McCarthy and John Stauffer (New York: The New Press, 2006), 114–44; On the broader context of black literary societies, see McHenry, *Forgotten Readers*.

[17] "Proposals for Publishing the Freedom's Journal," *Freedom's Journal*, March 16, 1827.

[18] McHenry, *Forgotten Readers*, 90.

[19] McHenry, *Forgotten Readers*, 85; Paul J. Polgar, "'To Raise Them to an Equal Participation': Early National Abolitionism, Gradual Emancipation, and the Promise of African American Citizenship," *Journal of the Early Republic* 31, no. 2 (2011): 229–58.

[20] "To Our Patrons," *Freedom's Journal*, March 16, 1827.

existence of racialized chattel slavery and advancing claims to the identity of "American" within the United States.[21]

Engagement with the topics of slavery and national citizenship made sense given the newspaper's desire to be a "medium of intercourse between our brethren in the different states of this great confederacy," but it was also necessitated by the extent to which black experiences were being shaped by the existence of the ACS in the 1820s.[22] The editor's recognition that black slaves were "brethren ... our kindred by all the ties of nature" reflected, among other connections, the manner in which the discourse of the ACS tied the fates of slaves and free blacks together in the mid-Antebellum period.[23] The ACS grew from a single organization in 1817 to over two hundred societies in 1831, with the aim of undertaking the colonization of African territory with free blacks transported there from the United States.[24] Claiming in its 1820 memorial to Congress that the free black population "are not, and cannot be, either useful or happy among us," the ACS called for "a separation; that those who are now free, and those who may become so hereafter, should be provided with the means of attaining to a state of respectability and happiness" through the project of their wholesale expatriation.[25] Nonetheless, speeches, such as Daniel Dana's in 1825 which avowed that the "great mass of African population in our country is corrupt and corrupting," seemed to confirm the view of many blacks that for many members of the ACS the immediate concern was the existence of a free black population rather than the existence of slavery.[26] And indeed against the backdrop of the development in the North of "a modern white supremacist political culture" in reaction to the very black social progress that gave rise to publications such as *Freedom's Journal*, the ACS plan met the desires of individuals like Dana to be rid of a black population they regarded as less than equals:

Detain them, then, no longer. This is not their country. Our very atmosphere to them is tainted. In every gale they perceive the hateful scent of *slavery*. ... Send them home; and send with them Christian instructions and privileges; let them feel that they are really

---

[21] Frederick Cooper, "Elevating the Race: The Social Thought of Black Leaders, 1827–50," *American Quarterly* 24, no. 5 (1972): 607.

[22] "To Our Patrons."

[23] "To Our Patrons." Gordon Fraser argues that *Freedom's Journal* and the later *The Rights of All* created an "emancipatory cosmology" that stretched across both free and enslaved portions of a black "quasi-national collectivity" in the 1820s. Gordon Fraser, "Emancipatory Cosmology: Freedom's Journal, The Rights of All, and the Revolutionary Movements of Black Print Culture," *American Quarterly* 68, no. 2 (2016): 263–86.

[24] Newman, *The Transformation of American Abolitionism*, 111.

[25] *Annals of Congress*, House of Representatives, 16th Congress, 1st Session, 1047–51.

[26] Daniel Dana, *A Discourse Addressed to the New-Hampshire Auxiliary Colonization Society, at Their First Annual Meeting, Concord, June 2, 1825* (Concord, NH: Shepard and Bannister, 1825), 8.

free; that they are surrounded with their equals; that the prize of knowledge, of virtue, of glory, is set before them; and you will find that Africans are men.[27]

In the South, the ACS-sponsored removal of free black populations addressed concerns, such as those expressed by Charles Fenton Mercer, over slave revolt, the perceived security threat of freeing a previously enslaved population, and any ensuing loss of property:

> The rapid increase of the free people of colour, by which their number was extended in the ten years proceeding the last census of the United States, from fifteen to thirty thousand, if it has not endangered our peace, has impaired the value of all the private property in a large section of our country [Virginia]. ... The habitations of our fathers have sunk into ruins; the fields which they tilled have become a wilderness. ... Those newly grown and almost impenetrable thickets which have succeeded a wretched cultivation, shelter and conceal a banditti, consisting of this degraded, idle, and vicious population, who sally forth from their coverts, beneath the obscurity of night, and plunder the rich proprietors of the valleys. They infest the suburbs of the towns and cities, where they become depositories of stolen goods, and schooled by necessity, elude the vigilance of our defective police.[28]

In the face of such sentiments, despite its being framed as a benevolent plan to end the slave trade and enable gradual emancipation of American slaves, the free black population regarded offers such as Caleb Cushing's in 1833 of a "secure asylum ... in the land of your fathers" as motivated less by concern for their welfare and more for their removal.[29]

The growth of the ACS and the attachment of powerful political figures to its agenda created additional impetus for black activists to articulate a notion of American citizenship that incorporated the black population.[30] C. Peter Ripley suggests that by "the late 1820s, blacks considered colonization to be as threatening as slavery and prejudice," and insofar as colonization worked to protect slavery and invigorated prejudice in its disavowal of black equality this fear was perhaps not misplaced.[31] At the core of the ACS project was a denial that the free black population were actually Americans. For white figures such as Dana, Mercer, and others, the removal of blacks from "our country" to "their country" was a crucial step in ensuring the protection of the inheritance,

---

[27] James Brewer Stewart, "The Emergence of Racial Modernity and the Rise of the White North, 1790–1840," *Journal of the Early Republic* 18, no. 2 (1998): 113; Dana, *A Discourse Addressed to the New-Hampshire Auxiliary Colonization Society*, 10.

[28] *First Annual Report of the American Society for Colonizing the Free People of Color, of the United States; and the Proceedings of the Society at Their Annual Meeting in the City of Washington, on the First Day of January, 1818* (Washington, DC: D. Rapine, 1818), 15.

[29] Quoted in Newman, *The Transformation of American Abolitionism*, 113.

[30] On the role of the ACS as a catalyst for this project, see Diemer, *The Politics of Black Citizenship*, 18–30.

[31] C. Peter Ripley, "Introduction to the American Series: Black Abolitionists in the United States, 1830–1865," in *The Black Abolitionist Papers: Volume III: The United States, 1830–1846* (Chapel Hill: The University of North Carolina Press, 1991), 3.

both in terms of territory and liberty, that the former had been gifted from their fathers. Black efforts to resist colonization therefore involved laying claim, as Thomas L. Jinnings did, to an American inheritance:

Our claims are on America, it is the land that gave us birth; it is the land of our nativity, we know no other country, it is a land in which our fathers have suffered and toiled; they have watered it with their tears, and fanned it with sighs.[32]

At Troy in 1829, Rev. N. Paul echoed that argument placing an emphasis on "our country ... our nativity ... our fathers" in countering the plans of colonization:

We claim this as *our country*, as the land of our nativity, and to achieve its independence, our fathers faced her enemies on the field of battle, and contended even unto death.[33]

Similar claims were offered in a letter to *Freedom's Journal* rejecting plans to celebrate New York abolition on the 5th of July and so leave the 4th to white Americans. Railing against the notion that the 4th of July was the preserve of whites alone, the correspondent also resisted the idea that distinct racialized conceptions of citizenship had meaning in the United States:

The event celebrated by the whites, is one in which we are interested, and have cause to rejoice, as well as they. Indeed many of our forefathers labored and shed their blood to produce it. And the event which we are specially called upon to celebrate, is one in which every white citizen, who has any regard to the honour, or welfare of his country, has cause to rejoice in as well as we.[34]

Following Forten's earlier "Letters" (and indeed reprinting them in *Freedom's Journal*), the free black community associated with *Freedom's Journal* sought to resist the erasure of black Americans' contribution to the creation and development of the United States and their corresponding claim to citizenship of it.

Reflecting this strategic claim, over the course of its brief life, *Freedom's Journal* contained original contributions and reprints that situated black claims to citizenship within a broader understanding of the meaning of the American Revolution and the documents associated with it. Within those discussions, references to and quotes from the Declaration of Independence worked to emphasize the commitments of the 1776 document to equality and push back against racial prejudice. For instance, Rev. Paul followed up his 1829 claim upon America with the view that "the Patriot" taught "by the pure principles recognized in the declaration of the independence of this country ... abhors such pitiful insolence and pride" as that contained in the ACS plan.[35] Some arguments, such as an 1827 *Freedom's Journal* article, echoed Forten in

[32] "Oration by Thomas L. Jinnings," *Freedom's Journal*, April 4, 1828.
[33] "The Truth and Nothing but the Truth," *The Rights of All*, September 18, 1829.
[34] "For the Freedom's Journal," *Freedom's Journal*, June 29, 1827.
[35] "The Truth and Nothing but the Truth."

highlighting the "strange inconsistency" between "that ever-memorable document (the Declaration of Independence) in which all men are declared to be born free and equal" and a nation that continues "to hold more than a million and a half of their brethren in the most cruel bondage" and in which free blacks "find their freedom to consist rather in name, than in reality."[36] Others made a similar point without direct reference to the Declaration, including a reprinted article from the *New York Observer* that stated that "the United States, where the torch of liberty was first kindled, ... are cherishing in their bosom nearly 2,000,000 of wretched slaves,"[37] and the Fourth of July poem "The Sorrows of Angola":

> Hail, the enrapturing Jubilee!
>   Tis fifty years to-day,
> Since this great nation was made free
>   From despotism's sway
>
> ...
>
> Now, Freedom's sons, in splendid trains,
>   Rush forth, to greet the day;
> But never strive to burst the chains,
>   Of captive – Africa![38]

Conversely, but in the same vein, William Hamilton's reprinted speech celebrating the end of slavery in New York State called the latter event a "victory obtained by the principles, such as are broadly and indelibly laid down by the glorious sons of '76; and are contained in the ever memorable words prefixed to the Declaration of Independence of these United States."[39] In these accounts the Declaration and the Revolution performed the well-worn function of offering a basis upon which to "call out" white America for its failure to live up to its own standards. By highlighting the hypocrisy, such interventions urged an acknowledgment that the Declaration of Independence obliged the United States to treat its black population as citizens.

Nonetheless, published in New York City against the complex backdrop of New York's gradual emancipation law, the somewhat unusual original State constitution of 1777, and the highly discriminatory revised State constitution of 1821, some material in *Freedom's Journal* evinced an understanding of the role of the Declaration of Independence that went beyond its use as a basis for highlighting hypocrisy by linking the Declaration to a broad, constitutional commitment to equality. Comparing the treatment of slaves in the District of Columbia to the Declaration of Independence, a reprinted piece noted:

---

[36] Consistency, "Serious Thoughts," *Freedom's Journal*, June 29, 1827.
[37] "The Revolt in Texas," *Freedom's Journal*, April 20, 1827.
[38] "The Sorrows of Angola," *Freedom's Journal*, June 8, 1827.
[39] "Extract from an Oration," *Freedom's Journal*, October 12, 1827.

It is certainly disgraceful that . . . we should behold human beings in the face of open day, under the sanction of a constitution which proclaims, that *"we hold these truths to be self-evident, that all men are created equal, and endowed by their Creator with certain inalienable rights; that among these are life, LIBERTY, and the pursuit of happiness,"* exposed to view:

> "chained foot to foot and hand to hand,
> Goaded along by scourge and brand."[40]

While performing a similar examination of conditions in Washington, DC, an editorial sarcastically noted:

Professions are nothing, when contradicted by daily practice. While the Constitution declares that all men are born free and equal, the wise corporation of the city of Washington in the plenitude of their power, are proper to prescribe the rights of a certain portion of the community, because the invertible decrees of the Creation have formed them somewhat darker than themselves.

. . .

The scriptures declare that all men are the workmanship of the same Almighty hand; reason that all men are by nature equal; the constitution, that all men have certain unalienable rights. [41]

In February 1828, a correspondent to the newspaper likewise claimed "'THAT all men,' are born free and equal is a position which I think few will deny has been recognized in its fullest extent in our happy Constitution."[42] Strikingly, in all three extracts, text from the Declaration of Independence is identified as drawn from the Constitution.

What is to be made of this identification is not entirely clear. In a wider American society in which the Declaration was increasingly read out loud and venerated, and in a narrower black society in which it was regularly mobilized for the purposes of highlighting white hypocrisy, the misidentification of the Declaration of Independence's most famous words as contained in the federal Constitution multiple times seems, if not evidence of a deliberate ideological strategy, certainly indicative of a way of thinking about the nature of the Constitution.[43] These references to the text of the Declaration of

---

[40] "Travelling Scraps," *Freedom's Journal*, August 29, 1828.
[41] "City of Washington," *Freedom's Journal*, November 16, 1827.
[42] J.H.V., "No Title," *Freedom's Journal*, February 8, 1828.
[43] The discussion here proceeds on the assumption that the authors in question are referring to the US Constitution. Although this cannot be stated definitively, the history of the US and New York constitutions and the context of the extracts are suggestive that this is the case. The wholesale incorporation of the Declaration of Independence into the preamble of the original 1777 constitution of New York State muddies the degree to which this idiosyncratic usage of the Declaration's text is incorrect – the writers here could well be referring to the Preamble of New York's 1777 constitution. But by 1827–28 that constitution had been superseded by one drawn up by a convention in 1821 that dispensed with the lengthy preamble and incorporated

Independence as existing in the constitution offer a productive understanding (or perhaps misunderstanding) of the nature of the federal Constitution. Ascribing to the constitutional document a textual commitment to equality is to imbue it with a substantial ideological content that is largely absent from the actual text. Foreshadowing Abraham Lincoln by several decades, these black authors seem to be engaged in reading the Constitution through the Declaration of Independence and thereby fleshing out the promise of a "more perfect union" with an understanding that "all men are created equal."[44] Linking the formal, institutional commitments of the Constitution with the ideological and symbolic commitments of the Declaration of Independence, the authors here create a potent ambiguity as to the content of the American founding and the space that it opens up for black Americans to claim citizenship in a manner reminiscent of the "constituent moments" theorized by Jason Frank.[45]

In this context, David Walker's *Appeal, in Four Articles; Together with a Preamble, to the Coloured Citizens of the World, But in Particular, and Very Expressly, to Those of the United States of America, Written in Boston, State of Massachusetts, September 28, 1829*, can be productively read as a wide-ranging claim upon American citizenship.[46] Peter Hinks positions the production of David Walker's *Appeal* within the "mainstream of the blossoming black reform movement of the late 1820s" and so similarly against the rise of the ACS and the "expanding body of laws and customs [which] reinforced blacks' subordinate place in America" from the 1820s forward.[47] In line with this, the *Appeal* follows Jinnings and others in staking a claim to the inheritance of America and in rejecting colonization. Drawing upon and quoting Reverend Richard Allen's letter to the *Freedom's Journal*, the *Appeal* noted that black Americans had as equal a claim to North America as

measures to strip free black men of representation in the absence of a freehold equal to 250 dollars. In a community that bore the brunt of that change, it seems unlikely that the writers of these pieces would have been unaware of the revision of the State's constitution. They may, however, have regarded the new constitution as illegitimate on this basis and continued to hold fealty to the 1777 constitution – but the context in which the Declaration's text is used in the previous quotes suggests that a reading audience will quickly identify and understand the references, which somewhat belies the idea that they rest on a personal principled rejection of the existing New York State constitution. The context of two of the quotes – in discussions of the existence of slavery in the District of Columbia – suggests that the authors are more likely referring to the federal Constitution. In that case, the commitments ascribed to the Constitution (that all men are created equal and that they hold unalienable rights) are literally incorrect, but highly suggestive in the ways discussed subsequently.

44 On Lincoln, see Maier, *American Scripture*, 202.

45 Jason Frank, *Constituent Moments: Enacting the People in Postrevolutionary America* (Durham: Duke University Press, 2010).

46 David Walker, *Walker's Appeal, in Four Articles: Together with a Preamble, to the Coloured Citizens of the World, But in Particular, and Very Expressly, to Those of the United States of America, Written in Boston, State of Massachusetts, September 28, 1829* (Boston: David Walker, 1830).

47 Hinks, *To Awaken My Afflicted Brethren*, 109, 204.

any white American. The reprints of Allen stated, "[w]e have *tilled* the ground and made fortunes for thousands ... This land which we have watered with *tears* and *our blood*, is now our *mother country*, and we are well satisfied to stay where wisdom abounds and the gospel is free."[48] Walker echoed and furthered Allen: "America is more our country, than it is the whites – we have enriched it with our *blood and tears*" (73), and earlier, "This country is as much ours as it is the whites" (62). He urged that white Americans "tell us no more about colonization, for American is as much our country, as it is yours" (79).

As did writers in *Freedom's Journal*, Walker mobilized the Declaration of Independence to highlight the hypocrisy contained within America's self-representation as an "Asylum for the oppressed of all nations" (82). Reflecting on efforts to stop the circulation of the *Appeal* in his third edition, Walker asked if "the United States is a Republican Government?" (82). Perhaps, he reasoned, the incendiary content of the *Appeal* that induced such repression was the extract of the Declaration of Independence that he included in it. Quoting the Declaration in the text, he drew the attention of white America to the gap between their own behavior and the commitments of the Declaration and called upon the wider world to witness the "declaration of these very American people, of the United States" (84). "See your Declaration Americans!!! Do you understand your own language? Hear your language, proclaimed to the world, July 4th, 1776" (85). As with others within the free black community, Walker placed emphasis upon the claim that "all men are created equal," reiterating and capitalizing the statement while enlarging "All" and "Equal" (85).

Alongside the rhetorical similarity, the *Appeal* also followed *Freedom's Journal* in offering performances of literary achievement, interpellating a black public sphere, and facilitating moments of reasoned judgment as enactments of the claimed citizenship. As with *Freedom's Journal* and *The Rights of All*, Walker's *Appeal* worked to challenge the notion of black inferiority by presenting evidence of literary achievement. On the very first page of the *Appeal*'s "Preamble," Walker establishes both his position as a black author through his membership of the "we" of the "coloured people of these United States" and his education through references to Josephus and Plutarch, and knowledge of classical Sparta, Egypt, and Rome.[49] Identifying himself as both black and well read, Walker challenged antebellum justifications of racial prejudice through this self-representation, a challenge that was inadvertently recognized by those who expressed doubt over his authorship of the *Appeal*.[50] Likewise, in addressing Thomas Jefferson's claims of black inferiority, Walker fulfilled his own desire to "see the charges of

---

[48] Walker, *Walker's Appeal*, 64–65.
[49] Walker, *Walker's Appeal*, 3. On the importance of literary character for Walker and others, see McHenry, *Forgotten Readers*.
[50] Hinks, *To Awaken My Afflicted Brethren*, 117–18.

Mr. Jefferson refuted by the blacks *themselves,"* and so demonstrated the capacity of black writers to engage Jefferson as equals.[51] In this sense, the title of pamphlet as expressed on the cover of the third edition, beginning *"Walker's Appeal ... "* and ending "Written in Boston, State of Massachusetts, September 28, 1829," operated to reinforce the significance of Walker's authorship for the argument of the text and to provide supportive information as to its provenance. Walker's demands of his readership and the dissemination of the *Appeal* worked to make visible a black public. Walker's famous expectation that "all coloured men, women, and children ... will try to procure a copy of this Appeal and read it, or get some one to read it to them" sought to incorporate all coloured people within a public and to address the weakness he identified in his speech to the General Colored Association in Boston (1828) that "we are disunited ... and, that the cause of which, is a powerful auxiliary in keeping us from rising to the scale of reasonable and thinking beings."[52] The deep penetration of the *Appeal* into the South and West and its merger of "the Southern African American culture of resistance and rebellious religion ... with flowering Northern culture of moral improvement" did much to make this public a national one.[53] Moreover, as Walker's demand that "Men of colour, who are also of sense" should *"go to work and enlighten your brethren"* and his appeal on behalf of *The Rights of All* show, he linked this public to the broader aim of proving "to the Americans and the world, that we are MEN, and not *brutes,* as we have been represented."[54] Crucially, as Melvin Rogers suggests, this identification of a black public to which an appeal was addressed affirmed the black population's "political standing as claimant and recipient [of the *Appeal,* and ...] presumes the equal capacity of actors to judge."[55] As Rogers documents, in framing the text as an "Appeal ... to the Coloured Citizens," Walker drew upon a genre in which the audience is recognized as holding the capacity to judge a supplicant and so identified the black population as holding the demotic rationality associated with freedom and citizenship.[56] At the same time, Rogers argues that the pamphlet required white opponents to acknowledge the author as a "judgment-making being" or to let the arguments go without response.[57] Thus, through the production and dissemination of the text, Walker's text called for and enacted modes of black citizenship.

The *Appeal* also advanced claims to citizenship, and in particular, American citizenship through the arguments offered and their arrangement. At the very

[51] See Article I, Walker, *Walker's Appeal.*
[52] "Address, Delivered before the General Colored Association at Boston, By David Walker," *Freedom's Journal,* December 20, 1828.
[53] Hinks, *To Awaken My Afflicted Brethren,* 116–72, 198.
[54] Walker, *Walker's Appeal,* 33, 76, 33. Original Emphasis.
[55] Rogers, "David Walker and the Political Power of the Appeal," 211.
[56] Rogers, "David Walker and the Political Power of the Appeal."
[57] Walker, *Walker's Appeal,* 219.

beginning of the "Preamble," Walker addresses himself to "My dearly beloved Brethren and Fellow Citizens" (3), reiterating the pamphlet's title's recognition of "coloured citizens," but the "Preamble" also discusses Walker's duty "to you, my country and my God," (5) so laying claim to the country itself. Acknowledging that support for colonization springs from a resistance to blacks being "set free in America," Walker frames the demands of his brethren as

nothing but the rights of man, viz. for them to set us free, and treat us like men, and there will be no danger, for we will love and respect them, and protect our country. (74–5)

A future of black and white citizens living in harmony is reiterated elsewhere with the following assurance:

Treat us like men, and there is no danger but we will all live in peace and happiness together. For we are not like you, hard hearted, unmerciful, and unforgiving. What a happy country this will be, if the whites will listen. What nation under heaven, will be able to do any thing with us, unless God gives us up into its hand? (79)

Moreover, as Timothy Patrick McCarthy has noted, the "formal elements of the *Appeal* make clear Walker's intention to incorporate blacks into the language and structure of American nationalism."[58] Pointing to the use of a preamble and articles as reflective of the US Constitution, McCarthy highlights the manner in which Walker emphasizes literacy as a prerequisite for calling the black population "into the tradition of American laws and letters, formally established in the writing of the Declaration of Independence and U.S. Constitution."[59] Using the founding documents of "this *Republican Land of Liberty*" to draw attention to the failings of the United States, Walker, McCarthy suggests, ultimately returns to the "beginning" and challenges "Christian America" to live up to the Declaration of Independence offering "not merely … a declaration of independence for African Americans, but … a demand for inclusion as well."[60]

Walker's *Appeal* offered then a complex and expansive reiteration of arguments emerging from within the free black activist grouping associated with *Freedom's Journal*. In his address to the General Colored Association at Boston, Walker had suggested the need

to unite the colored population, so far, through the United States of America, as may be practicable and expedient; forming societies, opening, extending, and keeping up correspondences, and not withholding any thing which may have the least tendency to meliorate our miserable condition.[61]

[58] McCarthy, "'To Plead Our Own Cause': Black Print Culture and the Origins of American Abolitionism," 136.
[59] McCarthy, "'To Plead Our Own Cause,'" 137.
[60] McCarthy, "'To Plead Our Own Cause,'" 137, 143.
[61] "Address, Delivered before the General Colored Association at Boston, by David Walker."

The *Appeal* seems to fall within the broad framework of such a project, emphasizing the spreading of literacy, forging a national black public, and urging resistance to slavery and black subordination via a vibrant black print culture. And like *Freedom's Journal* and *The Rights of All*, the *Appeal* situates itself within the American polity as it exists, but adopts a critical posture motivated toward its improvement. It would be erroneous to deny that during the 1820s free blacks were, as McHenry notes, "aware of themselves as a unified body, a distinct political entity with unique political concerns and objectives," but it would be equally erroneous to suppose that this awareness led to a complete rejection of American citizenship.[62] Instead, the group around Walker sought to articulate a national citizenship, linked to the founding documents of the United States, of which free black men in particular partook. Encapsulated in the justification for *The Rights of All*, the successor to *Freedom's Journal*, this outlook is captured in Samuel Cornish's position that:

Viewing this great Republick as composed of so many different grades and capacities, [he] considers that there is great room for, and that it is all important, that he as well as others, should contribute his mite towards the improvement of all its parts, every constituent must become perfect, as far as human perfectability [sic] goes, before the body politic can be made perfect.[63]

Although "especially ... devoted to the rights, & interests of the coloured population," *The Rights of All* does not reject the "great Republick" nor see their fate as distinct from its. Like the *Appeal*, it dismisses the ACS as not interested in the "three million that are now in the United States," and seeks instead to lay claim to membership of a national citizenry centered on an inclusive understanding of the founding and especially the Declaration of Independence.

2.2 BLACK CITIZENSHIP AND THE "RISE" OF WHITE IMMEDIATE ABOLITION

Histories of abolition have traditionally minimized the efforts of the black abolitionists in declaring the 1830s as the beginning of abolition in the United States, a framework that has endured even after revisionist efforts to document the activism of the 1820s and before.[64] Some scholars, such as Daniel J. McInerny, narrow down on a precise date of 1831 as the emergence of an immediate abolitionist movement to suggest that the "post-1831 movement

---

[62] McHenry, *Forgotten Readers*, 38–39.
[63] "To Our Patrons, and the Publick Generally," *The Rights of All*, May 29, 1829.
[64] Newman, *The Transformation of American Abolitionism*; William H. Pease and Jane H. Pease, "Introduction," in *The Antislavery Argument* (Indianapolis: The Bobbs-Merrill Company, Inc., 1965), xxii–lxxxiv; Lawrence J. Friedman, *Gregarious Saints: Self and Community in American Abolitionism, 1830–1870* (Cambridge, UK: Cambridge University Press, 1982).

stands as a distinct unit of study."[65] This approach gives rise to a variety of strategies to explain why 1831 marks a pivotal point for such study, often focusing on the influence of religion on white abolitionists, but equally exploring the internal politics of the gradualist abolitionist movement, Garrison's encounters with the courts, and/or his interaction with black abolitionists.[66] Nevertheless, recent scholarship is moving toward the consensus that "Evolution, not transformation, characterized the history of antislavery," and that whereas 1831 marks a decisive moment within Garrison's career, it was less decisive in terms of abolitionist thought.[67] Indeed, in her recent monumental study of the abolitionist movement, Sinha suggests that the abolitionists of the so-called neglected period of the 1820s "inaugurated many of the tactics and ideas used by their successors in the antebellum period."[68] Moreover, the apparent gap between the "militancy" of Walker and any approach taken by Garrison seems less visible in the pronouncements of the 1830s than in the subsequent historiography of such texts. Maria Stewart linked Walker and Garrison in exclaiming "God has raised you up a Walker and a Garrison," while Garrison himself reprinted the *Appeal* in the first six months of the *Liberator*.

Indeed, one of the key early texts of Garrisonianism can be productively understood as a continuity of, rather than departure from or moderation of, the 1820s abolitionism associated with *Freedom's Journal*. Garrison's publication of *Thoughts on African Colonization*, in 1832, offered a conduit by which the fruits of free black claims on citizenship flowed into the ideology of the movement developing around Garrison.[69] Drawing upon the opposition to

---

[65] Daniel John McInerney, *The Fortunate Heirs of Freedom: Abolition & Republican Thought* (Lincoln: University of Nebraska Press, 1994), 3.

[66] For a variations of such arguments, cf. Pease and Pease, "Introduction"; Ripley, "Introduction to the American Series"; Robert Fanuzzi, *Abolition's Public Sphere* (Minneapolis: University of Minnesota, 2003); Newman, *The Transformation of American Abolitionism*; David Brion Davis, *The Problem of Slavery in the Age of Emancipation* (New York, NY: Alfred A. Knopf, 2014), 185–90; David Brion Davis, "The Emergence of Immediatism in British and American Antislavery Thought," *The Mississippi Valley Historical Review* 49, no. 2 (1962): 209–30.

[67] Steven Mintz, "Introduction," in *The Problem of Evil: Slavery, Freedom, and the Ambiguities of American Reform*, ed. Steven Mintz and John Stauffer (Amherst: University of Massachusetts Press, 2007), 132. Even Newman in seeking to identify the "transformation" acknowledges that in the lead up to 1830 "African Americans developed an arsenal of strategies and tactics that diverged sharply from the learned and dispassionate legal/political activism of white abolitionists" and which fed into the white immediatism of the 1830s. Newman, *The Transformation of American Abolitionism*, 87.

[68] Manisha Sinha, *The Slave's Cause: A History of Abolition* (New Haven: Yale University Press, 2016), 191.

[69] William Lloyd Garrison, *Thoughts on African Colonization: Or An Impartial Exhibition of the Doctrines, Principles and Purposes of the American Colonization Society. Together with the Resolutions, Addresses and Remonstrances of the Free People of Color* (Boston: Garrison and Knapp, 1832).

the ACS that had galvanized the free black activist community in the 1820s, Garrison's *Thoughts on African Colonization* distilled the arguments that had convinced him to oppose colonization.[70] Despite a set of "introductory remarks" that made overbearing use of the first-person pronoun and the overlooking of *Freedom's Journal*, *Thoughts* as a whole was a faithful restatement of 1820s arguments against the ACS (Part 1), followed by a reprinting of black voices within that debate (Part 2).[71] It also echoed Walker's *Appeal* in framing its challenge as pursuing the core question of "whether it is not the sacred duty of the nation to abolish the system of slavery now, and to recognize the people of color as brethren and countrymen who have been unjustly treated and covered with unmerited shame" – which is to say, in equating abolition with the recognition of the black population as "brethren *and* countrymen."[72] Sinha has suggested that "a principled commitment to black equality" was what marked out an abolitionist from others with antislavery sentiments – if so, then *Thoughts on African Colonization* followed Walker's *Appeal* in making its claim to abolitionism within the framework of a shared claim to nationality.[73]

The reprints of the various black public meetings in *Thoughts on African Colonization* demonstrate that the arguments developed in the late 1820s in response to the ACS continued to be influential in the early 1830s. Both in the organization and presentation of the meetings and through the content of their statements, free black communities advanced a claim upon American citizenship. The meetings themselves were organized and presented in ways that accorded with the expectations of public political action in the early Republic. For instance, at the meeting at New Haven on August 8, 1831, "Mr. Henry Berrian was called to the chair, and Mr. Henry N. Merriman was appointed secretary," establishing the meeting as formally structured and having been brought to order. Thereupon, a series of resolutions were "unanimously adopted," the final one of which was that "the proceedings of this meeting be signed by the Chairman and Secretary, and sent to the Liberator for publication," ensuring that the meeting was both formally recorded and its content circulated within the republican printed sphere.[74] Other meetings, such as the one held in Trenton on November 30, 1831, appointed committees to draft addresses based on the resolutions passed, themselves often addressed to "colored citizens," enabling a further opportunity to engage in the demotic rationality Melvin Rogers associates

---

[70] Ripley, "Introduction to the American Series," 10.

[71] Davis, *The Problem of Slavery in the Age of Emancipation*, 189–90.

[72] Garrison, *Thoughts on African Colonization*, iv.

[73] Manisha Sinha, "Did the Abolitionists Cause the Civil War?," in *The Abolitionist Imagination*, ed. Andrew Delbanco (Cambridge, MA: Harvard University Press, 2012), 95.

[74] Garrison, *Thoughts on African Colonization*, Part Two, 30–31. On the republican print sphere, cf. Michael Warner, *The Letters of the Republic: Publication and the Public Sphere in Eighteenth-Century America* (Cambridge, MA: Harvard University Press, 1990).

with Walker's *Appeal*.[75] In the records of the meetings, the citizenship and respectability of the participants, as well as the size and public-ness of the events, is stressed in framing the meetings as instances of political activity in accordance with the expectations of antebellum political citizenship. As such the meetings and their circulation operated as performances of citizenship, undermining prejudicial arguments linked to the capacity of the black population to act as political participants, but more importantly attesting directly to the citizenship status of free blacks.

The content of the circulated records of the meetings also advanced claims upon citizenship, and, in particular, a national citizenship linked to the Declaration of Independence. Following the 1820s, the meetings laid claim to "our country," emphasized participation in the Revolutionary War, and highlighted the hypocrisy contained within a white attachment to the Declaration of Independence while testifying to their members' citizenship. A "public meeting of the colored citizens of New-York" issued "An Address to the Citizens of New-York," which stated:

The time must come when the declaration of independence will be felt in the hearts as well as uttered from the mouth, and when the rights of all shall be properly acknowledged and appreciated. God hasten that time. This is our home, and this is our country. Beneath its sod lie the bones of our fathers: for it some of them fought, bled, and died. Here we were born, and here we will die.[76]

In Rhode Island, "a respectable meeting of the colored people of Providence, R. I., duly appointed and publicly holden":

Resolved, That as our fathers participated with the whites in their struggle for liberty and independence, and believing with the Declaration of that Independence, "that all men are created free and equal ..." and as we have committed no crime worthy of banishment – Therefore

Resolved, That we will not leave our homes, nor the graves of our fathers, and this boasted land of liberty and Christian philanthropy.[77]

In Pennsylvania, "a respectable meeting of Afric-Americans [*sic*] convened pursuant to public notice" at Columbia viewed "all the arguments of [the advocates of ACS] as mere sophistry, not worthy our notice as freemen. Being citizens of these United States, we could call upon our brethren to awake from their slumber of ignorance."[78] In Pittsburgh, "a large and respectable meeting of the colored citizens" avowed:

That "we hold these truths to be self-evident: that all men are created equal, and endowed by their Creator with certain inalienable rights; that among these are life, liberty, and the pursuit of happiness" – Liberty and Equality now, Liberty and Equality forever!

---

[75] Garrison, *Thoughts on African Colonization*, Part Two, 45–48.
[76] Garrison, Part Two, 13, 17.   [77] Garrison, Part Two, 44–45.
[78] Garrison, Part Two, 31–32.

and that "we, the colored people of Pittsburgh and citizens of these United States, view the country in which we live as our true and proper home."[79] A similar use of the Declaration can be seen in resolutions arising from "a large, well informed and respectable meeting of the citizens of Harrisburg":

That we hold these truths to be self-evident, (and it is the boast declaration of our independence,) that all men (black and white, poor and rich) are born free and equal; that they are endowed by their Creator with certain inalienable rights; that among these are life, liberty, and the pursuit of happiness. This is the language of America, of reason, and of eternal truth.[80]

Moving in parallel, the claims furthered by the practices of the meetings themselves and claims made within the content of the meetings' resolutions thus followed the path offered by *Freedom's Journal, The Rights of All*, and the *Appeal* in advocating for recognition of black citizenship of the United States.

Nonetheless, within the resolutions and addresses of some of these meetings, the role of the Declaration of Independence in these arguments and the nation more widely seems to be undergoing something of an evolution. While the foregoing meetings fairly faithfully reproduced the Declaration as a pivot upon which to highlight white hypocrisy, other meetings move toward articulating a view of the document as a repository of constitutional guarantees and looked tentatively to the federal government to ensure them. An "Address" arising from the meeting in Lewiston, Pennsylvania, seemed to question the legitimacy of laws that conflicted with the Declaration in stating:

The Declaration of Independence declares, that "all men are born free and equal:" it does not say that the *white* man or the *black* man is free, – but all, without respect to color, tongues, or nation. We therefore consider all laws to enslave or degrade the people of color as contrary to the letter and spirit of this Declaration.[81]

In Brooklyn, "a numerous and respectable meeting of the colored inhabitants" resolved in familiar terms:

That we know of no other country in which we can justly claim or demand our rights as citizens, whether civil of political, but in these United States of America, our native soil: And, that we shall be active in our endeavors to convince the members of the Colonization Society, and the public generally, that we are *men*, that we are *brethren*, that we are *countrymen* and *fellow-citizens*, and demand an equal share of protection from our federal government with any other class of citizens in the community.[82]

But that meeting's "Address to the Colored Citizens of Brooklyn. (N.Y.) and its Vicinity" protested that the proceedings of the ACS were "a stigma upon our morals as a people, as natives and citizens of this country, to whom equal rights are guaranteed by the Declaration of Independence."[83] In Wilmington, Delaware, "a large and respectable meeting of the people of color" linked the

---

[79] Garrison, Part Two, 34–35.   [80] Garrison, Part Two, 40, 41.   [81] Garrison, Part Two, 49.
[82] Garrison, Part Two, 24.   [83] Garrison, Part Two, 25.

US Constitution and the Declaration in expressing the view that the project of the ACS was "wholly incompatible with the spirit of the Constitution and Declaration of Independence of these United States," while their "Address" rejected a plan "which we fear was designed to deprive us of the rights that the Declaration of Independence declares are the 'unalienable rights' of all men."[84] And in Massachusetts "a respectable meeting of the colored inhabitants of the town of Nantucket" resolved:

That we hold this truth to be self-evident, that all men are born free and equal; that we are men, and therefore ought to share as much protection and enjoy as many privileges under our federal government as any other class of the community.[85]

While by no means a clear shift nor a clear marker on a set trajectory, the missives of these latter meetings seem to point to a more robust role for the Declaration of Independence within the constitutional order. In doing so, they point to an understanding of citizenship as linked to the ability to make claims upon the "guarantees" of the Declaration of Independence.

2.3 CONCLUSION

Taken as a whole, the meetings reprinted in *Thoughts on African Colonization* depict a continuing black strategy of enacting and attesting to membership of a national citizenry. Following the arguments and developments of the late 1820s, these resolutions and addresses – and their reprinting in the *Liberator* and then *Thoughts on African Colonization* – provided a bridge between the citizenship claims of the free black abolitionists of the 1820s and Garrison. Located historically with reference to the Revolutionary War and drawing upon the Declaration of Independence, this national citizenship rendered the increasing popularity of the Declaration of Independence noted by Maier to more expansive ends than many white Americans envisaged. But they also accelerated the tendency noted by Maier to impart a substantive ideological content to the Declaration, beginning to look to the document as not only a proclamation of independence but also an articulation of what it meant to be American and to look to the federal government as institutionally responsible for the furtherance of the "American" spirit.

Some sense of such an understanding of the Declaration of Independence is hinted at in Garrison's own invocations of the document in *Thoughts on African Colonization*. Garrison included reference to the Declaration of Independence to highlight hypocrisy, but also linked it to a shared national identity by decrying white America's deprivation of "millions of their own countrymen of political and social rights."[86] He also drew directly upon the Declaration as a symbol of righteousness in his depiction of himself "with the Declaration of Independence in one hand, and the Bible in the other," and with

---

[84] Garrison, Part Two, 36, 37.   [85] Garrison, Part Two, 34.   [86] Garrison, Part One, 14.

his faith that "As long as there remains among us a single copy of the Declaration of Independence, or of the New Testament, I will not despair of the social and political elevation of my sable countrymen."[87] With time, the tendency to look to the Declaration of Independence as an articulation of what America was (or rather what it ought to be) would raise questions as to when America came to be America, how it should be presented to the wider world, and would ultimately draw forth rival articulations of the spirit of America in ways that would decisively shape notions of what it meant to have a constitution. Moving into the 1830s, the idea that the Declaration of Independence informed the aims and scope of the federal Constitution would provide the abolitionist movement with a way to read the Constitution in antislavery terms. Passing through the crucible of the debates over slavery in the District of Columbia, an even stronger association between the two documents would emerge for some abolitionists. Coming to be understood as revealing the spirit of the Constitution, the Declaration would be offered by the political abolitionists of the 1840s as evidence that slavery represented a betrayal of the spirit of the founding. But for now, it is enough to note that as the abolitionist movement entered the era of interracial immediatism, the wider abolitionist movement's sense of the Declaration of Independence and its significance was drawn from the arguments for and vision of national citizenship advanced by free black populations, themselves following the strategies and arguments of the late 1820s.

[87] Garrison, Part One, 14, 146.

3

Abolitionism and the Constitution in the 1830s

> We show no disrespect to our Constitution, therefore, by insisting upon the
> abolition of Slavery.
>
> *Abolition Principles* (1833)[1]

The 1820s were marked by a gradual reconsideration on the part of the second
generation of (white) Americans of their role in the world-historical events
associated with the American Revolution.[2] At the same time, free black
abolitionist communities in the North were enacting their identity as citizens
through political participation and claims-making upon the Declaration of
Independence. As might be expected, the interracial immediatist abolition
movement of the early 1830s drew on these developments in fashioning an
understanding of what the movement itself was doing and what the role of the
Declaration of Independence within American political life was.[3] The result was
a conception of abolition as the fulfillment of commitments made at the time of
the Revolution but which subsequent actions had left unmet. Viewing
themselves as not merely preserving, but fulfilling the revolutionary
settlement, abolitionists increasingly related their mission to the Declaration
of Independence, dating the nation's existence from the latter and coming to

---

[1] *Abolition Principles* (Providence Anti-Slavery Society, 1833), 2.
[2] See this book's Introduction for further discussion of this reconsideration.
[3] To treat the abolitionist movement of the earlier 1830s as a single bloc may seem to smooth over
significant differences, some of which foreshadowed the schism of the late 1830s. But to the extent
that there is little evidence that *they* saw themselves as distinct blocs in the earlier 1830s, and that
on the issues discussed here there was as much variation within the different clusters as between
them, this chapter examines the movement as a whole within the time period between Garrison's
Thoughts on Colonization and prior to the buildup to the 1836 election. Nonetheless, on the
differences between elements of the (white) movement, cf. Lawrence J. Friedman, *Gregarious
Saints: Self and Community in American Abolitionism, 1830–1870* (Cambridge, UK: Cambridge
University Press, 1982).

regard it as the fundamental expression of the spirit of the United States and the Americans who comprised its citizenry. They cast themselves as acting in parallel to the founding fathers, citing similarities between the characteristics demanded in 1776 and in the early 1830s and expressing concern for the possibility of transmitting an unfulfilled revolutionary settlement to posterity. These arguments were powerfully articulated in the Declaration of the National Anti-Slavery Convention that met at the end of 1833 and initiated the institutionalization of the movement through a national organization. The National Anti-Slavery Society, in particular, would seek to draw a connection between its aims and the completion of a project, initiated by the Declaration of Independence, of creating a nation defined by equality.

But the casting of the Declaration of Independence as a fount of liberty did not fully address the ambiguity of the revolutionary inheritance. Even if the Declaration offered a mechanism for understanding the Revolution as foreshadowing abolition, the US Constitution stood in stark contrast as the institutional support for slavery at the federal level. The abolitionists of the 1830s were faced with the problem of reconciling this difference if they were to hold the founding close. As previously noted, free black abolitionists had begun to advance arguments that tentatively linked the spirit of the Declaration of Independence (as they understood it) to constitutional guarantees, seeing in the Declaration the animating principles of the Constitution. The early 1830s would see the wider abolitionist movement more directly attempt to systematize such a relationship, arguing that the Constitution ought to be interpreted in accordance with the Declaration of Independence. Some would go further and argue that the Declaration was more fundamental than the US Constitution itself. Just as the earlier arguments had cultivated a sense of American national identity tied to the principle of equality, these variations furthered the association of the claim that "all men are created equal" with the American sense of self. This increasingly ideological formation of national identity set the stage for the conflict over the physical incarnation of that identity in the nation's capital detailed in the following chapters.

3.1   THE ABOLITIONISTS WITHIN POLITICAL TIME

Robert Fanuzzi has suggested that "the germane historical setting" for the abolitionists of the mid-1830s was the 1790s and its "radical democratic politics of artisan republicanism," which looked back to the American Revolution and its "unfilled promise."[4] In this reading of the movement, Garrison sought to fashion a role for the *Liberator* as a site of republican print politics geared toward enactments of individual independence, recursively seen in Garrison's breaks with fellow abolitionists, newspaper patrons, and subscribers, and ultimately the Union itself. Offering reiterations

---

[4] Robert Fanuzzi, *Abolition's Public Sphere* (Minneapolis: University of Minnesota, 2003), xxix.

of the Declaration of Independence in the many declarations of sentiment issued by Garrison and fellow travelers, the Garrisonian branch of the abolitionist movement sought to both "tap" the revolutionary spirit of 1776 and move beyond it through the radical print democracy associated with the Painite democratic-republican societies of the 1790s. If Fanuzzi is correct that the Revolution served as a historical framing for the maneuvers undertaken by Garrison in the 1830s and 1840s, it is also true that the Revolution worked as a touchstone for many of the abolitionists on an even more basic level. While Garrison may have engaged in an "ironic use" of the history of the Revolution, in the early 1830s most abolitionists made use of and understood their place in history in something less than an ironic sense. For such actors, their location in history was not one that offered the potential for the reemergence of revolutionary sentiments, but was instead one that positioned them generationally after a revolution initiated by the founders but before the posterity that would fully benefit – or not benefit – from it. Locating themselves within a historical period initiated by the American Revolution, the abolitionists shared many of the concerns of their generational cohort with regard to their own role in history. Whereas Fanuzzi argues that Garrison sought to capture and redeploy a mode of history drawn from the 1790s – that "Garrison wanted little else for the abolition movement than for it to have come too late … an epistemologically privileged position that put abolition on the side of progress, revolution, and popular democracy" – other abolitionists in the early 1830s seemed more concerned with directly tapping the spirit of '76.[5] But if they framed themselves as the successors rather than re-embodiments of the revolutionaries of 1776, they were still faced with the complex task of understanding the consequences of that legacy.[6]

William Snelling illustrated the potentiality of tapping the legacy of the Revolution in an address to the New England Anti-Slavery Society in 1833. Reprinted across three months in *The Abolitionist*, Snelling's speech urged his fellow abolitionists to think of their duty in relation to that of their fathers'. Meeting the accusation that abolition efforts would offend and irritate the South, Snelling declared, "Our fathers offended their English brethren when they threw the tea into the dock, and irritated them still more when, within cannon-shot of this hall, they taught their fellow subjects, that Americans would not submit to wrong."[7] With regard to the claim that individual exertions could

---

[5] Fanuzzi, *Abolition's Public Sphere*, xxiv–xxv.

[6] Jennifer Mercieca has discussed the "ironic partisanship" of the Antebellum period, by which Americans celebrated their democratic control over government and succumbed to their weakness in the face of party institutions. In a similar way, abolitionists found themselves celebrating the ideological legacy of the Revolution but, at the same time, constrained by the precise arrangements that arose from it. Jennifer R. Mercieca, *Founding Fictions* (Tuscaloosa: The University of Alabama Press, 2010).

[7] "Extracts from an Address Delivered before the N.E. Anti-Slavery Society, By Wm. J. Snelling, Esq. (Continued.)," *The Abolitionist* 1, no. 4 (1833): 53.

not make a difference, Snelling offered, "if our fathers had all thought so, the battle of Bunker's Hill [*sic*] would never have been fought, our independence would never have been achieved, Massachusetts would now be a British colony."[8] In these moments, Snelling, by comparing the failings of the present generation with the courage of the fathers', sought to mobilize the anxiety that the contemporary generation had with regard to their place in history to the furtherance of abolition in what was a superficially fairly mundane manner. But it is worth pausing to note that this mobilization only made sense and had any power because his audience understood themselves to be both linked to and distant from the prior generation, that is, subsequent to them within a linear and shared chronological space.

There is a complexity within Snelling's address that belies understanding it as merely an appeal to "live up to" their fathers. For one thing, the very challenge the abolitionists faced – the existence and continuation of slavery – was a product of the actions of that earlier generation. Snelling's address had early on conceded, "It is true that our fathers committed a grievous crime in bringing slaves to our shores. The original guilt was theirs, not ours."[9] The fathers were then not without sin, and their sin was shared and passed on to the current generation, who "stand with them in the relation of receiver and thief."[10] But, at the same time, the founding generation had left open the possibility of ending that relationship of sin: "The Constitution of the United States, indeed, recognizes slavery; but our fathers, who framed it, never said or thought that it would be criminal to wish to amend it."[11] As such Snelling's generation's inheritance was ambiguous at best – the founding generation had left both the crime and the means of addressing it as a legacy. Moreover, the possibility of addressing slavery meant that the current generation had the potential to surpass the founding generation. This potential is hinted at in Snelling's discussion of the Boston Tea Party, where he notes that "our fathers" taught their "fellow subjects" that "Americans would not submit to wrong." In this description, Snelling identifies the founding generation as *subjects* to the British monarch in the process of articulating what it means to be an *American* – submitting to no wrong. Whereas the founding generation aspired to not submit to wrong, and fell short in crafting a constitution that recognized slavery, Snelling's audience are interpellated as Americans, unable to recognize slavery and so destined to abolish it. They are, in this sense, already in the position of having transcended the founding generation. But once again, this only makes sense if they are understood to be chronologically after their fathers' generation. In this regard, they were not constrained to mere

---

[8] "Extracts from an Address Delivered before the N.E. Anti-Slavery Society," 73.
[9] "Extracts from an Address Delivered before the N.E. Anti-Slavery Society," 36.
[10] "Extracts from an Address Delivered before the N.E. Anti-Slavery Society," 36.
[11] "Extracts from an Address Delivered before the N.E. Anti-Slavery Society," 53.

"preservation" of the existing revolutionary settlement but had inherited the potential to expand upon it.

This ambiguous relationship with the founders and the founding, which paralleled the second generation's approach elsewhere, reoccurred in different ways within the abolitionist literature of the early 1830s. Aside from the appeals to the Declaration of Independence, which are discussed in more detail subsequently, the exact relationship between the present generation and their revolutionary fathers was a source of discombobulation. Trying to make sense of the 1833 riot in New York City that met attempts to create a New York City Anti-Slavery Society, *The Abolitionist* exclaimed, "What a chapter have I written in the history of republican America! What a tribute to the memory of our fathers, who poured out their blood like water to establish the principle, that 'All men are created equal.'"[12] These two short sentences conveyed the complexity of the project of positioning the abolitionists within the history of the United States. The first sentence located the events surrounding the riot within the time scape of "republican America," and that it was a chapter suggested that such a time was ongoing. The second sentence adopted a sarcastic tone to suggest the riot was a "tribute" to the proceeding fathers who had established the principle that "All men are created equal." But the riot, and the widespread resistance to abolition it represented, suggested that such a principle had not in fact been established, at least as the abolitionists understood that principle. Earlier in the same paragraph, the writer in dismay feared that the riot showed that the spirit of slavery had "poisoned the heart's blood of the *whole* American nation," excepting the "few, confessedly a handful of free citizens" that sought to abolish slavery.[13] The abolitionists were depicted here as the voices in the wilderness, seeking to overturn the consensus in favor of slavery that was resistant to even discussion of the issue. But if so, then it was far from clear that the riot represented a deviation from the legacy of the fathers. In suggesting that it was an unworthy "tribute," *The Abolitionist* was repurposing a revolutionary inheritance that had resulted in a society that was increasingly racializing questions of equality in order to portray resistance to racial equality within that society as illegitimate.[14]

A correspondent to *The Emancipator* on the subject of the 1833 riot similarly betrays an equivocal positioning of the abolitionists with relation to the legacy of the American Revolution. "An Abolitionist" locates the events in New York within a period of time initiated by the American Revolution, but also one whose end would be defined by emancipation. The correspondent wrote:

---

[12] "Riot in New-York," *The Abolitionist* 1, no. 11 (1833): 171.   [13] "Riot in New-York," 171.

[14] James Brewer Stewart, "The Emergence of Racial Modernity and the Rise of the White North, 1790–1840," *Journal of the Early Republic* 18, no. 2 (1998): 181–217. An index of this racialization can be seen in the attempts to predicate voting rights on race in the Northern states, see for example, Rhode Island's "Dorr Rebellion." W. Caleb McDaniel, *The Problem of Democracy in the Age of Slavery: Garrisonian Abolitionists & Transatlantic Reform* (Baton Rouge: Louisiana State University Press, 2013), 141–42.

Future generations will scarcely credit the record, that in the middle of the nineteenth century, in the fifty-eighth year of American independence, a proposal to establish an Antislavery Society in New-York, threw the whole city into a ferment ... so the fact must be written down, and transmitted to posterity. ... Were Antislavery societies to succumb beneath the violence of the present opposition, the emancipation of two millions of our fellow-men from worse than Egyptian bondage, would be delayed for one generation, at least.[15]

In dating the riot in a period of time measured from American independence, "An Abolitionist" – given the associations abolitionists regularly made between 1776 and equality – can be understood to be suggesting the incongruity of a riot against abolition fifty-eight years after the Declaration that "all men are created equal." But the writer's incredulity is also expressed in terms of an incongruity of such a riot with modernity ("in the middle of the nineteenth century") and a belief that future generations would not credit accounts of such. The notion of a "delay" and the supposed disbelief of future generations carry a sense of the inevitability of abolition (although to be sure, "at least" works to mitigate some of that conviction), indicating that slavery holds only a temporary status within the broad scope of the "modern" future. Put together, we are presented with an epoch of modern antislavery activity initiated by the revolutionary fathers' commitment to equality and culminating in the inevitable abolition of slavery at some future date.

But the position of "An Abolitionist" and his or her abolitionist peers within this period of time is marked by ambiguity. As with the coverage of *The Abolitionist*, the correspondent to *The Emancipator* finds the supporters of abolition assailed on all sides, belying a claim that the Revolution has established widespread support for the values motivating the abolitionists. The latter writer interprets the opposition to the meeting of the New York Anti-Slavery Society as "an omen of good to our cause," showing that abolition is a real threat to slave-holding interests, but also as a signal that abolitionism will be violently resisted – in words that echo Thomas Paine's, "An Abolitionist" declares "there are times, (and this the commencement of one) which try men's souls."[16] Invoking Paine's assessment of the Revolutionary War as a description of the period commencing with the New York riot, the author of this article would seem to be claiming that the abolitionist struggle parallels that of the founding fathers. Moreover, if we are to infer that the author sees Paine's *The Crisis* as a relevant textual invocation, then abolition is not the preserve of the unreliable and uncommitted "summer soldier" or "the sunshine patriot," a sense reiterated by the author's exhortation that "every true friend of the Negro ... buckle on his armor."[17] Abolition is not the uncomplicated carrying

---

[15] "Communications," *The Emancipator*, October 26, 1833.   [16] "Communications."
[17] Thomas Paine, "The Crisis: In Thirteen Numbers. Written During the Late War," in *Selected Writings of Thomas Paine*, ed. Ian Shapiro and Jane E. Calvert (New Haven: Yale University Press, 2014), 53; "Communications."

of the Revolution to completion; rather, it is instead a new struggle whose receptive audience is not the fathers who went before, but instead the "posterity" to come, who will marvel from their perch in a post-abolition future that there was ever a time that required a movement for abolition. As with Snelling, "An Abolitionist" seems to be balancing a claim upon the founding fathers' legacy with a commitment to transcending them.

Other abolitionist discussions of this period share "An Abolitionist's" and Snelling's concerns over the place of the movement within time and history. Regular consideration is given to the prospect of judgment by succeeding generations. Strongly aware that the founding fathers' failure to address slavery has been passed down to them, abolitionists in the early 1830s expressed apprehension that they would similarly fail their children and burden them with the punishment that slavery would surely bring. *The Emancipator* decried with foresight that the "procrastination of the removal of slavery will cast on succeeding generations ... the millstone of civil war."[18] Others argued that the sooner slavery was abolished, "the better may it be for us, our children, and our children's children."[19] They also recognized the gratitude and admiration that abolishing slavery might gain them from those succeeding generations. At the first convention of the National Anti-Slavery Society, Lewis Tappan urged the importance of recording the efforts of Garrison and Benjamin Lundy, editor of *The Genius of Universal Emancipation*, that "Posterity should know, that their fathers held such men ... to be highly esteemed."[20] Such efforts would ensure that "the coming generation shall hallow their memories, and rise up to call them blessed."[21] Conversely, Amos Phelps added, a failure to support such editors would mean "Posterity will write on our tomb-stones, as they look back on our past history, 'Perished by their own vices.'"[22]

Abolitionists in the early 1830s were then both highly aware of their location with the history of the United States and concerned by the constraints that location presented. It was within this framework that they sought to carve out a historic role for themselves. As much as figures such as Snelling sought to "tap" the Revolution in service of motivation and an ideological commitment to equality, the material experience of abolitionists suggested that they stood on shaky historical ground. Democratic power in the form of mobs and State legislatures presented an obstacle, not an aid, to their mission, suggesting that the Revolution's legacy was not wholly favorable to the abolitionist cause.[23] Nevertheless, they envisioned a future that would judge them harshly for not

---

[18] "Dissolution of the Union," *The Emancipator*, July 27, 1833.
[19] Samuel N. Sweet, "To the Editor of the Liberator," *The Liberator*, September 14, 1833.
[20] "American Anti-Slavery Society," *The Abolitionist* 1, no. 12 (1833): 182.
[21] "American Anti-Slavery Society," 182.   [22] "American Anti-Slavery Society," 183.
[23] For more discussion on this point, cf. McDaniel, *The Problem of Democracy in the Age of Slavery: Garrisonian Abolitionists & Transatlantic Reform.*

addressing slavery, particularly in light of the commitments of the Declaration of Independence. The ambivalence of the Revolution's legacy did not then allow the abolitionists to fully remove themselves from – or indeed, despite Garrison's efforts, to reimagine to any significant extent – the chronology that began with 1776. If they could not fully accept or reject the Revolution's legacy, a third option – transcendence – was suggested by the invocations of a Painite struggle. Moving beyond their fellow Americans who turned in the 1820s and 1830s to preservation as an appropriate response to the Revolution, abolitionists saw a role for themselves as the historic figures who redirected the United States toward the principles present, but waylaid, at the Revolution. Positioned between past and future, they were not trapped by their historical location but blessed with a historically important mission. Situating themselves within "a glorious era in American history," the abolitionists gathering around the National Anti-Slavery Society saw themselves as potentially reestablishing a society that more readily embraced the values of human equality that they saw as centrally American. But if such a posture worked to relate them satisfactorily to the Revolution, it left one element unclear. If it was their destiny to lead America to the true legacy of the Revolution, then how should they relate to the fathers who had not managed to?

3.2   MAKING SENSE OF THE FOUNDING FATHERS

In the same year as the National Anti-Slavery Society met for the first time, the difficulty of relating to the founding fathers surfaced in a minor conflagration over the nature of abolitionists' condemnation of George Washington. In July 1833, William Lloyd Garrison responded to claims made in the *Vermont Chronicle* by denying that *The Liberator* in May had pronounced George Washington "a hypocrite, a thief, a kidnapper, &c. and that he is now in hell."[24] Nonetheless, the issue raged on into September, when the *Vermont Chronicle* argued that it had only applied the "abstract principles" of *The Liberator* to the character of George Washington and disputed the claims of *The Genius of Universal Emancipation* that such inference was the work of the editor of the *Vermont Chronicle* alone.[25] In the September 14th issue of *The Liberator*, the editor was finally induced to meet the grounds of the accusation directly.[26] After reprinting the challenge made by *The Genius of Universal Emancipation* to the editors of the *Vermont Chronicle* on the front page, *The*

---

[24] "From the N.Y. American of July 11," *The Emancipator*, July 20, 1833; "Character of George Washington," *Vermont Chronicle*, May 24, 1833.

[25] "Character of Washington," *Vermont Chronicle*, September 6, 1833.

[26] The editorial suggests that Garrison would probably agree with its sentiments, although he did not write it; Garrison was in the United Kingdom during the summer of 1833. William Lloyd Garrison, "To the Patrons of the Liberator and the Friends of Abolition," in *The Letters of William Lloyd Garrison: Volume I: I Will Be Heard!*, ed. Walter M. Merrill (Cambridge, MA: The Belknap Press of Harvard University Press, 1971), 265. The letter was printed in *The*

Liberator offered an editorial comment that sought to set out *The Liberator*'s view of Washington in clear terms. Noting the view of the editors of *The Genius of Universal Emancipation* that "the writer in the Liberator merely stated an *abstract principle*, and therefore that the Chronicle was unfair in applying it to Washington," the editorial stated that it nonetheless found "this ground untenable."[27] With the disclaimer that "no one, except the correspondent of the Liberator," was responsible for the comments at issue, the editorial proceeded to set out its own view of the accusations against Washington:

[W]e will say frankly what we think of Washington as a slaveholder. We say, then, that he was guilty of violating the command, "Thou shalt not steal." In other words, he was guilty of *man-stealing*. ... It may be asked, if we mean to be understood as saying that Washington was a *thief*? We reply, *no*; not in the common acceptation of that word. ... Nor do we believe that the sin of mansteating necessarily made Washington a *hypocrite*. ... Will the Chronicle deny that slaveholding was a *stain* upon the character of Washington? ... This we say of all slaveholders, and we are ready to defend the proposition against any objections which can be brought against it.[28]

The editorial elided the question of whether Washington was in hell, only touching upon this accusation indirectly in hoping that he had repented his sins. This effort at drawing a line under the controversy, four months after it erupted, is a study in hesitation and equivocation, the like of which is not usually associated with *The Liberator*.[29] Washington is not a thief in the conventional sense, probably was not a hypocrite, and was guilty to the extent that any other slaveholder in the same position would have been. The *Vermont Chronicle* was not satisfied, accusing *The Liberator* evading the question of whether Washington was "a sinner of the first rank."[30]

The equivocation over condemning Washington was perhaps strategic, born of a desire on the part of abolitionists to avoid handing their opponents a stick to beat them within a society that revered the General.[31] But it can also be

---

Liberator of October 12, 1833. "To the Patrons of the Liberator and the Friends of Abolition," *The Liberator*, October 12, 1833.

[27] "Character of Washington," *The Liberator*, September 14, 1833.

[28] "Character of Washington."

[29] The editorial itself claims the delay in offering a direct response was due to "the peculiar course of the Editors of the Chronicle," which "made us desirous of waiting until they had enjoyed the full benefit of their misrepresentations." But it seems hard to credit that *The Liberator* waited until September to respond to an accusation made in May on the basis of a foresight that the accusation would ultimately damage the accuser.

[30] "The Genius of Emancipation," *Vermont Chronicle*, October 11, 1833. Upon his return to the United States after a summer in the United Kingdom, Garrison seemed to indirectly acknowledge the controversy, but did not elaborate upon the September 14th editorial, noting that "[t]he success of my mission seems to have driven 'the enemies of slavery *in the abstract*' to the verge of madness." "To The Patrons of the Liberator and the Friends of Abolition."

[31] George Washington was the most commonly toasted figure across celebrations of the Fourth of July during the early Republic even before the increasing attachment to the founders of the late 1820s. On the canonization of Washington, see François Furstenberg, *In the Name of the Father:*

interpreted as another instance of the abolitionists' lack of clarity as to how to relate to the founding fathers and the founding more generally. On one hand, George Washington – like Thomas Jefferson – had been a slaveholder and so deserved the unrestrained criticism of a movement mobilizing against slavery. On the other hand, in paralleling their own movement with that of the revolutionaries of 1776, abolitionists found themselves unable to wholly reject the leading figure of that earlier generation. This tension was captured in the following lines from a poem, "My Country," printed in *The Liberator* in early 1834:

> Can the name of "MY COUNTRY" – the deeds which we sing –
> Be honored – revered – 'midst pollution and sin?
> Can the names of our fathers who perished in fight,
> Be hallowed in story, midst slavery's blight?[32]

The challenge here was twofold: to make sense of how the founding fathers, as a group of men dedicated to liberty, could have allowed for slavery, and to navigate the contradiction that their actions gave rise to as an inheritance. One simple response was to deny that slaves were human and thereby to limit the scope of liberty to white men, thus enabling an embrace of the founders without qualification.[33] But as the previous chapter showed, such an approach was inimical to the abolitionist project. A more promising, if ultimately suspect, approach was to suggest, as a correspondent in *The Emancipator* did, that the founders would have extended freedom to slaves had they realized the hypocrisy of their actions. Seeking to reconcile the flaws of the "patriotic fathers" regarding slavery with their authorship of sentiment that "all men are created equal," the writer emphatically, if not convincingly, avowed, *"they did not know that negroes were MEN."*[34] More intellectually honest – but historically dubious – varieties of this argument suggested that the absence of the words "slave" or "slavery" from the constitutional document indicated recognition

---

Washington's Legacy, Slavery, and the Making of a Nation (New York, NY: Penguin Books, 2007); Catherine L. Albanese, *Sons of the Fathers: The Civil Religion of the American Revolution* (Philadelphia, PA: Temple University Press, 1976), 143–81. On Washington's own contribution to this process, see Paul K. Longmore, *The Invention of George Washington* (Berkeley, CA: University of California Press, 1988).

[32] "My Country," *The Liberator*, January 4, 1834.

[33] This was the tack taken in an article of the *Telescope* of Columbia, South Carolina, which declared slavery "ours by law and justice – we have inherited from our ancestors," while maintaining, "We are freemen, sprung from a noble stock of freemen." "An Incendiary Article," *The Liberator*, September 21, 1833. An approach echoed in the antirestrictionist responses to the use of the Declaration of Independence during the debates over Missouri's admission – see Chapter 1 of this book.

[34] "Connecticut versus Freedom," *The Emancipator*, August 3, 1833. Similarly misplaced optimism led a writer in *The Liberator* to suppose "that there was a degree of *machiavelism* practiced, in order to get the Federal Constitution through the Convention with the dead weight of SLAVERY upon it." "[For the Liberator.]," *The Liberator*, October 5, 1833.

that slaves would be granted status as free citizens in due course and the founding fathers were secretly antislavery men.[35] Such a line of argument foreshadowed the antislavery readings of the Constitution that animated political abolitionism from the 1840s onward, but in the early 1830s they were not as central to abolitionist debates as they would become.[36]

3.3 ABOLITIONISTS AND THE DECLARATION OF INDEPENDENCE IN THE EARLY 1830S

Instead, in the early years of the 1830s, abolitionists gravitated toward an understanding of the founding fathers and the founding that provided them with rhetorical tools to use against slavery and that both distanced themselves from the founders and capitalized upon the latter's legacy. Like the free black abolitionists of the late 1820s and the antislavery restrictionists during the Missouri Crisis, the abolitionists of the 1830s turned to the Declaration of Independence as a basis for claiming a revolutionary inheritance compatible with abolition.[37] Like the earlier abolitionists, the later activists interpreted the Declaration of Independence in terms that rendered it an expression of an American spirit in which equality, derived from natural law, was the central motif.[38] Using the Declaration as a touchstone, abolitionists mobilized accusations of hypocrisy and offered the Declaration as a basis for the creation of a more inclusive polity. They thereby "solved" the dilemma of their inheritance by understanding it as the initiation of campaign for liberty that it was their responsibility to take up and complete – they could both be the heirs of their forefathers and transcend the latter by bringing the promise of the Declaration to fruition.[39]

The choice to plant themselves on the Declaration of Independence was a shrewd one given the document's popularity in the period. The culmination of the transformations discussed by Pauline Maier had resulted in a material popularity for Declaration that made it a widely available point of reference as well as a culturally significant lever for public opinion.[40] Thus, one abolitionist

---

[35] "Dissolution of the Union."

[36] Helen J. Knowles, "The Constitution and Slavery: A Special Relationship," *Slavery & Abolition* 28, no. 3 (2007): 309–28. For further discussion of these tendencies, see Chapter 9 of this book.

[37] Not least because, to a great extent, these two groups overlapped (see further).

[38] There was awareness among the abolitionists of the early 1830s that the basis in natural law universalized these values, but that recognition does not seem to have mitigated claims that it comprised an "Americanism." The problem identified was rather the failure of America to live up to *its own* values. For further discussion on the Americanization of slavery and its opposition, see the next chapter.

[39] In 1834, Garrison would assert: "We will *preach* the DECLARATION OF INDEPENDENCE, till it begins to be put into practice." William Lloyd Garrison, *Address in Commemoration of the Great Jubilee, of 1st August*, 1834, 3.

[40] On this point, see the previous chapter. Pauline Maier, *American Scripture: Making the Declaration of Independence* (New York: Alfred A. Knopf, 1997).

could describe the widespread worship of the Declaration (as a precursor to highlighting the failure of America to live up to its values) in the following terms:

On this declaration hangs the existence of our government. – on this, a thousand orators, every fourth of July, pronounce an encomium; and a million of freemen laud its doctrine, and asseverate its correctness. … While this record stands on the pages of our national history – while its original hangs in one of the public offices at Washington, as a relic above all price – while ten thousand *fac-similes* grace the halls and parlors of our countrymen – and while our children are taught to read and reverence the names of those who "pledged their lives, their fortunes, and their sacred honor," in defence of its doctrines;[41]

The death of Charles Carroll of Carrollton, the last living signer of the Declaration of Independence, in late 1832, heightened the cultural currency of allusions to the Declaration. Carroll's death tapped into the sense of the passing of the revolutionary generation, the loss of guidance that passing entailed, and the transferring of responsibility for the Revolution to a post-revolutionary generation. In a reprinted extract of Governor Marcy of New York's Message of January 1833, the passing of Carroll was said to mean that "on us is devolved the high responsibility of preserving unimpaired the most valuable inheritance that one generation ever transmitted to another."[42] Although mourning the loss of the generation of the Declaration, Marcy looked to "the history of their lives, and their recorded precepts" for instruction as to fulfilling the "most difficult duty" that his generation owed to "those whom we have succeeded, to our age and to posterity." The abolitionists were not alone in puzzling over their inheritance or in tying it to their immediate political concerns.

Given this context, appeals to the Declaration of Independence were mainstays of abolitionist activism. A petition circulated as part of the campaign to abolish slavery in the District of Columbia utilized the Declaration of Independence and the failure to live up to it as the ideological framework for its challenge. Riffing from the famous lines of the Declaration of Independence, the petition noted that the conditions of slaves in the nation's capital were "not equal to other men" and that they were "for life, deprived of liberty, and the free pursuit of happiness."[43] John G. Whittier, the author of a key abolitionist tract of the early 1830s, "Justice and Expediency," was recorded as professing that the Declaration of Independence proclaimed all people free *"without distinction of color,"* and that the United States, for "more than half a century … have openly violated that solemn Declaration."[44] *The Emancipator* even went as far as mocking proslavery newspapers that celebrated the Fourth of July with "anti-slavery" toasts to the "Patriots and Sages of the Revolution," "Washington," "Jefferson,"

[41] "No Title," *The Emancipator*, May 25, 1833.
[42] "Extract from the Governor's Message," *The Globe*, January 10, 1833.
[43] "Slavery in the District of Columbia," *The Abolitionist* 1, no. 9 (1833): 139.
[44] "Whittier's Reply," *The Liberator*, August 10, 1833.

and the "Fourth of July '76."[45] The centrality of the Declaration also carried over into the constitutions of the emerging Anti-Slavery Societies, which invariably began with an acknowledgment of the "principles of our famed Declaration of Independence,"[46] "the principle laid down in the Declaration of Independence,"[47] or some similar variation.[48]

Indeed, the Declaration of Independence proved to be an important rhetorical support in the formal organization of immediate abolitionism carried out in Philadelphia in 1833. It was in the 1833 "Declaration of the National Anti-Slavery Convention" that the use of the Declaration of Independence was most developed and sustained. Aside from the invocation of a genre of "Declaration," the 1833 address, influenced by the free black abolitionists of the late 1820s and anxieties about succeeding the founding generation, placed the Declaration of Independence at the fore of the movement's ideology. The Convention's Declaration began by locating itself within a temporal order dating from the revolutionary struggles of 1776, noting: "More than fifty-seven years have elapsed since a band of patriots convened in this place to devise measures for the deliverance of this country from a foreign yoke."[49] It continued:

The cornerstone upon which they founded the TEMPLE OF FREEDOM was broadly this – "that all men are created equal; that they are endowed by their Creator with certain inalienable rights; that among these are life, LIBERTY, and the pursuit of happiness."[50]

Having in this way framed the Declaration of Independence as a progressive statement of freedom, the abolitionists in Philadelphia then connected the former to their project of immediate abolition through a claim that the latter was a culmination of the earlier national revolution whose spirit was embodied in the text of 1776. "We have met together for the achievement of an enterprise, without which, that of our fathers is incomplete," ran the 1833 Declaration, before adding that immediate abolition nonetheless "far transcends theirs, as

---

[45] "No Title," *The Emancipator*, August 3, 1833.
[46] "Constitution of the Female Anti-Slavery Society of Philadelphia," *The Liberator*, April 19, 1834.
[47] "Anti-Slavery Society," *The Emancipator*, October 5, 1833.
[48] "Anti-Slavery Society," *The Liberator*, December 21, 1833. A vivid variation of this acknowledgment came from the 1834 Constitution of the Colored Anti-Slavery Society of Newark: "and whereas the people of the United States assembled in the city of Philadelphia, on the 4th day of July, 1776, in the presence of Almighty God, declared that all mankind are created equal. .... Whereas it is our opinion, that if all the blood of our colored brethren, shed by the people of the United States, since the Declaration of Independence, was kept in a reservoir, the framers of that instrument, and their successors might swim in it." C. Peter Ripley, ed., "Constitution of the Colored Anti-Slavery Society of Newark," in *The Black Abolitionist Papers: Volume III: The United States, 1830–1846* (Chapel Hill: The University of North Carolina Press, 1991), 132–33.
[49] "Declaration of the National Anti-Slavery Convention," *The Abolitionist* 1, no. 12 (December 1833): 178.
[50] "Declaration of the National Anti-Slavery Convention," 178.

moral truth does physical force."[51] Returning to the Declaration of
Independence toward the end of the Convention's Declaration, the
Convention reiterated its understanding of abolition as part of the project
initiated in 1776 (as well as that of divine providence):

These are our views and principles – these, our designs and measures. With entire
confidence in the overruling justice of God, we plant ourselves upon the Declaration of
Independence, and upon the truths of Divine Revelation, as upon the EVERLASTING
ROCK.[52]

Like the earlier arguments of black abolitionists, the 1833 Declaration also
went beyond a focus upon slaves per se and identified the "coloured population
of the United States" as deserving of the "rights and privileges which belong to
them as men and as Americans" – which is to say that the Declaration identified
the free black and slave populations as constitutent parts of the American
citizenry.[53]

By the end of 1833, the various pressures on the growing abolitionist
movement had resulted in a strong attachment to the Declaration of
Independence. As the movement growing up around Garrison moved toward
institutionalization as a national organization, it continued to draw upon and
develop the arguments of *Thoughts on African Colonization* and especially the
discussion of the Declaration of Independence therein. In particular, the
National Anti-Slavery Society would seek to draw a connection between its
aims and the completion of a project, initiated by the Declaration of
Independence, of creating a nation defined by equality. Such a connection did
much to resolve the strategic and ideological problems faced by a movement of
reform-minded Americans living within the context of societal attachment to
the figures and achievements of the founding period. However, it left open the
issue of the relationship between the abolitionists and the other key textual

---

[51] "Declaration of the National Anti-Slavery Convention," 178.

[52] "Declaration of the National Anti-Slavery Convention," 179.

[53] That the "Declaration of the National Anti-Slavery Convention" came to follow closely the
arguments developed in *Freedom's Journal* and the black abolitionist speeches of the 1830s
should not perhaps be too surprising. As the previous account of Garrison's *Thoughts on African
Decolonization* suggested, Garrison – as the author of the Declaration – was both aware of and
drew upon black abolitionists to make his arguments in the early 1830s. Moreover, the recorded
signatories to the 1833 Declaration included prominent black abolitionists Robert Purvis, James
G. Barbadoes, and James McCrummell, while others were named as managers to the American
Anti-Slavery Society. It was not merely the case that black abolitionists influenced the thinking of
the immediate abolitionists of the early 1830s – the former comprised a significant part of the
latter. Richard Newman suggests Garrison's *Thoughts* was largely based upon the work of
James Forten and William Watkins. Richard S. Newman, *The Transformation of American
Abolitionism: Fighting Slavery in the Early Republic* (Chapel Hill: The University of North
Carolina Press, 2002), 113. On membership of the Convention, cf. *The Abolitionist* 1, no. 12
(1833): 177–78; "Declaration of the National Anti-Slavery Convention," *The Abolitionist* 1, no.
12 (December 1833): 180; Benjamin Quarles, *Black Abolitionists*, (New York: Oxford
University, 1969), 24–25.

legacy of the founding, the US Constitution. In comparison to the Constitution, the Declaration was easily incorporated into abolitionist rhetoric. But the fundamental problem of relating to the founding was significantly heightened in the case of the document which had entrenched the national compromise on slavery and which tied the abolitionists to the slaveholding Americans to their South. Moreover, having so closely drawn to themselves the revolutionary legacy of the Declaration of Independence, how could abolitionists disown the Constitution? Navigating this tension in the earlier 1830s gave rise to a burst of constitutional thought, and, specifically, attention to the relationship between the Declaration of Independence and the US Constitution. The result was the articulation of an understanding of the Declaration of Independence and the Constitution in which the former provided a framework for interpreting the "neutral" language of the latter.

3.4 IMMEDIATE ABOLITION AND THE CONSTITUTION

The complexity of abolitionist attitudes toward the US Constitution is evinced in two statements from Garrison in the early 1830s. Before free black audiences in 1831, Garrison thanked God for the existence of the Constitution and declared it "firm as the rock of Gibraltar, a high refuge from oppression."[54] The next year, in 1832, he described it in *The Liberator* as "dripping ... with human blood" and representing the "most bloody and heaven-daring arrangement ever made by men for the continuance and protection of a system of the most atrocious villainy ever exhibited on earth."[55] Garrison was perhaps more iconoclastic than many of his abolitionist peers when it came to the Constitution – he would famously come to condemn the Constitution as a "covenant with death" – but the incertitude encapsulated in the two quotes reflected the dualism of abolitionist attitudes toward the Constitution in the early 1830s.[56] On one hand, it was the Constitution that bound them to slaveholding. On the other hand, they believed – or wanted to believe – that

---

[54] William Lloyd Garrison, *An Address Delivered before the Free People of Color, in Philadelphia, New-York, and Other Cities, during the Month of June, 1831* (Boston: Stephen Foster, 1831).

[55] William Lloyd Garrison, "The Great Crisis!," *The Liberator*, December 29, 1832.

[56] Paul Finkelman, "Garrison's Constitution: The Covenant with Death and How It Was Made," *Prologue* 32, no. 4 (2000). During the 1830s, Garrison's relationship to the US Constitution was marked by equivocation as Garrison navigated complexities in his relationship to the Constitution and the founders; writing to Harrison Gray Otis in September 1835, Garrison would claim that the principles of abolitionists were neither "slightly or imminently dangerous to the constitution of the Union." In an earlier public letter to the same individual, he would accuse Otis of speaking as if the founding fathers could do no wrong, and then claim to be embodying "the free spirit of our fathers" in opposing Otis. William Lloyd Garrison, "To Harrison Gray Otis [September 19, 1835]," in *The Letters of William Lloyd Garrison: Volume I: I Will Be Heard!*, ed. Walter M. Merril (Cambridge, MA: The Belknap Press of Harvard University Press, 1971), 530–36; William Lloyd Garrison, "To Harrison Gray Otis [September 5, 1835]," in *The Letters of William Lloyd Garrison: Volume I: I Will Be Heard!*, ed.

the Constitution offered the framework within which to combat slavery through conversion of public opinion or legislative action.[57]

Abolitionists agreed that the institution of slavery was inherently sinful, and it was through the Constitution that this immorality spread to the souls of the abolitionists themselves.[58] The Constitution made the existence of slavery in the Southern States a sin for those in the North, as it required the latter's acquiescence and – more significantly for the abolitionists – potential active support for slavery. Fearful that a slave rebellion would see the Northern militias called into service in the South, abolitionists saw the congressional power to suppress insurrections as enlisting them as participants in the perpetuation of slavery. William Snelling told the New-England Anti-Slavery Society:

We have, by acceding to the Federal Constitution, solemnly and as a people, guaranteed the continuance of slavery. We, that is all of us between eighteen and forty-five, are liable to be called to suppress, what we should call rebellion, but what all other nations will call a glorious revolution.[59]

The *Anti-Slavery Reporter* in September of the same year, 1833, printed John G. Whittier's call for immediate abolition. Central to this claim were the North's constitutional ties to slavery. Whittier rejected the view that New England had no interest in slaveholding:

New-England is not responsible? Bound by the United States Constitution to protect the slaver-holder in his sins, and yet not responsible? Joining hand with crime – covenanting with oppression – leaguing with pollution, and yet not responsible![60]

The Constitution, Whittier asserted, bound the North's militia to active protection of the slave system. "Slavery is *protected* by the constitutional compact – by the standing army – by the militia of the free states."[61] The

Walter M. Merrill (Cambridge, MA: The Belknap Press of Harvard University Press, 1971), 496–504.

[57] As the 1830s progressed, this belief became harder to sustain, pushing and pulling the movement in two directions – either toward greater involvement in politics or a withdrawal from it. For further discussion of this point, see Chapter 9 of this book.

[58] The notion of slavery as sin was a central pillar of the abolitionist movement. The focus on immediate abolition reflected to an important extent an understanding of slavery not as a declining institution in need of a political solution but as a moral wrong demanding action on the part of professing Christians. At the annual meeting of the New-England Anti-Slavery Society in 1833, Rev. E. M. P. Wells listed his objections to slavery in order thus: "1. Slavery is inconsistent with Christianity. – 2. It is inconsistent with humanity. – 3. It is inconsistent with the principles of a republican government." "Annual Meeting of the New-England Anti-Slavery Society," *The Abolitionist* 1, no. 2 (1833): 17.

[59] "Extracts from an Address Delivered before the N.E. Anti-Slavery Society, By Wm. J. Snelling, Esq.," 35.

[60] John G. Whittier, "Justice and Expediency; or, Slavery Considered with a View to Its Rightful and Effectual Remedy, Abolition," *Anti-Slavery Reporter* (New York, NY, September 1833).

[61] Whittier, "Justice and Expediency."

constitutional requirement to return those held under service or labor was also understood by abolitionists to bind them to the immoral system. The October 1833 *Abolitionist* listing the proof that the "American nation ... approves and encourages slavery" made point number one that "The constitution of the United States binds, as far as it can, the people of the northern States, to restore runaway slaves to their owners."[62] Even as it rejected its moral authority, the First Annual Report of American Anti-Slavery Society concluded that through the constitutional requirement to return fugitives, Americans in the North had been "*hired* to abet oppression – to be the tools of tyrants."[63] Constitutionally tied to the South, Northern abolitionists identified the guilt of slavery as of the "nation, then, until we do something to amend our constitution and laws."[64] Immediate abolition was the only response to "all the iniquity of Slavery," for all the United States "are responsible for the shame and guilt of slavery."[65] Abolition was, said Garrison in 1834, "aimed at the redemption of the whole land ... We [are] all in bondage."[66] The Constitution, underwriting the Union of the sections, made the sin of slavery a stain on Northern as well as Southern souls.

Nonetheless, in the early 1830s at least, the Constitution's role in binding the abolitionists to slavery did not necessitate the former's rejection – indeed, it made engagement with it more morally urgent: "The fact that the Constitution of the United States allows and upholds slavery, instead of being a reason why each and every good citizen should not lift up his voice against it, is the very reason why a just God will not hold them guiltless for neglecting it."[67] While the early abolitionists identified the Constitution as central to their complicity in slaveholding, they also understood the text itself as a somewhat amoral framework for federal governance. Even as it bound them to slavery, it offered a means by which slavery might be addressed. The Providence Anti-Slavery Society declared themselves satisfied that "we have no other purpose but to overthrow a most unrighteous and cruel system, *by the means pointed out in the Constitution of the Republic*, for the improvement of our civil and social state" and argued that "[w]e show no disrespect to our Constitution, therefore, by insisting upon the abolition of Slavery."[68] The US Constitution was an important abolitionist resource insofar as it guaranteed the abolitionists the free speech needed to spread their literature, but also as it offered resources by which to problematize and

---

[62] "A Slaveholding Nation," *The Abolitionist* 1, no. 10 (1833): 158.
[63] *First Annual Report of the American Anti-Slavery Society* (New York, NY: Dorr & Butterfield, 1834), 58.
[64] "A Slaveholding Nation," 159.
[65] Whittier, "Justice and Expediency"; "A Slaveholding Nation," 159.
[66] *Proceedings of the New-England Anti-Slavery Convention, Held in Boston on the 27th, 28th and 29th of May, 1834* (Boston: Garrison and Knapp, 1834), 13.
[67] "From the (N.Y.) Emancipator," *The Liberator*, April 6, 1833.
[68] *Abolition Principles*, 2. Emphasis added.

harry slavery itself.[69] In their "Address to the People of the United States," New England abolitionists conceded, "It is true that slavery, as it exists in our country, is supported by law, and by the constitution as it is generally understood," but they questioned the belief that this required acquiescence.[70] "Ought it not," they asked, "to be to us the most powerful inducement, to use every means which the constitution has left us, to remove this fatal inconsistency with the vital principle of our social institutions?"[71] The *Anti-Slavery Reporter* argued, "while we confine ourselves within the strictest construction of the constitutional rights we do not intend to be precluded from urging any measure which the constitution warrants."[72] Such measures included the use of the constitutional protection of free speech to urge a constitutional amendment,[73] but more significantly they also involved the proffering of the Constitution as a basis for opposing slavery. Although unlikely to persuade slaveholders, abolitionists invoked constitutional clauses such as the ban on cruel and unusual punishments,[74] the privileges and immunities clause,[75] and the guarantee of republican government,[76] in order to juxtapose the Constitution and the reality of slavery. Furthermore, they emphasized the lack of specific reference to slavery in the constitutional document in order to challenge the view that it was inherently proslavery. At the American Anti-Slavery Society's Annual Meeting in 1834, Rev. Samuel J. May denied that the "constitution

---

[69] *Proceedings of the New-England Anti-Slavery Convention, Held in Boston on the 27th, 28th and 29th of May, 1834*, 68. The truth of this insight is perhaps witnessed by the decision of proslavery forces to target the exercise of the abolitionists' free speech as a primarily objective in the early 1830s. Cf. Christopher Childers, *The Failure of Popular Sovereignty: Slavery, Manifest Destiny, and the Radicalization of Southern Politics* (Lawrence, KS: University of Kansas Press, 2012), 76. Wiecek has argued that attempts to repress abolitionist speech contributed toward their "Manichaean outlook on the struggle between antislavery and slavery." William M. Wiecek, *The Sources of Antislavery Constitutionalism in America, 1760–1848* (Ithaca: Cornell University Press, 1977), 182.

[70] *Proceedings of the New-England Anti-Slavery Convention*, 65.

[71] *Proceedings of the New-England Anti-Slavery Convention*, 65.

[72] "Address," *Anti-Slavery Reporter* (New York, October 1833), 73.

[73] For example, Theodore Sedgwick, *The Practicability of the Abolition of Slavery: A Lecture, Delivered at the Lyceum in Stockbridge, Massachusetts, February, 1831* (New York: J. Seymour, 1831).

[74] *Proceedings of the New-England Anti-Slavery Convention*, 57.

[75] "To Peter Morse . . .," *Anti-Slavery Reporter* (New York, NY, June 1833), 15. Wiecek attributes this view to Theodore Dwight Weld's *The Power of Congress over the District of Columbia* (1838). Wiecek, *The Sources of Antislavery Constitutionalism in America*, 190.

[76] Whittier, "Justice and Expediency." This line of attack was perceived as most applicable to, and would become a central point of contention in, the creation of new states from Western territory. For discussion of this use, cf. Childers, *The Failure of Popular Sovereignty: Slavery, Manifest Destiny, and the Radicalization of Southern Politics*, chapter 3. See Chapter 1 of this book for its use during the Missouri Crisis.

sanctions slavery," as neither "slavery nor slaves are mentioned in the constitution. The words are not there."[77]

Maintaining that the US Constitution was a framework for abolition, while seeing it as the manifestation of "a villainous compact, which legalized manstealing," abolitionists in this period articulated a conception of the Constitution that tied it to the Declaration of Independence, as the black abolitionists of the 1820s had done.[78] This association was developed through several interlocking premises. The first was an understanding of the founding as incomplete with – or even corrupted by – the institutionalization of slavery that the Constitution represented.[79] The second was that the Declaration of Independence was a document of equal – if not more – importance to the Constitution in the expression of that founding. The third, drawing upon the first two, was that the Constitution could (*should*) be amended to bring it into line with the Declaration, to enable abolition and thus to bring the founding to its conclusion. This envisioning of the constitutional order had the advantage of enabling the abolitionists to reject the idea that they were bound to a Constitution that was morally corrupting, while also claiming the mantle of that same Constitution. Although conceptually distinct, in many actual abolitionist discussions, these three elements were often collapsed or rearranged such that the overriding argument was that the founding fathers had bequeathed a power of constitutional amendment or that it was self-evidently the duty of the present generation to constitutionally abolish slavery. For example, in discussing the ongoing case of Prudence Crandall in Connecticut, a correspondent to *The Emancipator* linked the two documents as sources of moral instruction without much elaboration as to the relationship between them: "Our Constitution and the Declaration of Independence, standing, as they do, opposed to the *practice* of our citizens."[80] However, there were more extended treatments of these issues that laid out a radical constitutional theory that posited an overt constitutional authority on the part of the Declaration of Independence.

As might be expected, the impetus for such theories was a reflection upon the burdens of supporting slavery that the Constitution placed upon abolitionists.

---

[77] *First Annual Report of the American Anti-Slavery Society*, 20.

[78] "African Repository," *The Liberator*, March 9, 1833.

[79] The Childs were important proponents of the "corruption" theory. David Lee Child identified slavery as the "original sin of the Constitution," while Lydia Child called the admission of slave representation into the Constitution "a wedge" and the attachment of the slavery to the Constitution the chaining of "the living and vigorous to the diseased and dying." David Lee Child, *The Despotism of Freedom: A Speech at the First Anniversary of the New England Anti-Slavery Society* (Boston: The Boston Young Men's Anti-Slavery Association for the Diffusion of Truth, 1834), 61; Lydia Child, *An Appeal in Favor of That Class of Americans Called Africans* (Boston: Allen and Ticknor, 1833), 109, 228.

[80] "Connecticut versus Freedom."

Garrison's "The Great Crisis!" of 1832 presented a typically outspoken iteration of this genre. There, Garrison offered a taste of his later forthright rejection of the Constitution *tout court*, with a rejection of the moral authority of a compact "formed at the sacrifice of the bodies and souls of millions of our race, for the sake of achieving a political object."[81] But while he decried the "sacred instrument ... *dripping as it is with human blood*," he also showed an unusual degree of equivocation in recognizing the compact "with feelings of shame and indignation." Rejecting the notion that an immoral agreement could ever be binding – "It was not valid then – it is not valid now" – Garrison did not reject the Union it represented per se. Instead, he called upon New Englanders to "agitate this question" and "to cease from giving countenance and protection to southern kidnappers," at the risk of the Union if necessary, but with the expectation that it would be the South that would depart, not the North: "Let them separate, if they can muster courage enough." But if he was willing to risk the Union and declaim the compact between the states, Garrison also held to "the spirit of Seventy-Six" as a source of redemption, noting that in the Constitution the founding generation had "trampled beneath their feet their own solemn and heaven-attested Declaration." The Union was not worth the price of complicity in slavery, but it was slavery, not the Union, that should be sacrificed.

Garrison was not alone in considering the limits of constitutional authority in the case of slavery. Seven months later, *The Emancipator* grappled with similar issues in an editorial entitled "Dissolution of the Union." In this editorial, Charles W. Denison, like Garrison, rejected the moral authority of an immoral compact.[82] Less comfortable with dissolution than Garrison, he placed weight upon the lack of an overt mention of slavery in the constitutional document to argue for transformation of the Union into "a union of entire justice to all, of every color, and of every clime." Just over a month later, the newspaper revisited the issue of the authority of the Constitution in a two-part essay, "United States Constitution."[83] Like the earlier editorial, this essay leaned upon the "peculiar *phraseology* of the certain important parts" of the Constitution in order to produce an interpretation susceptible to abolition. But beyond advancing this theory of narrow textual interpretation, the essay also elaborated a broader constitutional theory of the relationship of the Declaration of Independence and Constitution. Taking the contradiction between the constitutional settlement and the "demands of justice claimed by our fathers from the mother country," as they related to "the dearest rights of man" as a starting point of reflection, the writer pointed to the incorporation into the constitutional document of doctrines at odds with justice as evidence that "the American Revolution was incomplete." Identifying "a lingering darkness

---

[81] Garrison, "The Great Crisis!"   [82] "Dissolution of the Union."
[83] "United States Constitution," *The Emancipator*, August 31, 1833; "United States Constitution. (Concluded from Our Last)," *The Emancipator*, September 7, 1833.

around the first dawn of our national day … a darkness which is gathering blackness with every succeeding hour," the essay nonetheless contrasted this with the "redeeming spirit abroad." The codification and promulgation of the latter spirit could be seen as animating the lack of direct mention of slavery in the Constitution, creating "a warrant for the future enjoyment of true American liberty – a liberty which knows no distinction of color, condition, or clime."

The historical depiction of the founding as a Manichean conflict between the darkness of the constitutional compromise and the dawn of the Declaration of Independence set up Denison to both reject the constitutional legacy of slavery and claim the constitutional legacy of liberty. Positioning himself both as loyal son and dissident for universal liberty, the editor could call upon the spirit of revolutionary America as his inheritance:

[W]e take occasion to say, that the portion of [the Constitution] which aims at the preservation and the *integrity* of the Union, has our full and hearty assent. We take occasion further to say, that we yield to no man, living or dead, in our attachment to the institutions of our beloved but guilty land. Born among the hardy sons of revolutionary sires, and fed, from our cradle, with the stamina of legitimate democracy, we are for a firm and continued union of the people, on a just constitutional basis.[84]

But in characterizing the founding as a Manichean battle, the author was required to explain why liberty was to be taken as the "true" American legacy. This was achieved through an overt inclusion of the Declaration of Independence within the constitutional pantheon and its ascension over the Constitution:

It is certainly not statesmanlike to talk of *the Constitution* as the *origin* of our Union. The DECLARATION OF INDEPENDENCE is much more entitled to such a distinction. And that valuable document begins thus: "We hold these truths to be self-evident; that ALL MEN are created FREE and EQUAL" … The Constitution is merely a codicil to this will of freemen of the republic – an agreement by the parties as to the best mode of sustaining, protecting and carrying into practice the design of the declaration.[85]

Relegating the Constitution to "merely a codicil" to the Declaration had the effect of making the spirit of equality contained within the latter document the true legacy of the Revolution. The Constitution, far from the expression of the spirit of the compact, was in fact the administrative framework within which the Declaration's spirit was to be enacted – rendering any constitutional requirement at odds with that spirit an element of the "darkness" which it was the abolitionists' destiny to overcome. Positioning

---

[84] "United States Constitution."

[85] In the second half of the essay, Denison would use this framework to accept only express textual commitments to support slavery as constitutionally binding, establishing a very narrowly constrained space of noninterference in the subject of slavery. Arguing for a constitutional presumption in favor of liberty, the editor suggested a "literal construction" would support the abolitionists' efforts at defeating slavery. "United States Constitution. (Concluded from Our Last)."

the Declaration of Independence as a purer, and earlier, expression of the American spirit, Denison made it possible to read the Constitution against the earlier document and to identify its immoral requirements as errata within the American tradition.

Others made similar moves to place the Declaration on a par with, if not superior to, the US Constitution. Addressing the Reading Anti-Slavery Society, Horace Wakefield denied that abolitionists were attacking the US Constitution. Declaring that abolitionists "love the Constitution," Wakefield noted "there is another instrument which was promulgated long before, and which we love almost as well as that."[86] The offering of this observation in response to a charge of waging a war against the Constitution suggests that Wakefield believed that serving the aims of the Declaration made the charge of anti-Constitutionalism mute. Parallel claims that a failure to treat the Declaration with the same reverence as the Constitution was a central failure of non-abolitionist constitutional interpretations were scattered throughout abolitionist discussions: "That because the South holds slaves by the Constitution, we must not say a word about the clause in the Declaration of Independence ..., " "We wish the gradualists had half the regard for the declaration of independence and the commands of God, which they appear to have for the Union!"[87] In "Justice and Expediency," John Whittier made manifest the view that the Declaration ought to animate the Constitution and linked it to the legacy of the fathers:

[T]hey left us the light of their pure principles of liberty – they framed the great charter of American rights, without employing a term in its structure to which in after times of universal freedom the enemies of our country could point with accusation or reproach.

What is *our* duty?

To give effect to the *spirit* of our Constitution; to plant ourselves upon the great Declaration and declare in the face of all the world, that political, religious and legal hypocrisy shall no longer cover as with loathsome leprosy the features of American freedom; to loose at once the bands of wickedness – to undo the heavy burdens, and let the oppressed go free.[88]

Following Denison and Wakefield, Whittier read the Declaration of Independence as the spirit of the Constitution, collapsing the constitutional standing of the two documents and rendering the Constitution a framework for liberation. Developing the reading of the guarantee of equal rights into the Constitution initiated by the free black communities of the late 1820s and early 1830s, these abolitionists offered a reordering of the documentary legacy of the Revolution and the founding to provide a basis upon which to effect a constitutional abolition.

[86] "Reading Anti-Slavery Society," *The Liberator*, March 30, 1833.
[87] "Freedom of Speech," *The Liberator*, January 19, 1833; "Religious Intelligence," *The Liberator*, June 29, 1833.
[88] Whittier, "Justice and Expediency."

3.5 CONCLUSION

The early 1830s saw abolitionists grapple with an ambiguous founding legacy that embraced commitments both to universal equality and to a constitutional settlement that enshrined representation and practices of slavery. On one hand, the abolitionists of the 1830s sought to position themselves as the descendants of the revolutionaries of 1776, in terms of both enacting a revolutionary pursuit of liberty and locating their cause within the dominant frame of fidelity to the founding fathers. On the other hand, they recognized that the founding, and the US Constitution in particular, had erected institutional supports for slavery and continued to generate obstacles to its abolition. Encapsulated in the attachment to George Washington, the personification of the Revolution, the constituted federal government, and a slaveholder, abolitionists professed to "revere the character ... of Washington," while finding themselves repulsed by the Philadelphia convention which, under his presidency, had codified "a savage war upon a sixth part of our whole population."[89] They sought to navigate this tension by drawing upon the notions of a founding spirit proffered by restrictionists during the Missouri Crisis and a sense of national citizenship focused upon abolitionist readings of the Declaration of Independence developed within free black communities in the late 1820s. To wit, they tried to see themselves as tasked with neither the repudiation of the Revolution and founding nor with its preservation, but rather with its completion on the basis of the Declaration's commitment to universal equality.

To make sense of this historic role, the abolitionists of the early 1830s developed an understanding of the Constitution that relied upon its interpretation in correspondence with the Declaration of Independence. In such a way they could apply a presumption of liberty to the constitutional document and see in its indirect references to slavery an expectation of abolition. Moreover, in positing the coequal status of the Declaration of Independence and the US Constitution, the abolitionists could suggest that as the historically prior document, and the one containing more overt commitments to specific values of justice, the Declaration ought to be read as a guide to the meaning of the Constitution. Slavery could then be framed as an erroneous admission, "a fly-blow in the blossom," destined for removal.[90] Such a maneuver provided a mechanism by which to save the Constitution from itself – to ascribe to it a set of commitments that it only marginally alluded to, if at all – and so enable the embrace of a document and a founding that on its face stood in opposition to the values of the abolitionist movement. Mobilizing and circulating claims that "the Constitution of these United States ... hath made all men free and equal," the abolitionists of the early 1830s fashioned

---

[89] Child, *The Despotism of Freedom*; Garrison, "The Great Crisis!"
[90] Child, *The Despotism of Freedom*, 61.

a Constitution endowed with a spirit that served the purposes of their movement and enabled them to claim their revolutionary inheritance.[91]

The welding together of the free black reading of the Declaration of Independence and the Constitution and the broader evolving sense of the second generation of Americans as heirs to the founding era brought together two developing conceptions of American nationalism. In the first instance, free black advocacy of the Declaration of Independence had heightened in direct response to attempts on the part of advocates of colonization to deny the former's citizenship. Pushing back against such claims, free black activists enacted membership of the American nation through their claims-making upon the Declaration. In the second instance, the conception of a duty to complete the founding operated in part upon the notion that the second generation of Americans were uniquely bound to the revolutionary settlement and tasked with its preservation – an inheritance and responsibility that were theirs as a consequence of their American-ness. Both of these developments privileged a notion of American nationality that rested upon an ideological commitment to a set of values promulgated during the revolutionary era. In cojoining these traditions in response to their anxieties surrounding their relationship with the founding, the abolitionists came to advance a highly ideological sense of what it meant to be an American, and to impart to it a significance that would draw them almost inevitability toward the symbolism of failing to live up to that ideological nationalism within their national capital, Washington DC. Coupled with the particular constraints on national abolition generated by the constitutional document, this impetus would result in the District of Columbia emerging as a central focus for abolition in the early 1830s – a focus that would bring forth a response, and important constitutional innovations on the part of the defenders of slavery. To that focus, and the responses to it, we will later turn our attention. But first, it is necessary to explore the ways in which, at this very same moment in time, the US Constitution was becoming more central to defenses of slavery as well.

[91] Maria W. Stewart, *Productions of Mrs. Maria W. Stewart, Presented to the First African Baptist Church & Society, of the City of Boston* (Boston: Friends of Freedom and Virtue, 1835), 5.

4

The Slaveholding South and the Constitutionalization of Slavery

You may prove, if you can, that slavery is immoral, unjust, and unnatural, that it originated in avarice and cruelty, that it is an evil and a curse, and you still do not convince me that our slaves are not property, and as such, protected by our Constitution.

William Daniel Jr. (1832)[1]

In August 1831, the rebellion led by "General Nat" Turner shook Virginia to its core. Initiated in the early hours of Monday, August 22, the rebellion in Southampton County claimed the lives of at least fifty-five whites, over one hundred black people in the retaliatory violence that followed, and a further nineteen black persons deemed conspirators after trial and subsequently executed, including Turner himself.[2] The aftermath of the rebellion saw a reconsideration of the institution of slavery across the South, in which the giving way of the sense of slavery as an anomalous institution within a republican society to the articulation of more aggressive claim of slavery as a positive good accelerated.[3] The initial site of this reconsideration was Virginia

---

[1] Erik S. Root, ed., *Sons of the Fathers: The Virginia Slavery Debates of 1831–1832* (Lanham: Lexington Books, 2010), 97.

[2] For an account of the rebellion, cf. Lacy K. Ford, *Deliver Us from Evil: The Slavery Question in the Old South* (New York: Oxford University Press, 2009), 338–53.

[3] One scholar of the debates characterized them thus: "Virginians engaged in a unique discussion. . . . The forces of emancipation had a unique opportunity to end the peculiar institution. By the close of 1832, however, the possibility that emancipation could be effected for the Union, much less Virginia, closed." Erik S. Root, *All Honor to Jefferson?: The Virginia Slavery Debates and the Positive Good Thesis* (Lanham: Lexington Books, 2008), 211. For further details on Nat Turner's Rebellion and the ensuing debates as a turning point in proslavery thought, cf. Erik S. Root, "Introduction," in *Sons of the Fathers: The Virginia Slavery Debates of 1831–1832*, ed. Erik S. Root (Lanham: Lexington Books, 2010), 1–23; Christopher Michael Curtis, *Jefferson's Freeholders and the Politics of Ownership in the Old Dominion* (New York: Cambridge

itself, with the 1831–32 legislature drawn into an extended debate over the prospect of gradual emancipation in the State that foreshadowed the later 1835–36 congressional debates over slavery in the District of Columbia. In a series of events that would be echoed in 1835–36, the referral of a petition seeking gradual emancipation to a committee drew opposition from defenders of slavery who deemed it beyond the bounds of legitimate discussion. As would be the case in Congress in 1836, opposition to the petitions would backfire and, instead of suppressing the discussion, provided an opening for slavery's critics to publicly debate the institution.[4]

The ensuing debate over slavery opened with, and never moved very far from, a central concern with slaves as a form of property. Within the immediate Virginian debates, the meaning of holding property rights in slaves became a central point of contention. In the wider debate that followed, the centrality of property and the corresponding question of black personhood would be the overarching framework of debate. It would be upon the foundational claim that slaves were property that the early 1830s incarnations of the so-called "positive good" thesis of slavery would be developed. Moving from a position in which slavery was an anomalous evil within North America's republican societies to the view that slavery provided an important protection of republican government, white Southern intellectuals and polemists shifted from apology for slavery to celebration of it. As they did so, the sanctity of property rights both in slaves and more generally came to be interpreted as a measure of the Southern States' success in balancing freedom and order.[5]

University Press, 2012); John Ashworth, *Slavery, Capitalism, and Politics in the Antebellum Republic: Volume 1: Commerce and Compromise, 1820–1850* (Cambridge, UK: Cambridge University Press, 1995), 140; Ford, *Deliver Us from Evil: The Slavery Question in the Old South*, 359–60. Nonetheless, one ought to be careful in overstating the extent to which the reaction to Turner's Rebellion was a cause rather than symptom of change – already by 1829 John C. Weems was ready to stand on the floor of the House of Representatives and "to prove my right by every dispensation from God to man, to hold my fellow man as property." *Register of Debates, 20th Congress, 2nd Session*, 1829, 184. For an argument that 1831–32 was a crucial moment within Virginia's antebellum slavery debate but not a significant turning point, see Alison Goodyear Freehling, *Drift Toward Dissolution: The Virginia Slavery Debate of 1831–1832* (Baton Rouge: Louisiana State University Press, 1982). Fox-Genovese and Genovese suggest that proslavery militants themselves identified the 1830s as a crucial period in terms of the South becoming convinced of the militants' arguments but give significance to the Missouri Crisis as an earlier "turning point." Elizabeth Fox-Genovese and Eugene D. Genovese, *The Mind of the Master Class: History and Faith in the Southern Slaveholders' Worldview* (New York: Cambridge University Press, 2005), 87.

[4] Ford, *Deliver Us from Evil*, 366–67; Root, "Introduction," 8; Freehling, *Drift toward Dissolution*, 125–30.

[5] The increased attention to property rights in the enslaved also reflected a conceptualization of slaves as human capital and the economic significance of that "capital." One scholar of slavery and capitalism puts aggregated slave property at $577 million or 15 percent of national wealth in 1830. Rosenthal notes that scholars estimate "the amount of capital invested in slaves was massive, by some measurements as large or larger than the amount of capital invested in factories."

At approximately the same time, and not wholly inseparable from that development, the importance of constitutions within the white Southern imaginary grew. A drift away from the universalism of natural law and toward reliance upon American experience saw greater weight placed upon positive institutions. Skeptical of the destabilizing political forces they associated with the spread of industrial wage-labor relations, white Southern thinkers turned their attention to what among their own political arrangements might provide a bulwark against such pressures. Their constitutions, re-interpreted to reflect the hardy wisdom of statesmen not the abstract calculations of philosophers, offered one such resource. Shedding the belief that property rights existed only within society as a result of legislative statute, they looked to constitutions as the mechanisms by which those rights, "coeval" with society, were entrenched. Tapping the broader American turn toward valuing historical inheritances, the preservation of constitutions and constitutional arrangements became a motif of a Southern conservatism that made a commitment to slavery both an instance of the vitally important observation of constitutionally guaranteed property rights and as itself a mechanism of protecting those rights. The consequence was an intertwining of property, slavery, and constitutionalism such that each came to stand in for the others within political debate. A corresponding tendency to deny the personhood of slaves became as central, with significant consequences for constitutional politics in both the immediate and longer term.

The constitutionalization traced within this chapter proceeded then along two interrelated and reinforcing axes. In the first instance, slavery as an issue was "constitutionalized" through an overt association of slavery with constitutional rights. In the Virginian debates of 1831–32, the critics of slavery entertained the possibility that slavery was a public nuisance and thus resolvable through legislative action. Following the positive law theory of slavery, most notably advanced in *Somerset*, they regarded slavery as only holding a legal existence in territories where it was positively supported by legislation – remove the legislation and slavery had no legal basis. In response, their opponents advanced constitutional claims that made questions of positive law irrelevant. These latter advocates grounded their claims in constitutional law, and so pushed the debate into that realm. As is shown subsequently, an argumentative nexus of property rights, slavery, and constitutionalism had developed in the 1820s that provided an established framework for these claims.

Calvin Schermerhorn, *Unrequited Toil: A History of United States Slavery* (Cambridge, UK: Cambridge University Press, 2018), 1; Caitlin Rosenthal, *Accounting for Slavery* (Cambridge, MA: Harvard University Press, 2018), 3. On slavery as a proportion of southern capital, see Thomas Piketty and Gabriel Zucman, "Capital Is Back: Wealth-Income Ratios in Rich Countries 1700–2010," The Quarterly Journal of Economics 129, no. 3 (2014): 1301–3.

At a second level, constitutionalization proceeded in a greater attachment to extant constitutions and a call for their preservation as central objects of political life. If pushing debates over slavery into a constitutional realm was a useful strategy for such actors in the early 1830s in the face of moral or practical arguments for constraining slavery, it was also the case that constitutional preservation itself was deemed more urgent. As greater weight was placed upon institutional experience vis-à-vis abstract speculation, the existing social order was given greater politico-philosophical authority. Slavery, as a vital facet of existing Southern society, was located within a socio-constitutional order deemed to stand against agrarianism and the excesses of the wage-labor system of the North. These two developments, placed together, resulted in a conflux of slavery and constitution that made defense of each imperative to the other – constitutionalism became vital to defenses of slavery and slavery was interpellated in (increasingly urgent) defenses of constitutionalism.

4.1 CONSTITUTIONAL PROPERTY IN THE VIRGINIAN DEBATES OVER SLAVERY

Christopher Michael Curtis suggests that until the debates of 1831–32 Virginian legal culture had tacitly adopted a Blackstonian outlook on slavery.[6] Such an outlook regarded the holding of slaves as a positive rather than natural property right, which is to say, that slave property was created and supported by statute rather than claims raising from a hypothetical state of nature or universal practice. This approach worked effectively to place blame for slavery's existence in Virginia on the British colonial authority that had enabled slaveholding to take root there, while also allowing the Virginia slaveholders to pay lip service to ideas of universal liberty in the abstract.[7] But a positive law basis for slavery was vulnerable to legislative alteration when it was no longer deemed beneficial to the State as a whole.[8] As emancipationists challenged the notion that slavery was beneficial to the State as a whole – had not Nat Turner's Rebellion itself demonstrated it to be a great danger – the defenders of slavery in the Old Dominion were required to develop a justification for slavery on grounds other than positive law. The consequence of such an emancipationist challenge was, in Curtis's telling, "a more thorough conservative response that transformed the idea of slave

---

[6] Curtis, *Jefferson's Freeholders and the Politics of Ownership in the Old Dominion*, 128.

[7] Philip A. Bolling neatly encapsulated this view in his statement on the first day of substantial debate: "The question of abstract right is not a question now at all proper to be mooted – for the system of slavery, now existing in this commonwealth, is not a work of our hands, but a curse entailed upon us by our ancestors." Root, *Sons of the Fathers*, 38.

[8] Or at least those who held power via its "representative" bodies. On the significance of earlier debates over apportionment for the outcomes of the 1831–32 debate, see Ford, *Deliver Us from Evil*, 363–64.

ownership within republican political thought."[9] Within the immediate theater of the Virginian debate itself, this response took the form of an appeal to constitutional protections for slave property. This approach rejected any basis in natural law while simultaneously moving beyond the Blackstonian position. While supporters of emancipation argued that the Virginian Assembly could destroy slavery via statute, the defenders of slavery pointed to a higher, albeit not natural, law, in the form of constitutional prohibitions on uncompensated takings, as a counter to such efforts.

As noted, the debates on 1831–32 found their most proximate cause in the parliamentary maneuvering surrounding the reception of petitions calling for emancipation. The petitions in question had, in fact, already been received and referred to special committee when, on January 10, 1832, William O. Goode requested an estimated timeline for the committee's report on broad recommendations on slavery following the events of the Fall of 1831. The answer he received from the committee chair, William Brodnax – that the committee was considering two issues, the removal of free blacks and the gradual abolition of slavery in the State, and that of the two the latter was the more straightforward and could likely be reported upon within a week – obviously gave Goode pause.[10] The very next day he offered a resolution that called for the committee to "be discharged from the consideration of all petitions, memorials and resolutions, which have for their object, the manumission of persons held in servitude under the existing laws of the commonwealth, and that it is not expedient to legislate on the subject."[11] In justifying his motion, Goode claimed that it had become his duty to "arrest a misguided and pernicious course of legislation," as he was of the belief that "the Legislature of Virginia was now considering whether they would confiscate property of the citizens – a question which they had no right to act upon or consider."[12] Ironically, Goode's resolution provided the precise opportunity for considering that very question – his speech was met that day with three others arguing for the ending of slavery in Virginia in some form and a counter-resolution for a scheme of gradual emancipation.[13] From there an extended debate over slavery in the State raged in the House until January 25.[14]

Each of the three responding speeches on the first day of the debates contained elements of what would become the Virginian critique of

---

[9] Curtis, *Jefferson's Freeholders and the Politics of Ownership in the Old Dominion*, 129.
[10] Ford, *Deliver Us from Evil*, 367.   [11] Root, "Introduction," 9.
[12] Root, *Sons of the Fathers*, 26.
[13] In addition to three speeches in opposition to slavery, James G. Bryce urged the House to allow the committee to finish its work before taking up consideration of scheme of emancipation. Root, *Sons of the Fathers*, 37.
[14] Root, "Introduction," 13.

slavery – that it was un-American, subject to legislative destruction, and requiring of immediate attention. In the first instance, Samuel McDowell Moore offered a critique of slavery in which the "peculiar institution" was counter to America's republican heritage. Linking the sentiments of the Declaration of Independence to a claimed universal valuation of liberty, McDowell Moore condemned slavery as "a monster, on which freedom cannot look without abhorrence."[15] Fearing the negative judgment of world opinion and concerned for the "reputation of our ancestors," he called for a "determined effort to free our country from the odium of slavery."[16] Despite professing to take a view of slavery "as it affects the slaves themselves," McDowell Moore nonetheless seemed more concerned about the removal of the stain of slavery from Virginia's boundaries and proposed a scheme by which unemancipated slaves would be sold out of State by a given date.[17] In the second instance, Philip A. Bolling denounced slavery as "a curse" and asserted the right of society to destroy it. Bolling's speech evinced less concern with the ideological embarrassments of slavery and more for the burdens it placed upon white Virginians. In addition to the threat of slave revolt, Bolling pointed toward slavery's tendency to drive "the honest, industrious poor" from the State, as well as the entanglement of slaveholders in extensive systems of credit, showing considerable mental dexterity in reaching the conclusion that the real "bondsman" was the slaveholder – "the master of the slave absolutely belongs to the merchant, and has to labor – and labor hard – for their benefit."[18] Of significance to the ongoing debate was Bolling's suggestion that as a "nuisance," slavery was a legitimate subject of legislative destruction. Laying out a positive theory of property, Bolling asserted that "property was secured by the laws of society, and that the same society which secured property, had a natural right to destroy it, whenever it should become a nuisance to that society."[19] Despite seeming to define "nuisance" primarily in terms of threats of violence and relative economic deprivation, Bolling's positive theory of property contained the possibility of a broader mechanism for overcoming slaveholders' property claims through establishing slavery as an ideological or moral nuisance.

The contribution of the third speaker, Thomas Jefferson Randolph, to the debates came combined with a resolution calling for a scheme of gradual emancipation. This resolution sought to replace Goode's resolution calling for no further consideration of the petitions with a text committing the select committee to examination of a scheme of gradual emancipation. Randolph's plan, which was substantially the same as the plan for gradual emancipation offered by his grandfather, Thomas Jefferson, was a complex scheme for emancipation, under which those slaves born on or later than July 4, 1840,

---

[15] Root, *Sons of the Fathers*, 36.   [16] Root, *Sons of the Fathers*, 36.
[17] Root, *Sons of the Fathers*, 36.   [18] Root, *Sons of the Fathers*, 39.
[19] Root, *Sons of the Fathers*, 40.

became State property with a view to their manumission after reaching the age of twenty-one years for males and eighteen for females.[20] Randolph's scheme called for the transportation of freed black men and women from the State, reflecting the sentiments of the ACS, which retained support among leading Virginians despite the abolitionist attacks upon it.[21] Randolph's support for transportation also echoed Thomas Jefferson's starker views of the impossibility of cohabitation of free whites and free blacks within the same territory and simmering fear that slavery's resolution lay in servile insurrection.[22] With the latter fear in mind, Randolph urged Virginia to act on a plan for gradual emancipation lest "the bloody scenes of Southampton and St. Domingo" mark the coming of abolition.[23] Bolling had laid a stress upon the feelings of physical insecurity that Nat Turner's Rebellion had stirred among the white population, but in linking the events in Southampton County to the Haitian Revolution, Randolph offered a vision of an apocalyptical race war. Tying the fate of slavery to the prospect of bloody revolution, Randolph saw the ending of slavery as inevitable – the question was whether Virginia would act quickly enough for it to be on white terms. Instead of being paralyzed by the dangers contained within a plan of emancipation, for Randolph nothing but decisive action could meet the threat posed by the continuation of slavery as an institution.[24]

It was a combination of Bolling's and Randolph's positions that emerged as the main thrust of the emancipationists' case in the ensuing debate. As noted, Goode's initial resolution had been motivated by a fear that the legislature was moving toward the confiscation of property and Randolph's plan did nothing to assuage those fears with its proposal of State ownership of slaves born after 1840. It was immediately apparent that discussion of the Randolph plan necessarily incorporated debates over the nature and origin of property itself.[25] Within the debate emancipationists engaged the question of property along two dimensions in order to try to secure their policy goal. First, they

---

[20] After 1840 slaves born within Virginia to a female slave would be retained as the property of the Commonwealth, if not removed from the State, until the relevant ages and upon the completion of a period of hiring out to defray the costs of their transportation from the State. Root, *Sons of the Fathers*, 25. Regarding connection to Thomas Jefferson's plan, cf. Root, *All Honor to Jefferson?*, 140.

[21] The Fourteenth Annual Report of the ACS published in 1831 listed thirty local auxiliary societies in Virginia in addition to the State auxiliary. *The Fourteenth Annual Report of the American Society for Colonizing the Free People of Color of the United States. With an Appendix* (Washington, D.C.: James C. Dunn, 1831).

[22] Peter S. Onuf, "'To Declare Them a Free and Independent People': Race, Slavery, and National Identity in Jefferson's Thought," *Journal of the Early Republic* 18, no. 1 (1998): 1–46; Root, *All Honor to Jefferson?*, 140.

[23] Root, *Sons of the Fathers*, 41.

[24] Randolph seemed unconcerned by the gap between his call to take control of the issue and a scheme for emancipation that would emancipate its first slave in 1858 at the earliest.

[25] Curtis, *Jefferson's Freeholders and the Politics of Ownership in the Old Dominion*, 136.

suggested, following the positive theory of property sketched out by Bolling with regard to "nuisance," that society reserved the power to create and consequently destroy property. Emancipationists such as Charles J. Faulkner and John A. Chandler leant heavily on the future threat of slave revolt as the primary instance of nuisance to argue for an ending of slavery in the State:

Property is the creature of civil society. The gentleman from Brunswick, and the gentleman from Dinwiddie, hold their slaves – not by any law of nature – not by any patent from God ... – but solely by virtue of the acquiescence and consent of the society in which they live. So long as that property is not dangerous to the good order of society, it may and will be tolerated. But sir, as soon as it does become pernicious – so soon as it is ascertained to jeopardize the peace, the happiness, the good order – nay, the very existence of society – from that moment, the right by which they hold their property is gone.[26]

The positive theory of property, alongside the dictum *salus populi suprema lex esto*, enabled speakers to both acknowledge property in slaves and discount that acknowledgment as a curb on abolition.[27] In a subtler second line of attack, emancipationists attacked the notion that the slaves were actually property at all. On one hand, as Randolph's plan touched upon only slaves born after 1840, emancipationists questioned slaveholders' recourse to property rights in the case of slaves yet to be born.[28] On the other hand, some emancipationists took on a more expansive challenge to the assumption that slaves could ever be property. William B. Preston developed an argument on the basis of the personhood of slaves that each slave possessed "a *natural* right to regain his liberty," while George W. Summers asserted that men were made slaves only by force, which could in no way mitigate an unalienable and inherent right to freedom.[29] For both speakers, Virginia was obliged by such considerations to move toward emancipation unconstrained by the "mere law" Virginia had erected to support slavery.[30]

If these arguments sounded convincing to the emancipationists, their opponents met them with a barely contained astonishment that the emancipationists would countenance interfering with property rights. During an era in which liberty was increasingly defined in economic terms, a weakening of slave property claims was equated with an attack on liberty itself.[31] James

---

[26] Root, *Sons of the Fathers*, 106.

[27] Root, *Sons of the Fathers*, 164–65. Some speakers such as Thomas Marshall cast the public good in terms of economic considerations rather than public safety to reach the same conclusion regarding emancipation. Root, *Sons of the Fathers*, 113–14. *Salus populi suprema lex esto*, "the welfare of the people is the supreme law."

[28] On the role of this line of argument in the debate, cf. Curtis, *Jefferson's Freeholders and the Politics of Ownership in the Old Dominion*, 128–29, 138–40. William M. Rives raised the prospect that the "offspring" of current slaves were not protected to the same extent as extant slave property. Root, *Sons of the Father*, 59.

[29] Root, *Sons of the Fathers*, 137, 158.   [30] Root, *Sons of the Fathers*, 137.

[31] J. Mills Thorton, *Politics and Power in a Slave Society: Alabama, 1800–1860* (Baton Rouge: Louisiana State University Press, 1978), 57.

H. Gholson deemed the Randolph plan "unjust, partial, tyrannical and monstrous."[32] He suggested:

When the distant reader shall discover, that the Virginia Legislature, in the year 1832 is engaged in solemn debate on the questions, whether "private property can be taken for public use without compensation," whether "slaves are property," and whether "the increase of slaves is property," he will be lost in amazement, and will be ready to exclaim of us, "can these be the sons of the fathers?"[33]

Alex G. Knox described the suggestion that property could be taken by the State as "a power, new, unexpected, and revolutionary in its character."[34] William H. Roane raged against a "wild and dangerous crusade for *universal emancipation*," while asserting his "*absolute, vested*, and *indefeasible right of property*" in his "considerable" number of slaves.[35] Outside of the Assembly, Benjamin Watkins Leigh, writing as Appomattox, reminded readers that "[a]ll our institutions are founded on the principle, that every man's private property is absolutely his own," and that Randolph's plan was "founded on the violation ... of the rights of slave property as vested by existing laws."[36] As well as rhetorically powerful, taking the ground of property rights was an effective strategy for drawing support from more moderate figures within the House. William H. Brodnax was willing to decry slavery as a "transcendent evil" and bristled at attempts to impede discussion of emancipation as counter to the "spirit of the age," but even he regarded the Randolph plan as "monstrous in its features" insofar as it sought to infringe rights of property.[37] Figures more open to schemes of emancipation than Brodnax were equally hesitant to endorse any policy that weakened property rights in slaves.[38]

To counter the arguments offered by emancipationists, the opponents of the Randolph plan articulated a robust defense of property in slaves. In its most direct incarnations, this meant a rejection of the positive theory of property outlined by Bolling et al. that saw property as possible only after the existence of a society to create it. Moves toward that end were evident during the Virginia debates in attempts to locate the origins of property as coeval with the creation of society itself. For Gholson, private property was the "very ligament which binds society together," without which a return to the state of nature would be

---

[32] Root, *Sons of the Fathers*, 56.   [33] Root, *Sons of the Fathers*, 45.

[34] Root, *Sons of the Fathers*, 141.   [35] Root, *Sons of the Fathers*, 125.

[36] *The Letter of Appomatox to the People of Virginia: Exhibiting a Connected View of the Recent Proceedings in the House of Delegates, on the Subject of the Abolition of Slavery; and a Succinct Account of the Doctrines Broached by the Friends of Abolition* (Richmond: Thomas W. White, 1832), 47, 12.

[37] Root, *Sons of the Fathers*, 65–67.

[38] Robert D. Powell, for instance, suggested that while "slavery is an evil" and its removal was "most devoutly to be wished," he could not "go for that or for any other scheme, which does not recognize the right of property over this species or population." Root, *Sons of the Fathers*, 92.

desirable; without respect for private property there was "no civilization – no government."[39] Brodnax similarly argued that private property was "in some degree, the foundation, and the security of all other rights under government; for, no others can exist without it."[40] Watkins Leigh as Appomattox made the related claim that abandoning the principle of private property would be to destroy republican government.[41] These arguments had the advantage of positing property rights as more entrenched than "mere law" while – some rhetorical enthusiasm aside – not resting them on the fraught notion of a natural law of slavery.[42] Invoking natural law against the positive theory of property would have risked the unsavory consequence of an admission that slavery was just under natural law, a position that few beyond William H. Roane were willing to consider.[43] Even if that possibility could be evaded "in the abstract," it was still required to explain the significant distance between 1776's sentiments of universal liberty and equality and the idea that slavery was intrinsic to society itself.[44] Moreover, an unyielding right to property made little sense in a period increasingly debating the extent and nature of eminent domain.[45]

Against this backdrop, the robust defenses of property were framed not in absolute terms but rather as a resistance to the taking of property absent consent and/or compensation. Summarized by Rice W. Wood of Albemarle, the position of the opponents of the Randolph plan evolved toward the establishment of three fundamental commitments:

One of these is that the tenure by which this property is held must not be shaken. Another, that no man's property must be taken without his consent unless compensation is made for it. A third, that we must first remove the free colored population.[46]

There was little to debate in Virginia with regard to the third point – the Randolph plan already committed the State to the removal of freed blacks,

---

[39] Root, *Sons of the Fathers*, 44.   [40] Root, *Sons of the Fathers*, 67.
[41] *The Letter of Appomatox to the People of Virginia*, 47.
[42] Brodnax sounded close to an appeal to natural law when he argued that the "charter by which we hold our slaves ... is founded on the immutable principles of justice, which existed before the formation of political societies; it has received the approbation of man, and the sanction of his great Creator, and is written on our hearts." Root, *Sons Father*, 68.
[43] Roane candidly admitted that he was "not one of those who have ever revolted at the idea or practice of slavery, as many do." Root, *Sons of the Fathers*, 125.
[44] On this point, cf. Root, "Introduction," 17. This line of argument also cut against the notion that slavery had been forced upon the American colonists by the British Empire, which remained a central pillar of American efforts to discount their own complicity in the institution.
[45] Curtis notes that the "slavery debates took place at a time when eminent domain was undergoing a substantial reconceptualization." Curtis, *Jefferson's Freeholders and the Politics of Ownership in the Old Dominion*, 140; *Barron ex rel. Tiernan v. Mayor of Baltimore* (1833). For discussion of eminent domain, see William J. Novak, *The People's Welfare: Law & Regulation in Nineteenth-Century America* (Chapel Hill: University of North Carolina Press, 1996).
[46] Root, *Sons of the Fathers*, 131–32.

reflecting the growing consensus that a free black population represented a danger to slave society.[47] As such, it was the first two principles that were really of significance for the debate. Despite the apparent tension between them, the declaration of these two principles worked in unison to enable politicians opposed to emancipation to hold property sacred while acknowledging legitimate constraints upon it. Recognition of the legitimacy of some instances of eminent domain allowed figures like Gholson to appeal to the sanctity of slave property even as they conceded that what made the Randolph plan *"monstrous and unconstitutional"* was the lack of just compensation.[48] It also had the useful effect of separating the question of the justice of slavery from the justice of the Randolph plan. Thus, opponents of the plan were free to condemn slavery as an evil, keeping faith with 1776, while also resisting the efforts being made to end it. This moved them away from the unpalatable position of defending slavery as natural and from the associated position that ownership of slaves was antecedent to society itself. But it raised the question of where a right to just compensation – a right made effectual by positive law if ever there was one – came from?

In locating the basis of the claim for just compensation and in dating property to the formation of societies, opponents of emancipation were drawn toward the Virginian and US constitutions. As Gholson's reference to "monstrous and unconstitutional" suggests, he looked to locate just compensation among the constitutional protections afforded to white Virginians. Noting the similarity between the Fifth Amendment to the US Constitution and a corresponding clause in the 1830 Virginia Constitution, Gholson argued that it was these texts that shielded private property from the "rapacity of usurpation."[49] Despite the efforts of others to presage *Barron* v. *Baltimore* in pointing out

---

[47] Bonner suggests that during the 1830s, "Proslavery ideologues tended to shift the focus from the natural rebelliousness of degraded slaves to the threat posed by 'savage' blacks living apart from white masters." However, a fear of a free black population and its movement can be seen throughout the period of the early Republic in the numerous attempts to regulate black freedom of movement, particularly that of black sailors. Robert E. Bonner, *Mastering America: Southern Slaveholders and the Crisis of American Nationhood* (New York: Cambridge University Press, 2009), 18; Padraig Riley, *Slavery and the Democratic Conscience: Political Life in Jeffersonian America* (Philadelphia: University of Pennsylvania Press, 2016), 247; Brian Schoen, "Positive Goods and Necessary Evils: Commerce, Security, and Slavery in the Lower South, 1787–1837," in *Contesting Slavery: The Politics of Bondage and Freedom in the New American Nation*, ed. John Craig Hammond and Matthew Mason (Charlottesville: University of Virginia Press, 2011), 161–82.

[48] Root, *Sons of the Fathers*, 44, 47. Original emphasis.

[49] Root, *Sons of the Fathers*, 44. Article 3, Section 11 of the 1830 Virginian Constitution included the clause: "The Legislature shall not pass … any law impairing the obligation of contracts; or any law, whereby private property shall be taken for public uses, without just compensation." By comparison, the US Constitution's Fifth Amendment reads, "No person shall … be deprived of life, liberty, or property, without due process of law; nor shall private property be taken for public use, without just compensation." No such commitment was contained in the 1776 Virginia Bill of Rights. *Proceedings and Debates of the Virginia State Convention, of*

the irrelevance of the federal Bill of Rights to State regulation of property, the similarity of phrasing and the stronger association of the federal Constitution with the Revolution meant that slippage between the two constitutions continued.[50] But regardless of whether opponents of emancipation looked to the Virginian or federal Constitution, or to both, they shared a belief that the slave property was constitutionally protected. James C. Bruce denounced the Randolph plan as striking "at the very root of our constitution," while William Daniel Jr. would concede that slavery was "immoral, unjust, and unnatural" but not that it was unprotected by the Constitution.[51] Knox believed that the Randolph plan sought "to invade the sacred right of private property, and erect its empire upon the ruins of the Constitution."[52] Outside the House of Delegates Appomattox echoed the appeals heard inside the House, instructing his readers that the "constitution intended to secure all kinds of property to its owners, against the power of the public to take it away without compensation."[53] In his influential review of the Virginia debates, Thomas R. Dew rejected the Randolph plan with an allusion to the US Constitution and its sanction of the principle that no property be taken without "full and fair compensation."[54] Thus, even despite the limited applicability of the US Constitution to the internal debates over slavery in Virginia, opponents of emancipation in 1832 made a constitutional protection of private property a mainstay of their case for slavery.

4.2　SLAVERY AND CONSTITUTIONALISM IN THE 1820S AND 1830S

For the Virginian defenders of slavery, the appeal to constitutional provisions as the basis of property rights held distinct advantages over any basis in natural law. Aside from avoiding the aforementioned risk of seeming to recognize slavery as legitimate in the abstract, this mode of appeal positioned its advocates within a burgeoning school of thought that drew upon understandings of constitutions to defend slavery. Since at least the Missouri Crisis defenders of slavery had taken constitutional grounds in seeking to roll back attempts to contain or weaken the institution on moral or religious grounds. During the Missouri Crisis, Northern opponents of slavery read into

---

1829–30. To Which Are Subjoined, the New Constitution of Virginia, and the Votes of the People (Richmond: Ritchie & Cook, 1830), 899.

[50] For instance, see the speech of Alex G. Knox. For efforts to point out the Fifth Amendment's irrelevance, see the speeches of Charles Faulkner and William Preston. Root, *Sons of the Fathers*, 110, 136, 146. On the use of the Fifth Amendment in the Virginia debates, cf. Curtis, *Jefferson's Freeholders and the Politics of Ownership in the Old Dominion*, 140, 143.

[51] Root, *Sons of the Fathers*, 87, 97.　[52] Root, *Sons of the Fathers*, 141.

[53] *The Letter of Appomatox to the People of Virginia*, 16.

[54] Thomas R. Dew, *Review of the Debate in the Virginia Legislature of 1831 and 1832* (Richmond: T. W. White, 1832), 66.

the Declaration of Independence an antislavery national identity in which the nation was committed to freedom.[55] In response, defenders of slavery moved in the Missouri debates, and more firmly over the course of 1820s, to discount the association of the Declaration of Independence with the Constitution and to offer an understanding of the Constitution that supported slavery's continued growth.[56] At the level of constitutional interpretation, this resulted in the evolution of the understanding of the US Constitution as a compact between sovereign States that had informed the Virginia and Kentucky Resolutions of 1798–99.[57] Emerging from the Missouri debates, the intertwining of a States' rights constitution with ideas of territorial sovereignty that emphasized freedom in terms of property produced a constitutional interpretation that equated the emancipation of the enslaved (or even the restriction of slavery) as an unconstitutional constraint on property. At the same time, a declining emphasis on natural law claims was replaced by appeals to experience and a corresponding conservatism based upon positive institutions, and particularly property and constitutions. This conservatism worked to reinforce the idea that the United States had more effectively distilled universal values of liberty in its positive institutions than other nations, resulting in both the need to preserve constitutions and laws and to see wisdom in the practices – and primarily the institution of slavery – that grew up under them.

The proslavery appeal to the Constitution that followed the admission of Missouri unfurled as a conception of the Constitution as a compact between the States to create a governmental system that "still remains as at first, a Confederation of State Governments."[58] The notion that the US Constitution represented a compact between the separate sovereign States had remained a viable one throughout the early Republic. Both James Madison and Thomas Jefferson had been associated with the idea that the Constitution was a "compact, to which the States are parties" in their opposition to the Alien and Sedition Laws of the Adams administration.[59] And, in 1819, this view remained in sufficient vigor to require direct address by Chief Justice John Marshall in his opinion in *McCulloch* v. *Maryland*.[60] But the perception that the resolution of the Missouri

[55] George William Van Cleve, *A Slaveholders' Union: Slavery, Politics, and the Constitution in the Early American Republic* (Chicago: University of Chicago Press, 2010), 250–56; Riley, *Slavery and the Democratic Conscience*, 218–47; See also William M. Wiecek, *The Sources of Antislavery Constitutionalism in America, 1760–1848* (Ithaca: Cornell University Press, 1977), 119–21.

[56] Riley, *Slavery and the Democratic Conscience*, 240–41.

[57] Christopher Childers, "The Old Republican Constitutional Primer: States Rights after the Missouri Controversy and the Onset of the Politics of Slavery," in *The Enigmatic South: Toward Civil War and Its Legacies*, ed. Samuel C. Hyde (Baton Rouge: Louisiana State University Press, 2014), 12–29.

[58] David James McCord, "The Federal Constitution," *The Southern Review* 4 (1828): 450.

[59] *The Virginia and Kentucky Resolutions of 1798 and '99* (Washington, DC: Jonathan Elliot, 1832), 5.

[60] *McCulloch* v. *Maryland* (1819).

Crisis had worked to constrain the freedoms of States and territories resulted in an increasing attachment to the theory and the doctrine of States' rights associated with it as the 1820s proceeded.[61] On the basis that "the States, originally sovereign and independent, have never surrendered that sovereignty, except over a few definite and specified objects," defenders of slavery emphasized a "federal consensus" over slavery, to wit that interference with slavery in States was illegitimate.[62] Reaching an apex in South Carolina's threats of nullification and secession, this States' rights approach to the federal Constitution drew upon slogans of strict construction and the tradition of the Virginia and Kentucky Resolutions to equate constitutionalism with deference to proslavery state interests.[63] Shorn of the exaggeration of South Carolina, by the 1830s the compact theory of the Constitution as a confederation of sovereignties was a key component of Southern political thought.[64]

In a parallel development, proslavery advocates developed an understanding of the Constitution in which it served as a mechanism for protecting property rights. The stark reality of antebellum slavery as a brutal and extensive system of capitalist exploitation meant that slaveholders had a direct interest in "an unrivaled investment in the sanctity of private property rights."[65] The result was a series of modifications and innovations across a variety of legal fields that worked to support slavery and to functionally link its fate to that of the "rule of law" more broadly.[66] Rhetorically, the close association of property and slavery in Southern legal thought meant that robust defenses of the former served as effective bulwarks for the latter while resonating with the Jeffersonian right of the individual "to be

---

[61] Christopher Childers, *The Failure of Popular Sovereignty: Slavery, Manifest Destiny, and the Radicalization of Southern Politics* (Lawrence: University of Kansas Press, 2012), 77.

[62] "On the Constitution of the United States," *The Southern Review* 2 (1828): 273–320; Wiecek, *The Sources of Antislavery Constitutionalism in America, 1760–1848*, 129–31. Wiecek sees this approach emerging in South Carolina before radicalizing to the position that the federal consensus was more fundamental than even the Constitution itself (138).

[63] Manisha Sinha has argued that the South Carolinian position misrepresented both its own democratic aspirations and the nature of the Virginia and Kentucky Resolutions in order to fashion a conservative political ideology that was not wholly representative of the rest of the South. Manisha Sinha, *The Counterrevolution of Slavery: Politics and Ideology in Antebellum South Carolina* (Chapel Hill: The University of North Carolina Press, 2000).

[64] Michael O'Brien, *Conjectures of Order: Intellectual Life and the American South, 1810–1860* (Chapel Hill: The University of North Carolina Press, 2004), 848, 865–66.

[65] Sven Beckert and Seth Rockman, "Introduction: Slavery's Capitalism," in *Slavery's Capitalism: A New History of American Economic Development*, ed. Sven Beckert and Seth Rockman (Philadelphia: University of Pennsylvania Press, 2016), 14. James Oakes argues that the "distinguishing function of slaves in the South's market economy was to serve not only as a labor supply but also as capital assets. Consequently, the most distinctive feature of black slavery was the systematic effort to dehumanize the slaves by treating them as property." James Oakes, *The Ruling Race: A History of American Slaveholders* (New York: Alfred A. Knopf, 1982), 26.

[66] Alfred L. Brophy, "The Market, Utility, and Slavery in Southern Legal Thought," in *Slavery's Capitalism: A New History of American Economic Development*, ed. Sven Beckert and Seth Rockman (Philadelphia: University of Pennsylvania Press, 2016), 262, 276.

left alone to control their property as they saw fit."[67] With regard to constitutional theorizing, these strategic incentives were realized in a view of the Constitution as securing general property rights and sanctioning property rights in slaves. As the participants in the Virginia debates of 1831–32 would attest, society existed to protect property and constitutions existed to facilitate that protection. Bringing together the strong sense of private property and the constitutional "compact of States" theory, defenders of slavery tapped the popular support for property claims by conjuring up a constitutional vision in which any federal interference with slavery in the States represented an attack on property rights.

The conglomeration and evolution of a states' compact theory, strong property rights, and a defense of slavery can be readily seen in the development of Nathaniel Beverley Tucker's political thought from the Missouri Crisis onward. From the eminent Virginia Family of St. George Tucker and Henry St. George Tucker Sr., Tucker served as a federal judge in the Territory of Missouri prior to its admission as a State, returning to Virginia to serve as a State judge, before ending up a professor at William & Mary College.[68] While in Missouri, Tucker wrote a series of essays under the pseudonym "Hampden" in support of Missouri's statehood under a state constitution free from federal interference to curb slavery. Across these essays, Tucker unified the "compact of States" constitution with the constitutional protection of private property to the end of defending the supports of slavery offered in Missouri's State constitution. Setting out from the position that the Constitution represented a "compact between several *separate independent* states," he went as far as arguing that the admission of a new State marked a compact between the admitted State and the existing confederation.[69] To this formulation he added the view that the legitimacy of such a compact rested upon its origin in a "sovereign and independent act" on the part of the people of the Territory.[70] Equating freedom (for the white population) with the self-government that exists in the absence of any external interference, Tucker offered a defense of "territorial sovereignty" that would be used to support the western spread of slavery thereafter:

And would this [admission with a federally amended constitution] be freedom? would this be *self*-government? would a people this fettered and manacled, and carrying the badges of bondage about them, be worthy to be admitted into the company and fellowship of the *free, sovereign and independent states* of United America?[71]

[67] Riley, *Slavery and the Democratic Conscience*, 233; James Oakes, *Slavery and Freedom: An Interpretation of the Old South* (New York: Alfred A. Knopf, 1990), 72.

[68] "Recent Deaths," *New-York Daily Times*, September 18, 1851.

[69] Nathaniel Beverley Tucker, "No. I. To the People of Missouri Territory," *St. Louis Enquirer*, 1819. In doing so, he notably departed from the antirestrictionists in Congress.

[70] Nathaniel Beverley Tucker, "No. II. To the People of Missouri Territory," *St. Louis Enquirer*, April 14, 1819.

[71] Tucker, "No. II. To the People of Missouri Territory." On the significance of "territorial sovereignty" for slavery, cf. Childers, *The Failure of Popular Sovereignty: Slavery, Manifest Destiny, and the Radicalization of Southern Politics*, chap. 3.

Anticipating the association of individual freedom with "territorial sovereignty" that would animate the advocates of the proslavery Arkansas (1836) and Florida (1838) constitutions, Tucker linked meaningful self-government with a guarantee of private property, and property in slaves in particular. Articulating an extensive theory of property in slaves, he claimed that "a slave is as much the property of his master as any other article he can possess," and asserted the right of property in unborn slaves, dating that principle as "coeval with civil society."[72] To support this view of property in slaves, Tucker turned to the federal Constitution, noting the role of slaveholders in its creation.[73] He invoked the Fifth Amendment as a guarantor of slave property and allied that with the suggestion that abolition was unconstitutional as equivalent to a bill of attainder.[74] Putting the idea of framer intent to service in linking States' rights and property rights in slaves, Tucker argued that the framers "took care not to confer on congress any power to meddle with those subjects, whereon the feelings and interests of the several states were at variance."[75] Chief among these, he suggested, was that of domestic slavery.

But if Nathaniel Beverley Tucker was a zealot for a proslavery popular state sovereignty in 1819, by the mid-1830s – and safely back in the Old Dominion of Virginia – he increasingly personified the second trend within Southern constitutional thought of a turn against abstraction and toward institutional preservation. To be sure, Tucker's writing in 1819 had hinted at a concern that too much constitutional innovation would destroy the unprecedented "power and glory" experienced by the young United States.[76] But he proceeded to this point from a position in favor of self-government and the principle that "the people have the undoubted right to make, alter, and abolish their government according to their will and pleasure."[77] In the aftermath of the Virginian debates of 1831–32, Tucker would voice similar support for States' rights and private property in slaves, but they would be increasingly grounded upon a quasi-Burkean idea of preserving society as it is.[78] In writings spread across

---

[72] Nathaniel Beverley Tucker, "No. III. To the People of the Missouri Territory," *St. Louis Enquirer* 4 (April 28, 1819).

[73] Tucker, "No. III. To the People of the Missouri Territory."

[74] Nathaniel Beverley Tucker, "No. IIII. [*sic*] To the People of the Missouri Territory," *St. Louis Enquirer*, May 5, 1819.

[75] Tucker, "No. IIII. To the People of the Missouri Territory."

[76] Tucker, "No. IIII. To the People of the Missouri Territory." Fearing the danger presented by "high aristocratic notions" as well as "the demon of frantic democracy," he saw federal intervention in the State constitution as a mechanism by which the delicate balance between the sections of the nation might be upset.

[77] Tucker, "No. I. To the People of Missouri Territory."

[78] Edmund Burke's presence in the texts discussed here is worth remarking upon as an indication of this shift. Burke was directly quoted or alluded to approvingly by Tucker, Thomas R. Dew, and William Harper among others. A quote from Burke appeared on the title page of the contemporaneous proslavery pamphlet, *An Appeal ... By a South Carolinian. An Appeal to the People of*

the media of reprinted lectures, book reviews, and newspaper columns, Tucker developed a defense of the Virginian constitution that looked to experience, not abstraction, as the correct basis of constitutional design and which regarded universal suffrage as the proximate threat to the State's happiness. Never conceding Virginia's superiority in sovereignty or constitutional design to the federal Constitution, he brought together the Southern commitment to property in slaves and a desire for institutional preservation in an understanding of the institution of slavery as a crucial bulwark against the political degeneration inherent to republican government.

In a series of lectures reprinted in 1845, Tucker gave a systematic cast to the ideas and theories that he had developed since the Hampden essays.[79] Central to this system was a faith in experience and a belief that reform, if undertaken at all, should be hesitant and deferent to existing practice. With regard to constitutions, Tucker's views were guided by the conviction that governments were both the product of and ought to be judged against their specific historical situation; "that government is the creature of circumstance."[80] While denying that an abstract definition of the best government could exist – "There is no best in government. That which is best for one people is not best for another" – Tucker nonetheless believed that the original Virginian and US constitutions offered the best approximations of free government in their relative circumstances.[81] The reasons for this lay with the extremely favorable conditions the American colonies had found themselves in upon independence, but also crucially in the use made of the English and colonial experience by those framing those constitutions. Making use of history and allying it with "an utter disregard of theoretical perfection, and … an attention to expediency, fitness, and the actual condition of things," the founders had correctly identified the maxims appropriate for Virginian and American constitutional design.[82] Guided not by a concern for abstraction but by the circumstances with which they were faced, the framers succeeded where they did because they "were men of practical wisdom, learned in the school of experience; and,

the Northern and Eastern States, on the Subject of Negro Slavery in South Carolina. By a South Carolinian (New York, 1834).

[79] The lectures were individually dated in the collection from between 1839 and 1844 but as is discussed subsequently they systematized ideas seen in Tucker's writings from earlier in the 1830s.

[80] Nathaniel Beverley Tucker, *A Series of Lectures on the Science of Government, Intended to Prepare the Student for the Study of the Constitution of the United States* (Philadelphia: Carey and Hart, 1845), 56.

[81] Tucker, *A Series of Lectures on the Science of Government*, 64. Tucker designated the framers of the Virginia constitution as coming closest to the form of government most conducive to happiness, followed by the devisers of the federal Constitution. "In considering then, what government should be … we shall find ourselves following in great measure the footsteps of the authors of our institutions." Tucker, *A Series of Lectures on the Science of Government*, 49.

[82] Tucker, *A Series of Lectures on the Science of Government*, 220.

[took] experience for their guide."[83] He warned the rising generation against the seduction of the "common error" of thinking "themselves wiser and better than their fathers," and allowed for the occasional need for institutional amendment, but never in service of "a taste for mere theoretical symmetry and perfection."[84] What imperfections there were within the constitutions and institutions of Virginia had been shown by experience to support freedom and should be accorded corresponding reverence.

Among such "imperfections" domestic slavery stood out for both its conflict with abstraction conceptions of equality and its importance in preserving freedom. In 1819, Tucker had feared that the two extremes of "high aristocratic notions" and "the demon of frantic democracy" could equally result in federal interference in the Missouri constitution which, in turn, risked upsetting the delicate balance between the sections of the nation.[85] After the Virginia debates Tucker's concerns were much more focused upon the threats originating in democracy. Discounting the threat of aristocracy, he joined De Tocqueville in fearing that democracy would give way to the rule of ambitious individuals not to a ruling order. To the extent that "aristocracy" threatened the United States, it was in its ability to provide a foil for a demagogue. In the United States, there was "a danger in the name of aristocracy, but none of the thing itself."[86] For Tucker, the tangible threat to American society came in the form of a democratic people lacking sufficient commitment to property rights. Painting a vision of human nature as driven by material self-interest, he saw in the French Revolution the destabilizing force of "the lawless appetite of the multitude for the property of others."[87] Updating the republican distrust of the dependent man with the reality of industrial wage-labor, Tucker argued that the poorest in society, trapped in a cycle of working to reproduce their capacity for future labor, would always be susceptible to the temptation of using political power to redistribute property.[88] For this reason, he remained reluctant to extend the "sovereign principle of voting" to the hireling, whose "first and only use" of it "would be to sell it to the demagogue."[89]

Against the threat of a demagogue, slavery offered a twofold protection. Tucker looked to slavery as among the framers' deviations from theory in the light of practice that contributed to the preservation of liberty. On one hand, the existence of slavery ensured that "a jealous passion for liberty"

[83] Tucker, *A Series of Lectures on the Science of Government*, 259.
[84] Tucker, *A Series of Lectures on the Science of Government*, 232, 235.
[85] Tucker, "No. IIII. To the People of the Missouri Territory."
[86] Tucker, *A Series of Lectures on the Science of Government*, 95.
[87] Nathaniel Beverley Tucker, "Slavery," *Southern Literary Messenger* (Richmond, 1836), 337.
[88] Tucker, *A Series of Lectures on the Science of Government*, 335–36.
[89] Nathaniel Beverley Tucker, "Note to Blackstone's Commentaries," *Southern Literary Messenger* (Richmond, 1835), 230.

was kept aflame among the lowest white orders of society.[90] Selectively quoting Burke to support the view that the presence of slavery gives liberty greater nobility, Tucker envisioned slavery as a positive support for the spirit of freedom.[91] On the other hand, slavery ensured that the servile class of Virginian society were definitively removed from political activity, curbing the *"suicidal tendency* of freedom" to empower elements unattached to the rights of property.[92] Slavery created a class of individuals who were directed to menial labor, by force, and stripped of their legal personality.[93] For Tucker, this arrangement neatly ensured that the population in a position to participate politically would always be drawn from among those who had an investment in property rights. Wary as he was of universal (white male) suffrage, Tucker nonetheless believed it to be less destabilizing when allied to an institution of slavery. Enfranchisement of white men within a society that largely removed them from subsistence labor meant fewer voters "who have not a feeling sense of the importance and sanctity of the rights of property."[94] Although sanguine about the long-term hopes for property rights in a world succumbing to democracy, Tucker saw slavery as enabling the South to delay the day of reckoning.[95] In sharp contrast to 1819, if that brought upon the South the accusation of aristocratic tendencies, Tucker would weather them rather than face a "democracy of free labor and universal suffrage."[96]

Nathaniel Beverley Tucker's turn toward experience and positive institutions was echoed in other Southern thinkers of the time. Michael O'Brien has documented a shift in Southern constitutional thought during this period from the "old knowledge" of the commonwealth men and to the "the peculiarity of the American experience."[97] By the mid-Antebellum period, the rationalistic and universal sentiments that had led Thomas Paine to associate the American Revolution with "the cause of all mankind" were

---

[90] Tucker, *A Series of Lectures on the Science of Government*, 331.

[91] Tucker, "Note to Blackstone's Commentaries," 230. Tucker cut out Burke's aside that with regard to the American South "this sentiment ... has at least as much pride as virtue in it."

[92] Tucker, *A Series of Lectures on the Science of Government*, 331.

[93] On slavery and its relation to social death, cf. Oakes, *Slavery and Freedom: An Interpretation of the Old South*, 4–14; Orlando Patterson, *Slavery and Social Death: A Comparative Study* (Cambridge, MA: Harvard University Press, 1982).

[94] Tucker, *A Series of Lectures on the Science of Government*, 345.

[95] On Tucker's pessimistic attachment to the inevitability of degeneration, cf. O'Brien, *Conjectures of Order*, 870. In the lectures, Tucker offered the gloomy appraisal that "There is nothing good under the sun. Everything *but evil* carries in it the seed of its own destruction. That alone can be trusted to perpetuate itself. That alone, left to itself, remains unchanged; while, in every blessing that we enjoy, there is a something to enervate, to corrupt, or to lull into fatal security." Tucker, *A Series of Lectures on the Science of Government*, 144. Original emphasis.

[96] Tucker, "Note to Blackstone's Commentaries," 231.

[97] O'Brien, *Conjectures of Order*, 798, 783–870.

giving way to Romantic sentiments of American liberty as an essentially domestic project.[98] Distancing themselves from the excesses of the French Revolution, both in terms of the violence and the philosophical abstraction, thinkers such as John Taylor of Caroline, Abel P. Upshur, and Thomas R. Dew began in different ways to look to the American – and more exactly, the Virginian – experience for guidance. If Taylor can be taken as a transition figure – by delving into the canon of civic republicanism, O'Brien described him as making "political thought into a problem of American historicism" – Upshur more directly displaced the claims of universality by declaring that "Principles do not *precede*, but spring out of Government."[99] Such empiricism gave wider latitude to questions of societal justice than the relatively strict universalism of eternal natural rights. Judge William Harper, in rejecting the natural rights doctrine of the Declaration of Independence, responded to the claim that man cannot have property in man with a retort that "Certainly he may, if the laws of society allow it, and if it be on sufficient grounds, neither he nor society do wrong."[100] Abstraction and notions of natural law and even justice mattered less for the Southern thinkers associated with this empiricist turn than what they could derive from the American experience. Directly stated by a South Carolinian writer with regard to slavery, abstract questions of justice were irrelevant to the situation at hand – "It is sufficient for our purposes that we find them [slaves] among us."[101]

Nonetheless, the apparent relativism of this empirical approach always ended up back at a fundamental commitment to property. Thus could Thomas R. Dew join Tucker and his fellow Southerners in believing both that "circumstances give in reality to every political principle its distinguishing colour and discriminating effect" and that "from the days of the patriarchs down to the present time, the great desideratum has been to find the most efficient mode of protecting property."[102] Harper similarly asserted, "Property ... is the first element of civilization."[103] Dew arrived at his position by internalizing the view that property relations necessarily informed governmental structures, but others with less inclination for political economic analysis reached the same point through a cruder faith that property was what

[98] Thomas Paine, "Common Sense; Addressed to the Inhabitants of America, on the Following Interesting Subjects," in *Selected Writings of Thomas Paine*, ed. Ian Shapiro and Jane E. Calvert (New Haven: Yale University Press, 2014), 7.

[99] O'Brien, *Conjectures of Order*, 798, 803.

[100] William Harper, *Memoir on Slavery, Read Before the Society for the Advancement of Learning, of South Carolina, at Its Annual Meeting at Columbia. 1837* (Charleston: James S. Burges, 1838), 9.

[101] *An Appeal to the People of the Northern and Eastern States*, 9.

[102] Dew, *Review of the Debate in the Virginia Legislatire of 1831 and 1832*, 46, 66.

[103] Harper, *Memoir on Slavery*, 14.

separated them from the barbarians.[104] As with Tucker, Gholson and Brodnax, in stating that principles were coeval with society, Upshur was primarily concerned with the establishment of the sanctity of property. As good fortune would have it, in exercising this freedom of selecting first principles, Virginia and the United States had been shown to have best secured a desired balance of order and freedom – which was to say, they had best guaranteed property – and so it made sense to look to them, and certainly not to any abstractions, or worse still, foreign nations, for guidance on how to proceed.

The happy coincidence of property rights and experience served the interests of a slave system positioned within a liberal society and brought constitutionalism to the fore. At the heart of defenses of slavery in the Antebellum period was a deep attachment to property rights. While Paul Finkelman correctly points to race as the key to proslavery arguments – "[i]t served as the basis of all other defenses of slavery" – within the liberal culture of the antebellum United States it was claims to property rights that connected defenses of slavery to the wider political culture.[105] As James Oakes has argued, antebellum slaveholders came of age in a world imbued with capitalism and Lockean liberal values and came to share that world's understanding of freedom in terms of the exercise of rights.[106] Identifying slaves in terms of property put an ideological commitment to rights to work at both ends of the problem of justifying slavery in a liberal society. It gave the slaveholders a claim on "their" slaves that could be located within the wider understanding of property as one of the Lockean markers of self-hood, "life, liberty, and property." On a second level, by identifying slaves as property, it stripped the latter of the very claim to property in themselves and their own bodies that offered the strongest liberal counterargument to slavery.[107] As we saw, property rights was the *cri de coeur* of opponents of emancipation in 1832, and it echoed throughout debates over slavery in the 1830s and beyond. With the turn to experience and away from natural law as the basis of property rights, defenders of slavery increasingly looked to the positive institutionalization of property rights as the basis of claims to property. Within American political thought constitutions were the *ne plus ultras* of such institutionalization. And as national pressure was applied

---

[104] William Gilmore Simms, "Miss Martineau on Slavery," *Southern Literary Messenger* (Richmond, VA, November 1837), 654.

[105] Paul Finkelman, "The Significance and Persistence of Proslavery Thought," in *The Problem of Evil: Slavery, Freedom, and the Ambiguities of American Reform*, ed. Steve Mintz and John Stauffer (Amherst, MA: University of Massachusetts Press, 2007), 110; Oakes, *Slavery and Freedom*, 72.

[106] Oakes, *Slavery and Freedom*, 64–68; Oakes, *The Ruling Race*, 57–58. On the ways in which the debate over slavery was contained within a "liberal consensus," cf. David F. Ericson, *The Debate over Slavery: Antislavery and Proslavery Liberalism in Antebellum America* (New York: New York University Press, 2000).

[107] As Fox-Genovese and Genovese note, slaveholders were aware enough of the threat of this argument to repeatedly emphasize that they held no property in man per se, only in the labor and services of slaves. Fox-Genovese and Genovese, *The Mind of the Master Class*, 629.

to the institution of slavery in the 1830s, the institution of the US Constitution was increasingly central to such debates.

The close association of the US Constitution and property in slaves was an important thread within proslavery and anti-abolitionist writings of the early 1830s. Those offering a defense of slavery within the national arena saw the US Constitution as a crucial bulwark against the "fanatics" of the North. A correspondent in 1835 would claim, "The citizens of the South stand upon their rights. They are able to protect their domestic institutions by the shield of the [US] Constitution."[108] Harper was more forthright in stating that slavery was "guaranteed to us by the Constitution."[109] Advocates of slavery saw the link between the US Constitution and property in slaves as important to their position and went to work to show it to their audiences. J. K. Paulding's *Slavery in the United States* saw in abolition a war on the federal Constitution, a constitution that incorporated a guarantee of property in slaves "more complete as well as specific" than any other species of property.[110] When Edmund Bellinger condemned abolitionism as "a war against *the principles of constitutional liberty*," he seemed to be thinking of the latter as property in slaves.[111] Dew would cite congressional debates to show that the constitutional protections on property extended to slavery.[112] Offering "Thoughts on Slavery," an author in the *Southern Literary Messenger* suggested that the federal Constitution had expressly recognized slavery and sought to protect the "natural right of the master over the slave."[113] In so doing, the charter "itself legalizes, defends, maintains, and protects slavery."[114] And even when constitutional property was not named directly within defenses of slavery, the raising of the standard of the Constitution often denoted a heady brew of property rights, slavery, and States' rights that were not easily separated into their constituent parts. In 1838 a writer to the *Southern Literary Messenger* decried the efforts of abolitionists to ruin "domestic tranquility, private rights, public faith, and federal compact."[115] Slavery was, said that author, "distinctly recognized and protected under the federal compact, at the time of the adoption of the present constitution."[116] Even Thomas Cooper, as he leaned away from

---

[108] "Anti-Abolitionist Spirit at the North," *The Southern Literary Journal and Monthly Magazine* (Charleston, 1835), 128.

[109] "Reflections Elicited by Judge Harper's Anniversary Oration Delivered Before the South-Carolina Society for the Advancement of Learning, 9th Dec. 1835," *The Southern Literary Journal and Monthly Magazine* (Charleston, July 1836), 378.

[110] J. K. Paulding, *Slavery in the United States* (New York: Harper & Brothers, 1836), 12, 284.

[111] Edmund Jr. Bellinger, *A Speech on the Subject of Slavery; Delivered 7th Sept'r., 1835, at a Public Meeting of the Citizens of Barnwell District, South-Carolina* (Charleston: Dan. J. Dowling, 1835), 38.

[112] Dew, *Review of the Debate in the Virginia Legislatire of 1831 and 1832*, 66.

[113] "Thoughts on Slavery," *Southern Literary Messenger* (Richmond, December 1838), 742.

[114] "Thoughts on Slavery," 742.

[115] "Political Religionism," *Southern Literary Messenger* (Richmond, September 1838), 550.

[116] "Political Religionism," 550.

relying upon the federal government to defend slavery, talked of rights under the federal Constitution.[117] It would not have seemed at all incongruous to Southern readers in 1835 that a review article could remind readers that when it came to slavery, "he who most rigidly adheres to the principle of the Federal Constitution is ... the truest patriot," without much elaboration as to what the principle of the federal Constitution actually was.[118] By the mid-Antebellum period, property, slavery, and the federal Constitution were almost interchangeable when it came to mounting defenses of slavery and critiques of abolition.[119]

4.3 CONSERVATIVE FUTURES AND THE PERSONHOOD OF SLAVES

The support for the idea that knowledge came exclusively from experience, and from history as the record of the experiences of others, should not be understood as an indication that the temporal frame of reference for slaveholders was the past alone. The idea that the slaveholding South was a feudal anomaly among a forward-looking United States has come under attack in recent years, not least of all because there is scant evidence that any sizeable group in the South believed that to be the case.[120] Instead, like much of the rest of the nation, Southern slaveholders saw themselves as situated in a moment of rapid historical progress, buoyed along by a "spirit of the age" associated with the spread of enlightenment and material advance. And like the rest of the nation, they looked forward – not back – in anticipation of what that spirit would bring. In this vein, James H. Hammond would tell the House of Representatives in 1836 that as the result of the spirit of age the nation sat on the cusp of a new era:

---

[117] *The Crisis: Being, An Enquiry Into the Measures Proper to Be Adopted by the Southern States, In Reference to the Proceedings of the Abolitionists* (Charleston: Dan. J. Dowling, 1835), 21.

[118] "An Appeal to the People of the Northern and Eastern States, on the Subject of Negro Slavery in South-Carolina. By a South-Carolinian," *The Southern Literary Journal and Monthly Magazine* (Charleston, September 1835), 63.

[119] And thus with truth can Fox-Genovese and Genovese say that "Behind the endless constitutional wrangling lay a powerful defense of a particular theory of property." Fox-Genovese and Genovese, *The Mind of the Master Class*, 629.

[120] Beckert and Rockman in assessing recent historiographical trends suggest that recent years have seen "the history of the antebellum South ... rewritten as a quest for modernity and an embrace of progress." Genovese is quite clear that, with some hesitations, slaveholders saw material transformation, republican institutions, the spread of Christianity, and individual freedom as markers of "progress" and "embraced it as their own cause." Matthew Karp has provided a useful recent discussion of slaveholder attitudes toward modernity, with an emphasis on foreign policy. Beckert and Rockman, "Introduction: Slavery's Capitalism," 14; Eugene D. Genovese, *The Slaveholders' Dilemma: Freedom and Progress in Southern Conservative Thought, 1820–1860* (Columbia: University of South Carolina, 1992), 4; Matthew Karp, *This Vast Southern Empire: Slaveholders at the Helm of American Foreign Policy* (Cambridge, MA: Harvard University Press, 2016), 150–72.

Every close observer must perceive that we are approaching, if we have not already reached, a new era in civilization. The man of the nineteenth century is not the man of the seventeenth, and widely different from him of the eighteenth.[121]

Nonetheless, the context for Hammond's declaration – a speech opposing the reception of abolitionist petitions – points to the degree to which such attitudes were not seen as necessitating an opposition to the institution of slavery. Rather, for those advocating on behalf of slavery, their very concern for the future resulted in robust defenses of slavery. It was in these future-oriented defenses that a parallel argument to the idea that slaves were constitutional property – that slaves were not constitutional people – came out in its most urgent formulation.

As much as defenders of slavery looked to experience and history for positive guidance in the 1830s, they also sought to gather from their study warnings of what might befall their institutions if not administered wisely. Such study was all the more urgent, as their researches confirmed a belief that in the future the challenges would be greater than they were at present. If Southern conservatives saw in the French Revolution the dangerous results of reverting to abstraction over empiricism, they understood one facet of this dangerous abstraction to be realized in the replacement of organic social relations with a cold and rational cash nexus.[122] And to the extent that the cash nexus was bound up with the apparently unstoppable – and indeed broadly desirable – idea of progress as embodied in the industrial revolution, it would only become more threatening in the future. For William Harper, nineteenth-century capitalism meant an immiseration of the white working class as "competition is established. The remuneration . . . becomes gradually less and less; a larger and larger proportion of the product of his labor goes to swell the fortune of the capitalist."[123] Tying this process to the developments that gave rise to the various blessings of progress, Harper decried these necessary consequences of industrialization: "This inequality, this vice, this misery, this *Slavery*, is the price of England's civilization."[124] Such misery bred discontent, political instability, and the possibility of revolt or a class politics destructive of the sanctity of property. Harper was joined by Dew, Tucker, and others, in fearing a future characterized by (in Dew's words) "the dangerous vices of agrarianism, and legislative intermeddling between the laborer and the capitalist."[125]

In light of such a future, the understanding of slavery as an institutional support for liberalism gave the peculiar institution a heightened significance. In resisting a wage relationship between capitalist and laborer, slavery was seen to

---

[121] *Register of Debates, 24th Congress, 1st Session*, 1836, 2458.
[122] Genovese, *The Slaveholders' Dilemma*, 6.   [123] Harper, *Memoir on Slavery*, 16.
[124] Harper, *Memoir on Slavery*, 17. Original Emphasis.
[125] Thomas R. Dew, "An Address on the Influence of the Federative Republican System of Government upon Literature and the Development of Character," *Southern Literary Messenger* (Richmond, March 1836), 277.

retain the organic social relationship undermined by the cash nexus and to avoid the exploitation and immiseration of the worker deemed inherent to free labor.[126] With a willful lack of imagination, defenders of slavery suggested that as slaves were "paid" in kind they could never be inadequately compensated or made to suffer from states of scarcity.[127] Therefore, they ascribed to the slavery a capacity to mitigate exploitation and the political risks following on from it. Moreover, as briefly sketched out earlier with reference to Tucker, proslavery Southerners looked to slavery to engender among whites a spiritual support for property rights and to ensure that the most revolutionary class was excluded from political participation. By providing poor whites with a status definitively apart from the lowest in society and offering them the aspiration of socioeconomic advance, the institution of slavery was deemed to inoculate them to some degree against the "agrarian" attacks upon property seen in Europe and the North.[128] At the same time by identifying menial labor and the absence of political power with slavery, and assigning that dual status to a racial minority, the institution placed those most prone to agrarianism outside the formal political power structure. The consequence, as spelt out by Dew, was that the slaveholding South offered resources to sustain a republicanism of freedom and order absent elsewhere:

[I]n our slaveholding country the case is far different. Our laboring classes and menials are all slaves of a different color from their masters – the source of greatest distinction amongst freemen is taken away; and the spirit of equality, the true spirit of genuine republicanism may exist here, – without leading on to corruption on one side or agrarianism on the other.[129]

In this light, these Southern intellectuals did not see slavery as a holdover from a feudal past so much as pillar of support for the society to come. These associated fears and beliefs regarding the future were one element in the shift to a "positive good" defense of slavery over the Antebellum period.

It was against this backdrop that the slaveholding South reacted to the emergence of immediate abolitionism in the Northern states. To the extent that the shift to a "positive good" defense of slavery was a reaction to abolitionist pressure, it was at least in part a reaction to the perception that

---

[126] Within this literature implausible references to happy and contented slaves were everywhere, while the inherent exploitation within a master–slave relationship was never subjected to the same critical examination as the relations between the industrial capitalist and the wage laborer.

[127] Tucker, "Note to Blackstone's Commentaries," 229.

[128] Although concern over the threat of an interracial alliance of the dispossessed remained, as Keri Leigh Merritt has shown, and the ideological supports of sexual regulation, violence, and honor were mobilized to regulate the poor populations in the South. With time even the poorest whites would be politically disempowered in the service of preserving the social and political order. Keri Leigh Merritt, *Masterless Men: Poor Whites and Slavery in the Antebellum South* (Cambridge, UK: Cambridge University Press, 2017), 125–42, 162–78.

[129] Dew, "An Address on the Influence of the Federative Republican System of Government upon Literature and the Development of Character," 278.

abolitionism was one dimension of the coming political destabilization to which slavery offered a bulwark. Advocates of slavery saw embodied in abolitionism the wider revolutionary movement that progress would bring and the avowed rejection of property that would form its core. As such, abolitionism was condemned a foreign "contagion," and a part of the European "great party movement" against the organic forms of society.[130] As Tucker "reminded" his readers, "in that war against property [the French Revolution], the first object of attack was property in slaves."[131] Paulding likewise warned that the "furious zeal to give freedom to the blacks" was "laying the axe to the root of the fairest plant of freedom."[132] Abolition's threat was twofold. On one hand the abolitionist's denunciation of the property claims that slavery rested upon threatened to undermine the basis of the institution of slavery. On the other hand, in its recognition of the personhood of slaves, abolitionism sought to make citizens of the very group whose exclusion enabled the institution to function as a countervailing force against agrarianism. Slavery and its benefit as a bulwark against the destabilizing spread of the bourgeois cash nexus rested upon the nonrecognition of the enslaved as people and the corresponding recognition of them as property. Abolition sought to universalize its refusal to recognize slaves as a form of legitimate property and actively sought their recognition as people. For white Southern intellectuals, abolitionism was more than a misplaced sympathy for the "contented" slaves of the South – it was the cutting edge of a revolutionary spirit that sought to bring the destructive potential of progress into the South itself. The message of the abolitionists – that the slave was a person – was a conceptual threat to both the system of slavery and the value that slaveholders placed in the system as a counter to the excesses of progress.

Thus, in seeking to protect their system of slavery, Southern advocates deployed their rhetorical skills in the service of the de-personification of the slaves. Most directly, this involved the equation of slaves with property, as William H. Roane, for example, did in assuring his peer in the Virginia House of Delegates that he would not "touch a hair on the head of his slave, any sooner than I would a hair on the mane of his horse."[133] But it also meant, as the quote implies, the defining of a slave as an entity less than the white man. Here, the racial basis of American slavery was embraced. Often couched in the language of a hierarchy of races, characteristics and attributes were assigned to the slave population on the basis of the "now generally admitted" view that "the African

---

[130] *Register of Debates*, 1836, 726, 673. John Stauffer points to the slaveholders' fears of a worldwide emancipatory movement as an important element in shifting of the politics of slavery toward expansionism and a counterforce of abolitionism in the 1830s. John Stauffer, "Fighting the Devil with His Own Fire," in *The Abolitionist Imagination* (Cambridge, MA: Harvard University Press, 2012), 71.

[131] Tucker, "Slavery," 337.   [132] Paulding, *Slavery in the United States*, 10.

[133] Root, *Sons of the Fathers*, 124.

negro is an inferior variety of the human race."[134] Ordained by God or determined by phrenology, the distinctions between the races dictated that slaves "must remain, as in all times they have been, a separate order from ourselves."[135] The supposed inferiority was rendered into a further argument for slavery, as defenders of slavery argued that the institution served as a mechanism for black moral and intellectual development.[136] Such development was, of course, never expected to accrue to the point of ending black inferiority within a practical frame of time.

Time and time again, defenders of slavery linked the ending of slavery to a feared political agency of the then-freed black population. Invoking the specter of black political agency and a parallel decline of white political power, they tapped into the broadening white American fear of black citizenship in the period.[137] In these moments – often among the most emotive and most visually rich appeals – advocates of slavery suggested that the acknowledgment of the ex-slaves as political citizens would destroy the political institutions that the former held dear. Again race provided the grammar for such arguments. If the "Anglo-Saxon race [was] peculiarly constituted for freedom," the "black race" was "absolutely incapable" of republican liberty.[138] In the Virginia debate, William Brodnax asked his fellow representatives, through the Chair:

> With what feelings did *you* reflect on the spectacle, when you imagined to yourself a knotty-pated, sable African, usurping the chair, which you now occupy, and presiding over the deliberations of a negro assembly?[139]

Black political agency was linked to a loss of white political power and depicted as pregnant with violence. Reappropriating the very arguments that abolitionists used on behalf of black men against the existence of slavery and the slave trade in the District of Columbia, Robert Walker of Mississippi told the House of Representatives that the presence of a free black population in

---

[134] Harper, *Memoir on Slavery*, 36.
[135] *An Appeal to the People of the Northern and Eastern States*, 21; On divine sanction, cf. Tucker, "Slavery," 338. On phrenology, cf. "Slavery," *The Southern Literary Journal and Monthly Magazine* (Charleston, November 1835), 192.
[136] Simms, "Miss Martineau on Slavery," 656.
[137] Perhaps seeing this fear as the basis of cross-sectional opposition to "the fanatics," the *Richmond Enquirer* quoted with approval the view of F. A. Tallmadge, offered at an 1833 Tammany Hall meeting opposing abolitionism, that "if the blacks of the Southern States were at once to be set free, the whites would become slaves." "The Fanatics," *The Enquirer*, October 8, 1833. On the rise of racism in the North, cf. James Brewer Stewart, "The Emergence of Racial Modernity and the Rise of the White North, 1790–1840," *Journal of the Early Republic* 18, no. 2 (1998): 181–217.
[138] "Political Religionism," 559; "Natural History of the Negro Race, by Professor F. H. Guenebault," *The Southern Literary Journal and Monthly Magazine* (Charleston, October 1836), 151.
[139] Root, *Sons of the Fathers*, 75.

a post-Abolition District would "render it utterly impossible for any southern man to legislate here, except at the peril of his life."[140] In the background, the Haitian Revolution and the vital personhood of the Black Jacobin both provided confuting evidence of the possibility of black agency and animated the perception that it would result in bloodshed.[141]

The fear of black political agency brought advocates of slavery into conflict with a reading of the Declaration of Independence as enshrining universal equality. Across a variety of responses to this challenge, a common theme was the denial to the black population of personhood as understood within the Declaration's framework. A vanguard, of whom Harper was a central figure, opted to reject out of hand the Declaration's claim of natural equality of mankind as "utterly fanciful unphilosophical and unjust."[142] More common were two other approaches that had been posited during the Missouri Crisis. One made recourse to empiricist sentiments and suggested that the Declaration conveyed only an "abstract truth," not suited to actualization in an existing society.[143] Another held to the ideals expressed in the Declaration of Independence but resolutely denied the extent of its political equality reached to the inclusion of the black population.[144] At times, the historical instance of the Declaration itself was utilized to reemphasize racial inequality. In the *Appeal ... By A South Carolinian*, the very exclusion of black slaves from the Declaration was an indication of their status as property, while an article in the *Southern Literary Messenger* followed a longer chain of reasoning to reach the same end: that as Jefferson must not have had slaves in mind when writing the Declaration, the latter must not have been viewed as able to enter contracts, and as such were not considered capable of being political parties.[145] At their core, these arguments accorded with the broad thrust of proslavery thought in seeking to deny that slaves were people and to establish them as property.

4.4 CONCLUSION

It perhaps should not be surprising that at this time proslavery arguments regarding the Declaration of Independence would be reaching precisely the opposite conclusion as abolitionist arguments were about the same text. But to the extent that it highlights the manner in which battle lines were being drawn

[140] *Register of Debates*, 1836, 695.

[141] For a discussion of the centrality of fear of the Haitian Revolution to the proslavery political imagination, cf. Carl Lawrence Paulus, *The Slaveholding Crisis: Fear of Insurrection and the Coming of the Civil War* (Baton Rouge, LA: Louisiana State University Press, 2017).

[142] "Reflections Elicited by Judge Harper's Anniversary Oration Delivered Before the South-Carolina Society for the Advancement of Learning, 9th Dec. 1835," 380; O'Brien, *Conjectures of Order*, 948.

[143] *Register of Debates*, 1836, 2249.

[144] "Slavery," 189; Ericson, *The Debate over Slavery*, 19–20.

[145] *An Appeal to the People of the Northern and Eastern States*, 20; "Thoughts on Slavery," 742.

in the 1830s it is significant. Following the Virginian debates of 1831–32, the emerging "positive good" defense of slavery rejected or constrained the Declaration's commitment to political equality. A rejection in the mode of Harper's denoted a refusal to accept that the slave was the equal of the white man. A more "moderate" interpretation offered that the slave was "merely" not a political person. Both paths lead to the view that the salient identity of the enslaved was as property not person. Simultaneously, proslavery forces were discounting the claims of slave personhood and strengthening an ideological framework in which slaves were property under the federal Constitution. By comparison, abolitionists in the North in moving toward the theater of constitutional politics were drawing upon the Declaration of Independence to develop a constitutional interpretation supportive of action on slavery.

Associating slave property with constitutional protections became a powerful strategy in the mid-Antebellum period. As discussed earlier, constitutions, and the federal Constitution, in particular, became important sites for the establishment of rights and protections as natural law philosophies and strict legal positivism were replaced by a constitutionalism supported by experiential appeals. The turn to empiricism bolstered notions that property was "coeval" with society and that constitutions were the vehicles that enshrined property rights. Alongside and intertwined within these developments came a strengthening of a liberal understanding of freedom as the unconstrained accumulation and disposal of personal property. Connecting slavery to these trends enabled its defenders to capitalize upon them and transform the perceived threats associated with "progress" into arguments for the proliferation of the institution of slavery. The blending of constitutionalism, property claims, and slavery during the 1820s and 1830s made for a fertile environment in which "modern" defenses of slavery could take root.

But it also made control over interpretation of the federal Constitution a vital terrain within the debates over slavery. As the conflicting views over the Declaration of Independence indicated, the core of that debate was emerging as a philosophical conflict over whether slaves were understood to be people or property. On this point, the federal Constitution offered no textual resolution. The infamous three-fifths clause had fudged the fundamental question in service of a compromise between non-slaveholding and slaveholding States. The Missouri Crisis, to the degree that it incorporated the questions of black migration and transportation, had indicated the danger to the Union of applying pressure to this compromise, but its resolution in the "federal consensus" had displaced that tension into conflict over sectional, not individual, rights. Should it be revived in a form not so easily displaced into questions of state sovereignty, the question of whether slaves were property or people would require a more articulated response. And to resolve the tension constitutionally would necessitate stepping beyond the text. As we will soon see, the question of abolition in the District of Columbia presented exactly such a scenario.

5

Theories of the Federal Compact in the 1830s

In his seminal study of antislavery constitutionalism, William M. Wiecek argued that debates over slavery in the United States in the early Antebellum period largely operated within a "federal consensus."[1] This consensus held that, with regard to slavery, each State was free to regulate their own internal affairs as they saw fit and that the federal government was thus constrained from interference in the institution of slavery in the slaveholding States.[2] Undergirding this consensus was the notion of the Constitution as the product of a compact of the States in which each State, as a sovereign entity, entered into agreement with the others to combine limited surrendered powers in the federal government. In Wiecek's telling, over the course of the 1820s and 1830s, the federal consensus – or as it was sometimes labeled, the federal compact – faced greater pressure from a Southern "proslavery consensus," which expected the federal government's benevolence toward the slaveholding States and support for the expansion of slavery into the territories.[3] On the other side of the debate over slavery, abolitionists in the mid-1830s came to see the struggle between antislavery and slavery in Manichean terms and began to reject the idea of deference to the slaveholding States in federal matters.[4] Under these dual pressures, by the end of the 1830s, the federal consensus was fraying and represented a middle ground between proslavery and antislavery constitutional interpretations.[5] Assessing his tracing of the federal consensus's decline, Wiecek suggested that the 1830s "demonstrated that the federal

[1] William M. Wiecek, *The Sources of Antislavery Constitutionalism in America, 1760–1848* (Ithaca, NY: Cornell University Press, 1977).
[2] Wiecek, *The Sources of Antislavery Constitutionalism in America*, 83.
[3] Wiecek, *The Sources of Antislavery Constitutionalism in America*, 138–39.
[4] Wiecek, *The Sources of Antislavery Constitutionalism in America*, 169–84, 191–201.
[5] Wiecek, *The Sources of Antislavery Constitutionalism in America*, 200–201.

consensus, in its original form, had become too simplistic to be serviceable much longer as a pillar of the Union."[6]

Wiecek's account of the federal consensus's declension provides an important depiction of the fecund environment within which abolitionist constitutional thought would flower, but its narration of a linear decline in the power of the consensus underplays the extent to which the responses of those caught between the extremes of proslavery and abolition in the 1830s were themselves constitutionally creative. As the following discussion shows, the nature of the federal consensus/compact was not static throughout the 1830s and indeed its evolution may have had more profound implications for constitutionalism in the United States than either the Calhounite retreat into proslavery absolutism or the Garrisonian rejection of constitutional moderation.[7] In the remainder of the book, I argue that motivated by either political calculation or fears of the rupturing of the Union, Northern and Southern members of the broad coalition that compromised the mainstream of the Democratic Party in the 1830s articulated a vision of the constitutional compact as an inheritance from the actors of 1787–88, imbued with a "spirit of compromise" and transmitting a cross-sectional obligation to observe the understandings that had made such a compact possible.

I am not the first to identify the role of a spirit of compromise in the constitutional politics of this era. One exploration of this "spirit of compromise" has been offered by Peter B. Knupfer. Equating a spirit of compromise with a mode of responding to constitutional tensions, Knupfer has argued that "compromise – as a strategy and as a symbol" became intertwined with the idea of "constitutional unionism" in the Antebellum United States.[8] Associated with moderates navigating the sectional divides of the period, constitutional unionism understood the Union as limited by the Constitution and that its continuation was only possible through a civic attention to the "mutual affections" of its citizens.[9] Viewing compromise through the lens of statesmanship and a skepticism of political parties, Knupfer argues that Americans came to see legislative compromises over slavery as extensions of the Constitution's compromises – "indeed, as quasi-constitutional compacts reaffirming the compact of 1787."[10] With time, compromise came to be seen as a "custom," holding the authority of a principle with regard to constitutional law.[11] Knupfer suggests that the early Republic saw an important association of compromise, constitutional unionism, and a civic culture that prized moderation and statesmanship, before the symbolism of compromise was reshaped

---

[6] Wiecek, *The Sources of Antislavery Constitutionalism in America*, 200.

[7] Paul Finkelman, "Garrison's Constitution: The Covenant with Death and How It Was Made," *Prologue* 32, no. 4 (2000); William Lloyd Garrison, "The Great Crisis!," *The Liberator*, December 29, 1832.

[8] Peter B. Knupfer, *The Union As It Is: Constitutional Unionism and Sectional Compromise, 1787–1861* (Chapel Hill: The University of North Carolina Press, 1991), 3.

[9] Knupfer, *The Union As It Is*, 3.   [10] Knupfer, *The Union As It Is*, 17, 18.

[11] Knupfer, *The Union As It Is*, 18.

by the rise of mass democratic politics.[12] The value placed upon compromise during this period reflected an understanding of compromise as "an ethical imperative" if the Union were to survive.[13] Drawing on the template offered by the compromises reached in and around 1787, the early Republic turned to a spirit of compromise as a mechanism for preserving and augmenting the constitutional settlement of 1787.[14]

Nevertheless, Knupfer sees that model of navigating sectional tensions over slavery as reconfigured by the late 1830s and 1840s. As we have earlier seen, an appeal to conciliation and compromise formed part of the rhetorical arsenal deployed during the Missouri Crisis. But as competing "sectional constitutionalisms" arose around the fraught issue of slavery, political parties sought to absorb the threat of sectional tensions within their own structures and selection of political issues, and paid less homage to a "custom" of constitutional compromise.[15] The rise of interracial immediate abolitionism and a staunch and aggressive proslavery anti-abolitionism in the 1830s reframed compromise for those outside the moderate center as concession – a loss to the opposing side rather than a mark of superior political craft.[16] With that reframing, constitutional unionism came under siege and the centrality of a spirit of compromise to constitutional politics began to ebb. Scrambling to mobilize the constellation of civic virtues that had erected and then preserved the Union, moderates saw a new generation of party leaders instead emphasize the maintenance of the substance of historic compromises rather than any practices or customs of politics associated with them.[17] A tradition of compromise continued, but one in which the capacity of moderate leaders to reach new compromises was lauded as the craft of statesmen in the face of substantial disagreements.

In what follows, I argue that the 1830s saw a transformation of notions of a "spirit of compromise" rather than its diminishment. Where Knupfer sees compromise as a form of civic culture hollowed out by the rise of a sectional constitutionalism of slavery, I suggest that as the spirit of compromise became more tightly associated with the protection of substantive bargains, its relationship with the Constitution and with constitutional time made it both more fundamental to, and more productive for, the constitutional debates around slavery. The value of compromise had earlier lain in its being augmented across time – with each subsequent compromise particular patterns of behavior and modes of politics gained legitimacy and contributed to a constitutional understanding. In that view, by layering legislative compromises atop each other, with each attesting to the political value of the "virtue of moderation," compromise came to form a "legacy" of constitutional practice. In the words of a recent scholar, compromises operated as "de facto

---

[12] Knupfer, *The Union As It Is*, 20–21.   [13] Knupfer, *The Union As It Is*, 55.
[14] Knupfer, *The Union As It Is*, 56.   [15] Knupfer, *The Union As It Is*, 116–17.
[16] Knupfer, *The Union As It Is*, 161–65.   [17] Knupfer, *The Union As It Is*, 117.

constitutional amendments," with each extending compromise across time as itself an iterative process.[18] Instead, I suggest that in the course of the 1830s the "spirit of compromise" became associated with the Federal Compact itself, more so than the customary politics that arose from it. Rather than the animating ethos of a series of compromises across the history of the early Republic, the spirit of compromise came to be the web of understandings and postures that enabled the Compact of 1787. Reversing the view of the Union as being constrained by the Constitution, this subtle shift in the understanding of constitutional time depicted the Constitution as itself being the product of, and so constrained by, the Compact – understood as a spirit of compromise.

Whereas earlier versions of the federal compact had indeed been theorized since at least the Virginia and Kentucky Resolutions, these versions had for the most part rested upon an idea of retained sovereignty on the part of the compacting States.[19] The political debates arising from that view of the compact consequently concerned the extent of federal power under the Constitution and the institutional means of resistance to the exercise of powers not granted to the Constitution. In contrast, the 1830s compact theory associated with a "spirit of compromise" saw the compact not as the grant of powers formulated and ratified in 1787–88, but rather as the framework of beliefs and shared understandings that, in view of the proponents of the mid-1830s compact, made such a Constitution possible.

Each of the different approaches to the compact theory contained within them an associated view of what the founding had been and the consequences of that founding in the present moment for issues related to slavery. Discussions assuming a compact of States took as an initial point of inquiry the question of what powers had been granted to the federal government. From there, discussions could move to the identification of instances of federal encroachment upon the States and the just distribution of powers between the States and the federal government: Could the general government charter a national bank? Could the States resist a national tariff? David James McCord, writing in *The Southern Review* in 1828, spelled out the theory and the questions it raised in the following terms: "If that government be a union of States ... how can it be said, with any sort of reason or consistency, that such Legislatures, or State Governments, have no right or power to watch over and interest themselves in performance of the very trusts which they themselves have created?"[20] Such a framework suited

---

[18] Michael F. Conlin, *The Constitutional Origins of the American Civil War* (Cambridge, UK: Cambridge University Press, 2019), 161; Knupfer, *The Union As It Is*, 90.

[19] For instance, the Kentucky Resolutions declared that the various States "constituted a General Government for special purposes, delegated to that Government certain definite powers, reserving each State to itself, the residuary mass of right to their own self-government." *The Virginia and Kentucky Resolutions of 1798 and '99: With Jefferson's Original Draught Thereof. Also, Madison's Report, Calhoun's Address, Resolutions of the Several States in Relations to State Rights.* (Washington, DC: Jonathan Elliot, 1832), 15.

[20] David James McCord, "The Federal Constitution," *The Southern Review* 4 (1828): 452. In accordance with the set of questions raised by this model of the Constitution's creation – where

defenders of slavery well in 1820s and into the 1830s, when they looked to the federal government for noninterference and in which "strict construction" functioned effectively as "pro-slavery."[21] But by the mid-1830s, a distinct set of issues made such strict construction a less reliable mechanism by which to defend slavery. New questions emerged: Did a commitment to not abolish slavery in the District of Columbia exist in the absence of its expression in the constitutional text? Can a party to the compact expect other parties to that agreement to curb the freedoms of their own populations in the service of "foreign" domestic institutions? These new questions seemed less easily addressed by debates over express and implied powers and a commitment to noninterference in the States.

One response to these new questions was a strong articulation of the proslavery consensus identified by Wiecek – to come to view slavery as an untouchable property right, predating and consecrated, but not created, by a humanly constructed compact. In this view, the founding represented a bargain between the States (or sections) in which the North had accepted – and guaranteed to protect – the existence of slavery everywhere it was not explicitly barred from.[22] John C. Calhoun traced such a line of thought in his interventions in the debates over slavery in the District of Columbia during the mid-1830s. Particularly in the speeches surrounding the presentation of his six resolutions in the Senate in December 1837, Calhoun presented an aggressive articulation of the compact of States that married States' rights to a territorially expansive understanding of what such rights meant with regard to slavery.[23] While clinging to the framework of the Constitution as

the just limits of federal action ought to be placed – McCord deduced from this reasoning that the federal government held only powers expressly given.

21 This view was articulated by the Charleston *Mercury* in drawing a parallel between strict construction on fiscal powers and with regard to slavery. "The Sub-Treasury are the friends of *strict construction*, and this fact is not lost upon the Anti-Slavery men of the North, who know that so long as the Constitution is fairly administered and strictly construed, the cause of Abolition is hopeless." Quoted in Clyde N. Wilson, "Introduction," in *The Papers of John C. Calhoun: Volume XIV, 1837–1839*, ed. Clyde N. Wilson (Columbia: University of South Carolina Press, 1981), xxvii.

22 Clyde N. Wilson, "Introduction," in *The Papers of John C. Calhoun: Volume XIII, 1835–1837*, ed. Clyde N. Wilson (Columbia: University of South Carolina Press, 1980), xvi–xvii; William M. Wiecek, "'The Blessings of Liberty': Slavery in the American Constitutional Order," in *Slavery and Its Consequences: The Constitution, Race, and Equality*, ed. Robert A. Goldwin and Art Kaufman (Washington, DC: American Enterprise Institute, 1988), 39; Robert E. Bonner, *Mastering America: Southern Slaveholders and the Crisis of American Nationhood* (New York: Cambridge University Press, 2009), 62–67. John Ashworth points to the faith of Calhoun and his fellow advocates of the proslavery consensus that the mechanisms that the Constitution provided would support Southern slavery, if properly understood and activated. John Ashworth, *Slavery, Capitalism, and Politics in the Antebellum Republic: Volume 1: Commerce and Compromise, 1820–1850* (Cambridge, UK: Cambridge University Press, 1995), 136.

23 The fourth resolution asserted that "domestic slavery, as it exists in the Southern and Western States of this Union" was an inheritance that was "recognised" by the Constitution as an

a compact between sovereign States, the South Carolinian nevertheless expanded the resulting principle of noninterference in slavery beyond the scope of the slaveholding States so that it included anywhere slavery existed (or could be reasonably imagined to exist in the future). The fifth of those resolutions set out the view that action against slavery in the District or in the Territories was tantamount to interference in the States themselves.[24] Exhibiting his States' rights credentials, Calhoun drew upon the example of the Virginia and Kentucky resolutions, telling the Senate that opponents of the Alien and Sedition laws had guided his response in repelling the aggressions of abolitionists.[25] Writing to William Hendricks at the time, Calhoun stated that his object was "to rally all States rights men of any creed on the old State rights principles of '98."[26] Speaking on the fifth resolution in particular, Calhoun cited the "great and governing principles" of noninterference in other States or by the federal government (the "common agent of the States") to claim that to attack slavery in one State would be to attack it everywhere, "and in like manner, and for the same reason, to attack it here [the District], or in the Territories, is to attack it in the States."[27] Warming to this expansive view of the compact of States, Calhoun told the assembled Senators that he "regarded slavery, wherever it exists throughout the whole Southern section, as one common question, and is as much under the protection of the Constitution here [the District], and in the Territories, as in the States themselves."[28] Such an approach had the attraction of being direct and of appropriating the language of an accepted constitutional theory in the defense of slavery. But

"essential element" within the distribution of powers among the States. As such systematic attacks on this inheritance would represent a "manifest violation of the mutual and solemn pledge to protect and defend each other" that the States had given to each other upon entering the constitutional compact. John C. Calhoun, "Resolutions on Abolition and the Union," in *The Papers of John C. Calhoun: Volume XIV, 1837–1839*, ed. Clyde N. Wilson (Columbia: University of South Carolina Press, 1981), 32.

[24] Calhoun's proposed text read:

Resolved, That the intermeddling of any State or States, or their citizens, to abolish slavery in this District, or any of the Territories, on the ground, or under the pretext, that it is immoral or sinful; or the passage of any act or measure of Congress, with that view, would be a direct and dangerous attack on the institutions of all the slaveholding States.
   Calhoun.

[25] John C. Calhoun, "Remarks on His Resolutions on Abolition and the Union," in *The Papers of John C. Calhoun: Volume XIV, 1837–1839*, ed. Clyde N. Wilson (Columbia: University of South Carolina Press, 1981), 41.

[26] John C. Calhoun, "To William Hendricks (January 4th 1838)," in *The Papers of John C. Calhoun: Volume XIV, 1837–1839*, ed. Clyde N. Wilson (Columbia: University of South Carolina Press, 1981), 53.

[27] John C. Calhoun, "Further Remarks in Debate on His Fifth Resolution," in *The Papers of John C. Calhoun: Volume XIV, 1837–1839*, ed. Clyde N. Wilson (Columbia: University of South Carolina Press, 1981), 82.

[28] Calhoun, "Further Remarks in Debate on His Fifth Resolution," 82.

to be ultimately successful it also required an acceptance on the part of other (Northern) actors that the States' rights defense of slavery operated in geographical spaces hitherto excluded from noninterference.[29]

In contrast, a conception of the compact as encompassing the spirit of compromise present at the founding was both more ephemeral and more expansive. It created the potential to address a set of questions that did not fit easily within the debates over express and implied constitutional powers while maintaining that slavery outside the slaveholding States was a constitutionally distinct question from noninterference in the slaveholding States. This version of the compact provided an argument for opposing abolitionist activism and resisting abolition in the District of Columbia without conceding that slavery was everywhere and in all cases permitted. Whereas Calhoun saw abolitionist activity as a moral problem, those advancing a compact upholding a "spirit of compromise" saw it as political problem. Calhoun's response was to seek to cast abolition outside of the constitutional order as an illegitimate and fanatical attack upon the institutional arrangements constituted by the compact of States. For advocates of the spirit of compromise, abolition was to be addressed by the reanimation of values and shared sentiment that had made such a compact possible in the first instance. This approach could allow for Northern opposition to slavery in the abstract and avoided the need to accept the District and the Territories as constitutionally protected spheres of slavery, while also creating an imperative to not act against slavery therein. It reaffirmed the constitutional settlement as understood by the South, but without rewriting it in the eyes of the North. It created an expectation of individual behavior on the part of citizens without suggesting that any authority had the legitimate right to impose one.

Most significantly, the spirit of compromise compact did all this by positing that a spirit had existed at the time of the founding and that such a spirit could bind those who inherited the Constitution it had produced. For anti-abolitionists, all that was needed to ensure a return to national harmony was recognition by the abolitionists of the truth of this compact. Anti-abolitionists in Portland, Maine, noted, "The constitution of the United States it is well known, was the result of compromise," and resolved, "the Union must be preserved; and that the principles and spirit of the fundamental compact ... must be maintained holy and inviolate."[30] The abolitionist Rev. Samuel J. May sketched the argument "met with every where" in more begrudging terms:

---

[29] Analyzing the compact in these terms led Don Fehrenbacher to be skeptical that it amounted to any more than a forceful articulation of minority Southern opposition to interference. Don E. Fehrenbacher and Ward M. McAfee, *The Slaveholding Republic: An Account of the United States Government's Relations to Slavery* (Oxford: Oxford University Press, 2001), 69–81.

[30] *The Proceedings of a Meeting Held in Portland, ME. August 15, 1835, by the Friends of the Union and the Constitution, on the Subject of Interfering at the North and East with the Relations of Master and Slave at the South* (Portland, ME, 1835), 3, 6.

The alleged compact, it is urged, obliged our predecessors, who were the first parties to it, and obliges us, who have succeeded to the blessings of the "glorious union" they effected on this condition, silently to acquiesce in the continuance of that accursed system of physical oppression, civil degradation and soul-murder; nay more, to co-operate actively to enforce it, if at any time our Southern brethren may need our assistance.[31]

As the explanation of May suggests, the compact-as-spirit rested on the notion that there was continuity in the nature of constitutional compromise, that the commitments bound up in it were transferred from generation to generation. It took social obligations as existing in time and legitimated them by their connection back to a moment of creation. By contrast, the compact of States was relatively timeless. To be sure, the compact of States came into being at a specific historical juncture but each subsequent clash over its meaning was essentially timeless insofar as its justice was judged against a legalized set of institutional arrangements. Those debates took place within a framework of legalized rational distributions of power. For the compact as a spirit of compromise, debates were rooted instead in a quasi-romantic notion of reanimating a singular historical moment.

Crucially, it was also the case that this compact existed as much – if not more so – in practice and in a continuity of spirit than it did in the actual written Constitution. For those that advocated the spirit of compromise compact, the Constitution was not the product of interested negotiation and horse trading but an artifact of a mode of engagement – a spirit – that actualized the Preamble's commitment to form a more perfect union. This focus upon the spirit necessarily shifted the locus of constitutionality away from the impersonal and timeless written text and to the spirit of the time in which it was brought into being and of the individuals who carried out that task. As such it incorporated not merely agreements directly expressed in the text, but the assumed understandings that surrounded the Philadelphia Convention's final product. This view, in the words of a meeting of the citizens of Albany, avowed:

That the constitution of the United States carries with it an adjustment of all questions involved in the deliberations which led to its adoption, and that the compromise of interests in which it was founded, is binding in honor and good faith, *independently of the force of agreement*, on all who live under its protection and participate in the benefits of which it is the source.[32]

The compact theory did indeed represent a break with textual understandings of the Constitution. It raised, and defined as extratextual compromise, the spirit of

---

[31] Samuel J. May, "Slavery and the Constitution," *Quarterly Anti-Slavery Magazine* 2, no. 1 (October 1836): 73.

[32] Quoted in *Opinions of Martin Van Buren Vice President of the United States, Upon the Powers and Duties of Congress, in Reference to the Abolition of Slavery Either in the Slaveholding States or in the District of Columbia* (Washington, DC: Blair & Rives, 1836), 4–5. Original emphasis.

the Constitution at the expense of the text.[33] In the final analysis, it worked to make the intentions and commitments of the founding generation the very substance of the "Constitution" itself. With regard to the issue of slavery in the District of Columbia, this shift was entirely the point, undermining the clear textually derived authority of Congress in this area and prioritizing a particular conception of the spirit of the Constitution amenable to the designs of slaveholders.[34]

---

[33] Such a view was incorporated into the 1838 "Address of the Republican Members of Congress." Rejecting the notion of congressional abolition in the District of Columbia, the "Address" did not "deem it material, in coming to this conclusion, to inquire what the extent of its [Congress's] powers over this District; be they what they may, they are all conferred for special purposes, to be exercised, like all such powers, in subordination to the known objects for which they were granted. To pervert them to any other purpose inconsistent with the object of the grant, would be a violation of the Constitution, not less dangerous because not expressly forbidden." Clyde N. Wilson, ed., "Address of the Republican Members of Congress," in *The Papers of John C. Calhoun: Volume XIV, 1837–1839* (Columbia: University of South Carolina Press, 1981), 383.

[34] Of course, this was itself just one "reading" of the spirit of the Constitution.

6

Slavery, the District of Columbia, and the Constitution

In the *District of Columbia* ... the red ensign of the auctioneer of men, is stuck up under the flag which waves from the towers of the Capitol.

David Lee Child (1834)[1]

[Abolition] is a proposition ... to render the freemen of this District slaves ... whilst the wild spirit of fanaticism ... waves her black and blood-stained banner from the very dome, where now float the glorious kindred emblems of our country's Union.

Robert Walker (1836)[2]

By 1830, the District of Columbia and the practices of slavery and slave trading there were motifs within American antislavery literature and thought. In the late 1820s, national antislavery organizations orchestrated petition campaigns focused on the capital, critical newspapers reprinted accounts of slavery there, and, through the speech of Charles Miner, these concerns were penetrating onto the floor of Congress. The image of a slave coffle marching through Washington, DC, with the "temple of liberty" (Congress) as its backdrop was already a trope, thanks in part to the frontispiece printed in Jesse Torrey's 1817 *A Portraiture of Slavery*.[3] But in the 1830s the importance of the District of Columbia and slavery therein grew in the abolitionist imagination as their conception of its significance evolved. At the same time, changes in the way

---

[1] David Lee Child, *The Despotism of Freedom: A Speech at the First Anniversary of the New England Anti-Slavery Society* (Boston: The Boston Young Men's Anti-Slavery Association for the Diffusion of Truth, 1834), 14.

[2] *Register of Debates, 24th Congress, 1st Session*, 1836, 694.

[3] Jesse Jr. Torrey, *A Portraiture of Domestic Slavery, in the United States* (Philadelphia: John Bioren, 1817). On the significance of the frontispiece, cf. Padraig Riley, *Slavery and the Democratic Conscience: Political Life in Jeffersonian America* (Philadelphia: University of Pennsylvania Press, 2016), 200–202.

that defenders of slavery thought about the institution and about efforts at emancipation meant that the District took on greater significance for this group as well. By the mid-1830s, Congress would be rocked by the presentation of petitions regarding slavery in the District. As we will see in the next chapter, the result in 1836 was months of debate in both the House of Representatives and the Senate, bitter divisions, and a gag rule that satisfied neither extreme and exacerbated polarization. By contrast, the House of Representatives had disposed of similar petitions in 1831 with a summary report of less than a page. Between 1831 and 1836, the stakes of abolishing slavery in the District of Columbia and the stakes of resisting even a discussion of that topic had grown exponentially. Building upon the discussions of the last chapters, this chapter examines why it was that slavery in the District became so significant in the 1830s.

By 1836, the District of Columbia was a vital space within both the abolitionist and slaveholding imagination, and a vital cog within the slave economy. As a territory, the District was both a slaveholding locality and an important conduit for slaves being transported to the South and West from the surrounding area. This activity was supported by the federal government's creation of a legal regime that variously supported and refused to counter the structures that underwrote slavery in the District. In this way, the District drew the attention of abolitionists as a territory that implicated them in the sin of slavery through the federal government's oversight of the District, but which also afforded opportunities for federal action against slavery for the very same reason. Moreover, opponents of slavery identified the District of Columbia as symbolically important in the fight against slavery. The presence of slavery in the nation's capital stood as a tangible rebuke to the notion that the United States embodied values of liberty and republicanism. Perhaps nothing better attested to the fact that slavery was an American institution than its existence in Washington, DC. In the eyes of abolitionists, slavery and the slave trade within the federal city implicated all Americans in slavery's guilt. The implication of the whole people in the guilt of slavery in the District transformed the latter's conceptualization. The issue of slavery in the District came to be seen as national, constitutional, and urgent.

To the defenders of slavery, the District took on greater symbolism as they moved from apologizing for slavery to celebrating it. Changes in the national economy of slavery in the mid-Antebellum United States, particularly the massive transfer of slave populations west and south, made the District of Columbia more central to the political economy of slavery than the same territory had been at the beginning of the nineteenth century. At the same time, the moral sanction afforded to slavery by its practice in the nation's capital – or perhaps more accurately, the loss of sanction that abolition would bring – raised the stakes of protecting slavery in the District once "positive good" arguments became more common in the 1830s. Both changes, allied to a belief that abolition there was sought as a precursor to abolition nationally, meant that sensitivity to emancipation, or even regulation of slavery, within the ten miles square was greater in 1836 than it had been forty, or even twenty, years before.

This chapter follows the transformation of the issue of slavery in the nation's capital across four sections. The first section, located out of strict chronological order, steps back to provide the broad setting of a growing sense among abolitionists of the "Americanization" of slavery following the initiation of a gradual emancipation of slaves in the British Empire. The sense that slavery in the United States was a peculiarly national sin refocused the understanding of slavery in the country's capital from being an anomaly within a free republic to being the apogee of American slavery. Given the importance of the District for the domestic slave trade, examined in the second section, this reconceptualization was not without merit. In the mid-Antebellum period, the District of Columbia emerged as home to the nation's premier slave depot. The third section traces the ways in which immediate abolition and its reconceptualization of slavery within the District, in light of the trends discussed in the first and second sections, saw continuities but also important departures from the antislavery position on the District of Columbia in the 1820s. The final section examines the ways in which the District of Columbia grew in significance for defenders of slavery over roughly the same period. By 1835, the nation was primed for an unprecedented clash over the issue of abolition in the District.

6.1 THE AMERICANIZATION OF ABOLITION AND SLAVERY

In late September of 1833, news reached the United States confirming what abolitionists had long hoped for: the British Parliament had approved a scheme of gradual emancipation throughout the British Empire.[4] The move had been anticipated in the United States since at least the late 1820s, but it was still perceived as a significant milestone on the path to universal emancipation.[5] But the final arrival of the moment of legislative victory was greeted with as much nervousness as jubilation. On one hand, *The Abolitionist* reasoned that the example of the British Empire would provide an impetus for abolition in the United States: "When the British king put his name to the statute ... he signed the death warrant of slavery throughout the civilized world."[6] Believing the moral influence of the British abolition would be irresistible in the United States, the abolitionists looked forward to "the moral force of the great body of the

---

[4] "No Title," *Eastern Argus*, September 27, 1833; "No Title," *The Farmers' Cabinet*, September 27, 1833.

[5] An advocate of slavery had warned slaveholders in 1827 "*The British slaves will soon be free citizens.*" "From the Christian Spectator," *Freedom's Journal*, March 23, 1827; Robert Pierce Forbes, *The Missouri Compromise and Its Aftermath: Slavery and the Meaning of America* (Chapel Hill: The University of North Carolina Press, 2007), 268.

[6] "Abolition of Slavery in the British Colonies," *The Abolitionist* (Boston, October 1833), 156.

people" being roused to "exterminate at once and forever" the system of American slavery.[7] On the other hand, the action by the British government stood in stark contrast to the failure in the United States to secure any significant progress in terms of emancipation. The same issue of *The Abolitionist* admitted that: "This glorious act of the British nation, presents a mortifying contrast to the conduct of our own."[8] Whereas the British public had "for many years been exerting powerful efforts" to secure this victory, the journal noted despondently that Americans had "remained deaf to the cries of their oppressed fellow men, and insensible to the dishonor of their country."[9] As it became apparent that they waited in vain for a popular surge in "moral force" and that the United States would remain an outpost of slavery in the Anglo-American world, within the abolitionist mind, the dishonor associated with slavery came to be increasingly understood as a national one, and slavery as a particularly American sin.

The contrast with Britain and the British Empire was all the more pointed given that British monarchy was the very tyranny that American liberty was defined against. Even before 1833, the relative receptiveness of each nation to the abolitionist message had been of concern to abolitionists. Before leaving for the United Kingdom in early 1833, Garrison drew attention to both that comparison and its incongruity with the nations' respective political systems:

I propose to leave this free republican, christian country, and go to one in which there is a king and a proud nobility; but where my denunciations against the persecution and oppression of your color will be received, not as in this country with astonishment, and rage, and scorn, but with loud cheers – with thunders of applause![10]

The passage of the 1833 Act did nothing to alleviate those concerns. "Let it not be said," pleaded the October 1833 *Anti-Slavery Reporter*, "that in *free* America, truth and the sentiments of humanity, have less sway than in the monarchies of the old world."[11] The following year, the New-England Anti-Slavery Convention reiterated these concerns in attempting to rouse the American people, asking "Shall the United States, the free United States,

---

[7] "Abolition of Slavery in the British Colonies," 156.

[8] "Slavery and the Slave Trade in the District of Columbia," *The Abolitionist* (Boston, October 1833), 154.

[9] "Slavery and the Slave Trade in the District of Columbia." The year prior Garrison had told an audience of the African Abolition Freehold Society of Boston, "More heads are at work, more hands employed, more tracts and petitions printed and circulated, more funds raised, in one month, to effect the liberation of 800,000 British slaves, than have been in this country since the Declaration of Independence, to emancipate the two millions of slaves in our slave States." William Lloyd Garrison, *An Address on the Progress of the Abolition Cause: Delivered before the African Abolition Freehold Society of Boston, July 16, 1832* (Boston: Garrison and Knapp, 1832), 11.

[10] William Lloyd Garrison, *Address Delivered in Boston, New-York and Philadelphia, Before the Free People of Color, in April 1833* (New York, 1833), 19–20.

[11] "Address," *Anti-Slavery Reporter* (New York, October 1833), 74.

which could not bear the bonds of a King, cradle the bondage which a King is abolishing? Shall a republic be less free than a monarchy?"[12] The continued existence of slavery in republican America made the final question less rhetorical in nature than the Convention might have hoped. Far from being an absurdity, the trajectory of abolitionism in the United Kingdom and the United States in 1834 suggested that, at least with regard to black men and women, it would be the case that a republic was less free than a monarchy.

The contrast between American proclamations of freedom and the actual practice of human slavery was a source of discomfort to Americans opposed to slavery. The pseudonymous "Vigornius" wrote in the *Boston Recorder* in 1825 that slavery was not only indefensible "upon the general principles of right" but was also in "flagrant opposition to the genius of our government."[13] Making direct reference to the Revolution, the author offered a vision of "Americans signing a Declaration of Independence one day, and brandishing a Slave-Whip the next!"[14] In this, Vigornius was echoing John Wright, whose 1820 pamphlet branded slavery "Unsupported by Divine Revelation, a Violation of Natural Justice, and Hostile to the Fundamental Principles of American Independence" in its subtitle.[15] A sense that the American Revolution had struck a blow for freedom and that consequently the United States stood as an embodiment of liberty within a world of monarchies led to the view that the United States, more so than other nations, ought to root out the slavery in its midst. In *A Disquisition on Egyptian, Roman and American Slavery* published in 1831, Nathanial Field, as "Onesimus," wrote that with regard to the "heinous crime" of slavery, "above all people in the world, the Americans ought to be the most ashamed of it."[16] The root of that shame lay in the hypocrisy of a nation which had "declared to the world, in defiance of kings and despots, that men are by *nature* equal and free" and "staked the lives, fortunes, and sacred honour of her sages upon this maxim, and who [held] up the beacon of liberty to an astonished world," but which had failed to address slavery.[17] Lest Americans miss the discrepancy, the reproaches of the Irish champion Daniel O'Connell highlighted the distance between the rhetoric of the "asylum of mankind" and its reality. Americans could only fume as O'Connell named Bolivar a more virtuous revolutionary for liberty than General Washington and quoted their own

---

[12] *Proceedings of the New-England Anti-Slavery Convention, Held in Boston on the 27th, 28th and 29th of May, 1834* (Boston: Garrison and Knapp, 1834), 72.

[13] Vigornius, "Slavery No. IV," in *Essays on Slavery: Re-Published from the Boston Recorder & Telegraph, for 1825. By Vigornius, and Others* (Amherst: Mark H. Newman, 1826), 16.

[14] Vigornius, "Slavery No. IV," 16.

[15] John Wright, *A Refutation of the Sophisms, Gross Misrepresentations, and Erroneous Quotations Contained in "An American's" "Letter To The Edinburgh Reviewers"* (Washington, DC, 1820).

[16] Onesimus, *A Disquisition on Egyptian, Roman and American Slavery* (Louisville: Norwood & Palmer, 1831), 31.

[17] Onesimus, *A Disquisition on Egyptian, Roman and American Slavery*, 32.

Declaration of Independence back at them.[18] Even opponents of slavery who supported colonization recognized that slavery was ultimately "irreconcilable with every principle that constitutes this republic a glorious nation."[19] If the United States was indeed exceptional in terms of its commitment to freedom, slavery represented a severe instance of the nation failing in its world-historical role.

With the British program of gradual abolition, the juxtaposition of American freedom and American slavery began to lead to a morphing of the notion of American exceptionalism. The writers noted in the previous paragraph had assumed that what made the United States exceptional was its commitment to freedom, and that slavery was, therefore, an exceptional failing. After 1833, some abolitionists began to reverse that framing and ask the radical question: Was it actually its attachment to slavery that made the United States exceptional? And if so, then was it not the case that it was the claims that the nation represented the spirit of liberty that were most at odds with the nation's principles?

Such a revolutionary reconception emerged and caused much soul-searching at the New England Anti-Slavery Convention in 1834. The proceedings of the meeting noted Rev. John Blain's view that, to the sixth of the population held in bondage, "the 4th of July is no day of Independence."[20] How could it be, he asked, that "[w]hile the proud eagles of our country have been trumpeting long and loud the praises of liberty, a large portion of our fellow men enslaved and oppressed, have been toiling beneath the lash, in our very midst?" (7) After some diversions, Amasa Walker, a delegate from Boston, returned to the contrast noted by Blain with a resolution that emphasized the errancy of the United States. Walker asked the Convention to address the resolution:

That "THE LAND OF FREEDOM" is a phrase inapplicable to the United States of America, and ought not to be used by any real friends of universal liberty until slavery be abolished. (11)

Suggesting he was struck by the incongruity of its use at an abolitionist meeting, Walker said that the phrase "the land of freedom" seemed "a contradiction to the whole spirit and tenor of all we have done, and all we intended to do" (11). Conceding that "'The glorious land of liberty' had long been the boast of our people," Walker nonetheless demanded recognition of the fact "that we live in a land of Slavery, bitter, unalleviated Slavery" (11). It was not merely that the use of "the land of freedom" erased the guilt of slavery that motivated Walker, but that the phrase worked to set the United States apart from other nations:

---

[18] "Mr. O'Connell Holds …, " *Richmond Enquirer*, November 17, 1829. "At the Recent Meeting …, " *Newport Mercury*, February 13, 1830.

[19] A Citizen of New-York, *Remarks upon a Plan for the Total Abolition of Slavery in the United States* (New York: S. Hoyt & Co., 1831), 14.

[20] *Proceedings of the New-England Anti-Slavery Convention*, 1834, 7.

In contradistinction to other civilized nations, we call ourselves a *free* people. We point across the Atlantic to the empires of Europe, and thank God that we are not like other men.... But how empty, how vain, was this boast! Where shall we find slavery in its most aggravated and direful forms; in Europe or America? (11–12)

Challenging his listeners to find "a despotism like 'the despotism of freedom,'" Walker denied that among the "half-starved peasantry of Ireland ... The serfs of [Russia] ... the subjects of the Grand Seignor himself, do we find human degradation so complete and awful" as that of the American slave (12). "Let us," said the delegate, "frankly and honestly confess that we live ... in a land where the right of freedom depends upon the complexion of the skin" (12). The phrase "The Land of Freedom" was not merely unjust and improper, he asserted, but actively worked to "paralyze the public mind to the subject of slavery" (12).

It was a self deception; it was a concealment of a great and glaring fact; it tended to sear the consciences of men, and create a self complacency altogether unwarranted by the true state of the case. (12)

"Let us no talk about '*Southern Slavery*' and '*American Freedom*' ... but let the astounding conviction come home to our hearts, that, as a nation, we are polluted" (12). Walker urged the assembled delegates to "confess that, as a nation, we are disgraced" (12).

Walker's resolution and speech resulted in one of the few moments of genuine debate recorded in the published record of the Convention. Delegates pushed back against Walker's resolution in a variety of ways, beginning with Rev. Cyrus P. Grosvenor's claim that in the United States freedom was not dependent upon one's skin color.[21] Rev. Asa Rand of Lowell suggested that as the majority in the United States was free, the phrase "land of freedom" was indeed applicable (13). Against these positions, C. C. Burleigh argued that the Constitution sanctioned slavery and half the States of the Union supported it (13). Possibly trying to diffuse tension, William Oakes posited that in place of debating the United States as a land of freedom, the correct question was rather "whether this was a land of slavery" – which in his estimation it certainly was (13). A decisive intervention came in the form of Garrison's opinion that the resolution amounted to a "*self-evident proposition*" and that it was "an outrage upon common sense; it was consummate hypocrisy and glaring falsehood, to call ours a *free* country" (13). He "trusted the resolution would pass unanimously" (13). The latter is literally the last word in the debate as published – Walker's resolution was passed and adopted.

The way in which the episode is recorded in the published account of the Convention is both curious and insightful. Multiple resolutions were passed by

---

[21] Grosvenor argued that by siring slave children, slaveholders had ensured that many slaves were "as white, or even whiter" than their masters. *Proceedings of the New-England Anti-Slavery Convention*, 1834, 12.

the Convention and noted in its published account. Most of these are
accompanied with little evidence that they engendered debate. Often
a summary of their proposer's explanation for the resolution is attached, and
at times supportive speeches are very briefly recorded. Walker's resolution and
Grosvenor and Rand's discomfort with it stands out, therefore, as an unusual
moment of tension within the meeting. At the same time, that Garrison sought
a unanimous passage points to a desire to ensure outward unity on what was
clearly a contentious point. With all this in mind, it is easy to forget that the
substance of the resolution was on its surface fairly insignificant – whether
abolitionists should use the phrase "the land of freedom" to describe the
United States before the achievement of abolition. But arguably there was
a more fundamental question being debated: Was the United States to be seen
as exceptional because of its freedom, or because of its slavery? Those
committed to the former position would continue to recognize their own
country as being founded on a principle of freedom, and particularly so. Both
Grosvenor and Rand sought to hold on to the idea that America was
a particularly free nation while also acknowledging the reality of slavery.
Indeed, for both speakers, it was the very claim that the United States was a
land of freedom that offered hope for change in the future. A rejection of the
claim on freedom would be at the expense of those without liberty, but who
looked to a future in which they would enjoy it. Grosvenor and Rand offered
a view of American exceptionalism in which a heightened attachment to
freedom made it unlikely that slavery would survive in the United States,
especially without support from the broader world. In contrast to that
position, Walker and William Oakes saw the United States as exceptional in
its attachment to slavery, while Garrison offered the view that the whole nation
was held "in bondage" by the institution of slavery.[22] In their arguments we see
not slavery under pressure in a land of freedom, but freedom withering in the
face of slavery.[23] In the United States, "[t]hought – utterance – action – the
press – the pulpit – the bench – the bar – all were held in servile bondage."[24]
Their understanding of slavery was changing from the institution being an
anomaly within a republican America to it being the defining characteristic of
the United States. Or to put this in the language of later centuries, they were
increasingly seeing slavery as not "un-American," but rather essentially
American.

---

[22] *Proceedings of the New-England Anti-Slavery Convention, 1834*, 13.

[23] This view was sufficiently developed a year later that the Second Annual Report of the American
Anti-Slavery Society in 1835 would warn, "it is plainly impossible for a pure republican
government to subsist long upon a foundation of tyranny. Slavery is the *dry rot* to all the
props that can sustain a good government." *Second Annual Report of the American Anti-*
Slavery Society: With the Speeches Delivered at the Anniversary Meeting, Held in the City of
New-York, On the 12th May, 1835, and the Minutes of the Meetings of the Society for Business
(New York: William S. Dorr, 1835), 66.

[24] *Proceedings of the New-England Anti-Slavery Convention, 1834*, 13.

The identification of America with slavery proved to be the first step in coming to conceive of American abolition as aimed at the defeat of a peculiarly American form of slavery. Subtle changes in the aims of the movement across the 1830s highlight a reconception of slavery in national terms. The constitution of the New-England Anti-Slavery Society had committed it in 1832 to "effect the abolition of slavery in the United States."[25] In 1833, the national Anti-Slavery Society followed suit, committing itself to "the entire abolition of slavery in the United States."[26] The constitution of the Ohio Anti-Slavery Society shared these aims in 1835 by seeking "the entire abolition of Slavery throughout the United States."[27] But alongside the use of "in the United States" as a geographical locator of slavery developed a use of "American" as a prefix to identify a particular practice of slavery. In 1836, Rhode Island abolitionists would organize themselves into a society "for the extirpation of American Slavery," while in 1837 the Pennsylvanian Society "associated for the purpose of promoting the abolition of American slavery" and denounced "the slavery of the Southern states" as "a system of unparalleled oppression."[28] A pivotal moment in this transition can be seen in the New York Society's 1835 addresses. While the constitution of the New York Anti-Slavery Society followed the text of the national organization, the addresses issued by the State Society conceived of slavery in explicitly national terms.[29] In "To the Citizens of the United States," the Society took direct aim at *"the system of American Slavery,"* which held over two million humans as property.[30] Tracing the evolution of slavery within the Atlantic world, the Society offered slavery in the United States as its final and most outrageous stage:

At length, as the finishing stroke of the foulest policy which ever outraged heaven and disgraced the earth, the solemnity and authority of law were employed to protect and uphold an extensive and complicated scheme of theft, adultery and murder. THIS IS THE SCHEME OF AMERICAN SLAVERY. (27)

Issued at the same time, the address "To the Friends of Immediate and Universal Emancipation" made similar reference to the "system of America slavery" and committed the Society to never relax its "exertions till the system of American

---

[25] "New-England Anti-Slavery Society," *The Abolitionist* (Boston, January 1833), 2.

[26] "Constitution of the American Anti-Slavery Society," 1833.

[27] *Proceedings of the Ohio Anti-Slavery Convention. Held at Putnam, on the Twenty-Second, Twenty-Third, and Twenty-Fourth of April, 1835* (Beaumont and Wallace, 1835), 11.

[28] *Proceedings of the Rhode-Island Anti-Slavery Convention, Held in Providence, on the 2d, 3d, and 4th of February, 1836* (Providence: H. H. Brown, 1836), 7. *Proceedings of the Pennsylvania Convention, Assembled to Organize A State Anti-Slavery Society, at Harrisburg, On the 31st of January and 1st, 2d and 3d of February 1837* (Philadelphia: Merrihew and Gunn, 1837), 85, 87.

[29] *Proceedings of the New York Anti-Slavery Convention, Held at Utica, October 21, and New York Anti-Slavery State Society, Held at Peterboro', October 22, 1835* (Utica: Standard & Democrat Office, 1835), 10.

[30] *Proceedings of the New York Anti-Slavery Convention, 1835*, 23. Original emphasis.

slavery is utterly, universally, and forever abolished."[31] A year later, meeting at Utica, New York, the New-York State Anti-Slavery Society would reiterate the view that more than its geographical location defined slavery in the United States. Its 1836 address declared, "American Slavery is a pyramid of crime" and labeled the slaveholding States "the head quarters of cruelty for the world; the residence of duelling, the native land of Lynch law, where its professors reside and its scholars practice."[32] The shift was subtle, but the view of the United States as a place where slavery existed was being replaced by a view that a peculiar system of American slavery operated within the nation's borders (and constitutional order). What was exceptional about the United States was not its liberty, but its slavery.

6.2 THE DISTRICT OF COLUMBIA AND SLAVERY

Symbolically, at the heart of this system of American slavery stood the District of Columbia. The District of Columbia in the mid-Antebellum period was a vital territory of slavery within the United States. Although it was "home" to only a very small proportion of the nation's enslaved (something like 0.3 percent in 1830), the territory was a vital avenue for the domestic slave trade.[33] The status of Alexandria as slavery's port within the Chesapeake region, and the City of Washington as a land route to Alexandria, made the District of Columbia a hub within the massive population transfer of slaves to the South and West. It was also a space in which the oversight of the federal government implicated it in slavery as an institution. Through the administration of municipal jails and in the black codes established within the national territory, the federal government (through Congress) was directly engaged in the active support of slavery as an institution. Any tacit agreement to noninterference with slavery in the States that allowed for a lowering of sectional tensions did not extend to the District of Columbia, for within its boundaries Congress was facilitating slavery in the District, not refusing to become involved.

By the 1830s, the nation's capital was firmly enmeshed with the institution of slavery. The 1830 census counted 6,119 slaves within the District. The total had declined by 1840, but at that census 4,694 slaves were counted in the District.[34]

---

[31] *Proceedings of the New York Anti-Slavery Convention, 1835*, 30, 39.

[32] *Proceedings of the First Annual Meeting of the New-York State Anti-Slavery Society, Convened at Utica, October 19, 1836* (Utica: New-York Anti-Slavery Society, 1836), 42, 44.

[33] Myers Asch and Musgrove identify "the nation's capital [as] the largest slave-trading city in America in the 1830s." Chris Myers Asch and George Derek Musgrove, *Chocolate City: A History of Race and Democracy in the Nation's Capital* (Chapel Hill: The University of North Carolina Press, 2017), 48–49.

[34] "Abstract of the Returns of the Fifth Census, Showing the Number of Free People, the Number of Slaves, the Federal or Representative Number, and the Aggregate of Each County of Each State of the United States" (Washington, DC: Duff Green, 1832), 45. "Compendium of the

From those figures, in 1830 just over 15 percent of the District's population was enslaved, declining to about 11 percent in 1840.[35] Such proportions of slave population put the District in the lower range of slave territories in the period, but well above the Northern States embarking upon programs of gradual emancipation.[36] The decline in the District between 1830 and 1840 has led one historian of the District to conclude that "slavery as a local institution displayed steadily diminished vitality" over the period and that "the over-all climate of the ten-mile square promoted freedom as a natural state in preference to perpetual slavery."[37] It seems more likely that the decline in the census count of slaves in the District of Columbia between 1830 and 1840 reflects wider regional trends that worked to implicate the District more firmly with the institution of slavery. Stanley Harrold suggests that a shift in the regional crop from tobacco to wheat over the first third of the nineteenth century saw the Chesapeake region move toward free labor.[38] The consequence was an excess of slaves, who were sold or taken South.[39] Taken together, the District, Delaware, and Maryland contained over 15,000 fewer slaves in 1840 than in 1830, suggesting a significant removal.[40] One contemporaneous account by a visitor to Washington, E. A. Andrews, noted that "the planters in Virginia are selling

Enumeration of the Inhabitants and Statistics of the United States, as Obtained at the Department of State, from the Returns of the Sixth Census" (Washington, DC: Thomas Allen, 1841), 100–102. See also Constance McLaughlin Green, *The Secret City: A History of Race Relations in the Nation's Capital* (Princeton: Princeton University Press, 1967), 33; Letitia Woods Brown, *Free Negroes in the District of Columbia 1790–1846* (New York: Oxford University Press, 1972), 11.

[35] The District's total population was 39,834 in 1830 and 43,712 in 1840. "Abstract of the Returns of the Fifth Census," 45; "Compendium of the Enumeration of the Inhabitants and Statistics of the United States," 100–102.

[36] In 1830, Maryland was 23 percent enslaved, Missouri 18 percent, and the Territory of Arkansas 15 percent. In Delaware, approximately 4 percent of the population was enslaved in 1830. By contrast, in Illinois and Pennsylvania, the "non-slaveholding" States with the highest absolute number of slaves, the enslaved proportions of the population recorded in the census were, respectively, 0.5 percent and 0.03 percent. For the population of the United States as whole, the proportion enslaved was 16 percent. "Abstract of the Returns of the Fifth Census," 46–47.

[37] Woods Brown, *Free Negroes in the District of Columbia 1790–1846*, 13.

[38] Stanley Harrold, *Subversives: Antislavery Community in Washington, D.C., 1828–1865* (Baton Rouge: Louisiana State University Press, 2003), 4.

[39] That Maryland and Delaware saw similar declines in slave population between 1830 and 1840 suggests a regional structural change rather than Woods Brown's "climate of the ten-mile square" as the cause of the decrease in the District's slaves. Between 1830 and 1840, Delaware's slave population declined in absolute terms by 21 percent while Maryland's fell 13 percent. "Abstract of the Returns of the Fifth Census," 14–15; "Compendium of the Enumeration of the Inhabitants and Statistics of the United States," 30.

[40] Michael Tadman estimates that between 1830 and 1839 over 38,000 slaves were moved out of these three territories. Michael Tadman, *Speculators and Slaves: Masters, Traders, and Slaves in the Old South* (Madison: The University of Wisconsin Press, 1989), 12, 225–27; "Abstract of the Returns of the Fifth Census"; "Compendium of the Enumeration of the Inhabitants and Statistics of the United States."

their plantations as fast as possible, and removing with their slaves," but the development of a thriving domestic slave trade suggests that not all slaveholders moved with their slaves.[41] The same account noted that the District was "the very seat and centre of the domestic slave-trade" and that the adverts of slave dealers appeared "constantly" in the newspapers of Washington.[42] Walter Clephane notes that in 1836 three such adverts sought 1,200 slaves on a single day.[43] In the process of this sale of humans further south, the District of Columbia emerged as an important regional slave depot.

Regulations meant that the District of Columbia became more important to slavery as a node within the domestic slave trade's transportation network than as a slave market in the mid-Antebellum period. Laws in both Virginia and Maryland predating the cession of the District restricted importation of slaves and remained in force after Congress took responsibility for the District.[44] Among these, Maryland's 1796 law against the importation of slaves for the purposes of sale covered Washington County and was deemed in force in the 1834 case of *Lee v. Lee*.[45] Under that law, slaves imported for the purposes of sale were to be given their freedom. But while movement of slaves into the District risked their emancipation, slaveholders in the District could move and sell them internally without constraint and the movement of slaves *through* the District by slave traders was significant during the period. The latter possibility was taken advantage of in the mid-Antebellum period such that the District of Columbia became a center for the regional slave trade and by extension a critical hub of the national slave trade. Mary Beth Corrigan has described the District during the period in question as "the most active slave depot in the nation" and other scholars concur as to its importance.[46] In the mid-1830s, the most infamous slave-trading firm, Franklin and Armfield, estimated to Andrews that it was transporting from the District approximately 150 slaves every two months by sea and "a considerable number" over land to

[41] E. A. Andrews, *Slavery and the Domestic Slave-Trade in the United States*. (Boston: Light & Stearns, 1836), 119.

[42] Andrews, *Slavery and the Domestic Slave-Trade in the United States*, 122.

[43] Walter C. Clephane, "The Local Aspects of Slavery in the District of Columbia," *Records of the Columbia Historical Society, Washington, D.C.* 3 (1900): 235.

[44] Mary Tremain, *Slavery in the District of Columbia: The Policy of Congress and the Struggle for Abolition* (New York: G. P. Putnam, 1892), 31; Clephane, "The Local Aspects of Slavery in the District of Columbia," 224–25; "An Act Concerning the District of Columbia, Feb. 27" (1801), http://memory.loc.gov/cgi-bin/ampage?collId=llsl&fileName=002/llsl002.db&recNum=140.

[45] *Lee v. Lee* (1834); Mary Beth Corrigan, "Imaginary Cruelties? A History of the Slave Trade in Washington, D.C.," *Washington History* 13, no. 2 (2001): 8.

[46] Corrigan, "Imaginary Cruelties?," 5; Paul Finkelman, "Slavery in the Shadow of Liberty: The Problem of Slavery in Congress and the Nation's Capital," in *In the Shadow of Freedom: The Politics of Slavery in the National Capital*, ed. Paul Finkelman and Donald R. Kennon (Athens: Ohio University Press, 2010), 4; Don E. Fehrenbacher and Ward M. McAfee, *The Slaveholding Republic: An Account of the United States Government's Relations to Slavery* (Oxford: Oxford University Press, 2001), 66–67.

Natchez.[47] Another slave trader is recorded by Andrews as claiming to take at least forty slaves to South Carolina six times a year.[48] Whether or not these estimates were inflated by the slave traders or by Andrews, it seems likely that the volume of slaves passing through the District in the 1830s was a significant increase upon the "several hundred people" that Torrey, in his 1817 *Portraiture of Domestic Slavery*, claimed were annually collected in Washington for transportation south.[49] Certainly, the number of slaves moving through Washington, DC, itself was sufficient that from Torrey's account onward regular complaints of trains of slaves passing through the city are recorded.

During the early nineteenth century residents and visitors to the District of Columbia regularly referred to the transfer of slaves through the cities of Washington and Alexandria. As early as 1802, a Grand Jury in Alexandria complained of slave traders collecting "within this district, from various parts, considerable numbers of those victims of slavery," who, after confinement in the District, were then "turned out into our streets, and exposed to our view, loaded with chains as if they had committed some heinous offence against our laws."[50] The Grand Jury regarded the presence of a "traffic fraught with so much misery" a legitimate grievance and looked to the "imposition of civil authority" to stop the breakup of families the slave trade entailed.[51] The sight of a train of slaves while in Washington, DC, had shocked Torrey during the 1810s, as it had John Randolph, who in 1816 called for measures to put an end to the trade in the House of Representatives.[52] In the debate over Randolph's resolution, which was adopted, Charles Goldsborough attested to witnessing slaves marching through the streets of the city and that "it was a notorious fact this was the channel of transmission for them."[53] The

---

[47] Andrews, *Slavery and the Domestic Slave-Trade in the United States*, 142. Using a different source, the American Anti-Slavery Society claimed that the firm "according to their own statement" shipped over 1,000 slaves to New Orleans in 1834. "Slave Market of America" (New York: American Anti-Slavery Society, 1836). William Jay attributed the figure to Rev. Joshua Leavitt's January 23, 1834, letter. William Jay, "Inquiry in to the Character and Tendency of the American Colonization and American Anti-Slavery Societies," in *Miscellaneous Writings on Slavery* (Boston: John P. Jewett & Company, 1853), 157; cf. Tremain, *Slavery in the District of Columbia*, 50.

[48] Andrews, *Slavery and the Domestic Slave-Trade in the United States*, 148.

[49] Torrey, *A Portraiture of Domestic Slavery, in the United States*, 41.

[50] "Alexandria, Jan. 16.," *The National Intelligencer*, January 22, 1802. Mr. Miner would quote this complaint in Congress in 1829 and it was thereafter recycled into abolitionist literature. Tremain, *Slavery in the District of Columbia*, 49; William Jay, *A View of the Action of the Federal Government, in Behalf of Slavery* (New York, NY: J. S. Taylor, 1839), 80.

[51] "Alexandria, Jan. 16."

[52] Torrey, *A Portraiture of Domestic Slavery, in the United States*, 32–40; *Annals of Congress, 14th Congress, 1st Session* (House of Representatives, 1816), 1115–17.

[53] *Annals of Congress*, 1816, 1117. On Randolph's intervention, prompted most directly by the jumping of the slave woman Anna from a third-story window, cf. Robert H. Gudmestad, *A Troublesome Commerce: The Transformation of the Interstate Slave Trade* (Baton Rouge:

economic shifts within the region and contemporary observations suggest that the volume of slaves moving through the District increased over the 1820s. By 1827 the *Alexandria Gazette* complained, "Scarcely a week passes without some of these wretched creatures being driven through our streets."[54] A year later, the *National Intelligencer* printed a petition from citizens of Washington and Alexandria against the slave trade in the District alongside news that a bill had been offered in the House of Representatives to curb the use of enslavement as a means of meeting outstanding prison fees.[55] In 1829, Charles Miner read from a letter in the House of Representatives claiming "droves … of ten or twelve [slaves] all chained together" were brought into Alexandria almost every week.[56] In 1830, an article from the *American Spectator*, which was picked up by Lundy's *Genius of Universal Emancipation*, contrasted the procession that marched toward the Capitol celebrating French liberty with a train of slaves being marched the other way.[57] While these accounts seldom contained the hundreds of slaves that Franklin and Armfield boasted of, they pointed to a steady flow of tens of slaves through the towns of the District that indicates that census counts of 4,600–6,100 slaves in the District in the 1830s understates the entanglement of the District in the institution.

More than the numbers of slaves in and passing through the District, Congress's legislative neglect meant that the federal institutions of government played important roles in facilitating slavery in the District. Congress's wholesale adoption of the laws of Virginia and Maryland in 1801 meant that in Alexandria County Virginia's law at 1801 and in Washington County Maryland's law at 1801 remained in force thereafter. As well as therefore having two legal systems in place within the District, those legal systems were reliant upon congressional reform for substantial update. Despite pleas from Members of Congress that the District was taking up too much of the federal legislature's time, congressional tardiness in addressing its responsibility for the District was a recurring source of complaint from the citizens of the District.[58] The failure to meaningfully reform preexisting legal

---

Louisiana State University Press, 2003), 35–36. Torrey in *Portraiture* discussed the experiences of Anna.

[54] Jay, *A View of the Action of the Federal Government*, 81–82. Jay's source for the Gazette article may have been Charles Miner's 1829 speech in the House of Representatives. *Register of Debates, 20th Congress, 2nd Session*, 1829, 178.

[55] "District Subjects," *Daily National Intelligencer*, April 4, 1828; "Slavery in the District of Columbia," *Daily National Intelligencer*, April 4, 1828.

[56] *Register of Debates*, 1829, 180.

[57] "The Abominable Trade," *Genius of Universal Emancipation* (Washington, DC, December 1830).

[58] In 1819 members of the House of Representatives complained that "[w]e cannot much longer be expected to devote much of our time to the minor affairs of this little District," and that they were spending "too much of the national treasure in legislating for so small a portion of our country." *Annals of Congress, 16th Congress, 1st Session*, 1819, 794, 800. However, citizens of the District, particularly those in Alexandria, felt that Congress was failing to fulfill its obligations.

regimes that supported slavery has led one scholar to conclude, "rather than threaten slavery in the District of Columbia, Congress almost always protected it."[59] Several eighteenth-century Maryland laws remained in force in the District during the 1820s that had been subsequently revised in the early nineteenth century in Maryland proper. Among the most egregious was a law allowing for the sale of individuals jailed on suspicion of being runaway slaves in order to recoup jail fees.[60] Charles Miner had requested further information on this practice in his 1829 speech after identifying five cases during 1826–27 in which runaways were sold for jail fees and other expenses without proof that they were slaves.[61] In response to Miner's request, the Committee for the District of Columbia issued a report in late January.[62] While the report "strongly recommended" the continued use of public jails to facilitate the slave trade, an appendix offered evidence supportive of Miner's suspicions that individuals were being sold by the jails for fees when unable to prove their freedom.[63] In the Report's appendix, the District's Marshal, Tench Ringgold, calculated that between January 1, 1826 and January 1, 1829 the prison in Washington County had held 251 slaves for their owners and 78 as runaways.[64] Of the latter, eleven were proven to be free and one was sold for maintenance and jail fees. During 1826–27 Ringgold identified 101 persons of color committed to prison of whom 81 were slaves and 15 proven to be free. However, the remaining five were sold for maintenance and jail fees, "being unable to prove their freedom," one of whom, Josias or Si, was purchased by Tench Ringgold himself.[65] Although small numbers within the scale of the regional slave trade, the continued operation of this law in Washington

Mark David Richards, "The Debates over the Retrocession of the District of Columbia, 1801–2004," *Washington History* 16, no. 1 (2004): 59–60; A. Glenn Crothers, "The 1846 Retrocession of Alexandria: Protecting Slavery and the Slave Trade in the District of Columbia," in *In the Shadow of Freedom: The Politics of Slavery in the National Capital*, ed. Paul Finkelman and Donald R. Kennon (Athens: Ohio University Press, 2010), 149.

[59] Finkelman, "Slavery in the Shadow of Liberty," 10.

[60] "Slavery in the District of Columbia," April 4, 1828.   [61] *Register of Debates*, 1829, 176.

[62] The committee's chair, Mark Alexander, quickly – in just over three pages – disposed of any question of emancipation in the District as counter to the desires of the citizenry of the District and, therefore, unconstitutional. The committee did report a bill aimed at regulating the movement of slaves through the District and restricting free black migration into the District, but it did not become law. For a fuller discussion of the report and Miner's speech, see Chapter 7. "Report of The Committee for the District of Columbia, in Pursuance of Certain Resolutions of the House of the 9th of January, Memorials, &c. to Them Referred, Respecting Slavery with the Said District" (Washington, DC, 1829) [Hereafter, "Alexander Report"]; "H.R. 399" (1829).

[63] Alexander Report, 2.   [64] Numbers in this discussion taken from Alexander Report, 6–9.

[65] Ringgold defended his participation in these exchanges as in line with "the custom and the law" and preferable to the enslavement of free black individuals without their being registered in the docket of the jail and, therefore, having a chance to publicly assert their freedom. Nonetheless, at the time of the report he was holding $242.56 from the sale of individuals subject to claims by their proven owners. It was not made clear what would happen to such money in the event there was no claim made. Alexander Report, 7, 8.

County meant that the federal government was potentially enslaving and selling previously free individuals.

Beyond the operation of this law, the federal government and its oversight of the District facilitated the slave trade and slavery more broadly in numerous ways. As Ringgold's testimony indicated, the Washington County prison was regularly used to house slaves. In his 1829 speech, Miner suggested that between 1824 and 1828, 452 slaves had been held in the public jails for safekeeping, while 290 had been taken up as runaways.[66] As noted earlier, the Alexander Report did not dispute this practice and in fact deemed it desirable.[67] Moreover, congressional disinterest and delegation allowed for a racialized legal system to operate that constrained black freedom and simultaneously supported slavery. Numerous local laws worked to constrain the free movement of the District's black population and inhibit coordination and socializing. From 1820 the Corporation of Washington penalized "slaves, free negroes and mulattoes" for "nightly and other disorderly meetings" with imprisonment and whipping.[68] In 1827, a 10 pm curfew was imposed on the free black population as well as the requirement that they obtain permits for holding a dance in their homes.[69] In 1831, the City moved to restrict the employment of free blacks by only allowing them licenses for various types of driving.[70] Although Isaac M. Carey successfully challenged the latter provision after his arrest in 1836, challenges to the curfews were not successful.[71] The disruption these measures caused to abolitionist efforts is evinced by the fact that the District's abolition society ceased to meet after Georgetown followed Washington in adopting a black code in 1832.[72] After the so-called "Snow riot" of 1835, restrictions were further increased, and Washington City's police subjected to a fine of $50 and ineligibility from future office if they failed to enforce measures against black meetings.[73] Harrold points out that the City of Washington's police force was further used as tool to combat black resistance to the regime of

---

[66] *Register of Debates*, 1829, 176.   [67] Alexander Report, 2.

[68] Worthington G. Snethen, "The Black Code of the District of Columbia, in Force September 1st, 1848," in *Statutes on Slavery: The Pamphlet Literature, Series VII, Volume 2*, ed. Paul Finkelman (New York: Garland Publishing, Inc., 1988), 34. (Page numbers refer to pamphlet page numbers.)

[69] Snethen, "The Black Code of the District of Columbia," 40–41. This reform was part of a broader tightening of the Black Code. Myers Asch and Musgrove, *Chocolate City*, 69.

[70] Woods Brown, *Free Negroes in the District of Columbia 1790–1846*, 134.

[71] Woods Brown, *Free Negroes in the District of Columbia 1790–1846*, 135, 140.

[72] McLaughlin Green, *The Secret City*, 35.

[73] McLaughlin Green, *The Secret City*, 36–37; Snethen, "The Black Code of the District of Columbia," 46. The "Snow riot" (or "Snow Storm") saw several days of mobbing in Washington, DC, as white mobs attacked and destroyed free black establishments. The events get their name from the destruction of Beverly Snow's restaurant. On the more restrictive Black Code, cf. Myers Asch and Musgrove, *Chocolate City*, 81.

slavery within the District through its deployment as a slave patrol.[74] In an environment in which manumission suits had limited effect on the overall regime of slavery, physical resistance to slavery and running away proved vital mechanisms for challenging the institution. The use of the city's police to repress such behavior and to intercept escapes placed the District's authorities on the side of slavery over that of the enslaved. In addition to these directed measures, both federal and local laws enforced an environment of de facto and de lieu racial inequality that provided a social framework for slavery.[75]

By the early 1830s, the association of the District of Columbia with slavery was, therefore, of vital importance to the abolitionists. Within the framework of a nationalized institution of slavery, practices within Washington, DC, represented the intertwining of the United States with slavery. The coffles passing by the Capitol were the literal embodiments of a national slavery within the political heart of the country. But the District of Columbia was also the geographical location of a sustained interface between Congress and slavery that implicated federal government in the management and facilitation of slavery as an institution. In the jails administered by the federal government and the black codes of the corporations created by it, the federal government – and particularly Congress – did not withdraw from the evil of slavery but instead provided institutional support for it. The District, perhaps more than any other space in the nation, was the site of an enduring national institution of slavery. As the debates over slavery reached new peaks of passion and division in the 1830s, this made the District a significant territory for both the abolitionists and those defending slavery against them.

6.3 THE DISTRICT OF COLUMBIA AND ABOLITION

As the interracial immediatist abolition movement began to organize itself into the New England, and then American, Anti-Slavery Societies, slavery in the District of Columbia both linked and separated the activism of the 1820s and 1830s. As Miner's speech demonstrates, by the late 1820s, the issue of slavery and the slave trade in the District of Columbia was percolating up toward

---

[74] Harrold, *Subversives*, 46.

[75] In addition to the restrictions already discussed, the Black Codes reflected and gave credence to racial stereotypes and provided deferential social markers, including access to alcohol, requirements that free blacks gain permissions from "respectable citizens" for breaking curfew, and – curiously – forbidding free blacks from flying kites in Georgetown. Snethen, "The Black Code of the District of Columbia," 34, 41, 44, 53. In revising the District's criminal code in 1830, Congress revoked the death penalty for rape for all "free" individuals (retaining it for slaves). Efforts to limit the impact of that revocation to "free whites" alone were defeated not from an opposition to its intent but rather the difficulty of identifying who was white and who was not. *Register of Debates, 22nd Congress, 1st Session,* 1832. *Register of Debates, 21st Congress, 1st Session,* 1830, 822.

national prominence, primed for adoption as an issue by immediate abolitionists. But the speech also provides an index of a changing understanding of the District within antislavery circles. In 1829, Miner was no abolitionist in the sense of the free black immediatist movement of the 1820s or the wider biracial movement of the 1830s. Chief among his fears was that the slave trade would bring to the District a large black population who would curtail the future greatness of the capital. Identifying the black population as "a degraded caste," Miner congratulated Ohio on its productiveness while strongly implying that this was the result of its decision to constrain black immigration.[76] Regarding the District, he hoped that prudent regulations would see "the degraded caste ... gradually disappear, like darkness before the opening day."[77] Mixing such racial prejudice with antislavery sentiments did not preclude Miner from membership of the PAS, but it did place him outside an 1830s abolitionist movement committed to black citizenship.[78] When Charles Miner's 1829 speech was reprinted in 1832, even the committee of publication felt it was unsatisfactory in its timid approach.[79] Repackaged as an overview of slavery in the District, the speech was presented within an ideological sound review in October 1833's *The Abolitionist*.[80] There, the shocking information it conveyed was couched within an assessment that the people could secure immediate abolition in the District through their control over Congress. By the mid-1830s, this would represent the mainstream view among immediate abolitionists, who saw the District as a vital sphere within the fight against slavery, both for its potential success and because it tied them directly to the national sin of slavery.

Miner's speech was the culmination of over a decade of mobilization on the issue of slavery in the District of Columbia across the various strands of antislavery activity.[81] The regular reports of slave coffles in the District were contrasted to the nation's proclamations of freedom within antislavery literature, such as Torrey's *Portraiture* and John Wright's *A Refutation of the Sophisms, Gross Misrepresentations, and Erroneous Quotations Contained in "An American's" "Letter to the Edinburgh Reviewers"*

[76] *Register of Debates*, 1829, 181.   [77] *Register of Debates*, 1829, 181.

[78] Richard S. Newman, *The Transformation of American Abolitionism: Fighting Slavery in the Early Republic* (Chapel Hill: The University of North Carolina Press, 2002), 51. On the cohabitation of such views within antislavery, cf. Donald J. Ratcliffe, "The Decline of Antislavery Politics, 1815–1840," in *Contesting Slavery: The Politics of Bondage and Freedom in the New American Nation*, ed. John Craig Hammond and Matthew Mason (Charlottesville: University of Virginia Press, 2011), 267–90. Sinha suggests that what defined abolitionists was "a principled commitment to black equality." Manisha Sinha, "Did the Abolitionists Cause the Civil War?," in *The Abolitionist Imagination*, ed. Andrew Delbanco (Cambridge, MA: Harvard University Press, 2012), 95.

[79] Charles Francis Richardson and Elizabeth Miner Richardson, *Charles Miner: A Pennsylvania Pioneer* (Wilkes-Barre, 1916), 148.

[80] "Slavery and the Slave Trade in the District of Columbia."

[81] Newman, *The Transformation of American Abolitionism*, 51.

(1820).[82] Following the Missouri Crisis and drawing upon the elite petitioning campaigns in use since its founding, the PAS launched an extended petition campaign on the issue of slavery in the District of Columbia, believing it to be a territory over which the federal government had clear authority.[83] In 1828, the American Convention for Promoting the Abolition of Slavery called on the people of the United States to turn their attention to the District and seek the gradual extinction of slavery there.[84] Even as the antislavery movement was poised to fracture with the arrival of interracial immediatism, the District campaign drew all together. Lundy and Garrison emphasized the District strategy in the *Genius of Universal Emancipation*.[85] Among free black communities in the North, *Freedom's Journal* monitored and endorsed petition campaigns on the issue, publishing petitions drawn from around the country and eventually reprinting the Alexander Report.[86] Although the campaign ended in failure, and, Richard Newman suggests, actually exacerbated the latent divisions within antislavery, by the end of the 1820s, opponents of slavery recognized the District as a focal point for their campaign.[87]

The legacy of this mobilization around slavery in the District of Columbia was spelled out in the very first edition of Garrison's *Liberator*. But so too were the ways in which this mobilization was evolving in the hands of an immediatism which saw slavery as a national sin. In January 1831, Garrison selected abolition in the District of Columbia as the issue to announce his newspaper to the world. After a poem to commemorate *The Liberator* and the new newspaper's prospectus, two columns on the front page were dedicated to reprints of a petition circulating in Boston calling for gradual abolition in the District and the 1830 article published in the *Washington Spectator* detailing the transfer of slaves through the nation's capital.[88] With these reprints and the editorializing that accompanied them, Garrison drew on themes from the era of

---

[82] Wright demanded of his readership:

> Is not the great Council of the Nation, and the Temple of Independence and Liberty, insulted with such scenes, and the Representatives of the Country pested with the sight of bands of *fettered Slaves*, while they enter, or retreat from, the Edifice Sacred to the business of a free and independent nation?
>
> Wright, *A Refutation of the Sophisms, Gross Misrepresentations, and Erroneous Quotations Contained in "An American's" "Letter to the Edinburgh Reviewers,"* 28.

[83] Newman, *The Transformation of American Abolitionism*, 49.

[84] Reprinted in "ADDRESS, From the American Convention for Promoting the Abolition of Slavery &c. &c.," *Freedom's Journal*, December 20, 1828.

[85] Newman, *The Transformation of American Abolitionism*, 53.

[86] For instance, "[From the Georgetown Columbian]," *Freedom's Journal*, February 1, 1828; Alexander report: "Slavery in the District of Columbia," *Freedom's Journal*, February 21, 1829.

[87] Newman, *The Transformation of American Abolitionism*, 55.

[88] "District of Columbia," *The Liberator*, January 1, 1831; "The Slave Trade in the Capital," *The Liberator*, January 1, 1831.

Minerian critique of the District but also offered traces of what the abolitionists would add to that critique. The columns noted foreign criticism of slavery in the District and the shame that it brought to the "heart of the American nation."[89] The petition looked to action from Congress and called for gradual emancipation and the provision of education for the "free blacks and colored children" of the District.[90] Both the petition and the *Spectator* article made reference to the Declaration of Independence. But the framing of these pieces by Garrison foregrounded the implication of the nation as a whole, and by extension the "free" States, in the sin of slavery. There was a subtle shift from embarrassment at the scenes recounted to responsibility for them. "What," Garrison asked, "do many of the professed enemies of slavery mean, by heaping all their reproaches upon the south and asserting that the crime of oppression is not national?"[91] The District was "rotten with the plague, and stinks in the nostrils of the world," but it was also the "Seat of our National Government," a "national monument of oppression," and was under the authority of Congress and therefore under the authority of the American people as a whole.[92] The *Liberator* endorsed the existing petition campaign through its reprinting of the Boston petition and an earnest invitation for readers to sign it. But it also denigrated the "few straggling petitions" that had reached Congress as ineffectual and sought a new "vigorous and systematic effort."[93] Furthermore, the *Liberator* did not suppose that it was revealing anything unknown in recounting the practices of slavery in the District: "These facts are well known to our two or three hundred representatives ... they are known, if not minutely at least generally, to our whole population."[94] The pertinent issue was not interrogating the conditions of slavery in the District but asking why the American people had remained silent – "but who calls for redress?" – and whether the "'earthquake voice' of the people will this session shake the black fabric to its foundation."[95] Garrison prioritized the issue of slavery in the District of Columbia not because it was a national embarrassment (although of course it was), but because it was a theater within which the American people as a whole could act against slavery and crucially had not yet done so.

Conceiving of opposition to slavery in the District as a mobilization of the American people brought into focus several distinct but interrelated changes in opposition to slavery. Most immediately, it mapped onto a tactical change from petitioning as an elite activity aimed at persuading other elites and toward petitioning as a mass movement seeking to arouse national renewal. The PAS had undertaken an elite petitioning strategy over the course of the early Republic, which had done little to widen political participation beyond an establishment that could happily marry concern with slavery in the District

---

[89] "The Slave Trade in the Capital."   [90] "District of Columbia."   [91] "District of Columbia."
[92] "District of Columbia."   [93] "District of Columbia."   [94] "District of Columbia."
[95] "District of Columbia."

with support for colonization and even the institution of slavery itself.[96] In contrast, the petition campaigns undertaken by abolitionists in the 1830s were marked by the participation of historically excluded groups, including women and free blacks.[97] Secondly, the view of the District as peculiarly the preserve of the American people increased both the symbolic importance of the District and the potential for action within that territory.[98] As is discussed subsequently, it had long been the view that Congress had constitutional authority over the District and thus the practices of slavery therein. However, in emphasizing the people's authority over Congress, abolitionists created a space in which a national majority could legitimately act and opened up possibilities for popular national action against slavery. By the 1830s, action against slavery in the District could be seen by abolitionists as both national and constitutional. With the possibility of action came the suggestion of a corresponding guilt on the part of the American people for not acting – working to nationalize the sin of slavery in ways that paralleled its Americanization after 1833. The assignment of such a sin to the free States in the North made attention to the District a matter of urgency in ways that it had not been in the 1810s and early 1820s.

---

[96] Newman, *The Transformation of American Abolitionism*, 35–41.

[97] On the ways in which the petition campaign was an avenue for women's political participation, see Susan Zaeske, *Signatures of Citizenship: Petitioning, Antislavery, & Women's Political Identity* (Chapel Hill: The University of North Carolina Press, 2003). Although one should be careful not to overstate the opportunities for participation, cf. Steven Mintz, "Introduction," in *The Problem of Evil: Slavery, Freedom, and the Ambiguities of American Reform*, ed. Steven Mintz and John Stauffer (Amherst: University of Massachusetts Press, 2007), 133. Zaeske notes the opposition that female participation in petitioning generated in Congress. Zaeske, *Signatures of Citizenship*, 127–31. The opponents of abolition recognized the widening of political participation to include women and attempted to use it to delegitimize both the movement and the women involved in it. For instance, Senator Benjamin Leigh accused the women signing a petition in support of abolition as both being led astray by another "person" (presumably a man capable of undertaking such a scheme) and of being "unsexed" by the effort. Henry Wise asked the House of Representatives "what sort of a Government are we to have if women and priests are to influence our legislation?" In the same debate, James W. Bouldin suggested that "if they had husbands and children, they would find something else to do; I wish them all good husbands, and something better to do." *Register of Debates*, 1836, 186, 2032, 2170. On the deployment of tropes of masculinity within proslavery thought, cf. Patricia Roberts-Miller, *Fanatical Schemes: Proslavery Rhetoric and the Tragedy of Consensus* (Tuscaloosa: The University of Alabama Press, 2009), 103–26. Free black participation in petitioning, although muted under the PAS, had pedigree within the early Republic. A free black petition organized by Absalom Jones resulted congressional debate over its reception in 1800. *Annals of Congress, 6th Congress, 1st Session* (House of Representatives, 1800), 244.

[98] An 1833 article in the *American Quarterly Review* summarized this view with a belief: "The legislation of congress is but the echo of the people's voice. If the people really desire slavery to be abolished at the seat of government, congress will pass the statutes necessary to carry the object into effect." "ART. III – An Extract from a Speech Delivered by Charles Miner in the House of Representatives of the United States in 1829, on the Subject of Slavery and the Slave Trade in the District of Columbia: With Notes," *American Quarterly Review* 14, no. 27 (September 1833): 65. The article was later reprinted with edits in *The Abolitionist*. "Slavery and the Slave Trade in the District of Columbia."

The immediate abolitionist movement thus came to view action against slavery in the District as a matter national, constitutional, and urgent.[99]

The various parts of the notion that slavery was a national sin and that the District embodied that sin were not new in the 1830s, but they were pulled together with a new intensity and with a central motif of Northern responsibility for slavery in the District. Throughout 1827, the free black newspaper *Freedom's Journal* had reprinted articles that pinned the guilt of slavery on the nation as a whole interweaved with articles pointing out the incongruity of slavery in the capital of the United States. A reprint of a *Christian Spectator* essay declared that the "whole nation share in the disgrace of slavery, in the guilt of introducing it and perpetuating it."[100] And in November of the same year, *Freedom's Journal* spelled out the inconsistency of the City of Washington tolerating slavery and claiming the mantle of liberty:

We have always thought, perhaps erroneously, that if any spot on this planetary system should be sacred to the goddess of Liberty – to the rights of man – that spot should be our Capitol; ... Professions are nothing, when contradicted by daily practice.[101]

In these appeals, the practices of Washington, DC, were offered as illustrative of the corruptions of slavery, made all the more salient by their being carried out in the capital. There was little suggestion that slavery in the District implicated individual Americans living outside the capital in the latter's sins. As *Freedom's Journal* editorialized, "Slavery is certainly disgraceful in any part of the Union, but more particularly within the limits of the District of Columbia, under the immediate notice of Congress, and Ministers from the different governments of Europe."[102] Slavery in the District was symbolically significant and politically inconvenient but beyond that it was as much an evil as slavery elsewhere in the confederacy. Similarly, acknowledgment in the 1820s that questions of national popular sovereignty were at stake in debates over slavery in the District did not result in a sense of urgency or widespread guilt. The push for a petition campaign in the late 1820s came in part from recognition that the District was a unique territory in which the national people held sovereign authority. In 1828, the American Convention for Promoting the Abolition of Slavery identified the District of Columbia as *"the property of the nation"* and,

---

[99] And as such slavery in the District of Columbia provided a useful focal point for an abolitionist social movement that, in Benjamin Lamb-Books's words, "*was* the process of constructing slavery as a national moral problem." Benjamin Lamb-Books, *Angry Abolitionists and the Rhetoric of Slavery: Moral Emotions in Social Movements* (New York: Palgrave macMillan, 2016), 67.

[100] "People of Colour. (Continued)," *Freedom's Journal*, April 13, 1827.

[101] "City of Washington," *Freedom's Journal*, November 16, 1827.

[102] "Slavery in the District of Columbia," *Freedom's Journal*, February 1, 1828.

therefore, subject to popular control.[103] But it was concern for "the honor of the nation" rather than implication in sin that motivated it.[104] A year later, meeting in Washington, DC, the Convention went further, calling the District "the common property of the nation," and stating, "whatever enormity may be legally permitted therein, becomes the common concern of the whole confederacy."[105] Nonetheless, it was to gradual emancipation that it looked for a solution.

In contrast, by mid-1831 the same ideas were being drawn together to produce a potent sense of urgency on the question of slavery in the District. In June of that year, the *Liberator* pulled many of the strands together in a front-page article entitled "Slavery in the District of Columbia." The prompt for the article was a petition from the citizens of the District, which deferentially addressed the "Honorable Body" of Congress, and sought to "respectfully suggest ... the propriety of adopting measures" that would eradicate slavery "in a manner consistent with the safety and welfare of all concerned" within the District.[106] Garrison's response to a petition that could have been drawn from the files of the 1820s PAS was to impress upon it his own conception of the issue as a national question of morality and one that implicated in particular not the citizens of the District but those of "Massachusetts, New-York, or Pennsylvania."[107] As he had in the *Liberator's* first edition, Garrison stressed the guilt of the inhabitants of the free States, "who do not seem to perceive that they are parties to the toleration of the same system which they profess to consider unchristian."[108] They were "as guilty in permitting it to exist in the District, as they would be tolerate it in their respective states."[109] Slavery in the District was not a symbolically grievous instance of slavery – it was the site of slavery that linked the whole nation to that sin: "As long as the American government permits slavery to exist in the District, the Americans as a nation are the friends and patrons of slavery."[110] At the same time, however, Garrison believed in 1831 that the connection between the nation and slavery in the District would be the latter's undoing – because the authority in the District was the whole American people, abolition there would succeed with a concerted popular push. A month and a half later, *The Liberator* reaffirmed this view, stating, "Slavery in the District of Columbia is sustained in our national capacity: it

[103] *Minutes of the Adjourned Session of the Twentieth Biennial American Convention for Promoting the Abolition of Slavery, and Improving the Condition of the African Race* (Philadelphia: Samuel Parker, 1828), 17.
[104] *Minutes of the Adjourned Session of the Twentieth Biennial American Convention,* 19.
[105] *Minutes of the Twenty-First Biennial American Convention for Promoting the Abolition of Slavery, and Improving the Condition of the African Race* (Philadelphia: Thomas B. Town, 1829), 19.
[106] "Slavery in the District Of Columbia," *The Liberator,* June 18, 1831.
[107] "Slavery in the District Of Columbia."   [108] "Slavery in the District Of Columbia."
[109] "Slavery in the District Of Columbia."   [110] "Slavery in the District Of Columbia."

ought, therefore to be prostrated at a blow."[111] As optimism gave way to recognition that slavery in the District would not collapse with a single push, mortification at a continued entanglement in slavery grew.[112] In January 1832, *The Liberator* cried, "[i]t is in vain that we profess to be opposed to the continuance of slavery, while our insincerity is so manifest. Look at the District of Columbia, over which we have ample control!"[113] The situation in the District, along with the requirement to repress revolt in the States, led the paper to conclude, "We are guilty – all guilty – horribly guilty."[114]

The urgency prompted by the continued presence of slavery in the District of Columbia added energy to the long-standing identification of the District as space in which abolition could be pursued constitutionally. Pointing to the US Constitution's Article 1, Section 8 grant to Congress of the power to "exercise Legislation, in all Cases whatsoever" over the District, abolitionists identified congressional power to act against slavery within the District of Columbia. This view was more widespread in the early 1830s than it would be later, once the uses to which the abolitionists intended to put it became clear. Miner had asserted the power in 1829, as had petitions circulating in the late 1820s.[115] But so too had erstwhile opponents of abolition. Debates in Congress since 1800 had proceeded on the assumption of a power of "exclusive legislation" over the District, and this often included direct references to powers over slavery therein.[116] In 1816, John Randolph had supposed a congressional power to end the slave trade in the District.[117] The debates over Missouri had assumed congressional power over slavery in the District.[118] The 1829 Alexander report conceded the legitimacy of the view that "exclusive legislation" encompassed abolition, although it sought to resist its logic by suggesting that the population of the District did not desire abolition at that time.[119] Similarly, in 1831, the House Committee for the District of Columbia offered a very short report that evaded the question of constitutionality, and instead suggested that it was an "inauspicious moment" to consider action on slavery.[120] When William Jay stated in 1833, "Congress have full authority to abolish slavery in the District," he was voicing a conventional understanding of the relationship between Congress and slavery in the District. It was when he added, "and

---

[111] "What Shall Be Done?," *The Liberator*, July 30, 1831.
[112] In September 1831, the newspaper had suggested that what was needed was "One last, best effort now." "Petitions to Congress," *The Liberator*, September 10, 1831.
[113] "The Liberator and Slavery," *The Liberator*, January 7, 1832.
[114] "The Liberator and Slavery."
[115] *Register of Debates*, 1829, 176; "[From the Georgetown Columbian]."
[116] In the first debates over congressional power in the District, the division was on whether Congress was expected to actively assume its authority of exclusive legislation or whether it was implied absent action. *Annals of Congress*, 1800, 868–74.
[117] *Annals of Congress*, 1816, 1115–17.   [118] *Annals of Congress*, 1819, 230, 351, 992, 999.
[119] "Alexander Report," 3.   [120] *Register of Debates*, 1832, 1442.

I think it their duty to do so" that he (and the abolitionists) departed from the rest of the country.[121]

Throughout the early 1830s, the communications of the abolitionist movement reiterated the importance of the District as a site in which abolition could be achieved constitutionally. They were emphatic in claiming that Congress already held the power necessary to act in the District. In 1833, John Whittier declared it "clear. It is indisputable."[122] The next year, the New-England Anti-Slavery Society stated, "Congress ... has full and exclusive power to abolish slavery in the District of Columbia," while in 1835 John Dickson told the House of Representatives while presenting a petition on slavery in the District, "To the power of Congress over the District there is no limitation. It is undefined, unlimited, and absolute."[123] Time and again, the abolitionists drew a parallel between the powers of Congress over the District and the authority of State governments over their respective States. Doing so was an effective mechanism by which the arguments of anti-abolitionists – that the abolitionists had no business interfering with the "domestic institutions" of the States – were turned back against them. If State governments were wholly responsible for the regulation of slavery within their territory, then the equivalent authority – Congress – should also hold that power in the District. It was a way to distance the abolitionists from accusations that they sought to interfere in the States while also establishing the legitimacy of interference within the national territory in the District. In an 1835 "Address to the Public," the American Anti-Slavery Society systematized this viewpoint in a numbered list of "explanations and assurances":

1st. We hold that Congress has no more right to abolish slavery in the southern states than in the French West India Islands. Of course we desire no national legislation on the subject.

2d. We hold that slavery can only be lawfully abolished by the Legislatures of the several states in which it prevails, and that the exercise of any other than moral influence, to induce such abolition, is unconstitutional.

3d. We believe that Congress has the same right to abolish slavery in the District of Columbia, that the state governments have within their respective jurisdictions, and that it is their duty to efface so foul a blot from the national escutcheon.[124]

---

[121] "Letter from Hon. William Jay," *The Abolitionist* 1, no. 8 (August 1833): 119.

[122] John G. Whittier, "Justice and Expediency; or, Slavery Considered with a View to Its Rightful and Effectual Remedy, Abolition," *Anti-Slavery Reporter* (New York, September 1833); Frederick J. Blue, *No Taint of Compromise: Crusaders in Antislavery Politics* (Baton Rouge: Louisiana State University Press, 2005): 41

[123] *Proceedings of the New-England Anti-Slavery Convention, Held in Boston on the 27th, 28th and 29th of May, 1834* (Garrison and Knapp, 1834), 67; "Ladies' Petition," *The Emancipator* (New York, 24 February 1835). Such was the agreement and repetition of this point that British abolitionists were already repeating it as fact in 1833. "Prejudice Vincible," *The Anti-Slavery Reporter* (New York, June 1833).

[124] Ames, *Liberty*, 105.

At least in their publications, abolitionists seemed to believe that this view was widely shared. In a didactical dialogue between an abolitionist and a supporter of the ACS composed for September 1833's *The Abolitionist*, the colonizationist claimed, "An amendment of the Constitution is out of the question, against the will of the slaveholding states." However, his abolitionist opponent countered, apparently convincingly, "there is another consideration. Congress have the sole and absolute regulation of the District of Columbia."[125] In 1836, Lydia Child confidently stated, "Nobody disputes that Congress has constitutional power to abolish slavery and the slave trade in the District of Columbia."[126] Perhaps informed by the attitudes that had been prevalent at the start of the decade, abolitionists in the mid-1830s largely conceived that no substantial constitutional barriers existed to the abolition of slavery in the District of Columbia. Coupled with the urgency that arose from the people's control over the District, abolition in the national capital came to be seen as, in the words of Whittier, a *"constitutional* and necessary" measure.[127] The particular authority of Congress in the District made Northern abolition agitation not a choice but a duty. As news arrived from Britain of imperial abolition, that urgency only increased.

The intersection of an understanding of abolition in the District as constitutional and urgent with the "Americanization" of slavery occasioned by abolition within the British Empire produced a heightened sense of the symbolism of slavery in the capital.[128] The continuation of the institution in the nation's capital fed into the sense of slavery's Americanness and undercut attempts to frame the United States as a moral entity. The massive petition campaigns and their focus on the District of Columbia grew out of this milieu. Strategically, the campaign offered a way to attack slavery that abolitionists hoped would gain support from more moderate segments of society. Convinced that few in the North did not at least share their disgust at slavery in the nation's capital, the abolitionists hoped it would prove a galvanizing issue; "if we cannot "guarantee to each of the States a republican form of government," let us at least no longer legislate for a free nation within view of the falling whip, and within hearing of the execrations of the task-master, and the prayer of his slave!"[129] Symbolically, the campaign offered a chance for abolitionists to remove the stain of slavery from the national vertex. "To render this chosen land beloved by all, the pride and the glory of all," said Dickinson "we must first render it lovely."[130] The same year, in less Burkean language, the Vermont Anti-Slavery Society asked more pointedly, "How much longer shall the soil of the

---

[125] "Dialogue Between C, a Colonizationist, and A, an Abolitionist, on the Subject of the Anti-Slavery Society. (Concluded.)," *The Abolitionist* (Boston, September 1833), 133.

[126] Lydia Child, *Anti-Slavery Catechism* (Newburyport: Charles Whipper, 1836), 33.

[127] Quoted in Blue, *No Taint of Compromise*, 43.

[128] TenBroek notes the "great symbolic value" that the District held for abolition. Jacobus tenBroek, *Equal Under Law* (New York, NY: First Collier Books, 1965), 41.

[129] Whittier, "Justice and Expediency," 56.   [130] "Ladies' Petition."

District of Columbia be watered with the tears and fattened with the blood of Americans?"[131]

But more than those two considerations, the petition campaign allowed abolitionists to see themselves as atoning for the sin of slavery in the District. As early as the first meeting of the National Anti-Slavery Society in 1833, Samuel J. May called on his peers to "exert themselves to urge forward, without delay, the petition of Congress for the abolition of Slavery in the District of Columbia."[132] In the *Essex Gazette*, "Massachusetts" informed his readers that with regard to the District, "The time has gone by for empty profession. Men must *act* as well as *speak*."[133] As the Grimké sisters noted, petitioning was one avenue for "definite, practical" action.[134] These exertions were necessary to give abolitionists the moral authority to critique slavery.[135] But these efforts also served the purpose of allowing abolitionists to claim that they were engaged in combatting slavery – dividing themselves from the national sin as far as possible. The New Hampshire abolitionists suggested this more prosaic rationale in reflecting that even if petitioning made no difference, "[a]t least, we shall have the consciousness of having attempted duty."[136] Ohio's abolitionists were more explicit still in 1835: "We shall absolve ourselves from the political responsibility of national slave holding, by petitioning Congress to abolish slavery and the slave trade wherever it exercised *constitutional jurisdiction*."[137] By participating in the petitioning campaign, the association of abolitionists with the sin of slavery in their national capital was lessened. In a movement concerned with morality, this was not a minor consideration.[138]

---

[131] *First Annual Report of the Vermont Anti-Slavery Society. Presented at Middlebury, February 18. 1835* (Montpelier: Knapp and Jewett, 1835), 12. The identification of the slaves as Americans chimes with the wider abolitionist arguments about their humanity and citizenship. See Chapter 2.

[132] "American Anti-Slavery Society," *The Abolitionist* 1, no. 12 (1833): 184.

[133] Massachusetts, "No Title," *Essex Gazette*, July 12, 1834. Original emphasis.

[134] Ames, *Liberty*, 100.

[135] "Preliminary Meeting of Essex County Anti-Slavery Society," *Essex Gazette*, June 21, 1834.

[136] *Proceedings of the N.H. Anti-Slavery Convention. Held in Concord, on the 11th & 12th of November, 1834* (Concord: Lastman, Webster & Co., 1834), 32.

[137] *Proceedings of the Ohio Anti-Slavery Convention. Held at Putnam, on the Twenty-Second, Twenty-Third, and Twenty-Fourth of April, 1835*, 9. Original emphasis.

[138] For accounts emphasizing the religious dimensions of abolition, cf. Lawrence J. Friedman, *Gregarious Saints: Self and Community in American Abolitionism, 1830–1870* (Cambridge, UK: Cambridge University Press, 1982); William H. Pease and Jane H. Pease, "Introduction," in *The Antislavery Argument* (Indianapolis: The Bobbs-Merrill Company, Inc., 1965), xxii–lxxxiv. Reflecting on the distance between the nation's practice and Christianity, Garrison wrote in September 1835: "We must put away the unclean thing from our midst – it is a curse and contagion – it is fast hurrying us to ruin. . . . let us abase ourselves as did the inhabitants of Ninevah; let us bring forth fruits meet [*sic*] for repentance; let us cease to do evil and learn to do well." Implication in the sin of slavery would, of course, famously lead Garrison to reject the Constitution. William Lloyd Garrison, "To Peleg Sprague [September 12, 1835]," in *I Will Be*

As the mobilization around the petitions grew, it gained traction in Congress. In 1833, 1834, and 1835, the petition campaign resulted in divisions in the House of Representatives or the Senate over the disposal of the petitions.[139] The last provided the occasion for Dickson's speech. But as the petitions gained traction, they also drew the attention of opponents of abolition.[140] Just as the importance of the District for abolitionists grew in the 1830s, so too did it take on greater importance for the defenders of slavery. As the elected members assembled in Washington, DC, for the 24th Congress, this, alongside the petitions themselves, set the stage for the eruption of slavery as a congressional issue.

6.4 THE "THERMOPYLAE" OF SLAVERY

As noted earlier, the idea that Congress held authority over slavery in the District was held as conventional wisdom throughout the 1810s and into the 1820s. But by 1836 attempts at emancipation in the District of Columbia could no longer be countenanced by representatives of slaveholding States, who broke with that consensus. Part of the reason for this change lies with the emergence of the "positive good" defenses of slavery discussed in Chapter 4 – a simple but not insignificant explanation is that the ideological environment in which the discussions were taking place changed between 1816 and 1836; if slavery was a positive good then embarrassment over its practice in the District of Columbia was weaker. But it was also the case that the District took on greater symbolic and strategic importance for the opponents of abolition in the 1830s, prompting a more robust defense of slavery therein.

The fear of slave rebellion that animated much of the discussion in Virginia after Nat Turner's Revolt played an important role in raising the significance of the District for slaveholders.[141] Much as discussion in Virginia in 1831–32 had raised the prospect that gradual abolition would embolden violent demands for emancipation, so too was abolition in the District seen as an encouragement to future rebellion. A central element of this concern was the geographical location of the District in the midst of slaveholding States. As early as 1829, Representative John C. Weems suggested that Maryland and Virginia would have never ceded the District's territory if they had foreseen consideration of

---

Heard! *The Letters of William Lloyd Garrison, Volume 1: 1822–1835*, ed. Walter M. Merrill (Cambridge, MA: The Belknap Press of Harvard University Press, 1971), 525.

[139] *Register of Debates, 22nd Congress, 2nd Session*, 1833, 1585; *Register of Debates, 23rd Congress, 1st Session*, 1834, 198; *Register of Debates, 23rd Congress, 2nd Session*, 1835, 1141.

[140] In 1834 Senator Preston sought to reconsider a vote on referring the petitions to the Committee on the District of Columbia (the then expected practice) lest it result in the Committee issuing a report on the same. *Register of Debates*, 1834, 198.

[141] On the link between abolitionist efforts and slave revolt in the minds of slaveholders, cf. Carl Lawrence Paulus, *The Slaveholding Crisis: Fear of Insurrection and the Coming of the Civil War* (Baton Rouge: Louisiana State University Press, 2017), chap. 4.

abolition "in the midst of their slave population."[142] Thereafter, the consequences of abolition in the District for those two States were a recurring concern within congressional debates. The idea that abolition would trigger revolt elsewhere made the location of the District particularly concerning for slaveholders; writing in the *Charleston Courier*, Richard Yeadon Jr. suggested that the "mere discussion of the subject involves the safety of the South from internal commotion."[143] In 1830, Maryland and Virginia were collectively home to over 500,000 slaves, or approximately half the free population of those States.[144] Although a Northern politician, Senator James Buchanan vividly articulated slaveholder fears arising from the geographical location of abolition in the District:

You would thus erect a citadel in the very heart of these States ... from which abolitionists and incendiaries could securely attack the peace and safety of their citizens. You establish a spot within the slaveholding States which would be a city of refuge for runaway slaves. You create by law a central point from which trains of gunpowder may be securely laid, extending into the surrounding States, which may at any moment produce a fearful and destructive explosion.[145]

As this quotation suggests, the fear that revolution would be spread from an emancipated District to surrounding areas was allied with a belief that slaves would escape from slavery into the accessible free territory that abolition created.[146] The prospect filled slaveholders with dread. Senator Robert J. Walker offered a vivid and lengthy depiction of the apocalyptical scenes that would follow emancipation in the District:

It is a proposition, not merely to render the slaves of this District freemen, but, in its inevitable results and consequences, to render the freemen of this District slaves: to chain them to the ear of a despotic central power, whilst the wild spirit of fanaticism lashes her fiery steeds over the broken columns and shattered fragments of the constitution, and, driving onward in exulting triumph to the very Capitol of the nation, waves her black and blood-stained banner from the very dome, where now float the glorious kindred emblems of our country's Union. The mighty revolution proposed by these petitioners would make this District a den of thieves and assassins, of liberated slaves and blacks

---

[142] *Register of Debates*, 1829, 187.
[143] Richard Yeadon Jr., "Abolition in the District of Columbia," in *The Amenability of Northern Incendiaries As Well to Southern As to Northern Laws. Without Prejudice to the Right of Free Discussion: To Which Is Added an Inquiry into the Lawfulness of Slavery, Under the Jewish and Christian Dispensations;* (Charleston: T. A. Hayden, 1835), 34.
[144] "Abstract of the Returns of the Fifth Census," 46.   [145] *Register of Debates*, 1836, 84.
[146] The evidence garnered from the 1846 retrocession of Alexandria and the eventual abolition in the District in 1862 suggests these fears were not entirely misplaced. After 1846 the free black population of Alexandria decreased as that population moved to the relatively freer Washington. In 1862 Maryland's slave population fled their masters' grip and sought freedom in the District. Richards, "The Debates over the Retrocession of the District of Columbia, 1801–2004," 74; James Oakes, *Slavery and Freedom: An Interpretation of the Old South* (New York: Alfred A. Knopf, 1990), 187.

already free. .... This proposition would make the District an asylum for fugitive slaves from the States, the grand citadel of abolitionism, whence it would light the torch of the incendiary, and whet the knife of the assassin, upon the very borders of Virginia and Maryland.[147]

In the post-Turner environment, Walker's vision of a future District in which free blacks and runaway slaves congregated at the heart of the slaveholding Chesapeake offered a threat to both the property of slaveholding States and the lives of its citizens. Resistance to it was, in the view of slaveholders and their families, a matter of survival.

Another, but not unrelated, cause for greater concern over abolition in the capital was an attention to its symbolic value. By 1836, some opponents of abolition in the District saw the agitation over the issue there as part of a wider strategy to attack slavery nationally.[148] But advocates of slavery paralleled the abolitionists in moving toward seeing the institutionalized practices in the capital as holding a moral sanction. The fact that slavery existed in Washington, DC, moved from being an embarrassment to being an important indication of the nation's acceptance of the institution. A reversal of that situation would signal a rejection of slavery and embolden the abolitionists, giving moral authority to their cause. And as the abolitionists had chosen the District as the focus of their claim that slavery was a national sin, defenders of slavery were forced to a great degree to meet them on that ground. Representative James Garland believed that every "movement made in this House for the abolition of slavery within the District is a stepping-stone to the abolitionists to mount up to their work."[149] The belief that allowing discussion of abolition in the District gave a national moral sanction to opposition to slavery drove an unwillingness to condone what opponents of abolition regarded as "the mad spirit" of "artful, talented and enthusiastic leaders" and their views of the nation's capital.[150]

At the same time, the arguments being made to defend slavery in the 1830s made resisting abolition in the District more significant. As discussed in Chapter 4, the development of arguments for slavery in the 1830s located it as part of a network of constitutionally protected property rights. While such a defense provided defenders of slavery with a way to counter arguments that slavery lacked a positive constitutional basis, it tied slavery to a broader conception of property as sacrosanct. Abolition in the District of Columbia challenged that claim, suggesting that in areas under congressional authority there was

---

[147] *Register of Debates,* 1836, 694.
[148] In the House of Representatives, Representative Waddy Thompson Jr. claimed "the people of the universal South have for years regarded this question of emancipation in the District as identical with a proposition to emancipate the slaves of the whole South, and no human power can change that opinion." *Register of Debates,* 1836, 2006.
[149] *Register of Debates,* 1836, 2066.
[150] "Reflections Elicited by Judge Harper's Anniversary Oration Delivered Before the South-Carolina Society for the Advancement of Learning, 9th Dec. 1835," *The Southern Literary Journal and Monthly Magazine* (Charleston, July 1836), 376, 377.

provision for revising the regulations under which property was held or even destroying it (as property) outright. Despite abolitionists' repeated statements that they had no interest in federal legislative interference with slavery in the States, opponents of abolition believed the abolitionists saw it as the first step in a broader campaign against slavery.[151] A review of "The Partisan Leader" in an 1837 edition of the *Southern Literary Messenger* laid out this line of thought while decrying attempts at abolition in the District as an attack on property rights. Grounding property rights in the Constitution, the author saw their erosion in the District as their erosion more broadly:

The same constitution which guards the rights of property in the states, guards them also in the District of Columbia. That instrument gives Congress no authority to invade those rights any where.[152]

Given this, the review's author regarded the claim to power over property in the District as "but a pretence [*sic*] for the claim of the same power over the states."[153] In Congress, John C. Calhoun urged his fellow Senators to "meet this question as firmly as if it were the direct question of emancipation in the States," for if not arrested "the guards of the constitution will give way and be destroyed."[154] Mixing fears over personal safety with arguments about constitutional property, William C. Preston hoped that "portcullis of the constitution may be dropped between these men and our lives and property."[155] In crafting a defense of slavery on the grounds of constitutional property, the defenders of slavery committed themselves to policing the definition of the latter wherever it was challenged.

The cumulative result of these different strands was that Washington, DC, took on a symbolism for defenders of slavery that was absent in earlier periods. The historian Don E. Fehrenbacher has suggested that slavery was legalized in the District of Columbia "silently and almost casually" in the early days of the Republic, as cession and then the adoption of the existing States' laws created a space for slavery without much conscious reflection.[156] However, as a result

---

[151] Despite the distrust of their opponents, the abolitionists' broader strategy was actually to surround the slave States with inhospitable territory and have the isolation lead to slavery's end, rather than seek direct intervention. Cf. James Oakes, *The Scorpion's Sting: Antislavery and the Coming of the Civil War* (New York: W. W. Norton & Company, 2014). Such an approach had the advantage of according with the views of potential sympathizers, such as William Channing, who believed that the ending of slavery must come from the moral renewal of the slaveholding States. William E. Channing, *Slavery* (Boston: James Munroe and Company, 1835), 119, 127.

[152] "The Partisan Leader," *Southern Literary Messenger* (Richmond, January 1837), 80. *The Partisan Leader* was an 1836 fictional work by Nathaniel Beverley Tucker set in an 1849 secessionist future.

[153] "The Partisan Leader," 80.   [154] *Register of Debates*, 1836, 73.

[155] *Register of Debates*, 1836, 82.

[156] Don. E. Fehrenbacher, "Slavery, the Framers, and the Living Constitution," in *Slavery and Its Consequences: The Constitution, Race, and Equality*, ed. Robert A. Goldwin and Art Kaufman (Washington, DC: American Enterprise Institute, 1988), 14.

of abolitionist pressure and the shifts discussed in the last few paragraphs, by the mid-1830s the connection between the District and slavery was at the center of arguments over the institution in the United States. If the question of abolition in the District was an urgent one for abolitionists, it also became a crucial one for the defenders of slavery. Often deploying martial imagery, they saw the District as a vital theater in the "battle" with abolition; to lose there would mean being placed on the back foot in the wider conflict. Senator Gabriel Moore of Alabama believed that abolitionists had identified the District as "the most assailable point" and "an entering wedge to a great and general scheme of emancipation."[157] In Columbia, South Carolina, Yeadon posited that, should it come to pass, abolition in the District of Columbia "*must* be regarded as the commencement of war against Southern interests."[158] Given the significance of the subject, even the discussion of it was a "serious and perilous *action*" that "demands from the South *resistance* at the threshold – RESISTANCE NOW, AND RESISTANCE FOREVER."[159] In Congress, Calhoun evocatively suggested he would rather have his "head disserved from [his] body" than receive petitions calling for abolition in the District.[160] He was joined by Senator Black of Mississippi who told the Senate, "not as a threat, but as a true statement of public feeling," that the question of abolition in the District "never can be touched except with the point of the sword."[161] It was, said Calhoun, "our Thermopylae."[162] In the House of Representatives, Henry Wise turned to another classical and military allusion to suggest that if the House conceded to a congressional authority over slavery in the District, they would already be "beyond the Rubicon."[163]

6.5   CONCLUSION

Thus, by the mid-1830s, abolitionists and their proslavery counterparts had converged on the significance of the District of Columbia. Abolitionists, increasingly viewing slavery as a peculiarly national sin and seeing the District of Columbia as territory in which they carried a personal responsibility for it, came to believe that they held a duty to petition Congress for abolition there. Shifting from the elite petitioning against a national embarrassment that characterized the antislavery of the 1820s, abolitionists in the 1830s undertook a mass petitioning campaign that sought to relieve their guilt and expunge the national sin. They nonetheless accepted and repeated the 1820s

---

[157] *Register of Debates*, 1836, 477.
[158] Yeadon Jr., "Abolition in the District of Columbia." Original emphasis.
[159] Yeadon Jr. Original emphasis.   [160] *Register of Debates*, 1836, 484.
[161] *Register of Debates*, 1836, 650.
[162] *Register of Debates*, 1836, 775. Thermopylae was the classical battle in which the outnumbered Greeks held up the advancing Persian army on a narrow pass delaying the latter's march on Athens.
[163] *Register of Debates*, 1836, 2024.

belief that Congress's exclusive authority over the District meant abolition there was constitutional and unaffected by a commitment to not interfere with slavery in the States. The abolitionist view that the question of abolition in the District was national, constitutional, and urgent was countered by a proslavery view that abolition in the District would be the first step in a rollback of slavery throughout the nation. Unable to accept that slavery was obviously sinful while framing it as a positive good, the opponents of abolition saw any concession over the claim that slaves were property protected by the Constitution in the District as fatally weakening that argument as it pertained to the States. Neither side was prepared, or ideologically capable, of conceding ground to the other.

Between the two sides was a vast segment, probably the majority, of the population who saw no benefit at all to discussing the issue. Discussed more thoroughly in the next two chapters, this group contained the parts of the Democratic Party that would enter the 1836 presidential election committed to the Union and, as importantly, an effective cross-sectional partisan coalition. The growing significance and mobilization over the issue of slavery in the District of Columbia made the issue harder and harder to ignore. In Congress, that meant attempting to find a middle path through the demands of abolitionist sympathizers and proslavery fire-eaters that would have the effect of quieting the debate. In society outside of Congress, that meant finding a way to address the issue publicly that reassured Southern voters without alienating Northern voters. As we will see in the next two chapters, in attempting to do this, and at least temporarily succeeding in doing so, this middle segment would develop an understanding of the Constitution that countered the abolitionists' claim that Congress's power over the District was exclusive and unlimited. But the development of this understanding would be at the expense of the strict construction that the Democratic Party had believed itself to be the champion of under Jefferson and Jackson. The question of slavery in the District of Columbia would give rise to a conceptualization of constitutionality in which spirit played a transformed role.

7

The Congressional Crisis of 1836

What has happened here is enrolled already in the unchangeable records of time and eternity. *It is become history*. It cannot be recalled; it cannot be blotted from the memory; it cannot be expunged from the annals of the country.

Caleb Cushing (1836)[1]

The first session of the Twenty-Fourth Congress saw the tensions over slavery in the District of Columbia erupt on the floors of the House of Representatives and the Senate. In both chambers, the presentation of abolitionist petitions became a point of controversy and of congressional debate far beyond anything in the history of abolitionist congressional petitions up until that point.[2] In the House, the presentation of abolitionist petitions and contestation over their disposal grounded the petition process almost to a halt for nearly three months until the logjam was broken by the decision to refer all such petitions to a select committee on the subject of abolition. In the Senate, the debate over the

---

[1] *Register of Debates, 24th Congress, 1st Session*, 1836, 2323. Emphasis added.

[2] On the congressional debates arising from the petitioning campaign, cf. William W. Freehling, *The Road to Disunion: Volume 1, Secessionists at Bay 1776–1854* (New York: Oxford University Press, 1990), 308–36; William Lee Miller, *Arguing about Slavery: John Quincy Adams and the Great Battle in the United States Congress* (New York: Alfred A. Knopf, 1996); George C. Rable, "Slavery, Politics, and the South: The Gag Rule as a Case Study," *Capitol Studies* 3, no. Fall (1975): 69–87; David P. Currie, *The Constitution in Congress* (Chicago: The University of Chicago Press, 2005), 6–11; Robert P. Ludlum, "The Antislavery 'Gag-Rule': History and Argument," *The Journal of Negro History* 26, no. 2 (1941): 205–7; Daniel Wirls, "'The Only Mode of Avoiding Everlasting Debate': The Overlooked Senate Gag Rule for Antislavery Petitions," *Journal of the Early Republic* 27, no. 1 (2007): 115–38; Scott R. Meinke, "Slavery, Partisanship, and Procedure in the U.S. House: The Gag Rule, 1836–1845," *Legislative Studies Quarterly* 32, no. 1 (2007): 33–57. On petitioning as an antislavery tactic, cf. Richard S. Newman, *The Transformation of American Abolitionism: Fighting Slavery in the Early Republic* (Chapel Hill: The University of North Carolina Press, 2002).

presentation of the petitions – initiated in early January – was resolved in mid-March with a practice of tabling motions on the reception of each petition. Often depicted as a debate over free speech, the congressional debates over the petitions equally operated as a forum for discussing the relationship between slavery and the Constitution as it pertained to the District of Columbia. In the process of this discussion – and in its culmination in the House in the form of the Pinckney resolutions – a manner of thinking about the Constitution that privileged the spirit of compromise surrounding its composition was advanced. As actors in the Senate and House groped for a path around the polarizing and consuming issue of abolition, they moved away from reliance upon the text of the constitutional document and toward a constitutional spirit – embodied in the idea of "the compact" – as a way to navigate the apparent incompatibility of Southern and Northern understandings of the Constitution's guarantee of rights of property. In order to trace these discussions, the sections that follow sketch the process of the debates within each chamber before turning to a closer analysis of the constitutional issues raised by them. Finally, the chapter outlines the manner in which the invocation of "the compact" in the debates and in Pinckney's *Report* of May 1836 met the challenges of the abolitionist petitions and erected an understanding of constitutional faith that rested upon the reanimation of values deemed present in the debates of 1787–88.

7.1 THE DEBATE WITHIN THE HOUSE OF REPRESENTATIVES

The debate over abolitionist petitions in the Twenty-Fourth Congress (1835–37) was initiated in the House by the presentation of a petition from "sundry citizens of Massachusetts" by William Jackson (Massachusetts) on Friday, December 18, 1835.[3] Jackson's was not the first petition of the session, but it was immediately met with a motion from James H. Hammond (South Carolina) that it be rejected. Hammond sought an immediate rejection of the petition as a signal of its "impropriety" and to "put a more decided seal of reprobation" on abolitionist petitions generally.[4] He could not, said Hammond, "sit there, and see the rights of the South assailed, day after day, by ignorant fanatics."[5] In this, he was joined by Henry A. Wise (Virginia) who denied the right of Congress to interfere with slavery in the District and who urged a vote to reject the petition as a signal of that denial. The move of Hammond and its support by Wise transformed a routine disposal of

[3] *Register of Debates*, 1836, 1966.
[4] *Register of Debates*, 1836, 1966. Hammond had perhaps misunderstood the nature of the vote on December 16 to lay a motion to print a petition presented by John Fairfield (Maine) on the table as being a rejection of that petition. *Register of Debates*, 1836, 1963. However, Freehling suggests that personal ambition drove the motion. Freehling, *The Road to Disunion*, 310–19.
[5] *Register of Debates*, 1836, 1969.

abolitionist petitions into a hotly contested point of debate. Fearing the conflict that such a debate might give rise to, other members of the House sought to lay abolitionist petitions on the table – to "nail [them] to the counter, and thus silence debate" – a measure defeated that day but successfully prosecuted on December 21.[6]

However once raised and injected with political significance, the procedure for dealing with the petitions could not so easily be settled. John Quincy Adams pointed to the inconsistency of sending some petitions to the Committee on the District of Columbia (deemed the usual practice in such matters) where they "went to sleep the sleep of death" and tabling others.[7] With Hammond and Wise's demand for a decisive rejection of the petitions, and thus Congress's authority over slavery in the District, remaining unmet, Adams poured petrol on a smoldering fire by declaring that should they get the debate over slavery they sought, "every speech made by a Representative from north of the Mason and Dixon line, in this House, will be an incendiary pamphlet," a reference to the abolitionist literature that slaveholders were otherwise seeking to suppress.[8] Adams's statement resulted in further Southern calls for a decisive rejection of the "abusive petitions" and a clear statement of Congress's inability to act on slavery in the District of Columbia.[9]

Such a statement not forthcoming, the presentation of abolitionist petitions became a recurring point of contention until January 6, 1836, when Leonard Jarvis (Maine) offered a resolution that it was the opinion of the House that "the subject of the abolition of slavery in the District of Columbia ought not to be entertained by Congress ... [and that] it is the deliberate opinion of the House that [petitions praying for the abolition of slavery in the District] ought to be laid upon the table, without being referred or printed."[10] If Jarvis's aim was to end the debate over the petitions with a swift passage of the declaratory resolution, it failed. Instead of ending the debate over the petitions, Jarvis's resolution opened up a direct debate on the issue of congressional authority over slavery and the slave trade in the District of Columbia – a debate that by early February was touching upon questions of whether slavery was itself justifiable as an abstract idea and saw open threats of disunion should attempts be made at legislation upon the subject.[11]

It was against this backdrop that on February 4 Henry L. Pinckney offered a resolution that sought both to finesse the one offered by Jarvis and to give room for the House to proceed with other business. Pinckney's resolution read as follows:

[1] *Resolved*, That all the memorials which have been offered, or may hereafter be presented, to this House, praying for the abolition of slavery in the District of Columbia, and also the resolutions offered by an honorable member from Maine, with

---

[6] *Register of Debates*, 1836, 1980, 1987, 1996.   [7] *Register of Debates*, 1836, 2001.
[8] *Register of Debates*, 1836, 2002.   [9] *Register of Debates*, 1836, 2004, 2007.
[10] *Register of Debates*, 1836, 2135.   [11] *Register of Debates*, 1836, 2456.

the amendment thereto proposed by an honorable member from Virginia, and every other paper or proposition that may be submitted in relation to that subject, be referred to a select committee, [2] with instructions to report that Congress possesses no constitutional authority to interfere in any way with the institution of slavery in any of the States of this confederacy; [3] and that, in the opinion of this House, Congress ought not to interfere in any way with slavery in the District of Columbia, [4] because it would be a violation of the public faith, unwise, impolitic, and dangerous to the Union; [5] assigning such reasons for these conclusions as, in the judgment of the committee, may be best calculated to enlighten the public mind, to repress agitation, to allay excitement, to sustain and preserve the just rights of the slaveholding States and of the people of this District, and to re-establish harmony and tranquility amongst the various sections of the Union.[12]

Intended, in Pinckney's words, "for a decisive settlement of this question in the manner that I honestly think will best maintain the rights of the South and the peace and perpetuity of this Union," the resolution tried to incorporate Jarvis's rejection of a congressional power over slavery in the District of Columbia, Wise's desire for a substantive basis for that rejection, and the wider desire to deal with the petitions in a manner that would allow the House to proceed to other business.[13] Establishing a select committee with a specific remit to find against the petitions, the resolution bypassed the possibility of a report in favor of the petitions coming from the Committee for the District of Columbia as well as the constitutional concerns regarding the right to petition raised by a direct and immediate rejection of the petitions. Moreover, in passing responsibility to a select committee, the resolution moved the petitions from the floor of the House without individually voting on each, and delayed any reckoning on the issue of slavery in the District at least until a report was issued by the select committee. Although not immediately effective in this regard (see discussion of the votes subsequently), Pinckney's resolution ultimately worked to lessen the drama surrounding the issue such that it remained a peripheral issue between February 23 (when the disposal of subsequent petitions was determined to fall under the aegis of Pinckney's resolution) and May 18 (when the select committee, under the chairmanship of Pinckney, reported).

Pinckney's intervention came as the House was increasingly being divided into three distinct groupings by the issues arising from the presentation of the petitions, blocs which were themselves arranged around the sectional fault line of slavery.[14] In the first instance, a group making up just over a fifth of the 242

[12] *Register of Debates*, 1836, 2491–92. Numbers in parenthesis represent the five parts in which the resolution was broken down into for the purposes of voting on the resolution on February 8.

[13] *Register of Debates*, 1836, 2495.

[14] The following discussion examines the positions taken by Members of Congress within the debates over the petitions. Beyond and within the voting blocs discussed here were further factional calculations as to when and how to raise the issue as it related to the election of 1836. For discussion of the factional stakes, see Freehling, *The Road to Disunion*, 324–26, 331–36.

seats in the House expressed opposition to the notion that Congress had no power with regard to the regulation of slavery in the District of Columbia.[15] On February 8, 1836, the House voted on a resolution offered by Henry L. Pinckney which would go on to inform the work of the select committee created to respond to the petitions. To allow members to express support or opposition to distinct parts of the resolution, it was divided into five parts for the purposes of voting. The third of these five votes concerned the claim "that, in the opinion of this House, Congress ought not to interfere in any way with slavery in the District of Columbia." On this issue, the House divided 163–47 in favor of the clause.[16] A second vote on May 26, following the report of the select committee, supported the view "[t]hat Congress ought not to interfere, in any way, with slavery in the District of Columbia," by a vote of 132–45.[17] Fifty-six members of the House voted against the claim that Congress ought not to interfere with slavery in the District of Columbia on one or both of these occasions.[18] As might be expected, all fifty-six represented districts in nonslaveholding States. Every member of the Vermont, Rhode Island, and Massachusetts House delegations voted against the position that Congress ought not to interfere with slavery in the District of Columbia. Beyond these nineteen, other areas of abolitionist activity were represented among the fifty-six: seven of the Representatives hailed from Ohio, twelve from Pennsylvania, and ten from New York. Attitudes toward abolition varied within this group, extending from William Slade's advocacy of gradual abolition in the Capitol and the federal abolition of the slave trade between Southern States to John Quincy Adams's declaration that he was not personally in favor of the object of the petitions.[19] While no member of this Northern Slade-Adams bloc presented as an abolitionist per se, as a group they nonetheless represented the strongest critics of slavery within the House of Representatives debates in 1835–36.

A second grouping within the House comprised of those members who held out the hope of gaining a stronger counter to abolitionism than that offered in Pinckney's February resolution. A vote held on February 23 highlights this second bloc within the House of Representatives. This vote followed the successful adoption (on February 8) of Pinckney's resolution and the creation of

[15] Nonetheless, I label this group "skeptical" of such claims, as the bloc includes figures such as William Slade of Vermont whose views at this point in time are difficult to pin down. In December, Slade gave a speech in the House in which he stated, "The abolition of slavery which I would advocate is a gradual abolition." However, in a subsequent letter Slade made it clear that he believed that Congress could not interfere with ownership of slaves within the District, but could regulate or abolish the slave trade therein. *Register of Debates*, 1836, 2043, 4054.

[16] *Register of Debates*, 1836, 2500.   [17] *Register of Debates*, 1836, 4052.

[18] Six Representatives voted for the clause in February but reversed their position in May. The six with John Carr (Indiana), Joseph Henderson (Pennsylvania), Benjamin Jones (Ohio), Daniel Kilgore (Ohio), Amos Lane (Indiana), and Joshua Lee (New York). The remaining fifty voted consistently across both votes or were absent or did not vote on one or other occasion.

[19] *Register of Debates*, 1836, 2000, 2043, 4054.

a select committee to which "all the memorials which have been offered, or may hereafter be presented" on the subject of the abolition of slavery were to be directed.[20] The vote on February 23 concerned the question of whether a petition on abolition, presented after the adoption of the resolution, ought to be directed to the select committee. On February 15, George N. Briggs (of Massachusetts) presented a petition praying for the abolition of slavery in the District of Columbia.[21] It was immediately met with a demand to refuse its reception on the part of Wise. The Chair (future President James K. Polk) ruled that a motion offered by Wise to deny reception to the petition was in order. This reignited the debate over the petitions that Pinckney's resolution had been designed to suppress.[22] An appeal against the Chair's ruling was made and ultimately adjudicated on February 23 when the House voted to overrule the Chair by a majority of 147 against 56, establishing a practice of not allowing the question of reception to be raised upon the presentation of petitions and memorials regarding the subject of slavery in the District of Columbia.[23] The fifty-six can be understood here as resistant to the ending of debate over slavery in the District by the mechanism of referring the petitions to the select committee without debate. Of these fifty-six Representatives, eight – Timothy Childs (New York), Caleb Cushing (Massachusetts), William B. Calhoun (Massachusetts), Horace Everett (Vermont), Samuel Hoar (Massachusetts), Stephen C. Phillips (Massachusetts), David Potts, Jr. (Pennsylvania), and John Reed (Massachusetts) – had voted against the proposition that Congress ought not to interfere with slavery in the District of Columbia on February 8 and would do so again on May 26. As such it can be assumed that these eight Representatives desired to keep debate on slavery in the District alive with the hope of acting on the abolition of slavery or the slave trade in the ten miles square. The remaining forty-eight Representatives who voted in support of the Chair's ruling came from slaveholding States with four exceptions.[24] All forty-eight had taken the position of supporting parts of Pinckney's resolution asserting that the federal government ought not to interfere with slavery in the District and asserting the unconstitutionality of interference in slavery in the States or had adopted the even stronger position that the mere discussion of such powers was too great a concession to the powers of Congress.[25] As such these forty-eight

---

[20] *Register of Debates*, 1836, 2498.

[21] On the events of February 15, see *Register of Debates*, 1836, 2533–37.

[22] Mr. Manning of South Carolina stated as such during debate on February 23: "We hoped, by this resolution [Pinckney's], to stay debate, to prevent discussion, to keep down irritating, heart-burning invectives, and to unite Congress by a strong expression of its feeling and opinions, both as regards the States and the District of Columbia." *Register of Debates*, 1836, 2613.

[23] *Register of Debates*, 1836, 2620.

[24] Thomas L. Hamer (Ohio), George L. Kinnard (Indiana), Gorham Parks (Maine), and David Spangler (Ohio).

[25] See, for example, James H. Hammond's speech on February 8, 1836, stating that Pinckney's resolution is "abandoning the high, true, and only safe ground of our rights, to throw ourselves upon the expediency of this House." *Register of Debates*, 1836, 2495.

can be taken as a rough bloc of Representatives who sought a stronger statement against federal interference in slavery in the District and were willing to continue to differing degrees the discussion beyond Pinckney's resolution as approved on February 8.[26]

Between the fifth of the House of Representatives that were skeptical of claims that Congress could not interfere with slavery in the District and the fifth who sought a stronger counter to abolition in the District lay three-fifths of the House who believed that the issue was best avoided for the sake of the Union. This rump of the House comprised of those members who did not oppose the claim that "Congress ought not interfere in any way with slavery in the District of Columbia," and who also did not vote to block the transfer of subsequent petitions to the select committee on February 23. Given this definition is reliant upon the absence of two actions, it doubtlessly sweeps up individuals whose opinions were similar to either of the two groupings discussed previously but whose voting record did not completely reflect those positions.[27] Which is to say, that the rump was probably smaller than this broad characterization allows for – and, in actuality, the House was probably more divided than the raw vote tallies suggest.[28]

More significantly, however, was the fact that the rump itself was vulnerable to the same sectional polarization that divided the Hammond–Wise grouping from the Slade–Adams grouping. Represented in the figures of Leonard Jarvis and Henry L. Pinckney, the rump consisted of Northern and Southern parts with distinct views as to the risks presented by discussions of slavery in the District of Columbia. Jarvis advanced his resolution under the view that his Northern "constituents deprecated the agitation of this question. They consider

---

[26] Although the extent to which this bloc was united as to how that should occur is unclear – twenty-three of the forty-eight would ultimately vote in favor of the third of Pinckney's resolutions on May 26, 1836, to the effect that all petitions should be laid upon the table without debate or further action.

[27] Eighteen members had voted on either February 8 or May 26 (or both) for the idea the Congress ought not interfere in any way with slavery in the District but did not vote either way on February 23. As such they are counted within this middle group, but could well be more sympathetic to a stronger statement against interference than Pinckney's – absent their vote it would be unwise to too strongly ascribe to them a desire to end debate on this topic. Other members – seven in total – did not participate in any of the three votes, again placing them within this middle group, but it would be dangerous to read too much meaning into these missed votes.

[28] Six sitting members do not leave enough of a voting record to be positively located within one of the three groups. Of these six, two gave speeches that suggest they were among the Hammond–Wise grouping. Balie Peyton of Tennessee made a speech on January 19, 1835, stating that he regarded attempts to "baffle" the question of slavery in the District as an evasion that Southern members should resist. *Register of Debates*, 1836, 2224. In a similar way, Francis W. Pickens of South Carolina did not vote on any of the three occasions but gave a speech on January 21 in which he disclaimed any congressional power to interfere with slavery in the District and dismissed the Declaration of Independence's claim that "all men are created equal" as merely an "abstract truth" and "a doctrine of universal discord, confusion, and ruin" when applied to actual societies. *Register of Debates*, 1836, 2249.

it belongs exclusively to the southern States."[29] Jarvis's position reflected the views of Northern politicians who feared that the "agitation" of the abolitionists was putting the Union at risk and who sought to avoid further discussion of slavery as an acceptable price for preservation of the ties between North and South. Typified in Abijah Mann Jr.'s (New York) condemnation of the "few misguided men in the North," this group sought to reassure Southern politicians that there was not an extensive constituency for abolitionism in the North.[30] The South Carolinian Pinckney shared Jarvis's concern for national unity but also feared that Northern support for the South's peculiar institution of slavery was less robust than some in the South believed. Avowing his own rejection of a congressional power to interfere with slavery in the District of Columbia, Pinckney nonetheless believed that pressing the issue in the form of seeking a resolution to that effect would result in a defeat for the South on the floor of the House: "The South would be beaten, as it had been in the Senate on the question of reception."[31] Believing that it must be Northern politicians who defeated abolition, he decried the pressure for a vote on "abstract points," which would serve to "increase abolition, and drive our supporters from the field."[32] Others within the Southern delegation thought similarly, with Thomas Glascock (Georgia) conceding that while he believed interference with slavery in the District to be unconstitutional, "he knew several who would vote against any resolution declaring it unconstitutional ... but who would go heart and hand with the southern members against any such interference."[33] Better in this instance to forego the constitutional question and keep the congressional rump united – to force the issue might have seen a desertion of the Northern wing of the majority.

However, Pinckney's hesitation to offer a robust constitutional defense of slavery in the District of Columbia left him open to bitter attack from his Southern colleagues and an accompanying call for the South to stand united in a robust defense of slavery. Henry Wise was called to order after attacking Pinckney's actions as "treason to the South" and claiming to have "hissed him as a deserter from the principles of the South."[34] During the debates, Southern Representatives suggested that attempts to evade discussion of slavery were motivated by electoral considerations. Claiming that it suited leaders of the Democratic Party, and, in particular, Martin Van Buren, to suppress debates around slavery, members implied that the interests of the South were playing second fiddle to electoral expediency.[35] Upon the presentation of the select committee's report in May, John Robertson (Virginia) accused the

---

[29] *Register of Debates*, 1836, 2135.   [30] *Register of Debates*, 1836, 2019.
[31] *Register of Debates*, 1836, 3776.   [32] *Register of Debates*, 1836, 2495.
[33] *Register of Debates*, 1836, 2138.
[34] *Register of Debates*, 1836, 2534–35. Wise's antipathy perhaps reflected his position as an opponent of the Jacksonian Democrats as well as the particular policy Pinckney was pursuing. Freehling, *The Road to Disunion*, 332–33.
[35] *Register of Debates*, 1836, 2224.

committee of not having even attempted to locate a constitutional ground for opposing the petitions and instead having brought "a cargo of Albany notions" to the House.[36] For Hammond, Wise, and others, anything less than a constitutional basis for the noninterference of slavery in the District was a concession too far. In their view, only a constitutional prohibition on interference with slavery in the District would provide the timeless and definitive counter necessary to avoid abolitionist pressure.[37] Pinckney sought to chart a course between addressing the pressure for a robust defense of slavery in the District that threatened to peel Southern members from the rump and the fear that pressing for the rejection of the petitions might result in the unification of the North around the sanctity of the right to petition.[38] Pinckney's resolution and subsequent report was designed to hold together the cross-sectional rump and avoid a division of the House on sectional lines. It was against this backdrop that the debates on the floor of the House came to center upon the Pinckney resolution and subsequently upon the select committee report arising from them. And given these pressures, the subtext of the debates became the question of whether the House would condemn interference with slavery in the District of Columbia on constitutional or other grounds.

7.2 THE DEBATE WITHIN THE SENATE

The debate within the Senate followed such a similar path to that in the House that it is not necessary here to discuss it separately at length. However, there were some differences in its trajectory that make it worthwhile providing a brief account as a precursor to discussing the constitutional issues raised in Congress as a whole.

The debate over petitions in the Senate began in earnest in the Twenty-Fourth Congress a few weeks after that in the House, but was initiated in a proximate manner. On Thursday, January 7, Senator Thomas Morris of Ohio presented two petitions from that State praying for the abolition of slavery by Congress. Upon their presentation, Senator John C. Calhoun of South Carolina demanded they be read and then that a vote be taken on their reception.[39] His justifications for demanding a vote on reception of the petitions echoed those of his (close) colleague from South Carolina in the House (Hammond), with Calhoun denouncing the petitions as "a foul slander on nearly half of the States of the Union" and arguing that they prayed for "what was a violation of the constitution."[40] In contrast to the House, however, the immediate response to the move to not receive the petitions was to assess whether they raised an unconstitutional demand rather than to directly debate the constitutional

---

[36] An allusion to the Albany Regency, the New York political machine associated with Martin Van Buren.

[37] *Register of Debates*, 1836, 2026.   [38] *Register of Debates*, 1836, 2494.

[39] *Register of Debates*, 1836, 72–73.   [40] *Register of Debates*, 1836, 73.

right of petition. As a consequence of this, the debate over the petitions in the Senate placed more emphasis upon the constitutionality of the request to interfere with slavery in the District of Columbia.

Unlike the House, the impasse over the petitions in the Senate was broken not by reference to select committee but initially by a vote to receive an abolitionist petition followed by a vote to reject its prayer.[41] Subsequently, the Senate developed a *modus operandi* of tabling motions to reject the petitions thus avoiding having to directly vote upon receiving the petitions.[42] Nevertheless, it still took two months for the Senate to navigate the tensions in the chamber to reach that stage. It was not until March 9 that the initial vote was held on reception of the petition. The two votes – one to receive the petition and one to reject the prayer of the petition – indicate that similar alignments around the issue of slavery in the District of Columbia were present in the Senate as those seen in the House of Representatives. The first vote, on March 9, 1836, saw a division of the Senate on the question "Shall the petition be received?" with thirty-six votes in the affirmative and ten against. The ten votes against receiving the petition all came from the South, with both Senators from South Carolina, Mississippi, and Louisiana, being joined by one each from Alabama, Georgia, Tennessee, and Virginia.[43] In the second vote to reject the prayer of the petition the Senate split thirty-four yeas against six nays. The six were Samuel Prentiss and Benjamin Swift of Vermont, Daniel Webster and John Davis of Massachusetts, William Hendricks of Indiana, and Nehemiah R. Knight of Rhode Island. On the basis of these votes, the Senate seemed to be divided with approximately a quarter of the Senate committed to not receiving abolitionist petitions and a smaller faction committed to the idea that Congress ought to consider interference in slavery in the District of Columbia. As in the House of Representatives, between these two groups lay a rump of the chamber that wished to avoid the discussion for the sake of the Union. Within this group, opinions as to slavery varied from Thomas Ewing of Ohio's belief that "it a great evil in any community" to Felix Grundy of Tennessee's view that slavery rendered greater benefits to the slaves than the Northern wage system did to its poor.[44]

After these initial divisions over the issue of the petitions, the Senate moved to avoid further discussions. On March 16, Daniel Webster introduced further

---

[41] *Register of Debates*, 1836, 779, 810.   [42] *Register of Debates*, 1836, 838.

[43] Willie P. Magnum of North Carolina missed the vote but at a subsequent debate expressed a desire to vote to reject the petitions. *Register of Debates*, 1836, 835. Only one Senator – Benjamin W. Leigh – represented Virginia at the time of the vote: John Tyler had resigned on February 29 and his replacement, William C. Rives, took his seat on March 14. Tyler expressed the opinion in debate that the petitions should be referred to the Committee for the District of Columbia. *Register of Debates*, 1836, 89. In the previous Congress, Tyler had proposed penal reform within the District with the hope of ending slave trading therein. *Register of Debates*, *23rd Congress, 2nd Session*, 1835, 456.

[44] *Register of Debates*, 1836, 763, 754.

petitions along with Thomas Ewing, Benjamin Swift, and other Senators from the Mid-Atlantic States. In presenting these petitions, Webster claimed that – the previous months of debate apparently notwithstanding – "the unanimous opinion of the North is, that Congress has no authority over slavery in the States; and perhaps equally unanimous that over slavery in the District it has such rightful authority."[45] The newly arrived Senator from Virginia, William C. Rives, requested that the motion to not receive the petitions be laid upon the table until he could acquaint himself with the previous debates on the topic and the suggestions of his Southern colleagues as to the best approach.[46] The motion was never returned to, relieving the Senate of the need to debate and vote upon the reception of the petitions. Thus was the practice initiated of lying motions to receive the petitions regarding slavery in the District on the table, a practice extended over the session to incorporate petitions on slavery in the new Arkansas constitution.[47] As such, the Senate, unlike the House, avoided the need to openly debate its manner of disposing of the petitions. It never produced an equivalent of Pinckney's Report in the first session of the Twenty-Fourth Congress, even though both chambers ended up with approximately the same mode of dealing with abolitionist petitions.

7.3 THE CONGRESSIONAL DEBATE OVER SLAVERY IN THE DISTRICT OF COLUMBIA BEFORE THE TWENTY-FOURTH CONGRESS

The presentation of abolitionist petitions concerned with slavery in the District in the Twenty-Fourth Congress was not without precedent. Seven years earlier, the Twentieth Congress had seen the constitutional questions raised by abolition in the District brought into focus, if not resolved. As noted in the previous chapter, in 1829 the Representative from Pennsylvania, Charles Miner, requested that the House of Representatives consider a gradual plan of abolition for the District.[48] The House accepted Miner's resolutions calling for a review of slavery in the District of Columbia and such amendments to the laws as were deemed necessary (120 to 59), but instructed the relevant Committee "to inquire into the expediency of providing by law for the gradual abolition of slavery within the District, in such a manner that the interests of no individual shall be injured thereby" (114 to 66).[49] Miner's extensive preamble detailing the corruptions that any review might be expected to address and noting the

---

[45] *Register of Debates*, 1836, 834.   [46] *Register of Debates*, 1836, 836.
[47] *Register of Debates*, 1836, 1134–35, 1277.
[48] *Speech of Mr. Miner, Of Pennsylvania, Delivered in the House of Representatives. On Tuesday and Wednesday, January 6 and 7, 1829, On the Subject of Slavery and the Slave Trade in the District of Columbia.* (Washington, DC: Giles & Seaton, 1829).
[49] *Register of Debates, 20th Congress, 2nd Session,* 1829, 192. The commitment to gradual abolition and the provision that no interests should be injured made this resolution far less radical in reality than the apparent willingness to countenance an end to slavery suggests.

constitutional power of Congress to act against them was struck down with 37 votes in favor and 141 opposed.[50] Miner's speech gave occasion to a defense of slavery by John C. Weems of Maryland, himself a slaveholder with a self-confessed involvement in slave trading in the District, in which he defended slavery on biblical grounds, as "justified by the Almighty, and practiced by Abraham."[51] In the course of his speech, Weems also sketched out the lines of argument that would be deployed against the petitions in the Twenty-Fourth Congress.

Weems offered two main lines of argument for rejecting the claim that Congress could interfere with slavery in the District in 1829, both of which would be taken up in 1835–36 in expanded form as constitutional arguments. Drawing upon his belief in the sacred sanction of slavery, Weems argued against the idea of interference with the property rights of slaveholders. Resting the justification of ownership of others upon "both sacred and profane history," Weems attested to the "right of property in the human family, purchased with our money" and rejected the possibility that slaves held any claim to equality with the free white population.[52] Highlighting the racial prejudice that he attributed to the society around him – "negroes and mulattoes are not considered or treated as citizens – hardly as men" – Weems argued that slavery was a natural state and one recognized by the founding fathers:

I am now, sir, by promise to prove my right by every dispensation from God to man, to hold my fellow man as property – such as our worthy ancestors, framers of our constitution, considered them, when, in the declaration of rights, they are found to declare "all men to be born free and equal," all citizens of every country; masters as they were of thousands that were born and held in slavery. Had they an eye at all to slaves when they signed that instrument, they would have been hypocrites, altogether unworthy of being commemorated, nay, idolized, as they are by patriots, or others, honest men.[53]

Weems's claim here comes down decidedly upon the side of slaves as property rather than as persons. Avoiding charges of hypocrisy against the framers (and, by extension, himself) by embracing an exclusionary reading of the Declaration, Weems both protected slavery as a property relationship and located it within the series of considerations informing the founding. Weems did not take the step of claiming that ownership of slaves is sanctioned by or protected by the Constitution, instead being content to establish the historical precedent of property in other humans and showing it to be an established American practice. Nonetheless, in framing abolition of slavery as a question of the legitimacy of claims to own others, Weems located the issue of slavery in the

---

[50] *Register of Debates*, 1829, 192.
[51] *Register of Debates*, 1829, 185. Weems dismissed the "old hackneyed argument" that the Gospel's golden rule ("to do unto others as we would they should do unto us") revisited God's sanction of the early Israelites' practice of slavery.
[52] *Register of Debates*, 1829, 184.   [53] *Register of Debates*, 1829, 187, 184.

District of Columbia within discussions connected to the sanctity of property, a point that would be vital in 1835–36.

Drawing upon this foundation, Weems's second significant line of argument, briefly touched on at the end of his speech, rested upon the understandings held by Maryland and Virginia at the time of their cession of the territory that became the District of Columbia. Given the position occupied earlier – that slaves were property and that this relationship was wisely recognized at the time of the Founding – Weems argued that Maryland and Virginia could not have been understood to have envisioned emancipation at the time of cession. Linking this belief to fears of the consequences for the States should abolition take place within the District, Weems suggested that the States would have refused to cede the ten miles square had they believed that Congress would have considered emancipation of the slaves therein.[54] Once again not pursuing this line of argument to the point of a constitutional prohibition upon interference with slavery in the District of Columbia, Weems offered a basis for the arguments later offered in the Twenty-Fourth Congress that the nature of the cession created constitutional restraints.

Miner's resolutions, referred to the Committee for the District of Columbia, resulted in a report three weeks later rejecting the idea of abolition.[55] A scant four pages, excluding appendices, the Report concluded that "it is better not to disturb [slavery in the District], but leave it, where it now rests, with the laws, and the humanity of those who are interested in protecting and taking care of this species of property" (4).[56] In reaching this conclusion, the Report's author, Mark Alexander of Virginia, examined the constitutional questions raised by the prospect of abolition to an extent not undertaken by Weems but without reaching a definitive conclusion. Developing two strands of Weems's defense, Alexander noted the Constitution's vesting of exclusive power of legislation over the District in Congress, but also that it was "equally true that the rights of property were secured to the citizens by the laws and Constitutions of Virginia and Maryland, which deserve at least to be respected, if not held sacred, by the Legislature of the Union" (3). Without resolving that apparent tension, Alexander moved to note that the "exclusive power" of Congress over the District could not be understood to be a "greater power than is consistent with the general principles of the Constitution of the United States" (3). Such power ought to be wielded within "constitutional limitations," and it could, therefore, be supposed that within ceded territory it was not

---

[54] *Register of Debates*, 1829, 187.

[55] "Report of the Committee for the District of Columbia, in Pursuance of Certain Resolutions of the House of the 9th of January, Memorials, &c. to Them Referred, Respecting Slavery with the Said District" (Washington, DC, 1829). [Hereafter, "Alexander Report."]

[56] However, the Report did recommend measures to restrict the migration of free blacks into the District.

within the contemplation of the framers of the Constitution, nor is it within the spirit of that instrument to vest Congress with the power of prescribing rules by which property may be held, or the manner of its descent, different from that existing in the respective States. (3)

Alexander was thinking here of States surrendering territory for the purposes of erecting federal forts, magazines, and dockyards – he seemed unsure of applying this same logic to the District, clarifying that the committee "do not mean to say that Congress cannot change the rights of persons and of things within this District. ... But they mean to say, these cannot be abridged or taken away, independent of the consent of the People, without doing violence to the Constitution" (3). Arriving at this point – that the consent of the people of the District was necessary for changes in "the whole relations of society" to be undertaken constitutionally – Alexander could claim an implied constitutional prohibition on abolition at that moment (3). But this conclusion did not seem to arise directly from the premises he began with – the constitutional questions raised by the cession did not result in the need for democratic accountability, which, in turn, said nothing with regard to the issue of the actual reach of Congress's exclusive power of legislation. In this sense, the Report had worked to identify the crucial constitutional questions raised indirectly in Weems's speech – whether constitutional protections of property extended to ownership of slaves and whether such protections operated to constrain congressional authority in the District – but offered little light as to how to resolve them.

In the following sessions of Congress, these constitutional questions were not seriously grappled with again until 1835–36. In 1832, the House Committee for the District of Columbia rejected the prayers of abolitionist petitions with a three-paragraph "Report" concluding that it was an "inauspicious moment" to consider abolition in the District.[57] During the first session of Twenty-Third Congress in 1834, Ezekiel F. Chambers as Chair for the Senate Committee for the District of Columbia welcomed the reference of petitions to his committee in the confidence that "they would be productive of very little trouble" as he was pre-committed to finding them "misinformed as to the actual condition of the District."[58] In the following session in the House of Representatives, John Dickson of New York sought to open up a debate on the topic by addressing the 1829 arguments of John C. Weems and those of the Report of Mark Alexander. Presenting a petition from "ladies of the city of New-York" disclaiming the ability to interfere with slavery in the States but urging abolition in the District, Dickson joined them in seeking congressional action in the nation's capital. Citing Weems's view of the Declaration of Independence as not applying to slaves, Dickson reflected upon the intentions of the framers to draw the opposite conclusion:

---

[57] *Register of Debates, 22nd Congress, 1st Session,* 1832, 1442.
[58] *Register of Debates, 23rd Congress, 1st Session,* 1834, 198.

The wise framers of the Declaration of Independence, and the founders of this Republic, in accordance with the doctrines of heathen poetry and heathen philosophy, of the Scriptures, and of Revelation itself, in that immortal instrument, the enduring monument of their wisdom, proclaimed to an admiring world, as "self-evident, that all men are created equal, that they are endowed by their Creator with certain inalienable rights, that among these are life, liberty, and the pursuit of happiness." Did they mean slaves? Can any one doubt that they did? They spoke of man not as black, or white, but as embracing the entire species, all colors and all complexions.[59]

Proceeding from the assumption that slaves were men, not property, Dickson illustrated the ways in which laws in the District infringed citizenship and undermined claims that the nation was a republic. Avoiding discussion of property rights, the Representative from New York instead urged Congress to exercise its power to "render [the land] lovely" and to ensure that every man "no matter what complexion incompatible with freedom an Indian or an African sun may have burnt upon him ... stands redeemed, regenerated, and disenthralled, by the genius of universal emancipation" within the District.

Dickson addressed with equal directness the question of Congress's constitutional authority to undertake abolition in the District of Columbia. He argued that Congress had the power to abolish slavery in the District under Article 1, Section 8 of the Constitution, which granted power to Congress "to exercise exclusive legislation, in all cases whatsoever" over the District.[60] Dickson asserted Congress's power in the District to be "undefined, unlimited, and absolute, or it has no foundation and no existence." Equivalent to the power that State legislatures exercised within their respective States, Congress's power over the District matched the power "universally conceded to every state legislature to abolish slavery and the slave-trade within its own territory." There was, said Dickson, no connection between the fate of slavery in the States and abolition in the District. Furthermore, Dickson cited evidence of support for abolition among the population of the District. To his mind, the prayer of the petitioners was "reasonable; in accordance with the nature of man, and founded on the principles of eternal justice." Such arguments generated no further discussion of the issue, however. His prayer and the petition were met with a swift vote of 117–77 to lay the "whole subject on the table."[61]

7.4   THE DEBATE OVER SLAVERY IN THE DISTRICT OF COLUMBIA IN THE TWENTY-FOURTH CONGRESS

Between them, the debates of 1829 and the speech of Dickson in 1835 laid out the major points of the constitutional debate that followed the presentation of

---

[59] "Ladies' Petition," *The Emancipator*, February 24, 1835. Quotations from this speech are taken from *The Emancipator*'s reprinting of it. For the records contained within the *Register of Debates*, see *Register of Debates*, 1835, 1131–41.

[60] "Ladies' Petition."   [61] "Ladies' Petition"; *Register of Debates*, 1835.

petitions in the Twenty-Fourth Congress. Running through the debates over slavery in the District of Columbia was the question of whether slaves were people or property. Politicians sympathetic to the prayer of the petitions relied upon the Constitution's grant of power over the District of Columbia to Congress and the broader claims of equality contained within the Declaration of Independence to argue that abolition was constitutional and even desirable. Against them, proponents of slavery in the District laid stress on the restrictions upon Congress's power over property contained within the takings clause of the Fifth Amendment and deemed property foundational to the federal government.[62] Between these two groups lay the rump of Congress who wished to avoid discussion of this topic. In attempting to foreclose debate while avoiding the question of slaves' humanity, this group urged a recurrence to the values of compromise that they ascribed to the Constitution and the period of its creation.

The arguments offered in Congress in favor of a power to abolish slavery in the District of Columbia echoed the arguments for a textual reading of the Constitution informed by the commitments of the Declaration of Independence that had been developing within abolitionist circles since at least the previous decade. The supporters of the prayers of the petitions were careful throughout the debates to state that they had no imagination that Congress could interfere with slavery in the States. They also cleaved closely to the argument that the debates were really about the right to petition, attempting at least initially to avoid extended discussions on the constitutionality of abolition in the District. However, at different moments they did engage this topic, often under the guise of a disinterested concern for candor in "the expression of our real opinions on this question."[63] When they did so, the supporters of the prayers of the petitions read the Constitution as providing Congress with an exclusive power of legislation with regard to the District, one which included the ability to abolish slavery there. Echoing the text-focused interpretation of the Constitution under which abolitionists had mobilized to petition Congress, these politicians argued – as Dickson had in 1835 – that the powers granted under Article 1, Section 8 to "exercise exclusive legislation in all cases whatsoever" over the District of Columbia included abolition. For those sympathetic to abolition, this clause with its use of "exclusive" and "all cases whatsoever" provided unassailable support for the view that Congress could operate as the equivalent of a State government with regard to the District. Indeed, it was this view – that "Congress has primary and exclusive legislation over this District" – that informed Senator Morris's presentation of the petitions that drew Calhoun's ire.[64]

---

[62] The takings clause refers to the constitutional restriction on the taking of private property for public use without just compensation.

[63] *Register of Debates*, 1836, 670.   [64] *Register of Debates*, 1836, 74.

Believing that their constitutional claim was directly supported by the constitutional text, this group did not expound at length on constitutional theory or enter into complex readings of the Acts of cession. Instead, they laid stress upon a faith in the people themselves to read the constitutional document and reach the same conclusions as they did. Asserting the textual nature of their argument in this way, they both suggested the simplicity and thus honesty of their position and raised the specter of widespread popular support for the position in the North. In the House of Representatives, Samuel Hoar judged the language of the document "as comprehensive, as plain, as unambiguous, as any which could have been used to confer the power in question."[65] Linking this to Northern understandings with regard to abolition at the time of the Constitution's creation, he maintained that "it was clearly and fully believed, and indeed was doubted by no one, that language no more plain and explicit than the clause now under consideration did confer the power on the several Legislatures to abolish slavery."[66] Caleb Cushing placed his faith in the people to "look into any of the clauses of the constitution" and reach a decision that was "just, true, and patriotic."[67] He challenged that the proponents of slavery were afraid of such scrutiny in this instance: "Do they shrink from a fair and full examination of its merits and demerits?"[68] Senator Prentiss urged that the "people should not be blinded upon this subject, any more than upon any other."[69] In the House, William Slade believed that the "spirit of free inquiry" would result in the destruction of slavery.[70] As evidence of the apparent obviousness of this reading of the clause, the supporters of the petitions pointed to an allegedly widespread agreement on this point in the North. Senator Swift of Vermont claimed that "a very considerable portion" of his State agreed with the petitioners that "Congress [had the] power to abolish slavery within the District."[71] Senator Davis of Massachusetts advised that it would be "folly ... to disguise the fact that a vast majority of the people of the free States" viewed Congress as possessing a constitutional power to interfere with slavery in the District.[72] His Massachusetts colleague, Senator Daniel Webster, went further in believing it to be the "unanimous" opinion of the North that Congress possessed such authority.[73]

Allied to this argument was an attempt to frame the Declaration of Independence's recognition that "all men are created equal" as an American incarnation of a universal truth. The supporters of the petitions' prayers sought to identify the South as an outlier among a growing international consensus that slavery was manifestly wrong and a denial of the enslaved's humanity. Prentiss described the "opinion of all Christendom, the opinion of the civilized world,

[65] *Register of Debates*, 1836, 2254.   [66] *Register of Debates*, 1836, 2256.
[67] *Register of Debates*, 1836, 2331.   [68] *Register of Debates*, 1836, 2331.
[69] *Register of Debates*, 1836, 670.   [70] *Register of Debates*, 1836, 2061–62.
[71] *Register of Debates*, 1836, 301.   [72] *Register of Debates*, 1836, 807.
[73] *Register of Debates*, 1836, 834.

[as] becoming uniform and settled on the general subject of slavery."[74] In the House of Representatives, William Slade offered a panegyric on the "march of liberal principles" and reasoned that this march must end with "the great truth that 'all men are created equal'" and the abolition of slavery.[75] Much to the chagrin of the proponents of slavery, this group was joined by other Northern politicians – and, more distressingly, by some from slaveholding States – in viewing slavery as an evil.[76] The treatment of slavery as an anomaly requiring correction mapped onto the broader aim of the abolitionists to recognize the humanity of the slaves and to reject their treatment as property. Prentiss brought these several strands together in arguing that the "right of property in the persons of slaves is not the same, either in nature or extent, as the right of property acquired in things having a natural existence."[77] On this basis, he reasoned that Congress held the power to abolish slavery in the District without concerns over constitutional restraints on taking property.

Prentiss's concern to argue that slaves were not property in the sense of property "having a natural existence" addressed a central argument of the proponents of slavery in the District. Running through the arguments opposing congressional interference with slavery in the District was a commitment to the idea that slaves were property like any other. Within the immediate debates, this judgment was a crucial one insofar as slaveholders and their supporters argued that Congress's exclusive legislative power over the District was constrained by the Fifth Amendment prohibition "nor shall private property be taken for public use, without just compensation." Reasoning that slaves were property, supporters of slavery in the District argued that Congress could only "take" them for public use and with just compensation. In the Senate it fell to Calhoun to make the strongest articulation of this position:

The fifth amendment of the constitution offers an insuperable barrier, which provides, among other things, that "no person shall be deprived of life, liberty, or property, without due process of law; nor shall private property be taken for public uses without just compensation." Are not slaves property? and if so, how can Congress any more take away the property of a master in his slave, in this District, than it could his life and liberty? They stand on the same ground. The one, in the eye of the constitution, is as sacred as the other.[78]

Senator John P. King of Georgia concurred with Calhoun in arguing that the Fifth Amendment extended in reach to the States themselves such that the "States themselves had no power to take the slave from the owner, except for public use, and for a just compensation."[79] Senator Robert J. Walker of

---

[74] *Register of Debates*, 1836, 671.   [75] *Register of Debates*, 1836, 2062.
[76] For examples see the speeches of Senators Tallmadge (New York), Ewing (Ohio), and Clay (Kentucky). *Register of Debates*, 1836, 507, 651, 763, 786.
[77] *Register of Debates*, 1836, 669.   [78] *Register of Debates*, 1836, 97.
[79] *Register of Debates*, 1836, 481.

Mississippi focused upon the Fifth Amendment's requirement of "public use" in arguing that, "[t]o liberate the slaves of this District, even with compensation, would be equally a violation of the constitution; for, to liberate them, is not to take them for the use of the public."[80] Senator Benjamin Leigh (Virginia) agreed that abolition could not be understood as taking for "public use."[81]

Moving beyond this position, some proponents of slavery argued that any and all attempts to interfere with property in slaves went beyond the powers granted to Congress by the Constitution. For Senator Alexander Porter of Louisiana:

> The constitution was established, not merely in spirit, but in letter, in reference to this great interest of the South. The right to property which the petitioners sought to impair was recognised by that instrument.[82]

Senator Gabriel Moore of Alabama "was glad to know this property was secured and guarantied not only to the citizens of the District of Columbia, but to the citizens of all the slaveholding States by that sacred instrument, the constitution of the land, which we were all sworn to support."[83] Senator William C. Preston of South Carolina asked the Senate to "say, in language express and distinct, that this Government neither will nor can interfere with the constitutional rights of the slaveholder."[84] These rights reflected the fact that "the Government has the same power over this District that it has over a State, and it has no more."[85] Arguing that it was necessary and intended that members of Congress bring their property securely into the ten miles square, the Tennessee Senator Hugh Lawson White declared the "right of property in slaves in the States ... sacred, and beyond the power of Congress to interfere with, in any respect," thus rendering attempts at abolition in the District unconstitutional by extension.[86] A second variety of this argument suggested that such power was not included within the scope of Maryland's and Virginia's Acts of cession. For Leigh, Congress could only be understood to have "exclusive" legislative power in the sense of ordinary legislative authority. As such, Leigh argued that as Maryland and Virginia lacked the ability to abolish "slave property" under their own constitutions, it could not have been the case that such a power was constitutionally transferred to Congress by the cession.[87] Senator John Black of Mississippi similarly relied upon the cession in establishing a constitutional block to interference with slavery in the District.[88]

In the House of Representatives, the leaders of the opposition to the abolitionist petitions assumed a property in slavery but eschewed narrow arguments as to the constitutionally acceptable extent of congressional power over slave property in the District. Instead, they pushed back against the notion

---

[80] *Register of Debates, 1836,* 694.   [81] *Register of Debates, 1836,* 786.
[82] *Register of Debates, 1836,* 74–75.   [83] *Register of Debates, 1836,* 473.
[84] *Register of Debates, 1836,* 79.   [85] *Register of Debates, 1836,* 81.
[86] *Register of Debates, 1836,* 700.   [87] *Register of Debates, 1836,* 191–93.
[88] *Register of Debates, 1836,* 647.

that Congress could exercise power over property in slaves per se. Wise touched upon the Fifth Amendment argument but was more exercised by the existential threat he perceived in legislating abolition for the District.[89] Hammond cited it along with the recognition of slaves as property in the Constitution as evidence that abolition in the District of Columbia was "a violation of the letter and the whole spirit of the constitution."[90] But both Wise and Hammond seemed more concerned about abolition in the District as an indicator of the fate of slavery generally than as a question of congressional authority. Wise argued that it was a violation of the Fugitive Slave clause to push abolition in the District: "Admit this construction of unlimited legislation over the District, and it is plain and obvious that every fugitive slave, at least from the States ... will be free too soon for the safety of this Government."[91] The consequence would be that "[t]he faith, the compromise, the guarantee, the constitution, which our fathers pledged and made with each other, will be gone forever."[92] Hammond suggested that the moment the House legislated upon the subject "it dissolves the Union ... A revolution must ensue, and this republic sink in blood."[93] Hammond disputed the premise that slavery was an evil to be interfered with, stating that slavery "is no evil. On the contrary, I believe it to be the greatest of all blessings which a kind Providence has bestowed upon our glorious region."[94]

Other arguments against the prayer of the petitioners in the House made similar recourse to the position that slaves were not a distinct class of property. James W. Bouldin (Virginia) denied that the Constitution differentiated between property in slaves and property of other types, asking, "Can, then, the constitutionality of the proposed abolition be sustained, without showing a distinction between the property a man holds in a slave, and that which he holds in lands or horses? It surely cannot."[95] Any concession on this issue, Bouldin avowed, would "come at last to this point – that the property in a negro slave is no property at all."[96] If this came to be the case, then the Constitution held little value to the South. James Garland of Virginia held that "In relation to slaves, the constitution regards them as property, and guaranties its security."[97] Any interference in this right would be "a faithless violation of the federal compact, and utter disregard of the duties which you owe to it."[98] Francis Pickens (South Carolina) pointed to the recognition of slaves as private property in the Constitution while denying that such rights arose from the Constitution, declaring that property rights in slaves were held as "original rights, before and above the constitution."[99] The broad position taken by all these strands of the proslavery response was that slaves were property under the

---

[89] *Register of Debates*, 1836, 2024–27.   [90] *Register of Debates*, 1836, 2449.
[91] *Register of Debates*, 1836, 2028.   [92] *Register of Debates*, 1836, 2028.
[93] *Register of Debates*, 1836, 2456.   [94] *Register of Debates*, 1836, 2456.
[95] *Register of Debates*, 1836, 2224–25.   [96] *Register of Debates*, 1836, 2226.
[97] *Register of Debates*, 1836, 2071.   [98] *Register of Debates*, 1836, 2064.
[99] *Register of Debates*, 1836, 2246.

Constitution and so Congressional interference with slavery in the District of Columbia was unconstitutional.

Using property claims as the grounding of their opposition to the petitions held several significant consequences, however. In pitting a claim that slaves were property under the Constitution against the petitioners' view of slaves as human, the opponents of interference in the District ensured that the conflict between the two groups became tied at a fundamental level to the compromises embodied within the three-fifths clause of the Constitution. The question, left unresolved in 1787, over whether the enslaved were people or property under the Constitution was the core issue between those avowedly in favor of regulating slavery in the District and those avowedly opposed to it. This, in turn, had important implications for the debate. In the first instance, it left open three possible outcomes for the debate – an acceptance that slaves were people and an implicit rejection of slavery as an institution, an acceptance that slaves were property and an implicit rejection of their personhood, or a renewal of the compromises that had previously avoided an adjudication of this point. The second implication, arising from the first, was that a definitive constitutional resolution of the debate over slavery in the District would involve a division over the question of the personhood of slaves, a division that would likely be along sectional lines. As a consequence, for those members of Congress who valued union over the resolution of issues arising in association with slavery, some form of compromise that avoided a vote on the general question of property in slaves was the most desirable outcome. The initial attempts at avoiding discussion of the petitions within each chamber represented the first mechanism for achieving this outcome. Following its failure, a second mechanism for achieving this outcome was the attempt to enshrine the spirit of compromise that gave rise to the three-fifths clause as of equivalence to any textual constitutional obligation. The emergence of this mechanism was symbolized in the Twenty-Fourth Congress's commitment to "the Compact" of 1787. Such a commitment saw the congressional rump meet the abolitionists' reading of the Constitution with a reading of the Constitution imbued with the spirit of 1787–88.

7.5   THE "COMPACT" IN THE TWENTY-FOURTH CONGRESS

The challenge to the idea that slaves were property presented by the supporters of the petitioners had significant implications for the politicians seeking a suppression of the debate as a whole. As noted earlier, in both chambers the rump of members contained a suppressed line of friction between those of the North who wished to assure the South that they opposed the abolitionists and those of the South who wished to avoid forcing their Northern sympathizers to vote on an "abstract" constitutional point upon which the two groups differed. The question of the personhood of slaves proved to be one such "abstract" question for these groups and avoidance of congressional divisions on this basis was crucial to maintaining the unity of this central bloc. After the failure to "nail the petitions to the table," this group urged Congress to avoid discussion of the abstract constitutionality of abolition and instead appealed for moderation. Allied to these appeals was an attempt to reassure Southern representatives of the impossibility of congressional action on the question of slavery in the District of Columbia. Unable to sustain this position through invocation of a constitutional prohibition without inviting a vote that might rupture the coalition, they instead argued for the rekindling of a spirit of compromise that had animated the compromises of 1787. Stressing duty, forbearance, and faith, this group sought to draw equivalence between the agreements expressed within the text of the constitutional document and the spirit of comity that facilitated such agreements.

Such a position reflected and responded to the hesitancy of Northern politicians to embrace the claim that slaves were property like any other. That the view of the petitioners that Congress could abolish slavery in the District was widespread in the North was given credence by the hesitancy of Northern moderates to embrace the claim that slaves were constitutionally no more than property.[100] Even among some Northern politicians who opposed the prayer of the petitions there was doubt as to the extent of a right to property in slaves. In the House Joseph Ingersoll (Pennsylvania) represented such a tendency, offering skepticism that the property protected under the Acts of cession extended beyond land. It was not clear to him that a constitutional prohibition on abolition in the District existed – but this ambiguity made it all the more necessary to avoid discussion of the question.[101] Senator Isaac Hill of New Hampshire similarly saw the question of abolition in the District of Columbia as raising issues that threatened the Union. He feared that the agitation in Congress and reports of it in the newspapers would "create enough of excitement to effect every object of those who direct the movements of the abolitionists."[102] Senator John M. Niles of Connecticut challenged the view that rights to property in slaves were recognized in the Constitution by declaring that the prevailing view in the North was that Congress did have the right to legislate with regard to slavery in the District. He denied "an absolute, unqualified, indefeasible, right of property" in slaves, suggesting that slaveholders had "only an interest in their [slaves'] services" and that slaves were "regarded by the laws of all the States as human beings."[103] Nevertheless, Niles held to the view that until the States of Maryland and Virginia acted and the inhabitants of the District requested it, congressional attempts to abolish slavery in the District would be an abuse of power. Senator Garret D. Wall of New Jersey stressed that "one of the pillars of the most glorious temple of liberty which human wisdom has ever erected is based upon slavery; ... you cannot remove that foundation

---

[100] *Register of Debates*, 1836, 74, 807, 834.   [101] *Register of Debates*, 1836, 2015.
[102] *Register of Debates*, 1836, 488.   [103] *Register of Debates*, 1836, 520.

without destroying the whole edifice."[104] But he equivocated upon whether Congress had a constitutional power to interfere with it in the District.

While some Northern politicians reassured the South that they did recognize a right to property in slaves, Southern members of the centrist grouping within Congress nonetheless largely sought to avoid a debate focused upon textual interpretations given the hesitancy exhibited by Northern politicians. Senator Bedford Brown of North Carolina wished to avoid "opening the Pandora's box [of slavery] in the halls of Congress," and engaging in "a Quixotic expedition in pursuit of abstract constitutional questions."[105] Instead, he "was disposed to act upon this ... in that spirit of conciliation in which our federal Government had originated and without which it could not long survive."[106] In a similar vein, the Tennessean Felix Grundy stated a desire not to consider the constitutional stakes but rather found it more compelling that "the faith of the Government pledged not to interfere with this subject in this District, and [that] the faith of the Government should be preserved as sacredly as the constitution."[107] Richard I. Manning (South Carolina) represented the Southern segment of the Pinckney–Jarvis coalition in the House who similarly wished to suppress the debate but who also remained steadfast in the opinion that slaves were property. Making reference to both the Fifth Amendment and cession arguments, Manning asserted that Congress had no power to interfere with slave property "any more than it has to interfere with houses, or land, or any other description of property."[108] Nevertheless, Manning was cognizant that this constitutional interpretation was not held by "all the friends of southern rights" and thus it was better to forego the abstract question and re-embrace the "lofty and enlightened spirit of compromise" under which the federal government had been born.[109]

In this they were joined by Northern politicians for whom maintaining a cross-sectional coalition was more important than personal convictions as to the constitutionality (or morality) of slavery. Thus, Senator James Buchanan of Pennsylvania told the Senate "whatever may be my opinions upon the abstract question of slavery ... I shall never attempt to violate this fundamental compact" and later that "[a]lthough in Pennsylvania we are all opposed to slavery in the abstract, yet we will never violate the constitutional compact which we have made with our sister States. Their rights will be held sacred by us."[110] Senator Nathaniel Tallmadge of New York concurred as to the value of the compromises made at the time of the Constitution's adoption: "Those compromises are sacred. They must not, they cannot be interfered with without violation, not only of public faith, but of private rights."[111] Senator Garret Wall of New Jersey condemned abolitionism "[b]ecause it seeks, directly

[104] *Register of Debates*, 1836, 638.   [105] *Register of Debates*, 1836, 91.
[106] *Register of Debates*, 1836, 93.   [107] *Register of Debates*, 1836, 753.
[108] *Register of Debates*, 1836, 2615.   [109] *Register of Debates*, 1836, 2620.
[110] *Register of Debates*, 1836, 84, 781.   [111] *Register of Debates*, 1836, 507.

or indirectly, to violate the solemn compact of our ancestors … under a false and frenzied notion of humanity."[112] By returning to the issue of the right of petition, stressing "mutual forbearance and respect," and committing to the "federal compact, and the duties which, as a compromise, it enjoined," Ingersoll hoped that a disruption of the Union could be avoided.[113] The North, claimed Senator Isaac Hill, recognizing that interference with slavery "may involve the existence and welfare of the Union itself … understand[s] the obligations which the non-slaveholding States owe to the slaveholding States by the compact of confederation."[114] To substantiate this claim, Hill presented resolutions from meetings in New Hampshire that condemned interference with slavery as "faithless and dishonorable … against the letter and spirit of the sacred compact which binds us together."[115]

As some of the earlier quotations suggest, recurrence to the theme of an original compromise was often couched in terms of a return to the spirit that had made the Constitution possible in the first place. Abijah Mann Jr. linked the questions of duty and compromise to the original constitutional convention:

The Union and constitution, sir, were the result of cession and compromise. The subject under debate formed one of the points. We agreed; we entered into the compact with our southern brethren; and the question now presented by them to us – the real question (when the argument is pushed to the full extent) propounded to us of the North – is, whether we will live up to the bargain we have made, to the compact and union we have entered into?[116]

Richard Manning understood the commitment to respect Southern property to be a facet of the compromise that made the Constitution possible:

Under these compromises, in reference to the property of the slaveholding States, the constitution of the United States was adopted; … upon these, as their proper basis, rest the constitution and Government. These, then, under legitimate deductions of reason, are the spirit and life of the constitution and Government.[117]

Linking the contemporary debate back to the attitudes and commitments surrounding the drafting and ratification of the Constitution, these politicians expanded the scope of constitutional debate while also attempting to decouple it from the textual commitment to exclusive legislative power that those sympathetic to abolition within the District relied upon. Following but reconfiguring the invocations of compromise seen during the Missouri Crisis, the emphasis here was on honoring the original enabling compromise of 1787 rather than any following custom or tradition arising over the time since.

Although more readily serving the interests of the congressional rump, appeals to the Compact and compromise were not limited to those who wished to avoid discussion of slavery. James Garland, while wedded to the notion that slaves were

---

[112] *Register of Debates*, 1836, 643.   [113] *Register of Debates*, 1836, 2013.
[114] *Register of Debates*, 1836, 485.   [115] *Register of Debates*, 1836, 490.
[116] *Register of Debates*, 1836, 2019.   [117] *Register of Debates*, 1836, 2615.

property and among those who wished to prolong the debate in the House of Representatives, framed his opposition to the petitions in terms resonant with the themes of the Compact. Interference in the District would be "a faithless violation of the federal compact," declared Garland, who demanded the North show "fidelity" in the "discharge [of] your obligations."[118] Referring to the "sages of the Revolution," Garland suggested that the powers of Congress could not be interpreted to be in conflict with "the whole scope and intention of the framers of the constitution."[119] In the Senate, William Preston mourned the "plighted faith, the federal compact, … the friendship, and confidence, and sympathy, which should exist between us."[120] Similarly, Senator Porter argued "it was a violation of the compact to seek, either directly or indirectly, to shake the security which the slaveholding States had a right to look for under it," and reflected disappointedly on "how soon the wisdom and enlightened policy of the framers of the constitution were forgotten."[121] Senator Leigh joined them in stressing constitutional understandings grounded in 1787, suggesting that fair constructions of grants of power should be understood with "due consideration of the purposes of the trust for which they were conferred."[122] For Senator White the government could only succeed through administration "in the same spirit in which it was created":

When the constitution was framed, the great and leading interests of the whole country were considered, and, in the spirit of liberality and compromise, were adjusted and settled.[123]

This adjustment included slavery, and, therefore, for White, it was eminently clear that the intention had been to withhold a power to abolish slavery in the District of Columbia. In the House, Hammond similarly denied that the Constitution would have received the "sanction of a single slave State" if it had been suspected of giving Congress power over slavery in the District.[124]

It was against this background that the Pinckney committee offered its report on the issues raised by the debate over the petitions in the House. Pinckney's *Report … Upon the Subject of Slavery in the District of Columbia*, seeking to put to bed forever the issue of abolition in the District, provided an elaborate justification of noninterference in the District.[125] Following the instructions of his own resolutions to produce a report showing that interference in slavery in the States would be unconstitutional and the same in the District of Columbia would be "a violation of public faith, unwise, impolitic, and dangerous to Union," Pinckney later explained his purpose in the *Report* as being to show that "a violation of the public faith" was "substantially tantamount to

---

[118] *Register of Debates*, 1836, 2064, 2067.   [119] *Register of Debates*, 1836, 2070, 2072.
[120] *Register of Debates*, 1836, 81.   [121] *Register of Debates*, 1836, 75.
[122] *Register of Debates*, 1836, 194.   [123] *Register of Debates*, 1836, 698.
[124] *Register of Debates*, 1836, 2449.
[125] *Report of the Select Committee upon the Subject of Slavery in the District of Columbia, Made by Hon. H. L. Pinckney, to the House of Representatives, May 18, 1836* (Washington, DC: Blair & Rives, 1836). [Hereafter, "Pinckney Report."]

a positive declaration that the interference alluded to would be *unconstitutional.*"[126] The *Report* dealt initially with interference with slavery in the States, demonstrating the practice of noninterference and concluding with the hope that "all attempts in future to violate those sacred compromises, which lie at the very foundation of our constitutional compact, or to excite apprehension on this subject, will be effectually counteracted and defeated."[127] Turning to the issue of slavery in the District of Columbia, Pinckney hoped to harness the authority of "those sacred compromises" to shield Washington's slaveholders from regulation. Attempting to restrain congressional authority within the District by reading congressional action there as constrained by the intentions behind the Constitution, Pinckney argued that congressional authority over the District existed in order to secure the federal capital from outside interference by the State governments. As the regulation of slavery there did not involve considerations of the extent of State government power, it would be deemed a violation of the public faith to interfere with slavery in the District in a manner at odds with its treatment had the District remained within the borders of Virginia and Maryland. Cession of the District, read the *Report,*

was designed by the framers of the constitution, to enure to the benefit of the whole confederacy, and was made in the furtherance of that design; and if Congress, contrary to the obvious intent and spirit of the cession, shall do an act not required by the national objects, contemplated by it, but directly repugnant to the interests and wishes of the citizens of the ceded territory, and calculated to disturb the peace, and endanger the interests, of the slaveholding members of the Union, such an act must be in violation of the public faith. (9)

In such a way, Pinckney could argue that interference in the District was outside the powers of Congress despite the textual authority of the Constitution. But this did not show that exercise of such powers would be in any sense unconstitutional. To achieve this, Pinckney drew upon the discourse surrounding "the Compact" to articulate the view that something existed with greater authority than the textual constitution itself – the principles which the Constitution embodied:

The constitution, while it confers upon Congress exclusive legislation within this District, does not, and could not, confer unlimited or despotic authority over it. It could confer no power contrary to the fundamental principles of the constitution itself, and the essential and unalienable rights of American citizens. (10)

Driving his point home, Pinckney offered the view that a violation of the public faith was significantly more destabilizing than any act that was merely unconstitutional. A violation of the spirit of the commitments surrounding

---

[126] Pinckney Report, 3; Henry Laurens Pinckney, *Address to the Electors of Charleston District, South Carolina, on the Subject of the Abolition of Slavery* (Washington, DC, 1836), 7.
[127] Pinckney Report, 5.

the Constitution would undermine the very possibility of constitutional government and as such was more fundamental than any particular constitutional text:

Why are treaties regarded as sacred and inviolable? Why, but because they involve the pledge, and depend upon the sanctity of the national faith? Why are all compacts or promises made by Governments held to be irrevocably binding? Why, but because they cannot break them without committing perfidy, and destroying all confidence in their justice and integrity? (11)

As the great object of the Constitution had been to form a more perfect union, and as the District had been ceded to enable this – without the intention of surrendering powers over slavery to the federal government – and as the statesmen of the time (and since) had never considered the situation to be other than this, the *Report* regarded the understanding and intent of cession as holding higher authority than any constitutional text which could be interpreted to undermine this. Reaching beyond the committee's charge, the *Report* asserted that it had "no hesitation to say, that, in the view they [the committee] have taken of the whole question, the obligations of Congress not to act on this subject are as fully binding and insuperable as a positive constitutional interdict, or an open acknowledgement of want of power" (14). Which was to say, in effect, that the spirit of the Constitution was a stronger constraint than its words.[128]

7.6 CONCLUSION

Pinckney's *Report* did not satisfy his strongest critics in the South, but it did achieve the aim of foreclosing debate on the subject and soothing the divisions between North and South.[129] Supporters of the Administration and the Democratic Party's cross-sectional coalition, therefore, welcomed it. A correspondent to New Hampshire's *Portsmouth Journal of Literature and*

---

[128] Some of Pinckney's Southern colleagues found this claim wholly unconvincing. His colleague from South Carolina Waddy Thompson said he would rather commit the *Report* to "the flames or to the hangman" than the printer. John Robertson of Virginia accused the committee of replying on "speculative opinions of morality . . . in place of the plain provisions of a written law or compact." *Register of Debates*, 1836, 3758, 4032. Pinckney's own voters evidently felt the same way – he was ejected from office in the congressional election of 1836. Pinckney's support held up in the City of Charleston but beyond the parishes of St. Philip and St. Michael he garnered only 39 out of 351 cast votes. *The Southern Patriot*, October 14, 1836.

[129] At least within Congress – as the next chapter shows the debate was never wholly contained within its walls. Those at either extreme were predictably unsatisfied by the compromise at the heart of the *Report*. The abolitionist *Haverhill Gazette* believed that its "shallow hypocrisy and miserable party cunning will deceive nobody." After Pinckney's defeat in the 1836 election a Boston correspondent to the *Charleston Courier* noted that the *Report* saw the "Nullifiers from the South, and the Abolitionists of the North united in their opposition." "Mr. Pinckney's Report," *The Essex Gazette*, July 9, 1836; "Boston, Oct. 31, 1836," *Richmond Enquirer*, November 22, 1836.

Politics described the *Report* as "an able and interesting document" placing "the whole question in its true light" and likely to "gratify the north and the south."[130] The *Richmond Enquirer* welcomed the *Report* as "full of power and beauty" and "auspicious to the rights and interests of the South."[131] Read alongside the appeals to "the Compact" made in the process of the debates in the Senate and House of Representatives, the *Report* represented an attempt to elucidate and systematize a response – the compact – to abolitionist pressure on the constitutional text with regard to slavery in the District of Columbia. With Northern members of Congress unwilling to accept that slaves were mere property and politicians from North and South unwilling to risk the Union, the idea of the compact as a series of commitments of public faith and collective understandings intimately linked to the creation of the Constitution provided a mechanism by which to tie constitutional duty to noninterference with slavery. Ironically, the compact responded to abolitionist attempts to read the textual Constitution through the animating spirit of the Declaration of Independence by presenting an originary constitutional spirit that precluded abolition. In place of a spirit of 1776 manifesting as a commitment to equality, the compact offered a spirit of 1787–88 that gave weight to the compromises and commitments extant at the time of the Constitution's creation. As this pertained to slavery in the District of Columbia, it meant a renewed commitment on the part of the North to the reality of slavery in the South and an acquiescence in the dehumanizing three-fifths compromise and fugitive slave clauses. On the part of the South, it required once again that slavery and the enslaved not be directly acknowledged or protected by the Constitution lest it implicate the North in a system it deemed morally abhorrent (although tolerable amongst sister States) and destined for universal rejection. The compact tied the United States and its federal government to the compromises of 1787–88 not in the form of a textual legacy born of the people's authorization of their national government but rather as the spiritual inheritance of a brokered agreement between States, and more particularly between the representatives of the States present in Philadelphia in 1787.

Extending the obligations arising from the Constitution beyond the clauses of the Constitution, the debates of 1836 within Congress returned the question of slavery in the District of Columbia back to the intentions and understandings that had animated the Constitution's creation in 1787. As we have seen, one consequence of this was that the intentions of the framers became a crucial component in adjudicating the duties arising from the compact. Another was that actors in 1836 were able to suppress a discussion that threatened to resurrect the crucial division over the question of whether slaves were persons or property. While the compact offered a way to avoid a definitive resolution of this issue, it in no way settled the question, beyond linking contemporary

---

[130] "Washington, May 18," *The Portsmouth Journal of Literature & Politics*, May 28, 1836.
[131] "Mr. Pinckney's Report," *Richmond Enquirer*, May 24, 1836.

questions of slavery's regulation back to the intentions of 1787. As we will see, such a connection would be evident two decades later in Chief Justice Taney's *Dred Scott* opinion, which set the country on the path to a fundamental and bloody resolution of this question in favor of the personhood of slaves in the form of the Civil War. However, before turning attention to those later developments, the following chapter explores the contemporaneous invocation of "the compact" beyond Congress.

8

The Compact and the Election of 1836

> We doubted not the power by the *letter*, but we still doubt the power having been conceded *understandingly*.
>
> *New-Hampshire Sentinel* (1835)[1]

In late 1835, four days after William Jackson presented the petition in the House of Representative that led James H. Hammond to claim he could no longer sit there and "see the rights of the South assailed, day after day, by ignorant fanatics," the Raleigh *Register* told its readers that, with regard to the presidential election, "The cause of Judge White is the cause of the South."[2] By the time of the *Register*'s declaration, the Whigs in the South had been hammering the Democratic candidate and Vice President Martin Van Buren and praising Hugh Lawson White for months. White would go on to win only twenty-six Electoral College votes and poll under 10 percent of the vote, well behind Martin Van Buren's main rival William H. Harrison. Harrison secured seventy-three Electoral College votes while Van Buren claimed 170.[3] But White was Van Buren's chief rival in Alabama, Arkansas, Louisiana, Mississippi, Missouri, North Carolina, and Virginia, and won in Georgia and Tennessee.[4] Consequently, Van Buren effectively fought two presidential campaigns in 1836, one against Harrison in the North and West and one against

---

[1] "Herald of Freedom," *New-Hampshire Sentinel*, December 24, 1835.

[2] *Register of Debates, 24th Congress, 1st Session*, 1836, 1969; quoted in William J. Cooper, *The South and the Politics of Slavery 1828–1856* (Baton Rouge: Louisiana State University Press, 1978), 81.

[3] *Register of Debates, 24th Congress, 2nd Session*, 1837, 1656–57.

[4] Gerhard Peters and John T. Woolley, "Election of 1836," The American Presidency Project, accessed July 13, 2018, www.presidency.ucsb.edu/showelection.php?year=1836. The Legislature of South Carolina awarded its eleven Electoral College votes to Willie Person Mangum.

White in the South.[5] In the latter, the issue of slavery was highly significant and the candidates' positions on slavery in the District of Columbia became a litmus test.[6]

The emergence of the question of abolition within the District of Columbia in the presidential campaign of 1836 had profound consequences for the conception of the question and for the subset of constitutional questions that it represented. Over the course of the presidential campaign, Van Buren sought to hone his position on the question of abolition in the District through a series of letters and quasi-official campaign documents. In the course of these documents and in response to the pressures he faced from Southern Whigs, Van Buren's position on slavery in the District evolved. From an early position that abolition there would be inexpedient or impolitic, Van Buren shifted by his inaugural address to the position that such action was counter to "the spirit that actuated the venerated fathers of the republic."[7] At the same time, through campaign materials, public meetings, and official addresses, Northern Democrats developed the view that abolitionist activity aimed at altering the extant inter-State settlement on slavery was counter to the "spirit of deference, conciliation and mutual forbearance" that underwrote the federal compact.[8] Moving between the proslavery advocates of the South and the antislavery activists in the North, Van Buren Democrats – just as they did during the congressional debates over the petitions at the same time – navigated a middle path through the invocation of a spirit of compromise. And as with the debates analyzed in the previous chapter, this path operated to obscure the fundamental tension in the identification of the District's enslaved as both property and people. The idea of the federal compact as imbued with a spirit of compromise enabled Van Buren to successfully navigate the 1836 presidential election, but it also legitimized an appeal to spirit as a method of resolving constitutional disputes that had significant longer-term effects.

8.1 SLAVERY AND THE ELECTION OF 1836

Martin Van Buren's identity as a Northern politician created difficulties for his anointment as the heir to Andrew Jackson's cross-sectional Democratic mantle. Jackson had been the slaveholding victor at New Orleans and against the

---

[5] William G Shade, "'The Most Delicate and Exciting Topics': Martin Van Buren, Slavery, and the Election of 1836," *Journal of the Early Republic* 18, no. 3 (1998): 479.

[6] William Shade assesses that "Slavery was never the primary issue in the campaign, but because Van Buren was not a southerner, it was one that had to be handled carefully if he were to retain a constituency that he long strived to cultivate and without which victory was impossible." Shade, "'The Most Delicate and Exciting Topics,'" 479.

[7] "Inaugural Address of President Van Buren," *National Gazette*, March 6, 1837.

[8] "Communication from the Governor, Transmitting a Report and Resolutions Adopted by the Legislature of the State of Maine, Relative to the Subject of Slavery," *New York Senate Papers* No. 85, 1836, 3.

Seminole, but Van Buren, despite a family history of slaveholding, did not personify the defense of Southern institutions in anything like the same way.[9] The Jacksonian coalition that Van Buren hoped to marshal to his cause, like its Jeffersonian precursor, struck an awkward balance of promoting democracy in the North while protecting slaveholders in the South.[10] Jackson had managed this tightrope, in part by joining Southern slaveholders in regarding slavery as a settled issue and deprecating those who raised it.[11] But Van Buren appeared less reliable to Southern Democrats, despite having worked to establish and sustain the coalition in the 1820s.[12] Indeed, in his efforts to sustain a coalition of Northerners suspicious of Southern slavery and Southerners suspicious of perceived Northern democratic excess, Van Buren became the target of charges of unreliability and duplicity. Denounced as "a corrupt and vascillating politician," his Southern opponents charged him with being an ally to the South only insofar as it was in accordance with his immediate interests – and they suggested that such an alignment of interests could not be guaranteed in the future.[13] Playing on his reputation as a politician who shifted with the political wind, his critics asked whether he could be trusted with the presidency. David Crockett's campaign pamphlet denounced Van Buren as "a federalist to-day, a republican to-morrow, and a hypocrite always."[14] In comparison to the steadfastness of "Old Hickory," (Jackson) Van Buren's

---

[9] Joel H. Silbey, *Martin Van Buren and the Emergence of American Popular Politics* (New York: Rowman & Littlefield Publishers, Inc., 2002), 2.

[10] Padraig Riley, *Slavery and the Democratic Conscience: Political Life in Jeffersonian America* (Philadelphia, PA: University of Pennsylvania Press, 2016), 9; Donald B. Cole, *Martin Van Buren and the American Political System* (Princeton: Princeton University Press, 1984), 256; Leonard L. Richards, *The Slave Power: The Free North and Southern Domination* (Baton Rouge: Louisiana State University Press, 2000), 112.

[11] John Ashworth, *Slavery, Capitalism, and Politics in the Antebellum Republic: Volume 1: Commerce and Compromise, 1820–1850* (Cambridge, UK: Cambridge University Press, 1995), 333.

[12] George William Van Cleve, *A Slaveholders' Union: Slavery, Politics, and the Constitution in the Early American Republic* (Chicago: University of Chicago Press, 2010), 260; Richards, *The Slave Power*, 122–27.

[13] "The Van Burenites ...," *Fayetteville Weekly Observer*, August 4, 1836. A meeting of the citizens of Wake County, North Carolina, meeting to nominate political candidates cast their support for White while noting that Van Buren "is not one upon whom the South can rely with undoubting confidence upon this important subject." The subject was of course slavery. "White Meeting," *The Weekly Standard*, February 11, 1836.

[14] David Crockett, *The Life of Martin Van Buren, Heir-Apparent to the "Government" and the Appointed Successor of General Andrew Jackson* (Philadelphia: Robert Wright, 1837), 18. Other critics beat the same drum. "A Citizen of New York" wrote "His system of politics has been proverbially, non-committal. It has been a prominent trait in his policy, to float ostensibly with the majority, in favor of a measure, while his adherents have been found violently assailing it, and that too not only by his consent, but by his procurement." "Mr. Van Buren and the Slave Question," *United States' Telegraph*, March 27, 1835; Crockett, *The Life of Martin Van Buren*, 18; *Memoir of Martin Van Buren, Comprising an Account of the Intrigues by Which He Sought and Acquired the Nomination and Election to the Office of Chief Magistrate; Together with*

skills in coalition-building and politicking marked him as a presidential candidate upon whom the South could less readily rely. Whatever the truth of Martin Van Buren's personal convictions on the issues of importance to the South, his public persona in 1835–36 made him "a particularly vulnerable candidate in a presidential campaign that focused on sectional and slavery issues."[15]

Of the issues of importance to the South in 1835–36, none equaled slavery and the actions of abolitionists. By the mid-1830s, the aftermath of Nat Turner's Rebellion, British imperial gradual abolition, and the eruption of immediate abolitionism into the public mind had brought slavery to the fore of public debate in ways unseen since the Missouri Crisis. The skirmish over abolition petitions in early 1835 forced a House of Representatives' vote to lay them on the table and the reproduction and dissemination of John Dickson's speech in defense of the petitions by the abolitionist presses.[16] During the summer of 1835, the distribution of abolitionist materials in the US mail resulted in Southern protests, with President Andrew Jackson demanding federal action by the year's end.[17] Southern agitation over the actions of abolitionist "fanatics" and the belief that they were seeking to stir up slave rebellion brought the slaveholding South to fever pitch by mid-1835, and it did not subsequently die down ahead of the presidential election. Rumors of a white-led slave conspiracy in Mississippi in July 1835 only added to the frenzy.[18] In September 1835, the *Richmond Enquirer*, a newspaper erstwhile engaged in muting divisions between North and South for party political reasons, offered "Another Calm Appeal from the South to the North," which is suggestive of the level of anxiety across the slaveholding South. Demanding action from the North, the *Enquirer* asked:

Developments of His Political Character, By a Citizen of New York (New York: R. W. Roberts, 1838), 130–31.

[15] Cooper, *The South and the Politics of Slavery 1828–1856*, 52–53. M. Philip Lucas notes that historians continue to debate Van Buren's motivations during the 1820s. M. Philip Lucas, "Martin Van Buren as Party Leader and at Andrew Jackson's Right Hand," in *A Companion to the Antebellum Presidents 1837–1861*, ed. Joel H. Silbey (Malden: Wiley-Blackwell, 2014), 117. The contrast between Van Buren's reputation for politicking and Jackson's reputation for direct action may have also hurt him with a southern constituency in which the garnering of an honorable reputation was given public weight. Patricia Roberts-Miller, *Fanatical Schemes: Proslavery Rhetoric and the Tragedy of Consensus* (Tuscaloosa: The University of Alabama Press, 2009), 112–17; Jennifer R. Mercieca, "The Culture of Honor: How Slaveholders Responded to the Abolitionist Mail Crisis," *Rhetoric & Public Affairs* 10, no. 1 (2007): 69–70; Cooper, *The South and the Politics of Slavery 1828–1856*, 69–72.

[16] *Register of Debates*, 23rd Congress, 2nd Session, 1835, 1131–41; "Ladies' Petition," *The Emancipator*, February 24, 1835.

[17] Mercieca, "The Culture of Honor"; Lacy K. Ford, *Deliver Us from Evil: The Slavery Question in the Old South* (New York: Oxford University Press, 2009), 481–99; *Register of Debates*, 1836 Appendix, 1–12.

[18] Ford, *Deliver Us from Evil*, 489–93.

Do you intend to permit these madmen to pull down the edifice which was cemented with the blood of our forefathers? ... See the train of events that have already arisen! We have strengthened our police. We have been compelled to interrupt the public mails. We have held public meetings and organized committees of safety, as in the days of the Revolution, to watch the footsteps of the emissaries.[19]

The anxiety expressed by the *Enquirer* did not dissipate; by the year's end, over 150 anti-abolitionist public meetings had taken place throughout the South.[20] The heightened feelings with regard to slavery, and the corresponding concerns over the conduct of abolitionists meant that the presidential election of 1836 had little hope of escaping its gravity. With a degree of understatement, the *National Gazette* noted in mid-September 1835, "The Abolition-question is more and more mixed up with the Presidential question, in the Southern journals."[21]

The coming together of Van Buren's perceived unreliability and the tension over slavery worked to reinforce each other and presented a significant vulnerability to his presidential aspirations. The *National Gazette* followed up its comment on the mixing of the abolition and presidential questions, with the observation that "Mr. Van Buren's conduct and opinions in regard to the former are warmly discussed with reference to the candidateship."[22] In truth, the durability and truth of Van Buren's attachment to Southern interests had been raised by opponents well before the summer of 1835. As early as March 1835, the *United States' Telegraph* had reprinted an article from the New York *Courier* pointing to Van Buren's apparent hypocrisy in opposing abolition in Virginia while championing it in Connecticut.[23] This narrative meshed well with the charges of historical opposition to Southern interests promoted by Southern Whigs who pointed to Van Buren's association with Rufus King, and Van Buren's support for the enfranchisement of wealthy free blacks at the 1821 New York constitutional convention as evidence that he was an unreliable advocate for the South.[24] Alluding to Van Buren's lack of reliability as evinced by his behavior at the time of the Missouri Crisis, the

---

[19] "Another Calm Appeal from the South to the North," *Richmond Enquirer*, September 8, 1835. The *Enquirer*, as a Van Buren newspaper, was committed to soothing southern fears that Van Buren's Northern identity and the interests of the Northern wing of the Democrat Party were irreconcilable with southern interests.

[20] Ford, *Deliver Us from Evil*, 486.

[21] "The Abolition-Question ..., " *National Gazette*, September 18, 1835. Richards argues "In 1835 the American Anti-Slavery Society became the hottest issue in national politics." Richards, *The Slave Power*, 127; see also Cole, *Martin Van Buren and the American Political System*, 270.

[22] "The Abolition-Question ... " [23] "Mr. Van Buren and the Slave Question."

[24] Shade, "'The Most Delicate and Exciting Topics'," 467–68. Rufus King's opposition to the admission of Missouri as a slave State had tainted King, and by extension his associates, in Southern eyes. Ashworth, *Slavery, Capitalism, and Politics in the Antebellum Republic*, 378; Cooper, *The South and the Politics of Slavery 1828–1856*, 74. On King's actions during the Missouri Crisis and Van Buren's involvement with them, see Van Cleve, *A Slaveholders' Union*, 250–60.

Lynchburg *Virginian* asked whether slaveholders could entrust the protection of slavery to the "tender mercies" of the vice president.[25] In May, the *United States' Telegraph* ratcheted up the allegations by suggesting that Van Buren's election was advancing "under the promise, *express* or implied, that by his election the cause of anti-slavery will be advanced."[26] Such fears seemed justified following Van Buren's endorsement by the abolition-supporting *Oneida Standard and Democrat.*[27] Caught between a Southern section in which support of slavery advanced his cause and a Northern section in which it aroused suspicion, gains for Van Buren in the Northeast made him all the more vulnerable in the South. When the Boston *Courier* endorsed Van Buren because he was "northern man" and "not a slaveholder," the Winchester *Republican* vowed that the South would support Judge White "not on the grounds that he is a *slave holder*, but because the East is going over to Van Buren because he is none."[28] As the presidential contest proceeded, the actions necessitated to shore up support in the North made Van Buren increasingly vulnerable to accusations of double-dealing from the South.

The Winchester *Republican*'s statement that it was supporting Hugh Lawson White without regard to his slaveholding was probably a case of protesting too much. Over the course of the presidential campaigns, the Southern Whig press repeatedly emphasized White's Southern-ness, understood as indelibly linked to slaveholding. The Charleston *Mercury* proclaimed White the States' rights heir of Jackson in a widely reprinted column, noting "Judge White is a slave holder himself, and the citizen of a slave holding State, and therefore necessarily identified with us, and with all the South, upon that vital and absorbing subject."[29] The Nashville *Tennessean* reprinted a Georgian newspaper's framing of the Southern presidential election as a choice between "the Northern candidate with all his cherished Northern feelings and views, and Southern candidate, with all his cherished Southern feelings and Southern principles."[30] A few days later, while foregrounding the question of slavery in the District of Columbia, the same newspaper reprinted the *Columbia Observer*'s call on the "Freemen of the slave-holding States" to cast their votes "for a man whose interests are your interests, – who will prosper when you prosper, and fall when you fall."[31] By comparison, Van Buren's Northern identity was equated with a sympathy for abolitionism in ways that might have struck Northern readers as fantastical. The *United States' Telegraph* suggested in September 1835 that there was "no difference" between Van Buren and the

[25] Reprinted as "The Missouri Restriction – Jefferson and Van Buren," *Carolina Watchman*, April 23, 1835.

[26] "The Globe Say That Opposition Papers ...," *United States' Telegraph*, May 21, 1835.

[27] Cole, *Martin Van Buren and the American Political System*, 271.

[28] "The Succession," *Vicksburg Whig*, June 11, 1835.

[29] Cf. "From the National Gazette," *Pittsburgh Gazette*, May 1, 1835.

[30] "From the Southern (Ga) Recorder," *The Tennessean*, April 16, 1836.

[31] "The Difference," *The Tennessean*, April 19, 1836.

abolitionists Tappan and Garrison "except as to the time of action."[32] Throughout the Southern critiques of Van Buren, his identity as an outsider to the South was reinforced while White's Southern-ness was promoted as a security for the institution of slavery.[33] A public meeting in Perquimans County, North Carolina, praised White as "going heart and soul with the South against the Abolitionists" – in comparison, the political course of Van Buren "has been against the South."[34] Emphasizing the distinct identities of the candidates, different newspapers made a point of laying Van Buren's and White's opinions on slavery side by side, "[a]s the subject of Slavery is one of the most vital importance to the people of the South."[35] Attempts on the part of Van Buren's supporters to push back against this critique sought, in turn, to deploy the idea of Southern identity, either through endorsement by those of surer Southern pedigree or through attacks on White's own claims to be in tune with Southern values.[36] Despite the ultimate success of the Democrats in securing enough Southern support to gain the White House for Van Buren, the need to combat his depiction as a Northern politician without a natural sympathy for slavery remained a constant throughout the campaign.

---

[32] "Mr. Van Buren and Abolition." One correspondent even took the position that the destruction of the abolitionist convention at Utica, New York, by Van Buren lieutenant Samuel Beardsley was staged for political purposes. "Abolition," *United States' Telegraph*, November 10, 1835. The deployment of a southern identity as a proxy for support of slavery was utilized in Mississippi in similar ways to endorse the Democratic Senate candidate Robert J. Walker even as Democratic papers discounted its use in Van Buren's case. In October 1835, the *Weekly Mississippian* approvingly reprinted the Natchez *Free Trader*'s endorsement of Walker as "a *slave holder* and a *planter*, residing upon the banks of the Pearl, in the county of Madison, and the very center of the state." By comparison, his opponent, Plummer, was "a New Englander by birth and education ... in principle and predilections, and, who, notwithstanding his large purchase of Indian floats, never had and we understand never will own a slave in his life." "Robert J. Walker," *The Weekly Mississippian*, October 2, 1835.

[33] For instance, the Address of the Georgian Republicans' convention referred to the "ambitious schemes of the Northern candidate for the Presidency." In accepting a nomination for Governor of South Carolina, General Edward B. Dudley dismissed Van Buren as "not one of us. He is a Northern man in soul, in principle and in action." As evidence for this view, Dudley pointed to Van Buren's positions on the tariff and on slavery. "Georgia's Electoral Ticket," *Voice of Sumter*, June 7, 1836; "General Dudley," *Carolina Watchman*, March 5, 1835.

[34] "Perquimans County," *Weekly Raleigh Register*, June 7, 1836.

[35] "From the Washington Sun," *Selma Daily Reporter*, April 9, 1836; "The Difference"; "The Contrast," *Voice of Sumter*, August 9, 1836.

[36] An example of the first case is contained within John P. H. Claiborne's "Address to the People of Mississippi," offered by an author who attested to "as much southern feeling, as much regard for southern interests as any man." An example of the second lay in the attempts to smear White as having accompanied free blacks to the ballot box and on occasion linking arms with them. The reader was reassured that Van Buren had instead driven free blacks from the polls. "Address to the People of Mississippi," *Mississippi Free Trader*, July 29, 1836; "Judge White and the Free Negroes," *Mississippi Free Trader*, October 15, 1836; Cooper, *The South and the Politics of Slavery 1828–1856*, 89–93.

8.2   MARTIN VAN BUREN AND THE DISTRICT OF COLUMBIA
      IN THE ELECTION OF 1836

As noted in the previous chapters, the issue of slavery in the District of Columbia had been rising in salience for both supporters and opponents of slavery in the 1830s. As the presidential election of 1836 unfurled, the issue came to be significant as a litmus test for candidates regarding the broader issues of slavery and abolition. Just as Calhoun would frame the question of abolition in the District of Columbia as the South's "Thermopylae," Southern actors within the newspaper and pamphlet debates surrounding the 1836 presidential election saw the question of abolition in the District as a precursor to a wider scheme of abolition. In light of Van Buren's questionable loyalties to slavery, his position on the question of abolition in the District emerged as cudgel with which the Southern Whigs attempted to beat him. In response, Van Buren and his supporters attempted to finesse a position on the issue that would maintain his standing in both sections of the country. The result was an extended debate over the nature of congressional power over the District of Columbia in which the various positions evident within the petition debates were developed and given popular sanction.[37]

Southern defenders of slavery recognized the District of Columbia as a vulnerable territory for them as well as a symbolically important one. In the frenzied atmosphere of 1835–36, the possibility of abolition within the District took on heightened significance. Richard Yeadon's *Charleston Courier* article "Abolition in the District of Columbia" conceded the "strict *political* right of exclusive legislation" held by Congress over the District but simultaneously believed that any action with regard to the District "*must* be regarded as the commencement of a war against Southern interests."[38] For Yeadon, even discussion of the topic became a "serious and perilous *action*."[39] Similarly, the *Richmond Enquirer* warned the Abolitionists to "keep their hands from the

---

[37] The fact that the petition debates took place within the midst of the presidential election meant that the debates inside Congress could not be wholly separated from the debates taking place outside. Indeed, some Members of Congress harbored suspicions that the congressional debates were a Van Burenite attempt to quell the debate "out of doors." Representative Balie Peyton's reading of Van Buren's opinions on slavery during the House debate gives credibility to the views of Representative John Robertson that the outcome of the debates was, with reference to Van Buren's political base in New York, "a cargo of Albany notions." *Register of Debates, 1836*, 2223, 4032. The Van Burenite *Globe* newspaper expressed the belief that Whigs were stoking the issue in order to exacerbate tensions during the presidential race. "Saturday Morning, Aug. 29, 1835," *Extra Globe*, September 4, 1835; "What Is Duff Green About?," *Extra Globe*, September 18, 1835.

[38] Richard Yeadon Jr., "Abolition in the District of Columbia," in *The Amenability of Northern Incendiaries As Well to Southern As to Northern Laws. Without Prejudice to the Right of Free Discussion; to Which Is Added an Inquiry into the Lawfulness of Slavery, Under the Jewish and Christian Dispensations* (Charleston: T. A. Hayden, 1835), 34. Original emphasis.

[39] Yeadon Jr., "Abolition in the District of Columbia," 34. Original emphasis.

District of Columbia," while in 1836 Calhoun told fellow Southerners in Georgia that the "door must be closed" against interference "in the District of Columbia, or in the States or territories."[40] By the beginning of 1836, newspapers were reporting that legislatures in North Carolina, South Carolina, Georgia, and Virginia were debating and passing resolutions expressing the belief that action in the District was the first step toward broader national antislavery legislation.[41] Being aware that Abolitionists regarded the District as a constitutionally appropriate sphere for abolitionism, proslavery Southerners were especially sensitive to any legitimization that action in the District might bring for their opponents.

At the same time, the question of abolition in the District presented the Van Buren campaign with an opportunity as well as a potential vulnerability. Taking a strong stance against abolition in the District could enable Van Buren to signal his sympathy for the interests of the slaveholding South.[42] As early as March 1835, Thomas Ritchie, the editor of the *Richmond Enquirer*, forwarded to Silas Wright a request for more information on Van Buren's position on slavery and the District in particular. The request, which came from a member of the Virginia Legislature, suggested that many of the "administration members of the Virginia Legislature are anxious to know Mr. Van Buren's opinions on the subject of Slavery – Does he think it would be politic to abolish slavery within the District of Columbia? Does he think that the C. of the U.S. gives to Congress a right to interfere with relations between masters & slaves in any of the States?"[43] On March 14, the *Enquirer* published an apparent response, in the form of a letter from "an intimate friend of the Vice President," setting out Van Buren's view that it would be "impolitic" for Congress to legislate on slavery in the District of Columbia and that the Constitution denies Congress the right to interfere "with the relation between master and slave, in any of the States."[44] In addition to this letter provided by Silas Wright (hereafter the "Wright letter"), two further letters followed, on April 3 (the "Butler letter") and April 10 (the "Gwin letter"), seeking to address the question – the first from another of Van Buren's "most intimate friends" addressing a broad series of policy positions including the "Missouri

[40] "A Calm Appeal from the South to the North," *Richmond Enquirer*, August 14, 1835; John C. Calhoun, "To A[Ugustin] S. Clayton and Others," in *The Papers of John C. Calhoun: Volume XIII, 1835–1837*, ed. Clyde N. Wilson (Columbia: University of South Carolina Press, 1980), 263.

[41] "State Legislature," *Western Carolinian*, December 19, 1835; "General Assembly," *Newbern Spectator*, January 8, 1836; "South Carolina," *Arkansas Gazette*, January 26, 1836; "A Joint Report ...," *New-Hampshire Sentinel*, December 31, 1835; "The Abolition Question ...," *National Gazette*, January 25, 1836.

[42] Ashworth, *Slavery, Capitalism, and Politics in the Antebellum Republic*, 378.

[43] "Thomas Ritchie to Silas Wright, March 2 1835," in *Martin Van Buren Papers: Series 2, General Correspondence, 1787–1868; 1835; 1835, Jan. 1 – Jul. 6.* (Library of Congress, n.d.).

[44] "Mr. Van Buren's Opinions," *Richmond Enquirer*, March 14, 1835. The wording of the letter was slightly revised in its subsequent reprint in the *Extra Globe* in June.

Question," and the second a reprint of a July 1834 letter specifically on Van Buren's view of the "power of Congress over Slave Property in the Southern States."[45] All three letters were subsequently collated and reprinted as "Mr. Van Buren's Opinions" in a June 1835 edition of the *Extra Globe*.[46] Despite these early efforts, Van Buren's critics were not satisfied by his responses.[47] By August 1835, correspondents in Virginia and Georgia were warning Van Buren that Southern Whigs were attempting to use the issue of slavery to "inflame the minds and excite the prejudices of the people against you."[48] William Schley, writing from Georgia, nevertheless, suggested to Van Buren that "if this slave question does not produce a reaction against you," the latter would carry the presidential election.[49] Significantly, in these letters, Van Buren did not acknowledge a constitutional prohibition on congressional action against slavery in the District. To do so would have been to make an argument that rendered abolition in the District essentially impossible – if Congress could not abolish slavery in the District then it was not clear where such a power would reside. But perhaps more significantly within the context of 1835–36, such a position would have placed Van Buren in opposition to much of the North.[50] The Van Burenite *Mississippi Free Trader* warned those pressing the issue of the constitutionality of abolition in the District in the South that by "making this a test question, by denouncing and insulting all who cannot entertain this belief, they adopt a most efficient measure for diminishing the ardor, for quenching the zeal of those Northern men who are friends to the

---

[45] "Mr. Van Buren," *Richmond Enquirer*, April 3, 1835; "The Plans Exposed," *Richmond Enquirer*, April 10, 1835.

[46] "Mr. Van Buren's Opinions," *Extra Globe*, June 26, 1835. The Washington *Globe* served the role of the quasi-official organ of the Democrats during this period. Shade, "'The Most Delicate and Exciting Topics,'" 469.

[47] "Mr. Van Buren on the Slave Question," *Connecticut Herald*, April 21, 1835; "Mr. Van Buren's Letter – Slavery," *Richmond Whig*, September 25, 1835.

[48] "Richard Elliot Parker to Martin Van Buren, August 21, 1835," in *Martin Van Buren Papers: Series 2, General Correspondence, 1787–1868; 1835; 1835, July 7 – Dec. 31* (Library of Congress, n.d.); "William Schley to Martin Van Buren, August 22, 1835," in *Martin Van Buren Papers: Series 2, General Correspondence, 1787–1868; 1835; 1835, July 7 – Dec. 31* (Library of Congress, n.d.).

[49] "William Schley to Martin Van Buren, August 22, 1835." Van Buren responded with a letter that exudes some frustration at having to repeat his, by now widely disseminated, opinions on the matter. "Martin Van Buren to William Schley, September 10, 1835," in *Martin Van Buren Papers: Series 2, General Correspondence, 1787–1868; 1835; 1835, July 7 – Dec. 31* (Library of Congress, n.d.).

[50] William M. Wiecek, *The Sources of Antislavery Constitutionalism in America, 1760–1848* (Ithaca: Cornell University Press, 1977), 185–86. If Southern legislatures decried action against slavery in the District at the end of 1835, by the end of the following year the Vermont General Assembly had adopted resolutions affirming congressional authority over slavery in the District. In Pennsylvania, the Governor's Message noted the State's "unchanging" opposition to slavery in the District. "Resolutions," *Sentinel and Democrat*, December 30, 1836; "No Title," *Carlisle Weekly Herald*, December 15, 1836.

rights of the South."[51] For the remainder of the campaign, the vice president sought to navigate the pressures on both sides and remain faithful to the Northern Democrats without alienating the Southern Democrats.[52]

The result of this navigation was a gradually evolving position on the question of abolition in the District of Columbia. In the early part of 1835, Van Buren was seen to take the position that abolition in the District was "impolitic," "highly impolitic," or, indirectly, that he "would give it no countenance or support."[53] In October 1835, a fourth letter – Van Buren's response to William Schley's August letter (the Owasco letter) – was circulating widely in the press.[54] The Owasco letter was, in the assessment of the *Extra Globe*, "but a renewal of the declaration ... heretofore publicly announced" in the Gwin letter. Like the Gwin letter, the Owasco letter did not directly address the question of Congress's power vis-à-vis the District. Nonetheless, it did expand on the earlier letters in two significant ways. First, Van Buren claimed to have been explicit in regarding "agitating the question in the District of Columbia" as "against ... propriety."[55] This widened the sphere of his opposition to include abolitionist organizing on the issue of slavery in the Capital as well as congressional action on the same.[56] Second, he appended a "Preamble and Resolutions" from an Albany public meeting, stating that "I concur fully in the sentiments they advance."[57] The Resolutions, like the letter itself, did not take a position on the constitutionality of abolition in the District, but they did take a position on the constitutionality of interference between the slaveholder and enslaved in the slaveholding States. The first two resolutions stated:

---

[51] "Nullifiers & Abolitionists," *Mississippi Free Trader*, March 25, 1836.

[52] Shade argues that by the early summer of 1835 Van Buren's position on the issue of slavery seemed clear, but with regard to the narrower issue of slavery in the District of Columbia, I contend that Van Buren continued to pen responses and revise his position up to and including this inaugural address. That Van Buren's signature pamphlet on his position vis-à-vis the District was issued in 1835 then significantly revised and re-issued in 1836 belies the notion that his position was settled by mid-1835. Shade, "'The Most Delicate and Exciting Topics'," 471, 479. For discussion of the pamphlets see further.

[53] Respectively in the Wright letter, in its revised publication in the June 1835 *Extra Globe* reprinting, and in the Butler letter's equating of John Quincy Adams's position on the issue with Van Buren's.

[54] "The Letter of Mr. Van Buren," *Extra Globe*, October 9, 1835; "Wednesday, October 7," *Evening Standard*, October 7, 1835; "Mr. Van Buren and the Abolitionist," *Buffalo Whig and Journal*, October 14, 1835. The letter is named for the town in which it was composed.

[55] "The Letter of Mr. Van Buren."

[56] Although the position of the Democratic Party as being opposed to such organizing had been fully expressed in the Address produced by the Baltimore Convention at which Van Buren was selected as the Party's candidate. "Address. To the Democratic Republicans of the United States," *The Globe*, August 26, 1835.

[57] "The Letter of Mr. Van Buren."

Therefore Resolved, That we regard the Constitution of the United States as carrying with it an adjustment of all questions involved in the deliberations which led to its adoption; and that the compromise of interests in which it was founded, is, in our opinion, binding in honor and good faith, independently of the force of agreement, on all who live under its protection, and participate in the benefits of which it is the source.

Resolved, That under the Constitution of the United States, the relation of the master and slave is a matter belonging exclusively to the people of each State within its own boundary; that the General Government has no control over it; that it is subject only to the representative arrangements of the several States within which its exists; and that any attempt by the Government or the people of any State, or by the General Government, to interfere with or disturb it, would violate the spirit of compromise which lies at the basis of the federal compact.[58]

The Resolutions concerned the question of abolition within the slaveholding States, but the styling of the Constitution as "carrying with it an adjustment of all questions involved in the deliberations which led to its adoption" and the invocation of "spirit of compromise" provided for a more expansive understanding of constitutional obligation than the early letters had allowed for. Both developments provided a stepping-stone to the positions taken by Van Buren in early 1836.

The frenzied responses to the mail campaign and the emergence of extended congressional debates over abolitionist petitions kept the issue of slavery at the fore through the first half of 1836. A further letter in March 1836 reiterated Van Buren's opposition to interference with slavery in the slaveholding States and finessed his position on abolition in the District of Columbia. Initially written in response to an inquiry from several gentlemen from North Carolina, a March 6, 1836, letter (the "North Carolina letter") from Van Buren was sent by him to J. B. Mallory on March 11 with permission to seek its publication in the *Richmond Enquirer*. Along with the Butler letter and other documents, it was subsequently republished as a thirty-two-page pamphlet, *Opinions of Martin Van Buren, Vice President of the United States, Upon the Powers and Duties of Congress, in Reference to the Abolition of Slavery Either in the Slave-Holding States or in the District of Columbia.*[59] The North Carolina letter significantly expanded upon Van Buren's public position on abolition in the District of Columbia as stated in the earlier Wright and Owasco letters. The North Carolina letter reaffirmed Van Buren's support of the Albany Resolutions and stated that the vice president was "against the propriety" of interference "in any

---

[58] "The Letter of Mr. Van Buren."
[59] *Opinions of Martin Van Buren Vice President of the United States, Upon the Powers and Duties of Congress, in Reference to the Abolition of Slavery Either in the Slaveholding States or in the District of Columbia* (Washington, DC: Blair & Rives, 1836). Shade identifies this letter as "the Amis letter" after the principal recipient in North Carolina. The *Opinions* was itself a revision of the earlier 1835 pamphlet, "Mr. Van Buren's Opinions," which had contained the Wright, Butler, and Gwin letters as well as other materials. "Mr. Van Buren's Opinions," in *Martin Van Buren Papers: Series 2, General Correspondence, 1787–1868; 1835; 1835, July 7 – Dec. 31,* n.d.

manner, or to any extent" with slavery in the District of Columbia (4–5).[60] But it also made plain Van Buren's belief that there was no textual constitutional prohibition on congressional action in the District. "Thus viewing the matter, I would not, from the lights now before me, feel myself safe in pronouncing that Congress does not possess the power of interfering with or abolishing slavery in the District of Columbia" (5). But labeling this point "the abstract question of the legal power of Congress," Van Buren moved to quickly reassure Southern slaveholders that "there are objections to the exercise of this power, against the wishes of the slave-holding States, *as imperative in their nature and obligations,* in regulating the conduct of public men, *as the most palpable want of constitutional power would be*" (5; original emphasis).[61] As a result, said Van Buren, "I must go into the Presidential chair, the inflexible and uncompromising opponent of any attempt on the part of Congress to abolish slavery in the District of Columbia, against the wishes of the slave-holding States" (5). Drawing upon the Albany Resolutions, he justified this position as a consequence of the nature of the social compact. Believing that, if the possibility of abolition in the District had been envisaged at the time of the adoption of the Constitution, a specific exception from the power of "exclusive legislation" would have been added, Van Buren argued that:

3dly. I do therefore believe, that abolition of slavery in the District of Columbia, against the wishes of the slave-holding States (assuming that Congress has the power to effect it) would violate the spirit of that compromise of interests which lies at the basis of our social compact; and I am thoroughly convinced, that it could not be so done, without imminent peril, if not certain destruction, to the Union of States. Viewing the matter in this light, it is my clear and settled opinion, that the Federal Government ought to abstain from doing so, and that it is the sacred duty of those whom the people of the United States entrust with the control of its action, so to use the constitutional power with which they are invested as to prevent it. (6)

The *Richmond Enquirer* editorialized that the letter showed that "Mr. Van Buren holds ... that the abolition of slavery in the District, against the wishes of the slave-holding States, would destroy at once that compromise of interests *which lies at the basis of our social compact*" (3; original emphasis).[62] The *Enquirer* picked up and quoted Van Buren's commitment to being an "inflexible and uncompromising opponent" of abolition in the District.[63] If Van Buren had not reached the point of conceding to his critics the

---

[60] *Opinions of Martin Van Buren Vice President of the United States,* 4–5.

[61] The pro-Van Buren Democrat Representative John Claiborne would go even further in his "Address to the People of Mississippi," arguing that a "violation of the public faith by Congress involves a violation of the Constitution." "Address to the People of Mississippi."

[62] The inclusion of this framing within the pamphlet version of the letter suggests that Van Buren did not reject it.

[63] This phrase would later be adopted by the *Mississippi Free Trader* as the header to its editorial column. For example, "Thursday, October 27, 1836," *Mississippi Free Trader,* October 27, 1836.

unconstitutionality of congressional action in the District, he had traveled a significant distance from the Wright letter's position that such action was merely "impolitic."

Van Buren's ultimate campaign position held echoes of the wider debate over slavery in the District of Columbia within which he was maneuvering in 1835–36. The vice president's position that Congress could not act in the District against the wishes of the slaveholding States without violating "the spirit of that compromise of interests which lies at the basis of our social compact" fell short of the candid declaration of unconstitutionality that his opponents were pushing him toward. But by embracing arguments about "spirit" and "compromise" the position allowed Van Buren to move closer to the position of determined constitutional opposition to abolition in the District sought by defenders of slavery. For much of 1835, Van Buren and his surrogates had publicly held the various positions that interference with slavery in the District was "highly impolitic," "inexpedient," and that agitating the issue was "against … propriety." But careful wording obscured a precise opinion on the question of the federal government's authority over slavery in the District. A direct concession of the want of a *constitutional* power came only with the March 1836 letters, but was importantly allied with the charge that such action would violate "the spirit of the compromise of interests" which underwrote the constitutional compact. Perhaps more significantly, such a violation was rendered dependent upon the wishes of the slaveholding States. By the March 1836 letters, Van Buren had provided the slaveholding States with a moral veto on action to abolish slavery in the District, even if Congress was not faced with an explicit constitutional prohibition. Van Buren spelled out the real consequence of this position in his inaugural address with a promise to veto any bill aimed at abolition.[64]

Crucially, in the Inaugural Address, Van Buren marked a further evolution of his position by justifying his willingness to veto abolition in the District in terms of an overt founding spirit. Affirming his commitment to a veto, Van Buren told the assembly: "These opinions have been adopted in the firm belief that they are in accordance with the spirit that actuated the venerated fathers of the Republic, and that succeeding experience has proved them to be humane, patriotic, expedient, honorable, and just."[65] By the time of his entry into office in March 1837, Van Buren had reached a point of acting as though abolition in

---

[64] "Inaugural Address of President Van Buren." In his Farewell Address, President Andrew Jackson shared Van Buren's implied belief that abolition was at odds with the spirit of the founding, stating "all efforts on the part of the people of other States to cast odium upon [other State's] institutions, and all measures calculated to disturb their rights of property, or to put in jeopardy their peace and internal tranquillity, are in direct opposition to the spirit in which the Union was formed, and must endanger its safety." "Farewell Address of Andrew Jackson to the People of the United States," *Evening Post*, March 7, 1837.

[65] "Inaugural Address of President Van Buren."

the District was unconstitutional, even if the textual support for such a belief was absent.[66]

8.3 THE CONSTITUTIONAL COMPACT AND THE DEBATES OVER ABOLITION IN THE 1836 ELECTION

Van Buren's willingness to veto bills aimed at abolition within the District of Columbia placed him in alignment with the defenders of slavery in terms of policy but out of alignment with them in important ways with regard to the justification for such a policy. While many defenders of slavery in the South held fast to a Calhounite notion that a compact of States forbade federal interference with slavery in any form, Van Buren and Northerner Democrats began to articulate an understanding of the constitutional compact in which a spirit of the founding played a more prominent role. At foundational level, the debates over abolition in the District in Congress and within the 1836 presidential election were about the nature of the constitutional compact. Abolitionists and those sympathetic to them looked to the precise phraseology of the constitutional text to locate an extensive authority over the District in the hands of Congress. As noted in earlier chapters, they also looked to read the apparently neutral text of the Constitution in correspondence with the Declaration of Independence in order to generate the possibility for an expansive constitutional future in which slaves were recognized as citizens. By comparison, opponents of abolition in the District of Columbia rendered the Constitution as the textual product of a series of compromises agreed between the States. In the 1830s, the temporal nature of these compromises emerged as a point of contention. On one hand, Calhoun and others saw the compromise as an emerging practice in which, for example, concurrent majorities checked each other. On the other hand, a tight

---

[66] It is incumbent on me to note that Van Buren's conception of the obligations of the Constitution as transcending the text were limited here to the question of abolition in the District. On the broader question of constitutional government per se, Van Buren paid lip service to strict construction and the time-honored couplet of "letter and spirit" – albeit contextualized by the importance of cession and compromise and the intention of the framers:

For myself, therefore, I desire to declare, that the principle that will govern me in the high duty to which my country calls me, is a strict adherence to the letter and spirit of the constitution, as it was designed by those who framed it. Looking back as a sacred instrument carefully and not easily framed; remembering that it was throughout a work of concession and compromise; viewing it as limited to national objects; regarding it as leaving to the people and the States all power not explicitly parted with; I shall endeavor to preserve, protect, and defend it, by anxiously referring to its provisions for direction in every action. To matters of domestic concernment which it has intrusted to the Federal Government, and to such as relate to our intercourse with foreign nations, I shall zealously devote myself; beyond those limits I shall never pass.

"Inaugural Address of President Van Buren."

association of compromise with 1787 saw that moment as the compromise that continued to obligate future political actors. For both, the Constitution served as a tangible monument to a moment of past negotiation and settlement. But the latter vision of the Constitution looked not forward to multiple possible constitutional outcomes, but backward to a historic moment, the agreements of which must be honored. Van Buren's promise to veto bills aimed at abolition in the District reflected the view that the Constitution was a historical bargain to be maintained.[67] But his position that the Constitution did not forbid congressional abolition in the District textually placed him closer to the abolitionists than the South would have liked. Instead, in the absence of a clear textual support for that original bargain, Van Buren made recourse to the spirit that informed the bargain. The position that Van Buren and other Northern Democrats eventually adopted took elements of constitutional thought in common circulation – the idea of the compact and the notion of compromise as a mode of constitutional discourse – and reimagined the constitutional compact as not an institutional or legal framework for adjusting federal distributions of power but rather as a spirit, extant at the moment in which those bargains were struck, exemplifying for the current generation, and obligating them to, an ideal of inter-State relations in which abolition was illegitimate. But this reconfiguration of the compact was not restricted to the Van Buren campaign. Within the popular opposition to abolition in the District, such a view of the constitutional compact was unevenly spreading in the mid-1830s.

In popular discourse, Southern opponents of congressional abolition in the District often couched their objections in terms of opposition to the machinations of Northern abolitionists or, specifically, Van Buren, and at the register of a reaction to, rather than any dialogue with, claims of a congressional power over the District or slavery more generally. As such, there were often only halting elaborations of the constitutional basis for such a conclusion. In such a vein, a July 1835 meeting in Richmond, Virginia, suggested that abolition in the District would be "a wanton and obvious violation of the compact between the States."[68] A Hugh Lawson White meeting in Raleigh, North Carolina, accused the people of the Northern States of "disregarding the guarantees of the Constitution" and cited Van Buren's limited opposition to abolition in the District as evidence of his unsuitability as a presidential candidate.[69] In one instance, a reprint in *The Tennessean* zeroed in on Van Buren's concession that Congress possessed the

---

[67] Bonner has suggested that an important strand of Southern thought in the Antebellum period was a reassessment of whether the bargain at Philadelphia in 1787 had been a good one. Robert E. Bonner, *Mastering America: Southern Slaveholders and the Crisis of American Nationhood* (New York: Cambridge University Press, 2009), 68–70.

[68] "Publick Meeting at the Capitol," *Evening Standard*, August 12, 1835.

[69] "White Meeting."

power to abolish slavery in the District and rejected the existence of such a power by reversing the logic of the debate being carried out everywhere else. If Congress possessed a power to take slave property in the District, *The Tennessean* argued, then the inescapable conclusion was that it possessed such a power over the States as well – in voting for Van Buren Southerners would be "forging the chains with which [their] limbs are to be fettered."[70] Why power to interfere in the States would be equivalent to that in District was not explained, a significant omission given that everywhere else debates on the topic were marked by widespread and repeated observations that the federal government did not possess the power to intervene in the States. However, in channeling something more akin to a feeling than a detailed legal argument, *The Tennessean* was not out of step with much of the Southern opposition to abolition in the District.

When elaborations of the constitutional basis for regarding interference in slavery as unconstitutional were present, they explored a variety of constitutional arguments with greater and lesser credibility. Two of the more credible arguments were that the Fifth Amendment barred taking of private property without compensation and that the States of Maryland and Virginia would not have ceded the territory for the District if they had envisaged the possibility of abolition.[71] As was seen in the previous chapter, these lines of argument would feature within the congressional debates over the petitions. But, while they were present within the newspaper attacks on Van Buren over the District, the extent to which these arguments were only two within a variety of pseudo-constitutional arguments is striking.[72] Perhaps because these two arguments offered only qualified constitutional arguments and so implicitly accepted a congressional power of abolition in the District, it was more usual for Southern critics of Van Buren to construct arguments that developed – when they didn't merely assert – an absolute constitutional prohibition on abolition in the District.[73] Such arguments traced multiple routes to the conclusion that abolition in the District was fundamentally unconstitutional, but they often shared the important assumption that such a conclusion was feasible because of

---

[70] "The Difference."

[71] The latter argument was repeatedly regularly although why the intent of Maryland and Virginia held constitutional authority was not systematically explained. In *Pinckney's Report*, the question was more carefully dealt with by arguing that betrayal of the two States amounted to a "violation of the public faith" and by tying the understanding of the two States to the broader intention of the framers in allowing for cession of the ten miles square (see previous chapter).

[72] For example, "Mr. Van Buren's Letter on the Subject of Abolition," *United States' Telegraph*, March 19, 1836; "District of Columbia," *Richmond Enquirer*, September 4, 1835.

[73] These two arguments were only qualified arguments in the sense that they left the door open to abolition in different circumstances; if Congress was in a position to provide compensation for these takings, or if Maryland and Virginia were no longer in opposition to such a measure, then presumably Congress could act. Such fears were not without some substance; when in 1862 Congress did enact abolition in the District it would do so under a scheme of compensation and while capacity of the two States to object was significantly diminished.

a historically shared understanding of the impermissibility of such action at the moment of the Constitution's creation. Just as Van Buren would come to invoke "the spirit of that compromise of interests which lies at the basis of our social compact," some of these arguments came to locate the authority for a proslavery reading of the Constitution in the notion of an understanding supplemental to, or in some cases more fundamental than, the precise wording of the constitutional text.

Within constitutional arguments that drew upon the notion that interference with slavery was limited by agreements struck at the time of the nation's founding there were distinct argumentative strands. One strand was the arguments that saw respect for contractual relations as intertwined with the creation of the federal compact. For instance, a public meeting reported in the Tuscaloosa *Flag of the Union* looked to the "formation and adoption of the Constitution" as the origin of an agreement that no body had authority to "dissolve or impair" the relations between master and slave.[74] Another strand followed the understanding of the Constitution as an institutional agreement between States. This view, espoused by John C. Calhoun, held firm to the spirit of '98 and the Virginia and Kentucky resolutions but grafted an aggressively proslavery federal conclusion onto the sovereignty of the States.[75] But a further strand drew upon the sense that there was a spirit of the Constitution that transcended either an obligation to observe contractual relations existing at the founding or the legal-rational institutionalization of federalism emerging from it. This strand anticipated and, in some cases, developed alongside Van Buren's understanding that the question of slavery in the District of Columbia could be resolved by appeal to a spirit of compromise.[76] However, among those pressuring Van Buren from the slaveholding South for a more proslavery or anti-abolitionist posture, the separation of these different strands and their relationship with States' rights and strict construction was not always clear.

Southern actors during the electoral campaign stated in various ways the belief that the agreement of noninterference in the slaveholding States, which they ascribed to the Constitution, extended to the District as well, often with that obligation arising from the notion that the founding represented a bargain between North and South and that the spirit undergirding that bargain held political authority. But the different models of the compact blended into one another as authors sought to present their most compelling argument. For instance, in late September of 1835, the *Richmond Whig* offered arguments

[74] "Public Meeting," *Flag of the Union*, November 14, 1835.

[75] Looking at this strand, Don Fehrenbacher remained unconvinced that the compact amounted to more than an aggressive retort to potential interference. Don E. Fehrenbacher and Ward M. McAfee, *The Slaveholding Republic: An Account of the United States Government's Relations to Slavery* (Oxford: Oxford University Press, 2001), 69–81.

[76] For example, at the end of 1835, the Georgia Legislature was reported as viewing interference with slavery in the District as in "conflict with the spirit of the Constitution." "No Title," *New-Hampshire Sentinel*, December 31, 1835.

against the constitutionality of abolition in which the notion of a foundational compact of the States took precedence over the express textual grant of congressional authority over the District of Columbia. Taking particular exception with Van Buren's claim that abolition was not permissible "without a change of Constitution," the newspaper argued that textual amendment was not competent to adjust the original principles of the federal compact.[77] The *Whig* was arguing that the foundational principle of slaveholding was itself prior to and more authoritative than the constitutional text. But a month later, a different article from the same paper was circulating which "emphatically" denied that Congress held a power over the District equivalent to that which a State legislature held over a State.[78] Instead, the Richmond newspaper took the position that, as the "Federal Constitution is a federative compact among sovereign powers," when it came to the District, "a mere municipal appendage," Congress held only the powers that were positively ascribed to it in the Constitution.[79]

At different moments a clearer articulation of the idea that understandings and extratextual agreements informed the parameters of legitimate action on slavery could be observed. Although willing to circulate the useful arguments offered by the *Whig*, the *Telegraph* could be more forthright in its invocation of understandings said to inform the actions of 1787–88. In October 1835, the *United States' Telegraph* reprinted a letter claiming that the States south of Virginia would never have agreed to the federal compact if they had believed it allowed for abolition.[80] A year later in the fall of 1836, the *Telegraph* made an explicit connection between the compact and the ability to regulate slavery, defining any attempt to interfere with slavery as "an assault on the constitution itself."[81] To do so, the *Telegraph* turned to the "time of the adoption of the federal constitution" and asserted that during this period the slaveholding States had "required a positive recognition of their rights to hold slaves."[82] On this basis, the newspaper claimed that slavery became part of the federal compact, and crucially "a part, without which, the compact itself never would have been ratified." From here, it concluded that any "attempt, therefore, to interfere with the question of slavery, being an attempt to abridge the rights secured under the compact, is an assault on the constitution itself."[83] The editor of the *Telegraph*, Duff Green, took the opportunity presented by a prospectus for a literary company to elaborate this approach to the compact. Dated to September 1836, the prospectus claimed that the "question of slavery, as it now exists in the United

[77] "Mr. Van Buren's Letter – Slavery."
[78] "Mr. Van Buren and the District," *United States' Telegraph*, October 19, 1835.
[79] "Mr. Van Buren and the District."
[80] "The 'Magnanimous South,'" *United States' Telegraph*, October 28, 1835.
[81] "At the Time of the Adoption of the Federal Constitution …, " *United States' Telegraph*, September 16, 1836.
[82] "At the Time of the Adoption of the Federal Constitution … "
[83] "At the Time of the Adoption of the Federal Constitution … "

States, was, so far as the rest of the world and the non-slaveholding States are concerned, adjusted at the time of the adoption of the federal constitution."[84] Green claimed that the rights of the slaveholding States were "admitted and guarantied" by the other States, and that absent such recognition the Constitution could never have been ratified. "The Union was a measure of compromise ... and the attempt to disturb the original agreement by introducing any modification of it, is to be met and put down by the same considerations which were so conclusive at the time of its adoption."[85] Moving beyond the pointed anti-Van Burenism of the newspaper articles, the prospectus reflected a willingness to see the relations between the States as inflected by the posture of compromise ascribed to the founding.

Nevertheless, the extent to which the States' rights compact was clearly divisible from the spirit of compromise compact in Southern thought was limited. Seeking to throw up any and all obstacles in what they believed to be the abolitionists' path south through the District, defenders of slavery were less careful in parsing constitutional theories than they might have been. A year before it embraced the compact of 1787, the *United States' Telegraph* rejected Van Buren's "plighted faith" in favor of its own belief that "an express provision of the Constitution, and ... the act of cession" showed that Congress had no power over slavery in the District.[86] In a similar vein, Virginian Democrats continued to present Van Buren as a disciple of strict construction of the Constitution even as the candidate's position regarding the District evolved toward a constitutional intentionism informed by the spirit of compromise that had actuated the founders.[87] The overriding imperative of resisting abolitionism made the coherence of constitutional opposition something of a second-order consideration. Consequently, while the theory of the compact as imbued with a spirit of compromise was present in Southern discussions, it often lacked clarity or was easily conflated with the compact of States.

Instead, and perhaps unsurprisingly, it was in the North and among political elites seeking to bridge the tensions between the Northern and Southern sections of the country that the most coherent invocations of a spirit of compromise can be observed. In the North, public meetings expressed opposition to interference in the District of Columbia although they hesitated in identifying such measures as counter to the text of the Constitution. For instance, an anti-abolition meeting at Troy considered "all attempts to induce Congress to abolish Slavery in the District of Columbia, in reference to the question of Slavery, as unwise, inexpedient, and incendiary."[88] In other meetings, elements of the

---

[84] "Prospectus," *United States' Telegraph*, October 3, 1836.   [85] "Prospectus."
[86] "Mr. Van Buren's Letter on the Subject of Abolition."
[87] "The Address of the Central Corresponding Committee to the Citizens of Virginia," *Richmond Enquirer*, August 2, 1836.
[88] "An Anti-Abolition Meeting ...," *National Gazette*, September 21, 1835.

argument that the Constitution rested upon a spirit or incorporated a series of implied agreements were more evident in addresses and resolutions. At Cincinnati, a "Great Anti-Abolition Meeting" argued that the "union of the States ... could only have been effected in the first instance, by a patriotic sacrifice, mutual forbearance, and a decided spirit of compromise."[89] The meeting claimed that by the leaving of the question of slavery to the States, "the implied guarantee was thus promulgated, that slave property should be held sacred by the Constitution and be protected by the Laws." With regard to the District, this resulted in the view that congressional legislation was "not expedient" because it would result in depriving citizens of property in slaves, "which right we believe is secured to them by the Constitution and laws of the land." In Chautauqua County, New York, a "democratick meeting" resolved that such interference was "unjust ... inexpedient ... [and] if not unconstitutional, as violating the spirit if not the letter of that common charter of our rights."[90]

Moreover, Northern meetings were more willing to articulate the view that the compact itself consisted of or was tied to a spirit of compromise. In Portland, Maine, a meeting stated its belief that no power was granted to the "General Government to interfere in any respect" with the subject of slavery.[91] This reflected their belief that the Constitution was "the result of compromise" in which the differences between the States were "adjusted" prior to ratification. The Portland meeting resolved that "the Union must be preserved; and that the principles and spirit of the fundamental compact which constitutes the People of our happy country one people, must be maintained holy and inviolate, as the ark of our political salvation." In New Haven, a meeting of citizens resolved that the Constitution "as the basis of our national compact was formed in a patriotic spirit of mutual concession, and that any citizen who attempts to undermine its foundations, is an enemy to the best interests of his country."[92] Nearby Hartford, Connecticut, called for the Constitution to be interpreted "in the same spirit of conciliation and compromise in which it was framed" and viewed it as "a violation of the spirit of the Constitution" for citizens of one State to seek to effect a change in domestic relations in another.[93] Later that year, the *Richmond Enquirer* noted with approval that a meeting at Rochester, New York, had resolved that inter-State appeals on the subject of domestic slavery were "a violation of the spirit of the compact under which the States are united" and that the "Union of these States [was] a contract binding upon the consciences of their citizens."[94] Time and again, Northern public meetings turned to the language of compromise, conciliation, and spirit in

[89] "Great Anti-Abolition Meeting in Cincinnati," *United States' Telegraph*, 1836.
[90] "Thursday, October 1," *Evening Post*, October 1, 1835.
[91] "Anti-Slavery – Abolition," *The Globe*, August 26, 1835.
[92] "Meeting at New Haven," *Connecticut Courant*, September 21, 1835.
[93] "No Title," *The New-London Gazette, and General Advertiser*, September 30, 1835.
[94] "Proceedings of Meeting at Rochester, NY 24th Instant," *Richmond Enquirer*, October 6, 1835.

order to articulate an opposition to abolitionist activity and the prospect of abolition in the District of Columbia.

A bridge between these public addresses and the rhetoric being honed by the Van Buren campaign was the series of messages and communications generated by the political institutions of the States. A flurry of official communications between the States in 1836 provided an opportunity for State Governors to place on record their views of the constitutional questions being raised by abolition. These were used to give the notion of a compact imbued with a spirit of compromise an official imprimatur. Van Buren convinced Governor Marcy of New York to use his gubernatorial message to challenge abolition and to deliver a speech for a Southern audience.[95] Marcy devoted nearly a third of the message, ostensibly on the issues facing the State of New York, to remarks on slavery and abolition, reminding his audience that slavery had existed in almost every State of the Union at the time of the founding and that the founders had "delegated to Congress no power to act on this subject" beyond a power to prohibit the importation of slaves beginning in 1808.[96] The New York location of Marcy's message resulted in more attention being given to the question of "managing" the abolitionist activity in that State that so offended the South than the prospects for congressional action.[97] However, without directly alluding to the question of slavery in the District, Marcy declared, "Legislation by Congress would be a violation of the Constitution by which that body exists … The powers of Congress cannot be enlarged so as to bring the subject of slavery within its cognizance, without the consent of the slaveholding States."[98] Further on, he turned to the obligations arising from the federal compact to which New Yorkers "cherish[ed] unabated attachment." The advantages of the Union bound the people of New York, said Marcy, "to a course of fraternal conduct towards their sister States, and lay them under the highest and most sacred obligations to fulfill in good faith … all duties it imposes on them, and to abstain from all practices incompatible with these duties, or contrary to the spirit of any of its provisions."[99]

A rash of communications and resolutions followed, each affirming Marcy's position to one degree or another, and most reiterating an understanding of the constitutional compact as originating in a spirit of compromise that ought to continue to be honored. The following day, in Massachusetts, Governor Edward Everett echoed the sentiment that the compact bound Northern

[95] Shade, "'The Most Delicate and Exciting Topics'," 472–73.

[96] William L. Marcy, "To the Senate and Assembly," in *Journal of the Senate of the State of New-York, At Their Fifty-Ninth Session, Begun and Held at the Capital, in the City of Albany, the Fifth Day of January, 1836* (Albany: E. Croswell, 1836), 27.

[97] The mail campaign, seen as having one of its sources in New York City and particularly the Tappan-led activity centered on Nassau Street, and the violent disruption of the Utica meeting by a Samuel Beardsley-led anti-abolitionist mob, likely made abolitionism within the State a more immediate concern for Governor Marcy than the question of congressional action in the District.

[98] Marcy, "To the Senate and Assembly," 28.   [99] Marcy, "To the Senate and Assembly," 31.

citizens to a recognition of and respect for slavery, and that such action accorded with the intentions of the founding generation. Everett told the Legislature there that the "compact expressly recognizes the existence of slavery ... Every thing that tends to disturb the relations created by this compact is at war with its spirit."[100] He called upon his fellow citizens to "imitate the example of our fathers, the Adamses, the Hancocks, and other eminent patriots of the revolution" who had entered the Union "on the principle of forbearance and toleration on this subject."[101] The Legislature and Governor of Maine stated on behalf of that State that the "federal compact owed its origin to the spirit of deference, conciliation and mutual forbearance, which pervaded the then independent States."[102] The Kentucky General Assembly denounced interference in the States as "at war with the solemn sanctions of that instrument which binds us together," the abolition mail campaign as "a violation of the original basis of the federal compact," and abolition in the District as amounting to "a breach of the implied faith of the nation, towards the citizens of that District."[103] Michigan's legislative bodies resolved that the acts within the non-slaveholding States, "having for their object an interference in the rights of the slaveholder, are in direct violation of the obligations of the compact of our Union."[104] In Virginia, the Legislature offered resolutions that spoke of the "intimate and sacred relations that exist between the States of this Union" and rejected the constitutionality of congressional abolition in the District.[105] North Carolina expressed the belief that abolition in the District would be a breach of faith towards the States who had originally ceded the territory.[106] In Georgia the General Assembly claimed that the District of Columbia was the common property of the whole American people and that any interference with slavery there would be "unauthorized by, and contrary to the spirit of that sacred charter of American liberty."[107]

---

[100] Edward Everett, *Address of His Excellency to the Two Branches of the Legislature on the Organization of the Government, for the Political Year Commencing January 6, 1836* (Boston: Dutton and Wentworth, 1836), 29–30.

[101] Everett, *Address of His Excellency to the Two Branches of the Legislature on the Organization of the Government*, 30.

[102] "Communication from the Governor, Transmitting a Report and Resolutions Adopted by the Legislature of the State of Maine, Relative to the Subject of Slavery," 3.

[103] "Communication From the Governor, Transmitting Resolutions from the Legislature of Kentucky on the Subject of Abolition Societies," *New York Senate Papers No. 79*, 1836, 5.

[104] "Communication From the Governor, Transmitting a Preamble and Resolutions of the Legislature of Michigan, in Relation to Slavery," *New York Senate Papers No. 77*, 1836, 4.

[105] "Communication From the Governor, Transmitting a Copy of Certain Resolutions of the General Assembly of the State of Virginia," *Documents of the Assembly of the State of New-York, Fifty-Ninth Session, No. 246*, 1836.

[106] "Message From the Governor, Transmitting a Preamble and Resolutions from the Legislature of North-Carolina," *Documents of the Assembly of the State of New-York, Fifty-Ninth Session, No. 22*, 1836.

[107] "Communication From the Governor, Transmitting a Copy of a Preamble and Resolutions Passed by the Legislature of the State of Georgia," *Documents of the Assembly of the State of*

Others questioned these claims, but as they did so they acknowledged the widespread endorsement of the "spirit of compromise." In the midst of the messages, Rhode Island abolitionists were already complaining of being charged with violating ancient compacts, the latter being "built entirely on implication."[108] Characterizing the environment they faced, their "Report on the Constitution" claimed that ""We abide by our compact" is the motto of the Pro-slavery party at the North, and "you are violating your fathers' compact," is the charge made against us in the South."[109] The evolving sanctioning of the notion of the compact as imbued by the spirit of compromise by the Democratic Party over the course of the year did little to change the situation. By early 1837, as Van Buren prepared to take office, the abolitionist N. P. Rogers would complain that "You cannot advance in direction of the castle of this pet-monster of the republic – slavery ... – but your ears are assailed from every quarter, with cries of, 'Compact' – 'Pledge to our Southern brethren' – 'Guaranty of their peculiar institutions' – 'the great compromise."[110] While the messy conceptualization of the compact evident in the Southern Whig attacks on Van Buren did not disappear, in the North a conceptualization of the compact in terms of a commitment to a spirit of compromise was significantly crystalized and legitimized by the end of 1836.[111]

New-York, Fifty-Ninth Session, No. 109, 1836. Nonetheless, with regard to abolitionist activity, the General Assembly also claimed "the perpetuity of this glorious Union ... is only to be ensured by a strict adherence to the letter of the Constitution" – which was interpreted to require the North to "crush the traitorous designs of the abolitionists" and put to an end their "impertinent, fanatical and disloyal interference with matters settled by the Constitution."

[108] *Proceedings of the Rhode-Island Anti-Slavery Convention, Held in Providence, on the 2d, 3d, and 4th of February, 1836* (Providence: H. H. Brown, 1836), 71.

[109] *Proceedings of the Rhode-Island Anti-Slavery Convention, Held in Providence, on the 2d, 3d, and 4th of February, 1836*, 70.

[110] N. P. Rogers, "The Constitution," *Quarterly Anti-Slavery Magazine* 2, no. 6 (January 1837): 145.

[111] Over the course of 1836, Pennsylvania would push back, with its antislavery Governor Ritner using his end of year message to reaffirm that opposition to slavery at home, in the Territories, and in the District of Columbia – "the very hearth and domestic abode of the national honor – have ever been, and are the cherished doctrines of our State." "Governor's Message," *Carlisle Weekly Herald*, December 15, 1836. Ritner's gesture moved John Greenleaf Whittier to pen the poem "Ritner," which began:

> Thank God for the token! one lip is still free,
> One spirit untrammelled, unbending one knee!

Ritner's message followed the mid-year introduction of resolutions into the Pennsylvanian House that Congress held the power to abolish slavery in the District and that it was "expedient" for it to do so. The author of the resolutions was Thaddeus Stevens. In November the General Assembly of Vermont resolved that Congress did have the power to abolish slavery in the District. But neither Ritner nor Stevens reflected the mainstream of American thought on this issue. John Greenleaf Whittier, "Ritner," in *Anti-Slavery Poems: Songs of Labor and Reform* (Boston: Houghton Mifflin and Company, 1892), 47–50; "Pennsylvania Legislature," *Gettysburg Compiler*, June 14, 1836; "Resolutions."

8.4 CONCLUSION

It would be an overstatement to claim that that the presidential election cycle of 1835–36 was dominated by the question of slavery in the District of Columbia or even by slavery and abolition. Especially beyond the South, other issues – the Bank, the Tariff, Internal Improvements, and the legacy of the Jackson administration – provided grist for the mills of the campaigns. But it would be equally disingenuous to argue in 1836, as the *Middlebury Free Press* attempted to, that the question of abolition was "not directly involved in the approaching presidential election."[112] The nature of the Democratic Party's cross-sectional coalition and the tumultuous atmosphere resulting from abolitionist activity and its repression made the issues of slavery and abolition a potential pitfall for Van Buren in 1836. Once the Southern Whigs identified the District of Columbia as a pressure point for Van Buren, addressing it became unavoidable. During the campaign the question of abolition in the District was a source of recurrent discomfort for Van Buren, necessitating repeated attempts to quell a Southern breakaway over the issue. Over the course of those attempts, the candidate's position on the question underwent a sharpening that resulted in a declaration, after Van Buren's victory, of an "inflexible and uncompromising" opposition to abolition in the District "in accordance with the spirit that actuated the venerated fathers of the republic." The invocation of a spirit of the founding as a curb on presidential action – and indeed necessitating a presidential veto – built upon a campaign which had seen recourse to "spirit," and particularly a constitutional "spirit of compromise." In Northern public meetings and through the formal messages and addresses of Northern Governors, a conceptualization of the federal compact as containing within it an obligation to the spirit of compromise upon which it was founded gained ground and was legitimized. The campaign literature issued by Van Buren, in which the obligation to avoid a violation of "the spirit of that compromise of interests which lies at the basis of our social compact" was deemed of equivalence to a direct constitutional prohibition, had placed a similar stress on spirit as constraining and guiding inter-State relations. And, if not fully separated from the enduring conception of the compact as an agreement between States, similar notions of understandings more fundamental than the constitutional text itself were sporadically evident in the slaveholding States as well. By the end of the presidential election cycle, abolitionists would voice their frustration at the persuasive nature of such arguments.

In one important way the election of Van Buren resolved the question of abolition in the District of Columbia. The Little Magician's commitment to a presidential veto ended what small hope might have existed that abolition in the District could be achieved in the short term through the federal legislative

---

[112] "Mr. Van Buren and Slavery," *Middlebury Free Press*, March 29, 1836.

process. By the time of the 1840 election, the political and antislavery environment had changed. Van Buren again faced Harrison in that campaign, but there was no rival Southern candidate to press him on slavery in the same way as Hugh Lawson White had. Moreover, with the abolitionist movement splintering, James Birney ran as a Liberty Party candidate and Van Buren was freed from any accusations that he was the abolitionist candidate for the White House. While the slave trade in the District would be abolished under the 1850 Compromise (once the 1846 retrocession of Alexandria returned the regional headquarters of the slave trade to Virginian territory), it would not be until the Civil War and 1862 that Congress would abolish slavery in the District.[113] To the extent that the language of the compact as a spirit of compromise was mobilized with the aim of allowing Van Buren to reach the White House given the existence of the issue of abolition in the District in the 1836 campaign, it succeeded. To the extent that advocates for slavery applied pressure on Van Buren regarding the District as part of a battle for slavery at the threshold of its territory, they succeed in defusing whatever momentum the abolitionists were building on the issue and made the District safe for slaveholding for another twenty-five years. A candidate's position on abolition in the District of Columbia would not serve as a litmus test in the same way in future presidential campaigns.

If the deployment of the compact as a spirit of compromise helped to politically contain the question of abolition in the District of Columbia, it nonetheless had consequences that extended beyond that issue and that election. In his inaugural address, Van Buren was careful to apply the notion of a spirit of the founding to the specific question of abolition in the District. Nonetheless, his critics quickly identified the move as holding significance for broader questions of constitutional interpretation.[114] Moreover, others during the election were already extending the concept to cover wider categories of abolitionist activity and to protect their own constitutional legitimacy. While the issue of abolition in the District had brought the spirit of compromise approach to the compact into focus, the idea of a constitutional spirit, and its association with the founding generation, did not exhaust itself in that theater. In reality, the idea of a spirit of the compact was a response to a wider problematic of which abolition in the District was merely one example: How to address constitutional issues deliberately or inadvertently obscured in the constitutional text in the pursuit of a bargain in 1787 but which called for constitutional responses and thus decisive clarification at a later time? The

---

[113] A. Glenn Crothers, "The 1846 Retrocession of Alexandria: Protecting Slavery and the Slave Trade in the District of Columbia," in *In the Shadow of Freedom: The Politics of Slavery in the National Capital*, ed. Paul Finkelman and Donald R. Kennon (Athens: Ohio University Press, 2010), 141–68. In advocating for the Compromise of 1850, Daniel Webster cited the retrocession as a reason that there was no further need for a slave trade in the District. Crothers, "The 1846 Retrocession of Alexandria," 167.

[114] See the discussion at the beginning of the next chapter.

question of slavery in the District may have been a "*casus omissus*" in the constitutional text, but that observation provided no guidance in itself of how to navigate the question constitutionally.[115] As we have seen in the previous chapter, the final resolution of the question of abolition in the District rested upon a willingness to decisively recognize the enslaved as either persons or property – the essential ambiguity of the Constitution left unresolved, but recognized, in the three-fifths clause. A return to 1787–88 through a constitutional spirit and the associated idea of an intention on the part of framers provided one mechanism by which to adjudicate this. Van Buren had opened the door to such a decisive adjudication but retreated from its final consequence by acknowledging a conflict between the spirit of the Constitution and the constitutional text but then personally proclaiming the text while acting in accordance to the spirit. But once acknowledged, however haltingly, this was not an idea that could be easily shut out. In the afterlife of the election of 1836, the idea of a constitutional spirit distinct from the text would emerge as a powerful concept within American constitutional debate and specifically within its attempts to negotiate the legacy of the three-fifths clause.

[115] An omitted case. The *Richmond Enquirer* identified the question as such in the reprint included in the 1836 *Opinions* pamphlet. *Opinions of Martin Van Buren Vice President of the United States*, 3.

9

The Afterlife of the Compact of 1836

The duty of the court is to interpret the instrument they have framed with the best lights we can obtain on the subject, and to administer it as we find it, according to its true intent and meaning when it was adopted.

Chief Justice Robert Taney (1856)[1]

This shield, which God has given us to put over the head of the slave, we have, traitorously, made the protection of the slaveholder.

Gerrit Smith (1844)[2]

As noted at the end of the previous chapter, abolitionists in the mid-1830s had grown frustrated at being met with "the compact" at every turn. They had two potential options in responding to this. The first was to identify and reject the argument that a spirit of the founding could be substituted for the constitutional text. The second was to accept the premise that the spirit could be holding over the constitutional text and seek to fashion an abolitionism within that framework. To a striking extent, the second response proved to be the dominant strategy among abolitionists. One strand of such a response is represented in the increasing Garrisonian rejection of the Constitution as a legitimate authority given the historical context of its creation. Setting aside the claim that the constitutional text contained no direct invocation of slavery, Garrisonians moved to accepting the characterization of the document's creation as a grand bargain over slavery. Forcefully spelt out in the American Anti-Slavery Society's 1844 Address, this posture led to the conclusion that the only just response to the Constitution was to withdraw support for it. A second strand of abolitionism similarly accepted the idea that the Constitution should

[1] *Dred Scott* v. *Sandford* (1857).
[2] Gerrit Smith, *Gerrit Smith's Constitutional Argument* (Jackson & Chaplin, 1844), 16.

be understood with reference to the spirit that animated it. Given voice by Samuel P. Chase this strand claimed that the Constitution represented an attempt by antislavery founders to grapple with the reality of slavery in their historical moment and to construct an institutional apparatus that would provide a path toward its extinction. Equally willing to incorporate the idea that the spirit of the founding should guide constitutional understanding, they nonetheless sought to challenge the characterization of that spirit as protective of slavery.

In concert with these developments, after 1836 supporters of slavery began to refine their own understanding of the role of spirit in constitutional interpretation. Moving away from appeals to a spirit of compromise and the understandings enabling the compact embodied in the Constitution, political figures made appeals to the recognition of slavery within the historical moment of the founding. Inverting the demands of free black activists in the 1820s for constitutional recognition as citizens, opponents of abolition instead prioritized the recognition of slavery as a constitutional institution and denied enslaved people recognition as anything other than property. Given judicial sanction in the cases of *Prigg* v. *Pennsylvania* and *Dred Scott* v. *Sandford*, the pseudo-doctrine of recognition presented a highly restrictive understanding of constitutional spirit as the measure of constitutionality. Grounded in the attitudes of those framing and ratifying the Constitution, it offered a historically contextualized "intention" as a means for recovering constitutional meaning. Disregarding changes in public opinion or the flexibility/ambiguity of the text, this mode of constitutional interpretation tied the Constitution back to non-textual indications of the intent of 1787–88. Calcifying and historicizing the notion of constitutional spirit, it produced the aggressively proslavery constitution that would be articulated by Chief Justice Taney from the bench in *Dred Scott*. To different ends, both abolitionists and their opponents would gravitate in the 1840s toward a view of the Constitution as correctly understood only with reference to the attitudes that were prevalent at the time of its creation. As these historical attitudes were identified and categorized through the historical record, they would take on the character of the various framers' and ratifiers' intentions for the Constitution. Thus the legacy of the compact of 1836 in the 1840s would be a legitimization of the original intentions of those who crafted the Constitution in 1787–88 as the arbiter of constitutional meaning.

9.1 WILLIAM LEGGETT AND THE REJECTION OF CONSTITUTIONAL SPIRIT

In antislavery circles, Van Buren's Inaugural Address was received with recognition that his language regarding the District of Columbia marked something significant. First reactions focused upon the promise to veto any bill proposing abolition in the District of Columbia. In the *Liberator*'s initial response to the inaugural address, Garrison bristled that the first act of the new President was to make a "solemn pledge" to "rivet the chains of those who groan in bondage."[3] Comparing Van Buren to the Pharaoh, Caligula, and Nero, Garrison condemned him as a disgrace to America and a mockery of republicanism.[4] The *Emancipator*'s assessment of the address sensed something new in Van Buren's position and declared, "we can neither respect the man nor his principles. . . . There is neither honesty, nor republicanism, nor manhood in the position he has now taken."[5] Two weeks after its initial reaction, the *Liberator* reprinted an article from William Leggett in which the latter noted, "Mr. Van Buren is the first President of the United States who, in assuming that office, has held up his veto power, *in terrorem*, to the world."[6] Leggett's criticism was welcomed by the *Atlas* who saw him as an erstwhile die-hard Democrat and so interpreted his attack on the Inaugural as proof that Van Buren was out of step with his wider constituency.[7] Leggett's article, more so than those of the *Liberator* or the *Emancipator*, linked Van Buren's promise to use the veto to the notion of a spirit that actuated the fathers of the republic.[8] Leggett noticed something new and altogether unwelcome in Van Buren's use of the concept of a constitutional spirit in the latter's Inaugural Address.

   Leggett, although warming to the abolitionist cause slowly over the course of the 1830s, had earlier considered the consequences of invoking a spirit as a mode of constitutional interpretation.[9] In September 1835,

---

[3] "Martin Van Buren," *The Liberator*, March 11, 1837.   [4] "Martin Van Buren."

[5] "The New President . . . , " *The Emancipator*, March 9, 1837.

[6] "Character of the Inaugural – By One of the President's Friends," *The Liberator*, March 24, 1837.

[7] The *Liberator* lifted Leggett's article from the *Atlas*. In fact, as is discussed subsequently, Leggett's attacks on the Democrats' positions vis-à-vis the abolitionists had been bringing him into conflict with the Party apparatus since at least 1835.

[8] It is not clear whether the editor of the *Atlas* or Garrison fully appreciated the critique that Leggett offered of the Inaugural Address. Whether in error or in an attempt to shorten Leggett's article, a crucial paragraph of Leggett's article (in which he highlighted the dangers of a constitutional spirit) was left out of the *Liberator*'s reprint. For the complete version (used in the discussion below), cf. William Leggett, "Commencement of the Administration of Martin Van Buren," in *A Collection of the Political Writings of William Leggett, Volume 2*, ed. Theodore Sedgwick Jr. (New York: Taylor & Dodd, 1840), 250–56.

[9] Leggett would attest in 1835 that "the whole scheme of immediate emancipation, and of promiscuous intermarriage of the two races is preposterous, and revolting alike to common sense and common decency," but by 1837 declared to his readers "We are an Abolitionist" and asserted "there never was a band of men, engaged in any struggle for freedom, whose whole course and conduct evinced more unmixed purity of motive, and truer or loftier devotion to the great cause of human emancipation." In an 1838 letter, Leggett offered his view that "Abolition is, in my sense, a necessary and a glorious part of democracy." On Leggett's conversion to abolition, see Jonathan Earle's discussion in *Jacksonian Antislavery & the Politics of Free Soil, 1824–1854*. William Leggett, "Riot at the Chatham-Street Chapel," in *Democratick Editorials: Essays in Jacksonian Political Economy*, ed. Lawrence H. White (Indianapolis: Liberty Fund, 1984), 192; William Leggett, "Progress of Fanaticism," in *Democratick Editorials: Essays in Jacksonian Political Economy*, ed. Lawrence H. White (Indianapolis: Liberty Fund, 1984), 212, 216; William Leggett, "Copy of a Letter from Wm. Leggett, To –," in *A Collection of the Political*

writing for the *Evening Post*, Leggett had reflected upon the extent and consequences of there being a spirit of the Constitution. On September 4, Leggett wrote of his support for an abolitionist address, "with a single exception" that he did not agree that it was the duty of the Congress to abolish slavery in the District of Columbia.[10] Accepting that Congress had the constitutional power to do so, Leggett nonetheless believed that a "spirit of conciliation and compromise should govern in the matter, as it did in the formation of our sacred *Magna Charta*."[11] The following week, Leggett broadened his reflections to take in the pressure being placed upon abolitionists not to upset their Southern brethren. Here he was more fully on the side of the abolitionists, but again the spirit or sentiments of the founding were a crucial element in arriving at such a view. He rejected the idea that the abolitionists were obliged to refrain from discussion of slavery by the federal constitution "in letter or spirit."[12] Any other conclusion could only be reached through an inadequate study of the Constitution itself and "those documents which illustrate its history, and the sentiments, motives and policy of its founders."[13] But two days later, his apparent exasperation at the use of the idea of a spirit of the compact to foreclose debate led him to address the value of spirit directly. In an editorial on September 9, Leggett decried attempts to erect slavery as a positive good and forbid discussion of it as a "violation of the spirit of the federal compact":

What a mysterious thing this federal compact must be, which enjoins so much by its spirit that is wholly omitted in its language – nay not only omitted, but which is directly contrary to some of its express provisions![14]

To drive home his point, he suggested that such an interpretation of the Constitution was at odds with the attitudes that had informed the founding generation.[15]

Writings of William Leggett, Volume 1, ed. Theodore Sedgwick Jr. (New York: Taylor & Dodd, 1840), 335; Jonathan H. Earle, *Jacksonian Antislavery & the Politics of Free Soil, 1824–1854* (Chapel Hill: The University of North Carolina Press, 2004), 22–23.

[10] William Leggett, "The Anti-Slavery Society," in *Democratick Editorials: Essays in Jacksonian Political Economy*, ed. Lawrence H. White (Indianapolis: Liberty Fund, 1984), 201. While White dates this editorial to September 7 in the collection, it was actually printed on September 4.

[11] Leggett, "The Anti-Slavery Society," 202.

[12] William Leggett, "Abolitionists," in *Democratick Editorials: Essays in Jacksonian Political Economy*, ed. Lawrence H. White (Indianapolis: Liberty Fund, 1984), 207.

[13] Leggett, "Abolitionists," 207.

[14] William Leggett, "Slavery No Evil," in *Democratick Editorials: Essays in Jacksonian Political Economy*, ed. Lawrence H. White (Indianapolis: Liberty Fund, 1984), 209, 210.

[15] "But the sentiments which Jefferson, and Madison, and Patrick Henry freely expressed are treasonable now, according to the new reading of the federal compact." Leggett, "Slavery No Evil," 210.

Illness placed Leggett's career at the *Evening Post* on hold in the fall of 1835, constraining his ability to develop these reflections in print.[16] Nonetheless, they foreshadowed the critique that he would level against Van Buren in 1837. In the September 1835 articles, Leggett adopted two divergent but intertwined positions: (1) that there could be no spirit of the compact at odds with the text, and (2) that the attitudes evidenced at the founding proved that the anti-abolitionists' understanding of the spirit was incorrect. These positions were divergent insofar as the success of one argument negated the need for the other. But they were mutually reinforcing within a broader vision of seeing the text and spirit as ultimately identical. Leggett's efforts in showing that the attitudes of the founding generation were at odds with the positions taken by the anti-abolitionists in 1830s worked, not to correct an understanding of the spirit, but to tie the spirit more closely to the text. The danger, as Leggett came to see it, was that unless the spirit was tightly bound to the text it offered an expansive and subjective mode of interpreting the Constitution. At stake in September 1835 was the prospect that, for slaveholders, a spirit of the compact could incorporate ever-greater requirements of support for slavery on the part of the North. By fall of 1835 the North was "[n]ot only ... told that slavery is no evil, but that it is criminal towards the south, and a violation of the spirit of the federal compact, to indulge even a hope that the chains of the captive may some day or other ... be broken."[17] Leggett feared that were this claim accepted, the "next claim we shall hear from the arrogant south will be a call upon us to pass edicts forbidding men to think on the subject of slavery, on the ground that even mediation on that topic is interdicted by the spirit of the federal compact."[18] Spirit, as a mode of constitutional interpretation divorced from the text, was too capacious and perhaps too capricious to ensure that constitutional government did not amount to the whims of a dominant faction.

The concern that spirit without text was wholly unanchored informed Leggett's charge against Van Buren's Inaugural Address. Leggett acknowledged, and approved, Van Buren's concluding commitment to govern strictly in accordance to the letter and spirit of the Constitution.[19] But he

[16] Theodore Sedgwick gave illness as the reason that Leggett left the *Evening Post* in fall of 1835, an explanation that Lawrence H. White concurs with. Both authors also note that Leggett's willingness to confront the Democratic Party in print created a challenging environment for the newspaper. In October, the *Post* reported that the Democratic Republican General Committee meeting at Tammany Hall had voted to censure the newspaper and resolved to no longer publish their proceedings therein as a result of the *Evening Post's* continuing discussion of abolition. Theodore Jr. Sedgwick, "Preface," in *A Collection of the Political Writings of William Leggett, Volume 1*, ed. Theodore Jr. Sedgwick (New York: Taylor & Dodd, 1840), xiv; Lawrence H. White, "Forward," in *Democratick Editorials: Essays in Jacksonian Political Economy*, ed. Lawrence H. White (Indianapolis: Liberty Fund, 1984), xiii; William Leggett, "The Committee and the Evening Post," in *A Collection of the Political Writings of William Leggett, Volume 2*, ed. Theodore Sedgwick Jr. (New York: Taylor & Dodd, 1984), 76–80.

[17] Leggett, "Slavery No Evil," 209.   [18] Leggett, "Slavery No Evil," 209.

[19] Leggett, "Commencement of the Administration of Martin Van Buren."

discounted the commitment on the grounds that it stated nothing more than was demanded by the presidential oath of office, and that the single meaningful discussion of the Inaugural Address – regarding slavery in the District of Columbia – suggested just the opposite. Honing in on Van Buren's promise to veto legislation abolishing slavery in the District of Columbia, Leggett suggested that nothing "but the clearest warrant of constitutional obligation could possibly excuse" such a step.[20] Van Buren had, however, failed to show where the constitutional text supported such a position, instead offering that his course would be in accordance with the spirit that actuated the venerated fathers of the republic. Van Buren, Leggett charged, "does not pretend that such a spirit has made itself palpable and unequivocal in any of the written provisions of the instrument which he has sworn to maintain."[21] Given the promise to govern in accordance with this unmoored spirit, what was constitutional amounted to little more than Van Buren's personal opinions. If the president were not willing to list everything he believed to be constitutional and unconstitutional at the outset, "conjecture may go widely astray, since there is no other very certain mode of ascertaining what is not, in Mr. Van Buren's belief, according to 'the spirit which actuated the venerated fathers of the republic.'"[22]

Leggett regarded Van Buren's implicit rejection of strict construction as making the latter's future course unknowable. Van Buren sought to adopt the spirit of the Constitution as his guide and so "to steer by the uncertain light of the spirit," but, reasoned Leggett, the result is that "we are tossed about on a sea of vague conjecture, and left to the mercy of winds and waves."[23] Turning to the history of the early Republic, Leggett located an adherence to the spirit in deviations from the Jeffersonian ethos:

Hamilton was guided by the *spirit* in proposing the first federal bank; but Jefferson adhered to the *letter* in his argument against that evil scheme. The high tariff system claims for its paternity the *spirit* of the Constitution; but the advocates of a plan of equal taxation, adjusted to the actual wants of the government, find their warrant in the *letter*. The internal improvement system, the compromise system, the distribution system, and every other unequal and aristocratic system which has been adopted in our country, all claim to spring from the *spirit* of the Constitution; but Andrew Jackson found in the *letter* of that instrument his rule of conduct, and it was fondly hoped that his successor meant to emulate his example. Appearances now authorize a fear to the contrary.[24]

A recourse to the spirit of the Constitution marked attempts to (in Leggett's view) move against the democratic will and expand the reach of the federal government in support of aristocratic elements of society. Van Buren's

---

[20] Leggett, "Commencement of the Administration of Martin Van Buren," 253.
[21] Leggett, "Commencement of the Administration of Martin Van Buren," 253.
[22] Leggett, "Commencement of the Administration of Martin Van Buren," 253.
[23] Leggett, "Commencement of the Administration of Martin Van Buren," 253–54.
[24] Leggett, "Commencement of the Administration of Martin Van Buren," 254. Original emphasis.

deployment of the spirit to support a veto of abolition in the District of Columbia could be understood in a similar vein, as an attempt to overcome or subvert the perimeters of the federal government as established by the textual constitution. In asserting that the spirit commanded him to veto, Van Buren claimed a constitutional power not textually bestowed on the executive. One consequence of such lawlessness was elaborated in the final part of Leggett's editorial. Under the capacious spirit of the Constitution and in line with Van Buren's anti-abolitionism, the proslavery mobs attacking alleged abolitionists throughout the nation were the "true friends of the Constitution" and suitably "animated by 'the spirit which actuated the venerated fathers of the republic.'"[25] Shorn of the anchor of the text, the spirit allowed the Constitution to be whatever the strongest asserted it to be. In ways perhaps not widely appreciated at the time, Leggett saw in Van Buren's Inaugural Address not just an unsatisfactory or immoral position vis-à-vis slavery in the District but the emergence of a mode of constitutional interpretation that threatened to undermine the Constitution's primary function. As Leggett identified it, Van Buren's conceptualization of the compact in terms of spirit was a significant shift in Democratic constitutional discourse.

9.2 ABOLITIONIST RECONCEPTIONS OF THE SPIRIT

Nonetheless, if Leggett identified a great danger for constitutional government in Van Buren's move toward spirit, his view was somewhat idiosyncratic. Both within abolitionist circles, and beyond them in the wider political discourse, Van Buren's action was not immediately understood in those terms. As noted earlier, the first reactions of the *Liberator* and the *Emancipator* focused upon Van Buren's support for slavery in the District and the perception that his veto threat was arbitrary. Such views took the notion of a spirit that actuated the founding fathers to be at best a fig leaf for an arbitrary rejection of abolition or at worst as further confirmation that the Constitution was hopeless proslavery. However, one important reaction to the compact as a spirit of compromise came in the form of attempts to refute the characterization of the spirit of the compact as proslavery. As noted in earlier chapters, since the 1820s abolitionists had occasionally sought to read the constitutional text in accordance with what they perceived to be the spirit of the founding. Prior to 1836, this had largely meant construing the text as a commitment to the principles of the Declaration of Independence, rendered as the idea that all men were created equal. But from the mid-1830s, a more robust articulation of a pro-abolition founding spirit was developed in response to the compact arguments offered by defenders of slaveholding.

Already in the midst of the 1836 campaign some abolitionists were growing tired of the ways in which invocations of the supposed compact were working to

---

[25] Leggett, "Commencement of the Administration of Martin Van Buren," 256.

restrict discussion of and opposition to slavery. The Rhode Island Anti-Slavery convention at the beginning of 1836 chaffed at being lectured on "the *'compact'* and of the *'compromise'* which was entered into when the U.S. Constitution was formed."[26] But in place of a rejection of the legitimacy of offering the sentiments of 1787 as binding upon actors in 1836, the Rhode Island abolitionists – in a "Declaration and Expose" – instead sought to show that the spirit of 1787 was in tune with their own abolitionism. Disputing the views attributed to the founding, these abolitionists offered the resolutions against slavery made in the State during the ratification as evidence of the antislavery ethos of the founding and denounced the idea of a solemn compact to defend slavery as an "impudent pretension" (52). Against a conception of the compact as a compromise over slavery, the convention mobilized a rival understanding of the founding, premised on the antislavery of Franklin, Rush, and Jay, and urged their countrymen to *"regain the ground which liberty occupied in 1787"* (29; original emphasis). In the face of the compact offered by opponents of abolition, the Rhode Island abolitionists sought to deploy an understanding of 1787 as supportive of abolition.

The work begun in the "Declaration and Expose" was followed by a "Report on the Constitution" which considered the anti-abolitionist formulation of the compact more directly and developed a rival understanding of it. Considering the efforts of the opponents of abolition to suppress the discussion of slavery, the Rhode Island abolitionists suggested that the former claimed slavery's exception to the demands of free expression without "referring to any provision in the National Constitution."[27] Instead, anti-abolitionists sought to mobilize "the allegation of a supposed national compact, made between the different States, when they first entered into a National Confederacy, and confirmed by the subsequent adoption of our present General Constitution" (70). The temporal division between the creation of the compact and the Constitution's "subsequent adoption" reaffirms the earlier division between the provisions of the Constitution and the compact – the abolitionists are here supposing that the proslavery compact is not to be found in the constitutional text, but in the understandings and compromises that form a penumbra to the text of 1787. Lest this be missed, or the abolitionists acceptance of the (limited) authority of these non-textual elements of the founding, they continued by asserting their own fidelity to the founding fathers:

[Y]our committee cheerfully declare, that their fathers' principles, their fathers' examples and their fathers' compacts, are things sacred in their eyes. If we do not regard them as binding authority in all things, we yet hold them in great reverence. (70–71)

---

[26] *Proceedings of the Rhode-Island Anti-Slavery Convention, Held in Providence, on the 2d, 3d, and 4th of February, 1836* (Providence: H. H. Brown, 1836), 50. Original emphasis.

[27] *Proceedings of the Rhode-Island Anti-Slavery Convention, Held in Providence, on the 2d, 3d, and 4th of February, 1836*, 70.

The Report disagreed that the proslavery understanding of the compact was a correct interpretation of those attitudes. The proslavery compact after all was "a compact built entirely on implication. It has never been recorded" (71). The Report argued for a broader attempt to recover the attitudes of the founding fathers, utilizing the constitutional text, the meager available evidence of discussions that took place in Philadelphia convention, and the actions of founders to combat slavery after the creation of the US Constitution. Taken altogether, the understanding of the Constitution most appropriate to the issue at hand was one that recognized, as the abolitionists did, the "old landmarks of Freedom" and which sought to ensure that they were "tenaciously defended" (71). The constitutional text, read as an expression of intent – "There is a manifest effort in the construction of sentences, to avoid every appearance of sanctioning the institution of slavery" – accorded with the "but slight sketches of the debates in this Convention" and the "avowed object" of the leaders of the early Abolition Societies (72–73). The result was the conclusion that the claimed compact to noninterference with slavery was "nothing less than an atrocious libel on the characters of the illustrious dead, invented to deprive the living of their dearest and most invaluable privileges" (74). By excavating the beliefs and attitudes of the founders, an antislavery understanding of the Constitution could be offered to counter the proslavery compact.

A year later, N. P. Rogers was both complaining of the ubiquity of the proslavery "Compact" and seeking to explain the founding and Constitution in ways that refuted the notion that they were marked by a proslavery spirit of compromise. Rogers took the position that the constitutional text provided no sanction for slavery, even if the founders had intended such a sanction – "it is possible they conceived it in their hearts . . . But they did not succeed in reducing their compromise to writing."[28] Rogers viewed slavery as unsupported by the constitutional text whatever the actual practice of the United States since the founding.[29] But he went further than the standard abolitionist approach of highlighting appropriate clauses of the text and pointing to the absence of the words "slave" and "slavery" to refute the assertions of the proslavery compact. Rogers instead framed those typical clause-based arguments with an initial section undertaking a close reading of the Preamble to the Constitution to "gather some inklings of their *intent* . . . some means of conjecturing their *purpose*."[30] Read against the backdrops of the Declaration of Independence and the States' Bills of Rights, Rogers discovered in the Preamble antislavery and democratically expansive potential. Enshrining a commitment to "secure the blessings of liberty to ourselves and our posterity," Rogers saw the Preamble as incorporating black as well as white within the framers' posterity:

[28] N. P. Rogers, "The Constitution," *Quarterly Anti-Slavery Magazine* 2, no. 6 (January 1837): 146.
[29] Rogers, "The Constitution," 147.   [30] Rogers, "The Constitution," 147.

Go to the gloomy gang that drag the heavy foot to the toils of the plantation. "Posterity" linger there rank and file. Go to your federal city and there see the posterity of these constitution-mongers gracing the *coffle* ... There are the posterity of the framers of the Constitution – of this same "ourselves," and these are the blessings of liberty secured to them by the Constitution if it sanctions slavery.[31]

In this, Rogers followed the arguments by which free black abolitionists advanced a claim on the part of black Americans to the inheritance of the Revolution discussed in Chapter 2, and like those claimants, he made recourse to the Declaration to support such a claim. But in his reading of the Preamble – despite his assertion that abolitionists would "hold the [advocates of a pro-slavery Constitution] to the deed [the text]" – Rogers gave credence to a mode of argument that moved beyond those earlier arguments in a nuanced way. Rather than viewing the Constitution as a disembodied text, and interpreting it in correspondence with the Declaration of Independence, Rogers read the constitutional text as a written record of the intent of historically specific actors. The Declaration operated, as the States' Bills of Rights did, as "indications of the *quo animo* of the times," as corresponding indications of intention.[32]

If Rogers was moving toward reading the constitutional text as a record of a historically specific intent, other abolitionists were similarly adjusting their approach to the text. Rev. Samuel J. May shared Rogers's complaint that the "alleged compact" was "met with every where. ... flippantly iterated by thousands, who never read the Constitution of the United States."[33] And like Rogers, May rejected the notion that the constitutional text provided any sanction for slavery. But in an article spread over two editions of the *Quarterly Anti-Slavery Magazine* he also undertook an investigation of the intentions and conduct of the framers with the hope of exonerating them "from the tremendous responsibility that is laid upon them" by the invocation of the proslavery compact.[34] Tracing an argument that anticipated Rogers's, May examined the articles of the Constitution offered as evidence of a compromise over slavery with an eye to reconciling them with the "avowed

---

[31] Rogers, "The Constitution," 149. Rogers seems to have meant this figuratively. He does not betray support for the belief that the sexual relations of antebellum slavery meant that members of such coffles were potentially the literal posterity of some framers – although other abolitionists did enrage defenders of slavery by pointing out the treatment the latter dealt to their own children. For example, Lydia Child, *An Appeal in Favor of That Class of Americans Called Africans* (Boston: Allen and Ticknor, 1833), 37; Angelina. E. Grimké, *Appeal to the Christian Women of the South* (New York: American Anti-Slavery Society, 1836), 12–13.

[32] Rogers, "The Constitution," 147. "Quo animo" as the legal phrase referring to an inquiry into the intent or motivations of an actor.

[33] Samuel J. May, "Slavery and the Constitution," *Quarterly Anti-Slavery Magazine* 2, no. 1 (October 1836): 73. The second part of the article appeared in the April 1837 edition of the magazine. Samuel J. May, "Slavery and the Constitution," *Quarterly Anti-Slavery Magazine* 2, no. 7 (April 1837): 226–38.

[34] May, "Slavery and the Constitution," October 1836, 74.

sentiments and purposes of the framers."[35] Read in their historical context and in correspondence to the Preamble, May deemed it "impossible not to perceive the pains which the framers of these [constitutional] articles took to avoid any explicit recognition of slavery."[36] Foregrounding intent, by the start of the second half of the article in April 1837, May hoped that he had "made it apparent . . . that the Magna Charta of our civil liberties was not intended to be, and is not, by any fair construction, instrumental to the continued oppression of the colored people of the land."[37] In case questions still lingered, May pointed to, as the Rhode Island abolitionists had, the "subsequent conduct of some of these men" to show that the Philadelphia convention had gone as far as it could have in avoiding national institutional support for slavery. Although he had earlier noted the meager evidentiary basis for rendering opinions on the conduct of the Philadelphia convention, May read the convention's intent to be in accordance with an ascribed spirit of the times, asserting, with reference to 1787, "There was a spirit then abroad in our land which threatened to extirpate every vestige of oppression; and the men who devised the plan of our general government were careful not to throw any impediment in its way."[38] Reversing Marshall's dictum that the intent should be garnered from the text, May undertook an extended effort to understand the text as a record of the intent he expected the framers to have held.

As these three attempts – Rhode Island, Rogers, and May – suggest, within the abolitionist movement of the mid-1830s, some attempts to meet the proslavery compact upon its own grounds of an animating spirit of 1787 were being undertaken. In contrast to Leggett's rejection of spirit as a legitimate basis for constitutional interpretation, these efforts sought to develop an account of the founding wherein spirit could be deployed in support of abolition. In doing so, Rogers, May, and the Rhode Island abolitionists recalled the earlier arguments of free black abolitionists who had sought to read the Constitution in correspondence with the Declaration of Independence. But in a significant way, they approached the Declaration from a different vantage point. Whereas the abolitionists of the 1820s had seen the Declaration of Independence as a document conjoined to the Constitution and informing the textual interpretation of the latter, Rogers and his fellow travelers saw the Declaration as further evidence of the spirit of the times that produced the Constitution. Indeed, the latter approach positioned even the constitutional text itself as a record of intent, a further instance of the project of distilling and preserving the spirit of the founding in written form. While Leggett believed that spirit would ultimately undermine the stability of the constitutional text,

---

[35] May, "Slavery and the Constitution," October 1836, 84.
[36] May, "Slavery and the Constitution," October 1836, 89.
[37] May, "Slavery and the Constitution," April 1837, 226.
[38] May, "Slavery and the Constitution," October 1836, 79; May, "Slavery and the Constitution," April 1837, 228.

these abolitionists saw in the text an imperfect attempt to capture the then-stable – and to their minds, abolitionist – spirit of the founding.

9.3 SPIRIT AND INTENT IN THE ABOLITIONIST COMPACT

At the 1837 Annual Meeting of the American Anti-Slavery Society, to judge by the Report produced by the Meeting, Van Buren's Inaugural Address was fading as an issue. In an Annual Report stretching to ninety-one pages, only six were given over to the Inaugural Address. However, in this "official" response of the movement to the Inaugural Address, the two approaches sketched earlier came together in a condemnation of Van Buren's "unconstitutional" use of his veto authority and a rejection of the claim that the founding was animated by a proslavery spirit. The Report echoed the initial abolitionist responses to the Inaugural Address in viewing Van Buren's threat to use the veto as a new and unwelcome development within American constitutional practice. Van Buren's position was "arrogant and unconstitutional," and a departure from all previous Presidents who had wielded the veto to avoid "acquiescing in the violation of an instrument which [they] had sworn to support."[39] The Inaugural Address instead pledged Van Buren to veto constitutional measures "out of regards to the interests or will of a section of the country," reducing the veto to a political offering within cross-sectional coalition building (100). In line with Leggett's view that this new-fangled understanding of the Constitution risked undermining the very protections for which the Constitution was valued, the Report saw in Van Buren's veto promise one more indication that it was "slavery, and not the Constitution, which govern[ed] the United States" (89).

But as this suggestion that slavery had replaced the Constitution indicates, the Report also cleaved to a view of the Constitution as itself antislavery, or at least neutral with regard to slavery. The Report dissented from Van Buren's interpretation of the founding, and specifically the latter's view of the founders' intent. If Van Buren believed that the founding fathers took into account, and sought to avoid disturbing, the peculiar slaveholding institutions of the South, then the Report avowed with "regard to the intent of the framers of the Constitution, the President has certainly taken things as they are not" (102). It was not the case that the framers had sought to leave slavery undisturbed – rather "They looked upon slavery as an institution which must soon become extinct" and equipped Congress with the powers necessary to accommodate and, in the case of the District of Columbia, enact such an extinction (102). Foreshadowing the "Slave Power" thesis of the 1840s, the Report asserted that the subsequent growth of slavery in the United States was not a reflection of the framers' intention, but an idiosyncratic working out of the experiment "which

[39] *Fourth Annual Report of the American Anti-Slavery Society, with the Speeches Delivered at the Anniversary Meeting Held in the City of New York, On the 9th May, 1837. And the Minutes of the Meetings of the Society for Business* (New York: William S. Dorr, 1837), 99, 100.

they only commenced" (102; original emphasis).[40] Van Buren's claim that subsequent time had proven the value of the framers' policy was "not true" (102). Pointing to the international condemnation of American slavery, the Report saw the consequence of the founders' experiment as a willingness to accept a system of cruel oppression along with the growing prosperity of the nation that the founding generation could not have predicted. At the end of the Report, the Society could still hope to "stand not only upon the safe foundation of the law of God, but fully upon the Constitution of their country" (122), having noted along the way that "Slavery is unknown to the Constitution" (116).

Overall, the 1837 Report offered a pointed but somewhat hesitant rejection of Van Buren's commitment to the constitutional spirit of the founders. As penned by the Society's Secretary of Domestic Correspondence Elizur Wright Jr., the Report did not go as far as either May or Rogers in interrogating the founding to reveal an antislavery spirit, settling instead for a stated refutation of Van Buren's understanding of the framers' intention.[41] The Report, if taken as expression of the sentiment of the abolitionist movement, seemed to reflect a desire to address the infringements of free speech and expression rather than address the issues of constitutionality raised by the Inaugural Address.[42] This hesitancy was perhaps a harbinger of one dimension of the schism within the movement that would shortly arrive. On one hand, figures such as May, Rogers, and Rev. Orange Scott believed that an antislavery spirit of the founding could be offered to counter the spirit of compromise that Van Buren and others were mobilizing. But, on the other hand, at least since Garrison's "The Great Crisis!" in 1832, elements of the abolitionist movement had recognized some truth in the claim that 1787 represented an "infamous bargain" and thus regarded conceptualization of the Constitution as the legacy of the framers with suspicion.[43] While the focus of constitutional debate was the text or when the proposition of a grand bargain was conceived to be binding only for issues of slavery in the States, this difference was not crucial.[44] As the

[40] On the "Slave Power" thesis, see Eric Foner, *Free Soil, Free Labor, Free Men: The Ideology of the Republican Party before the Civil War* (Oxford: Oxford University Press, 1995), 90–98.

[41] Such an approach was not absent from the Meeting itself, where Rev. Orange Scott was noted as having offered "a very ingenious and satisfactory argument, to show that the Declaration of Independence spoke the true sentiments of the country; and that Constitution of the United States, so far from guaranteeing slavery, is and was designed to be wholly incompatible with its perpetuity" (16).

[42] On the ways in which Garrison, in particular, welcomed the opportunity to frame the conflict between free and slaveholding States as one of free speech, see Robert Fanuzzi, *Abolition's Public Sphere* (Minneapolis: University of Minnesota, 2003), 7, 21–27.

[43] William Lloyd Garrison, "The Great Crisis!," *The Liberator*, December 29, 1832.

[44] As noted elsewhere, a consensus existed which extended to most abolitionists that the federal government could not interfere with slavery in the States. In the early 1830s, the question of

spirit of the founding became pivotal for discussions of slavery in the District of Columbia, and potentially the territories, this difference took on greater salience. The Report perhaps reflected such a tension in its adoption of – but nonengagement with – the position that an antislavery spirit had animated the founding. Insofar as it seemed to embrace both the Leggett and May–Rogers responses to the Inaugural Address, it marked a semiofficial evasion of the question of how to respond to a presidentially endorsed proslavery constitutional spirit.

Whatever possibility of evading that question existed in 1837 would be shattered just a few short years later. Writing the Report in May of 1837, Elizur Wright Jr. could not have anticipated the revelations that would come with the publication of Madison's notes from the federal convention in 1840. In 1836, Rev. Samuel J. May had looked forward "with eager expectation to the report about to be published from the manuscript of the late James Madison," but this expectation was surely deflated when the published notes failed to vindicate his belief that the Philadelphia convention contained no bargain over slavery.[45] Instead, Madison's notes confirmed the suspicions of the Garrisonians and set the defenders of an antislavery Constitution to task in elucidating a theory of the Constitution that preserved their faith in its antislavery identity. The result was a fertile period within the development of abolitionist constitutional thought – but one that grappled with the central question of the spirit that has animated the founders.

One strand within abolitionist constitutional thought that emerged would be the outright rejection of the Constitution that came to be associated with Garrison. Exemplified in Charles Lenox Remond's speech in Boston, this strand held that "knowledge of the origin and progress, and ... experience of the present practical workings of the American Constitution" did not sustain the view that it was "a glorious means to a glorious end" and

whether or not the existence of slavery was "approved or encouraged by" the US Constitution remained unsettled, as is indicated by a 1834 debate between correspondents within the pages of the *Liberator*. "Political Action," *The Liberator*, November 29, 1834; "The National Compact," *The Liberator*, December 6, 1834; "The National Compact – Again," *The Liberator*, December 13, 1834; "The National Compact," *The Liberator*, December 20, 1834. Even two years after Garrison's "The Great Crisis!" the *Liberator* reprinted without comment the claims of the New-York Young Men's Anti-Slavery Society that "The provisions of the Constitution fully and fairly carried out, would cripple and destroy slavery." "Extracts From an 'Address of the New-York Young Men's Anti-Slavery Society, to Their Fellow-Citizens,'" *The Liberator*, November 29, 1834.

[45] May, "Slavery and the Constitution," October 1836, 79. May would later state "the publication of the 'Madison Papers' ... I confess, disconcerted me somewhat. I could not so easily maintain my ground in the discussions which afterwards agitated so seriously the Abolitionists themselves – some maintaining that the Constitution was, and was intended to be, proslavery." Quoted in Helen J. Knowles, "The Constitution and Slavery: A Special Relationship," *Slavery & Abolition* 28, no. 3 (2007): 323.

instead urged dissolution of the Union.[46] Having roots within the Garrisonian affinity for disunion, this constitutional approach seized upon Madison's notes to bolster the position that the founders had created a proslavery constitution.[47] Wendell Phillips's *The Constitution a Pro-Slavery Compact* argued that a compromise was made in 1787 "between freedom and slavery" and that "our fathers bartered honesty for gain, and became partners with tyrants."[48] As the alternative title of Phillips's work (*Selections from the Madison Papers*) suggested, it drew upon the historical evidence available to show that the Constitution was informed by a proslavery sentiment. Elaborated in an 1844 Address of the American Anti-Slavery Society, this argument posited "No just or honest use of [the Constitution] can be made, in opposition to the plain intentions of its framers, *except to declare the contract at an end, and to refuse to serve under it.*"[49] Taking the American Constitution as the "exponent" of the national compact, the Address, signed by Garrison, Phillips, and Maria Weston Chapman, denied the legitimacy of interpreting the constitutional text so as to "harmonize" with the objects of the Preamble.[50] The Constitution's language was *"not to be interpreted in a sense which neither of the contracting parties understood,* and which would frustrate every design of their alliance – to wit, *union at the expense of the colored population of the country."*[51] The Address objected to the idea that the values of the Declaration of Independence might be read into the Constitution, seeing the spirit represented by the Declaration as never having been understood to extend to the enslaved:

The truth is, our fathers were intent on securing liberty to *themselves*, without being very scrupulous as to the means they used to accomplish their purpose. They were not actuated by the spirit of universal philanthropy; and though *in words* they recognized occasionally the brotherhood of the human race, *in practice* they continually denied it.[52]

Committing wholly to the view that the spirit that animated the framers was in no way antislavery, the Garrisonians nonetheless saw that spiritual frame as the key to interpreting the subsequent requirements of the Constitution. It was not without reason that one holder of enslaved persons saw Phillip's *The*

---

[46] C. Peter Ripley, ed., "Speech by Charles Lenox Remond, Delivered at Marlboro Chapel, Boston, Massachusetts, 29 May 1844," in *The Black Abolitionist Papers: Volume III: The United States, 1830–1846* (Chapel Hill, NC: The University of North Carolina Press, 1991), 443–44.

[47] William M. Wiecek, *The Sources of Antislavery Constitutionalism in America, 1760–1848* (Ithaca: Cornell University Press, 1977), 240, 242.

[48] Wendell Phillips, *The Constitution a Pro-Slavery Compact: Or, Selections from the Madison Papers* (New York: American Anti-Slavery Society, 1845), v, viii.

[49] As reprinted in Phillips, *The Constitution a Pro-Slavery Compact*, 104. Original emphasis.

[50] As reprinted in Phillips, *The Constitution a Pro-Slavery Compact*, 104, 105. Original emphasis.

[51] As reprinted in Phillips, *The Constitution a Pro-Slavery Compact*, 105. Original emphasis.

[52] As reprinted in Phillips, *The Constitution a Pro-Slavery Compact*, 105. Original emphasis.

Constitution a Pro-Slavery Compact, minus a few paragraphs, as a useful defense of their position.[53]

On the opposite side of the abolitionist debate was a group that the preeminent scholar of antislavery constitutional thought has identified as proponents of a radical antislavery constitutionalism. This group sought to resist the idea that the Constitution has been animated by a proslavery spirit but did not fully forego the idea that such a spirit, appropriately understood in terms of an antislavery sentiment, might inform constitutional interpretation.[54] Evident in the writings of May and Rogers in 1836–37, this group understood the Constitution to be antislavery and that, in the words of Rev. Orange Scott, "the Constitution of the United States, so far from guaranteeing slavery, is and was designed to be wholly incompatible with its perpetuity."[55] This grouping gave rise to George W. F. Mellen's *An Argument on the Unconstitutionality of Slavery* in 1841. Dismissed by one scholar as consisting of "ill-constructed, half-baked ideas," Mellen's work nonetheless reflected the challenge radical antislavery constitutionalists faced in reconciling their constitutional interpretation to the historical record.[56] Mellen, whose eccentric behavior distanced him from other abolitionists, produced a carefully selected historical account that showed that the founders "left no word by which slavery could be justified or maintained in the Constitution of our country."[57] Covering the proceedings of the Philadelphia convention and *The Federalist Papers,* as well as the State conventions in Massachusetts, New York, Virginia, North Carolina, and Pennsylvania, Mellen reached the surprising conclusion that "the subject of slavery was fully commented upon, and the Constitution

---

[53] Foner, *Free Soil, Free Labor, Free Men,* 86; Wiecek, *The Sources of Antislavery Constitutionalism in America, 1760–1848,* 240.

[54] An important exception to this was Lysander Spooner, whose natural law-based argument for the unconstitutionality of slavery denied any role for contemporary intention or spirit in constitutional interpretation. For Spooner, intentions were to "be gathered entirely from the words, which [the people] adopted to express them." Lysander Spooner, *The Unconstitutionality of Slavery* (Boston: Bela Marsh, 1845), 135. Nonetheless, Spooner's influence as a representative of the antislavery strand of constitutional thought has grown with time. In the 1830s and 1840s, his positions were more radical than most of the movement and his position vis-à-vis the abolitionist movement was as an "outsider." Knowles, "The Constitution and Slavery," 320; Wiecek, *The Sources of Antislavery Constitutionalism in America, 1760–1848,* 227.

[55] *Fourth Annual Report of the American Anti-Slavery Society, with the Speeches Delivered at the Anniversary Meeting Held in the City of New York, On the 9th May, 1837. And the Minutes of the Meetings of the Society for Business,* 16; cf. Wiecek, *The Sources of Antislavery Constitutionalism in America, 1760–1848,* 253.

[56] Helen J. Knowles, "Seeing the Light: Lysander Spooner's Increasingly Popular Constitutionalism," *Law and History Review* 31, no. 3 (2013): 536.

[57] G. W. F. Mellen, *An Argument on the Unconstitutionality of Slavery, Embracing an Abstract of the Proceedings of the National and State Conventions on This Subject* (Boston, MA: Saxton & Peirce, 1841), 18; On Mellen's eccentricity, see Wiecek, *The Sources of Antislavery Constitutionalism in America, 1760–1848,* 256.

was formed with the full understanding of its nature, and the people of that day did not and would not, in any shape give their sanction to the system."[58] Mellen's claims might seem fabulous, but his instinct to retell the founding as a moment of antislavery sentiment was not out of step with other radical abolitionist constitutionalists.

As noted earlier, May and Rogers made similar, if more circumspect, claims that the Constitution's creation was informed by an antislavery spirit. Others including James G. Birney, upon whom Mellen had relied in developing his own argument, made arguments that looked to the presence of an antislavery spirit at the founding to refute claims of slavery's constitutionality. Birney wrote in 1838 of a public sentiment at the time of the Constitution's formation in favor of emancipation, and of a subsequent growth in the institution of slavery in opposition to "the Constitution according to its original intent."[59] That same year, Theodore Dwight Weld's *The Power of Congress over the District of Columbia* made an argument against the constitutionality of slavery in the nation's capital through consideration of the precise powers of Congress.[60] To do so, Weld dedicated a quarter of the text to showing "by testimony, that at the date of the United States' constitution, and for several years before and after that period, slavery was rapidly on the wane."[61] In a Postscript challenging the notion that Virginia had ceded territory for the District of Columbia with the understanding that slavery would be secure therein, Weld offered a dubious pantheon of antislavery Virginian founders – "Washington, Jefferson, Wythe, Patrick Henry, St. George Tucker, and all her most illustrious men" – who, he claimed, were at the time of cession advocating for the abolition of slavery.[62]

Within the same radical abolitionist grouping, William Goodell's 1844 *Views of American Constitutional Law* took defenders of slaveholding to task for ignoring the "*spirit* of the Constitution" in advancing arguments based upon "compromises, compacts, guaranties, and understandings."[63] Instead of

---

[58] Mellen, *An Argument on the Unconstitutionality of Slavery*, 426. Mellen did exempt from this claim the unavoidable counterexample of the twenty-year tolerance of the slave trade. That concession reflected the "strong opposition made by South Carolina and Georgia."

[59] *Correspondence between the Hon. F. H. Elmore, One of the South Carolina Delegation in Congress, and James G. Birney, One of the Secretaries of the American Anti-Slavery Society* (New York: American Anti-Slavery Society, 1838), 59, 31.

[60] Theodore Dwight Weld, *The Power of Congress over the District of Columbia* (New York: American Anti-Slavery Society, 1838).

[61] Weld, *The Power of Congress over the District of Columbia*, 25. For details of the testimony, cf. 25–36.

[62] Weld, *The Power of Congress over the District of Columbia*, 49. Some sense of the distance covered by abolitionists in the 1830s is given in the gap between Weld's assertion in 1838 that Washington was an antislavery founder and the heated debates in 1833, discussed in Chapter 3, as to whether or not Washington was "a hypocrite, a thief, a kidnapper, &c. and [...] now in hell."

[63] William Goodell, *Views of American Constitutional Law, in Its Bearing upon American Slavery* (Utica: Jackson & Chaplin, 1844), 20, 19. Original emphasis.

recognizing the "*grand* intention to '*secure liberty*,'" Goodell argued that defenders of slavery fell back on "*supposed intentions and 'understandings'* to eke out the construction."[64] Developing among the most sophisticated responses to the slaveholders' arguments regarding a compromise of 1787, Goodell carefully delineated "strict construction" and "the spirit of the Constitution" as distinct "courts" or modes of constitutional interpretation and detailed comprehensive but distinct antislavery arguments for both. After showing that strict construction rendered an antislavery Constitution, Goodell turned his attention to the spirit of the Constitution, as derived from the document itself and then from the external evidence drawn from history. Seeking the latter spirit in "the spirit of the age," he equated it to the "spirit of seventy-six" and challenged his critics to plead that "'the spirit of the Constitution' of 1787–9 is NOT identical with the 'spirit of seventy-six,'" – and concluded that the "prevailing 'spirit of the age' that produced the Federal Constitution, was an *anti-slavery* spirit, and that this spirit was manifest in the leading minds by which the Constitution was projected, and adopted as well as framed."[65] In case of doubt, Goodell referred his readers to Weld's 1838 discussion of the language of the period's eminent statesmen.[66]

Between the Garrisonian embrace of a proslavery spirit and the radical attempt to understand the spirit as antislavery, a moderate mainstream of abolition position held that both a recognition of and opposition to slavery had informed the Constitution's creation.[67] In such a reading of the framers' intent, the practical existence of slavery in the States had been acknowledged in the mechanics created by the Constitution's clauses, but the absence of direct textual acknowledgment and the aspirations of the Northwest Ordinance pointed to a belief in the coming end of the peculiar institution.[68] Building upon a belief that slavery could only be legal under positive law, the moderate

---

[64] Goodell, *Views of American Constitutional Law*, 20. Original emphasis.

[65] Goodell, *Views of American Constitutional Law*, 103, 106. Original emphasis. In linking 1776 to 1787–89, Goodell argued that the Declaration of Independence represented the first national constitution. Goodell, *Views of American Constitutional Law*, 138–42; Wiecek, *The Sources of Antislavery Constitutionalism in America, 1760–1848*, 264–65.

[66] Like Weld, Goodell produced a pantheon of antislavery founders – "Dr. Rush, John Jay, Alexander Hamilton, and Benjamin Franklin" and as well as James Wilson and George Washington. To those, Goodell added the following individuals who believed that slavery was a waning system whose fall should be speedy: "Madison, Pinckney, and Jay, but also of Patrick Henry, Grayson, Tucker, Wythe, Pendleton, Lee, Blair, Mason, Page, Parker, Randolph, Iredell, Spaight, Ramsay, Martin, McHenry, Chase, Bayard, Rodney, Rawle, Buchanan, Wilkinson, Pleasants, McLean, Anthony, Bloomfield, Galloway, Johnson, Dawes, Scott, Gerry, Rice, Brown, Campbell, &c. &c." Interestingly, Jefferson was identified by Goodell as among the anti-federalists who resisted the antislavery Constitution's adoption. Goodell, *Views of American Constitutional Law*, 104–5, 108.

[67] William M. Wiecek, "'The Blessings of Liberty': Slavery in the American Constitutional Order," in *Slavery and Its Consequences: The Constitution, Race, and Equality*, ed. Robert A. Goldwin and Art Kaufman (Washington, DC: American Enterprise Institute, 1988), 36–37.

[68] Wiecek, *The Sources of Antislavery Constitutionalism in America, 1760–1848*, 210.

abolitionists accepted the legitimacy of the federal consensus that the national government could not touch slavery in the States. But they allied this belief with the view that the federal government equally did not have the power to establish slavery anywhere within its territory, rendering slavery in the District of Columbia unconstitutional.[69] Traced by Eric Foner in the constitutional thought of Samuel P. Chase, this strand of abolitionist thought sought to convince Americans that "anti-slavery was the intended policy of the founders of the nation, and was compatible with the Constitution."[70] The subsequent history of the nation was one of betrayal of those initial intentions, with the rise of the "Slave Power" corrupting and subverting the antislavery Constitution.[71] Over time, a fairly stable series of events – the Louisiana Purchase, the Purchase of Florida, the Admission of Missouri, and a plot to admit Texas – came to represent the milestones on a path away from the Constitution's original antislavery spirit.[72]

More politically engaged than its two rival strands of abolitionist constitutional thought, this approach became the dominant line of thought of the Liberty Party and then the Republican Party. Therein, abolition came to be understood as the recapturing of an earlier antislavery spirit associated with the founding generation. Nominating James G. Birney and Thomas Morris to its ticket, the Liberty Party of 1844 resolved to represent the "true principles of American liberty, or the true spirit of the Constitution of the United States."[73] Fleshing out those terms, that Convention further resolved, "That it was understood in the times of the Declaration and the Constitution, that the existence of slavery in some of the States, was in derogation of the principles of American Liberty."[74] In Pennsylvania, the State Liberty Party asserted that it was "in its principles, the same party as that which, in 1787, formed our own federal Constitution" and invited citizens to join the Party in "restor[ing] to our country those principles

---

[69] Wiecek, *The Sources of Antislavery Constitutionalism in America, 1760–1848*, 209–10.

[70] Foner, *Free Soil, Free Labor, Free Men*, 73. See also Rogers M. Smith, *Civic Ideals: Conflicting Visions of Citizenship in U.S. History* (New Haven: Yale University Press, 1997), 248.

[71] Foner, *Free Soil, Free Labor, Free Men*, 87–91. The idea of the "Slave Power" is said by Foner to come into vogue in 1838–39 with Thomas Morris's speeches in the Senate, but the historical account of slavery's advance in the face of Congress's "unfaithfulness" to the intentions of the framers is present in Birney's March 1838 letter to F. H. Elmore. *Correspondence between the Hon. F. H. Elmore, One of the South Carolina Delegation in Congress, and James G. Birney, One of the Secretaries of the American Anti-Slavery Society*, 29–34; On Morris, see Foner, *Free Soil, Free Labor, Free Men*, 90–91.

[72] "Address of the Liberty Party of Pennsylvania to the People of the State," *The American Intelligencer* (Philadelphia, September 1844), 3–4. *Correspondence Between the Hon. F. H. Elmore, One of the South Carolina Delegation in Congress, and James G. Birney, One of the Secretaries of the American Anti-Slavery Society*, 32–34.

[73] Horace Greeley and John F. Cleveland, eds., "Liberty Party National Convention, 1843," in *A Political Textbook for 1860* (New York: The Tribune Association, 1860), 14.

[74] Greeley and Cleveland, "Liberty Party National Convention, 1843," 14.

which our fathers so labored to establish."[75] The Party's literature reassured readers of the "strong anti-slavery sentiment," which animated the country at the time of the Constitution's creation and adoption, explaining the continuation of slavery in terms of a faithless and perverted administration of the Constitution.[76] Such was the spread of this approach to constitutional history that Gerrit Smith saw value in challenging his readers with the question "Is the Constitution pro-slavery, because the Government of the United States has, almost from its beginning, been administered for the advantage of slavery?" – presumably confident in hearing "No!" in response.[77] This attitude did not abate with the disintegration of the Liberty Party; Foner argues, "Almost every Republican believed that it had been the intention of the founding fathers to restrict slavery and divorce the federal government from all connection with it."[78]

The consequence of the publication of Madison's Notes for abolitionist constitutionalism was a significant turn to the founding and its spirit. Garrisonians embraced their suspicions of a grand bargain and merged that constitutional history with an affinity for disunion. Radical abolitionist constitutionalism drew upon an ascribed abolitionist spirit of the founding to see a constitutional obligation to abolish slavery throughout the nation. Finally, moderate abolitionists followed their radical brethren in seeing the presence of an antislavery spirit in founding America but tempered that observation with a willingness to recognize the capacity for State law to create slavery within the States. Crucially, no major strand of abolitionism picked up the possibility offered by Leggett of an outright rejection of the legitimacy of spirit within constitutional interpretation.

9.4 PROSLAVERY ARGUMENTS FOR "RECOGNITION" AFTER 1836

If the invocation of a spirit of compromise prompted abolitionists to turn toward a spirit of the founding as a support for antislavery, that tendency had an effect, in turn, on the opponents of abolition. The argument that a spirit of the founding constrained constitutional interpretation was vulnerable to a counterargument that that spirit was itself antislavery. As abolitionists were actively developing this counterargument, defenders of slavery looked to the claim that slavery had been "recognized" at the time of the Constitution's adoption as a way of characterizing prevailing values in 1787 as accepting of, if not promoting, slavery. Reviving the arguments offered in Virginia in the

---

[75] "Address of the Liberty Party of Pennsylvania to the People of the State," 1, 15.
[76] Smith, *Gerrit Smith's Constitutional Argument*, 14. See also Alvan Stewart, *The Creed of the Liberty Party: Or, Their Position Defined, in the Summer of 1844* (Jackson & Chaplin, 1844), 3.
[77] Smith, *Gerrit Smith's Constitutional Argument*, 4.
[78] Foner, *Free Soil, Free Labor, Free Men*, 84; Wiecek, *The Sources of Antislavery Constitutionalism in America, 1760–1848*, 217–19.

early 1830s, this position emphasized that property claims upon slaves predated but were secured by the Constitution. The argument that slavery had been recognized in the Constitution provided a surer argument in two important ways. First, it directly linked slavery to the Constitution as text; by highlighting the fugitive slave clause and three-fifths compromise, defenders of slavery located "recognitions" of slavery within the text that could be offered against the argument that slavery was not directly mentioned. Second, recognition anticipated and addressed the counterargument that the "spirit" at the time of the founding was antislavery; whatever may have been the beliefs of the founding generation as to the long-term fate of slavery, they had acknowledged in these clauses the practical existence of slavery in North America during the 1780s. Importantly though, the move to recognition did not mean a shift of focus away from the historical moment of the founding. Instead, it reified that focus in the form of a determined attempt to understand the nature of the recognition undertaken in 1787–88. Portending the landmark Supreme Court decisions of *Prigg* v. *Pennsylvania* (1842) and *Dred Scott* v. *Sandford* (1857), the search for concrete proof of a constitutional recognition of slavery foregrounded the intent of the framers.

The potential for the arguments developed around the spirit of compromise to be turned back upon the opponents of abolition was signaled in William Slade's speech in Congress in late 1837. Following the resolution of the House of Representatives debates with the initiation of the Pinckney gag rule in 1836, the first weeks of subsequent congressional sessions were marked by attempts to have petitions received. In early 1837, these attempts had resulted in attempts to censure John Quincy Adams and a resolution that enslaved persons lacked the right to petition the House.[79] In December 1837, William Slade attempted again to have memorials against slavery in the District referred by the House to committee.[80] Accompanying his request, he offered a speech justifying the prayer of the petition, a move that was met with decided opposition. Slade's speech was interrupted throughout, but when he sought to show that slavery was inconsistent with the values held by leading Virginians during the revolutionary period the House moved to adjourn and the Southern delegations withdrew, cutting the speech short.[81] Nevertheless, the text of his full intended speech was reproduced and circulated in pamphlet form, giving publicity to his argument that the Constitution "as it was understood by its framers, and as it appears when thrown into the strong light of the period which gave it existence" was actually a concession to slavery made in the context of

---

[79] *Register of Debates*, 24th Congress, 2nd Session, 1837, 1684–86, 1733–34.

[80] *Congressional Globe*, 25th Congress, 2nd Session, 1837, 41.

[81] *Congressional Globe*, 25th Congress, 2nd Session, 41; William Slade, *Speech of Mr. Slade, of Vermont, on the Abolition of Slavery and the Slave Trade in the District of Columbia, Delivered in the House of Representatives of the U.S. December 20, 1837*, 1837, 9.

a strong belief that it would facilitate the gradual expiration of the institution.[82] Slade's speech, although not offering the systematized argument that the spirit of the founding was abolitionist that he would develop by 1840,[83] showed the potential for turning arguments grounded in concession, compromise, and an implied faith of 1787 back against slavery. Quoting liberally from Jefferson, Madison, and Franklin, and even invoking Washington, Slade offered a compelling illustration of the dangers for advocates of slavery in relying too extensively upon a spirit of the founding to delegitimize abolition.

By the time of Slade's speech, some opponents of abolition had already developed arguments that could incorporate the historical facts alluded to by Slade and others. If at the beginning of 1837, opponents of abolition condemned the latter as "a violation of that spirit of compromise in which the Constitution was framed," Calhoun's Resolutions in the Senate a year later positioned abolition in "manifest violation of the mutual and solemn pledge to protect and defend each other" that the States had made upon entering the constitutional compact.[84] This was a subtle difference, but it pointed to a sense of the moment of compacting as enshrining a series of commitments. Calhoun's Resolutions hinged upon the idea that

domestic slavery, as it exists in the Southern and Western States of this Union, composes an important part of their domestic institutions, inherited from their ancestors, and existing at the adoption of the Constitution, by which it is recognised as constituting an important element in the apportionment of powers among the States . . .[85]

Which was to say that slavery was both recognized by the Constitution and through that recognition removed from the scope of congressional interference. That this argument gelled with claims that Virginia and Maryland possessed an expectation that slavery would not be abolished in the District of Columbia – by framing abolition in the District as *de facto* interference within the previously recognized slavery in those States – surely made the argument more attractive. Indeed, the argument that the Constitution had "recognized" slavery was well worn in the congressional debate over the petitions by the time it was directly invoked in Calhoun's Resolutions.[86] As we have seen, it was put forward during

---

[82] Slade, *Speech of Mr. Slade, of Vermont, on the Abolition of Slavery and the Slave Trade in the District of Columbia*, 23.

[83] See discussion at the outset of this book's Introduction.   [84] *Congressional Globe*, 37, 98.

[85] *Congressional Globe*, 98.

[86] In February 1837, Senator Tipton stated, "Our forefathers, in framing the federal constitution, recognised the existence of slavery in a portion of the States of this confederacy, by permitting slaves to be enumerated in apportioning representation on the floor of Congress." Senator Rives argued, "It is sufficient for me to know that domestic slavery, whether an evil or not, was an institution existing at the time of the adoption of the constitution; that it is recognised and sanctified by that solemn instrument." In the House, Aaron Vanderpoel promised the South that "We of the North, the great mass of the North, will fulfill the compact to the letter and spirit. We recognised your property in slaves when we entered into solemn covenant and union with you."

the Missouri Crisis. But, in the late 1830s, this recognition took on added significance insofar as recognition of slavery moved from indicative of the nature of the Federal compact and to a core facet of the compact itself. Recognition in 1787 was itself the origin of a constitutional obligation to not interfere with slavery.

But the recourse to recognition did little to resolve the fundamental and animating conflict between slavery and abolition, the question of whether a slave was a human being or property.[87] In fact, the recognition of slavery as a "constitutionalized" argument enabled defenders of slavery to fall back to the perceived stronghold of property rights. As they had in Virginia in 1831–32, arguments in which the Constitution secured slave property rather than created it lent themselves to an appeal to natural rights. As tenBroek argued, this approach tapped into the broad consensus that constitutional grants of legislative power were "curtailed by [the] extraconstitutional and unexpressed limitations of natural law and natural rights" as well as by the textual amendments.[88] But the appeal to natural rights only served to focus debates on slavery in the District on the moral question at its heart – for abolitionists, the laws of nature forbade ownership of another human being; for slaveholders, the laws of nature forbade government interference in property claims vested in another human being. The argument for recognition of slavery ultimately regressed to an argument over the recognition of the enslaved's humanity. Such a debate became actualized in debates over the constitutional recognition of firstly slaves, and latterly all black persons, as citizens of the United States. It is perhaps not surprising, then, that the principal flashpoint within the debates over petitions in 1837 concerned the right of slaves to petition Congress – a right recognized as pertaining to citizenship.[89] In 1837, the questions of recognition of slavery and recognition of slaves as citizens were jointly resolved by the House of Representatives through commitment to the idea that enslaved people played no part in the compact of the Constitution – that the slaves lacked the right of petition "secured to the people of the United States by the constitution."[90] By recourse to the events of 1787–88, the House ascertained that slavery was recognized and that slaves were not at the time of

---

Richard French noted, "At the time of the adoption of the constitution, slavery existed in the States. And are we of this age better than those who waded through the Revolution? ... Did they not recognise the right of property in slaves, and guaranty it by that instrument?" *Register of Debates*, 706, 722, 1727, 1659.

[87] William E. Channing conceptualized this debate and espoused the Abolitionist position on this question with the statement that "this claim of property in a human being is altogether false, groundless. No such right of man in man can exist. ... This position there is a difficulty in maintaining on account of its exceeding obviousness." William E. Channing, *Slavery* (Boston: James Munroe and Company, 1835), 14.

[88] Jacobus tenBroek, *Equal under Law* (New York: First Collier Books, 1965), 50.

[89] The suggestion that Congress ought to receive petitions from slaves was, said Representative Holsey, "an outrage upon the genius and spirit of the constitution." *Register of Debates*, 1620.

[90] *Register of Debates*, 1733–34.

the Constitution's adoption. As such, the debates of the late 1830s did not ultimately move much beyond the fundamental debates over black and slave citizenship of the 1820s and early 1830s, but they did displace those debates from the present and into the past.

Invoking the recognition of slavery at the time of the Constitution's adoption addressed the argument trialed by Slade that the spirit of the founding was antislavery, but it made only slight changes to the temporal framework adopted by 1836 arguments grounded in a spirit of compromise. The use of recognition countered Slade's suggestion – that concession and compromise only indicated that there was antislavery sentiment in 1787–88 – by accepting the premise and offering the compromise as evidence of an explicit acknowledgment of slavery in the States during that moment. To the extent that it worked to discount the value of evidence of antislavery sentiment among Franklin, Jay, Madison, and others, recognition was an effective argument. But at the same time, as a mode of constitutional argument it "double-downed" on the importance of 1787–88 by making the contemporaneous perception of a grand bargain over slavery central to a present-day delegitimization of abolitionism. In short, recognition only worked if you could show that slavery had indeed been recognized in 1787–88. Traveling a different route, the opponents of abolitionism had arrived at the same point as May, Birney, and Chase – attempting to recover an intention on the part of the founding generation in order to adjudicate the present constitutionality of interference with domestic slavery.

9.5 PROSLAVERY JURISPRUDENCE AFTER 1836

The turn to the founding for constitutional meaning saw abolition's opponents, both proslavery and anti-abolition, place increased value on the intention of the framers. The majority of the white population in the antebellum United States accepted that the founding had created a constitutional order sanctioning slavery and regarded such an order as the intent of the framers.[91] Whatever the suppositions of moderate and radical abolitionist constitutionalism, white America as a whole shared a Garrisonian understanding of the founding, even if they differed in the conclusions to draw from that understanding. As the constitutional arguments developed in and after 1836 moved from the popular to the judicial sphere, it would be in the form of a belief that a recognition of slavery (and the corresponding nonrecognition of slaves) had animated the founding. The two seminal slavery cases of the Antebellum period (*Prigg* and *Dred Scott*) would be grounded in the notion that contemporary slavery was legitimized by attitudes prevalent during the nation's founding.

The case of *Prigg v. Pennsylvania* (1842) hinged upon the recognition of fugitive slaves as property and made recourse to the founding to support that

---

[91] Wiecek, "'The Blessings of Liberty,'" 24, 38.

position.[92] Edward Prigg, a slave-catcher, was indicted for the kidnapping of Margaret Morgan under Pennsylvania law but appealed to the US Supreme Court on the grounds that the relevant State law was void as the US Constitution charged Congress with the power to legislate for fugitive slaves, a power taken up in the 1793 Fugitive Slave Act.[93] The US Supreme Court ruled in favor of Edward Prigg, producing seven different opinions along the way and explicitly recognizing slavery as a constitutionally protected institution for the first time.[94] Rendering an opinion on behalf of the Court, Justice Story combined attention to the constitutional text with historically grounded understandings of its nature and object. Seeing the fugitive slave clause as a necessary concession to the slaveholding States at the time of the Philadelphia convention, Story regarded it as a "positive and unqualified recognition of the right of the owner in the slave."[95] While the case produced a variety of opinions, the balance of the Court saw nothing inaccurate in Story's turn to an account of historical bargaining. The different opinions reflected distinct views regarding the balance of power and responsibility between the States and the federal government that arose from that bargain, with Justice Story delivering an opinion that regarded the power of legislation to be exclusively in Congress.[96]

The justices' dissents and concurrences principally addressed Story on the relative balance of legislative power between the federal and State governments, with all except Daniel and the uncommunicative Baldwin

---

[92] *Prigg* v. *Pennsylvania* (1842). Barbara Holden-Smith argues that in his opinion for the Court Justice Story "subordinated the claims of black people to human dignity to the claims of slaveholders to their property." Barbara Holden-Smith, "Lords of Lash, Loom, and Law: Story, Slavery, and Prigg v. Pennsylvania," *Cornell Law Review* 78 (1993): 1146. Leslie Friedman Goldstein offers a reading more sympathetic to Story as an opponent of slavery in Leslie Friedman Goldstein, "A 'Triumph of Freedom' After All? Prigg v. Pennsylvania Re-Examined," *Law and History Review* 29, no. 3 (2011): 763–96. Robert M. Cover argues that in Fugitive Slave cases Justice Story saw his primary responsibility as upholding the Constitution regardless of his own moral position. Robert M. Cover, *Justice Accused: Antislavery and the Judicial Process* (New Haven: Yale University Press, 1975), 170–71.

[93] On the case, cf. H. Robert Baker, *Prigg v. Pennsylvania: Slavery, the Supreme Court, and the Ambivalent Constitution* (Lawrence: University of Kansas Press, 2012); Melvin I. Urofsky, *Supreme Decisions: Great Constitutional Cases and Their Impact* (Boulder, CO: Westview Press, 2012), 61–74; David P. Currie, *The Constitution in the Supreme Court: The First Hundred Years 1789–1888* (Chicago: University of California Press, 1985), 241–54.

[94] Urofsky, *Supreme Decisions*, 67–68.

[95] *Prigg* v. *Pennsylvania*, 41 U.S. at 611–12, 613. Paul Finkelman suggests that in *Prigg*, Story produced a "creative, but historically inaccurate, original intent analysis of the Constitution's Fugitive Slave Clause." Paul Finkelman, "Story Telling on the Supreme Court: Prigg v Pennsylvania and Justice Joseph Story's Judicial Nationalism," *The Supreme Court Review*, 1994, 256.

[96] *Prigg* v. *Pennsylvania*, 41 U.S. at 622.

explicitly accepting the premise that the fugitive slave clause represented a compromise struck by the framers of the Constitution.[97] Chief Justice Taney understood the right of property in slaves as "recognized" by the "national compact," a recognition that created obligations "equally binding upon the faith of every State in the Union."[98] Thompson likewise assumed a shared knowledge that

> this provision was the result of compromise between the slaveholding and non-slaveholding States; and it is the indispensable duty of all to carry it faithfully into execution according to its real object and intention.[99]

Wayne noted that all the justices concurred that the fugitive slave clause was "a compromise between the slaveholding and the non-slaveholding States" before being guided by the "condition of the States when the Constitution was formed, by references to the provision itself, and [...] the Constitution generally," in reaching the conclusion that Congress held the sole power of legislation with regard to fugitive slaves.[100] Even in departing with his brethren on the constitutionality of the Pennsylvanian law, Justice McLean declared, "That the Constitution was adopted in a spirit of compromise is matter of

---

[97] Finkelman describes Story's opinion as a "fabricated" history, "that elevated the fugitive slave clause to central compromise of the Constitutional Convention," while Holden-Smith argues the claim that the fugitive slave clause was central to the debates at the Philadelphia convention "lacks supporting evidence" and follows Don Fehrenbacher in suggesting that the claim is belied by the inaction of the First Congress on a mechanism of implementation. Paul Finkelman, *Supreme Injustice: Slavery in the Nation's Highest Court* (Cambridge, MA: Harvard University Press, 2018), 145; Holden-Smith, "Lords of Lash, Loom, and Law," 1130. Elsewhere Finkelman describes the opinion as "intellectually dishonest, based on inaccurate historical analysis, judicially extreme ... and inhumane." Finkelman, "Story Telling on the Supreme Court," 249. Dissenting from Story's reasoning, if not the final outcome of the appeal, Chief Justice Taney believed that congressional authority did not negate State responsibility to protect masters seeking the recapture of slaves. *Prigg v. Pennsylvania*, 41 U.S. at 633. Among the other justices, Justice Thompson regarded State legislation aimed at asserting the property rights of slaveholders as necessarily in accordance with the Constitution, while Justice Daniel argued that the property rights of the slaveholder were more secure with supportive State legislation. Justice Wayne joined Story in regarding the legislative power as residing exclusively in Congress. Justice Baldwin's taciturn dissent left the grounds of his disagreement with Story ambiguous. Justice McLean's opinion dissented from the Court's in regarding the Pennsylvanian law as an acceptable effort to protect free blacks from illegal rendition. Nevertheless, H. Robert Baker notes, discussed nowhere in the opinions was the fact that Margaret Morgan's child (also returned to Maryland by Prigg) was born in Pennsylvania and therefore free. Baker, *Prigg v. Pennsylvania*, 151. See also Holden-Smith, "Lords of Lash, Loom, and Law," 1146.

[98] *Prigg v. Pennsylvania*, 41 U.S. at 628, 633. Baker suggests this usage indicates Taney's sympathy for the theory that the "implied conditions of the Constitution" restrained action against slavery. Baker, *Prigg v. Pennsylvania*, 150.

[99] *Prigg v. Pennsylvania*, 41 U.S. at 634.   [100] *Prigg v. Pennsylvania*, 41 U.S. at 637, 638.

history."[101] McLean excepted, the justices then moved from this originary compromise to a constitutional recognition of slavery and an associated commitment to noninterference in the perceived property rights of the slaveholder. In Wayne's description:

> One of the parties, consisting of several States, required as a condition, upon which any Constitution should be presented to the States for ratification, a full and perfect security for their slaves as property when they fled into any of the States of the Union; ... The representatives from the non-slaveholding States assented to the condition. ... When the three points relating to slaves had been accomplished, every impediment in the way of forming a Constitution was removed. The agreement concerning them was called, in the convention, a compromise; the provision in respect to fugitives from service or labor was called a guarantee of a right of property in fugitive slaves, wherever they might be found in the Union. The Constitution was presented to the States for adoption with the understanding that the provisions in it relating to slaves were a compromise and guarantee, and, with such an understanding, in every State it was adopted by all of them.[102]

By returning to the Philadelphia convention and the adoption of the Constitution, the justices showed a compromise over, and, therefore, recognition of, slavery had taken place. From this recognition, they derived the recognition of a right of property in enslaved people and the corresponding denial of their personhood. Edward Prigg could escape Pennsylvanian justice because the constitutional recognition of slavery trumped the State's duty of protecting free persons within its borders.[103]

The issue of recognition recurred in *Dred Scott* v. *Sandford* (1857), in guise of the legal question of standing.[104] While the case would see the Supreme Court rule the Missouri Compromise unconstitutional, setting in train a series of events culminating in the Civil War, it also adjudicated the question of whether or not Dred Scott held citizenship "within the meaning of the

---

[101] *Prigg* v. *Pennsylvania*, 41 U.S. at 660.

[102] *Prigg* v. *Pennsylvania*, 41 U.S. at 638–39. The other two points of agreement concerned the three-fifths compromise and the temporary extension of participation in the international slave trade.

[103] The legal notion that the founding had been supportive of slavery had roots in the period before *Prigg* v. *Pennsylvania*. Judge Daggett's charge in the second trial of Prudence Crandall had drawn upon the contemporary attitudes found at the founding to suggest "slaves were not considered citizens by the framers of the Constitution" and to extend this exclusion to encompass "slaves, free blacks, or Indians." The State Supreme Court of Errors reversed Daggett on appeal. A year before in 1832, Attorney-General Roger Taney had drawn on an understanding of the framers' intention in offering his opinion that Black Americans "were not looked upon as citizens by the contracting parties who formed the Constitution." "Miss Crandall's Second Trial," *The Abolitionist* 1, no. 11 (November 1833): 163; Smith, *Civic Ideals: Conflicting Visions of Citizenship in U.S. History*, 256; Carl Brent Swisher, *Roger B. Taney* (New York: The Macmillan Company, 1935), 154; Finkelman, *Supreme Injustice: Slavery in the Nation's Highest Court*, 184.

[104] *Dred Scott* v. *Sandford*, 60 U.S. 393

Constitution of the United States."[105] Chief Justice Taney answered that question by denying Dred Scott's citizenship, and in the words of Rogers Smith attempting to "write Jacksonian racism into the nation's laws."[106] At the center of Taney's ruling on this aspect of the case was an appeal to the founders' nonrecognition of black Americans as citizens. In relying upon the founders' opinions, Taney affirmed an understanding of the Constitution as a mechanism for binding contemporary American society back to the bargains and attitudes of the founding era. Implicitly acknowledging the ambiguities of the constitutional text, Taney shored up the slaveholding Constitution through the incorporation of ascribed founding-era racial understandings into the constitutional corpus.

Taney sought to ascertain whether the framers and ratifiers had ever envisaged black citizenship. To do so, Taney turned to the nation's founding period, and particularly the attitudes and views prevalent in that period, and defined the "duty of the court" to be the interpretation and administration of the Constitution "according to its true intent and meaning when it was adopted."[107] Ignoring all manner of evidence, he concluded, "no one seems to have doubted the correctness of the prevailing opinion" that black people were recognized only as property in the colonial

---

[105] *Dred Scott* v. *Sandford*, 60 U.S. at 427. At stake was the question of whether Scott was a citizen of Missouri under the US Constitution and, therefore, able to pursue a diversity suit in the federal courts. On the connection to the War, see Jenny Bourne, "Dred, Panic, War: How a Slave Case Triggered Financial Crisis and Civil Disunion," in *Congress and the Crisis of the 1850s*, ed. Paul Finkelman and Don Kennan (Athens: Ohio University Press, 2012), 159–202. For summaries of the case, see Currie, *The Constitution in the Supreme Court*, 263–73; Harold M. Hyman and William M. Wiecek, *Equal Justice under Law: Constitutional Development 1835–1875* (New York: Harper & Row, 1982), 172–97; Urofsky, *Supreme Decisions*, 75–90.

[106] Smith, *Civic Ideals*, 199. Taney's ruling is widely regarded as among the worst, if not the worst, in US legal history. David Currie notes, "*Scott* has been widely lamented as bad policy and bad judicial politics. What may not be so well recollected is that it was also bad law." For Urofsky it holds "a unique place in American constitutional history as the worst example of the Supreme Court trying to impose a judicial solution on a political problem." A more sympathetic reading has been offered by Mark A. Graber who suggests, "Taney's constitutional claims in *Dred Scott* were well within the mainstream of antebellum constitutional thought." Perry Miller likewise argued that Taney believed he was "adhering to the native American tradition." Currie, *The Constitution in the Supreme Court*, 264; Urofsky, *Supreme Decisions*, 75; Mark A. Graber, *Dred Scott and the Problem of Constitutional Evil* (Cambridge, UK: Cambridge University Press, 2006), 28; Perry Miller, *The Life of the Mind in America: From Revolution to the Civil War* (New York: Harcourt, Brace & World Inc., 1965), 221–22. See also Gerald Leonard, "Law and Politics Reconsidered: A New Constitutional History of Dred Scott," *Law & Social Inquiry* 34, no. 3 (2009): 747–85.

[107] *Dred Scott* v. *Sandford*, 60 U.S. at 405. Finkelman describes Taney's use of "a slanted history" to achieve this aim. With regard to the rest of the opinion, Finkelman accuses Taney of offering "an unsophisticated historical claim that was a thinly disguised political argument designed to destroy the Republican Party and any opposition to the spread of slavery into the territories." Finkelman, *Supreme Injustice: Slavery in the Nation's Highest Court*, 204, 217.

period leading up to the founding.[108] Anticipating an obvious rejoinder, Taney dismissed the idea that the black population had been on the mind – "in the eyes and thoughts" – of those who framed the Declaration of Independence.[109] Offering the language of the Constitution as proof that public opinion had not changed on this question, Taney asserted that it was "obvious" that black Americans were "not even in the minds of the framers of the Constitution" and "not in the contemplation of the framers," when it came to citizenship.[110] The subsequent action of these men, in the creation of a law of naturalization and of the militia, further indicated a solely white conception of citizenship.[111]

Having established that the framers and adopters of the Constitution had no idea of recognizing black citizenship, Taney then moved to claim that subsequent changes in public opinion had no bearing upon this question. Tacitly conceding that (white) public opinion had evolved since 1787, Taney nonetheless rejected the import of such a change for constitutional interpretation: "No one, we presume, supposes that any change in public opinion or feeling, in relation to this unfortunate race, in the civilized nations of Europe or in this country, should induce the court to give to the words of the Constitution a more liberal construction in their favor than they were intended to bear when the instrument was framed and adopted."[112] Such an approach would have ruled out black citizenship when allied with an explicit textual rejection of such citizenship. But, of course, the text was ambiguous on this point – which may be why Taney moved to anchor his rejection of Scott's citizenship in meaning and intent and not text alone. Having rejected the power of contemporary public opinion, Taney suggested that opinion at the time of the founding was binding on the Court. The Constitution must, said Taney, be interpreted in accordance with its understanding at the time of its adoption:

It is not only the same in words, *but the same in meaning*, and delegates the same powers to the Government, and reserves and secures the same rights and privileges to the citizen; and as long as it continues to exist in its present form, it speaks not only in the same

---

[108] *Dred Scott* v. *Sandford*, 60 U.S. at 408. Justice Curtis's dissent (beginning at 564) systematically demolished the notion that free blacks lacked recognition as citizens at the time of founding, and pointed out that it was "doubtless" the case that at least some of them, via the franchise, had played a part in ratifying the Constitution. *Dred Scott* v. *Sandford*, 60 U.S. at 576.

[109] *Dred Scott* v. *Sandford*, 60 U.S. at 409.   [110] *Dred Scott* v. *Sandford*, 60 U.S. at 411, 423.

[111] *Dred Scott* v. *Sandford*, 60 U.S. at 419–20. With regard to the Militia Act, Taney made the forced argument that the Act's identification of membership of the militia as extending to "free abled-bodied white male" citizens was indicative that citizenship was only intended to extend to the white population. Clearly, if only whites could be citizens then that qualification would have been redundant – "able-bodied" and "male" were obviously designed to identify a subset of the citizenry for militia service.

[112] *Dred Scott* v. *Sandford*, 60 U.S. at 426.

words, *but with the same meaning and intent with which it spoke when it came from the hands of its framers* and was voted on and adopted by the People of the United States.[113]

While not acknowledging the possibility that the text and meaning could deviate from one another, Taney nonetheless foreclosed the antislavery potential of such deviation by tying contemporary political actors to the intents and understandings of actors in 1787–88 as well as to the (ambiguous) text. The ascription to the founding generation of a belief that black Americans could not be citizens ruled out black citizenship regardless of the text's capacity for such a recognition. It made race-based citizenship constitutionally binding, as well as the former's corollary of race-based exclusion from citizenship rights.

In Taney's opinion in *Dred Scott* the earlier notion of a spirit of compromise had evolved into a proslavery conception of the meaning and intent of the framers and ratifiers. Upon the basis of race-based citizenship, Taney erected a constitution favoring a vibrant and expanding institution of slavery. The recognition of slavery in 1787–88 provided the foundation for the claim that racially determined chattel slavery had been acknowledged and guaranteed by the Constitution. The widespread call of 1836, for a return to the spirit of moderation and compromise that had informed the Constitution, had calcified into a demand that the recognition of slavery inherent in such a compromise become the controlling understanding of the Constitution's relationship with slavery. At least for Taney, that recognition brought the constitutional text into alignment with the intentions and meanings ascribed to it in 1787–88; the Constitution acknowledged slavery in the three-fifths and fugitive slave clauses, providing a textual record of the intention to guarantee slavery.

9.6 CONCLUSION

Martin Van Buren's invocation of a spirit that had actuated the fathers set the stage for an evolution of the antislavery and proslavery constitutional thought in the decade following the 1836 election. While William Leggett recognized the potential for "spirit" to unmoor the Constitution from any universal meaning, others like Samuel J. May responded by initially challenging the idea that the constitutional spirit in question opposed immediate abolition. The subsequent publication of Madison's notes set back the project of proclaiming the founding a moment of antislavery action and sharpened the emerging divergence between a Garrisonian rejection of the Constitution as a "covenant with death" and a political abolitionist belief that the Constitution provided a framework for the ultimate extinction of slavery. Nevertheless, in distinct ways the period saw abolitionist understandings of the Constitution becoming increasingly defined by a belief that the latter could only be adequately comprehended through reference to the attitudes and intentions prevalent at the founding. The

---

[113] *Dred Scott v. Sandford*, 60 U.S. at 426. Emphasis added.

creation of rival historical accounts, the generation of new pantheons of the founding generation, and – at least among non-Garrisonians – a plea to return to the values of the founding became hallmarks of abolitionist constitutional thought in the early- to mid-1840s.

This transformation, in turn, created a response on the part of abolitionism's opponents. Seeing the potential for constitutional spirit to be mobilized in support of abolition, slaveholders and their allies offered an increasingly restrictive conception of the founding spirit and its role in constitutional adjudication. The defenders of slavery placed emphasis upon the "recognition" that slavery had received in 1787–88. As a concept, "recognition" allowed these actors to accept the premise of a discussion over the desirability of slavery in 1787–88 and offer that very discussion as evidence of a constitutionalized guarantee of slavery in the document that was produced. The very lack of a direct textual acknowledgment became not a weakness for slavery, but indirect evidence of the intention of the framers and ratifiers to preserve the institution of slavery under the Constitution. Allied with the argument that the fugitive slave clause and temporary constraint on regulating the slave trade were themselves evidence of the "federal consensus" on slavery, the use of recognition worked to establish a constitutional protection of slavery in the States and a constitutional presumption against abolition elsewhere. That the recognition of slavery was predicated upon the nonrecognition of the enslaved population's personhood and upon their identification solely as property only served to bolster the "constitutional" character of the protections offered to slaveholders.

Throughout these responses, a common thread was the formulation of the Constitution as a historical artifact, defined by the historical motivations of its authors. Both Garrisonian and non-Garrisonian abolitionists saw the Constitution by the mid-1840s as the product of a historical compromise – their disagreement was on the nature and subsequent development of that compromise. Likewise, "recognition," and its judicial enactment in *Prigg* and *Dred Scott*, was premised upon a series of attitudes and intentions pertaining to a particular historical moment. None of the varied responses to Van Buren's invocation of spirit (with the exception of Spooner) took direct issue with the notion that a historical account of the founding provided the framework for interpreting and implementing the values of the Constitution in the present. Indeed, by the 1840s, historical spirit seemed to rule supreme.

Conclusion

[T]he dead have no rights, they are nothing.

Thomas Jefferson (1816)[1]

Over the course of the debates around slavery and abolition in the 1820s, 1830s, and 1840s, the notion that the US Constitution was best understood with reference to the spirit that animated its creation underwent transformation. The free black writers in the 1820s had taken the sentiments expressed in the Declaration of Independence as the basis for a spirit of the founding that looked forward to universal equality. But by the 1840s the nation, beyond a relatively small section of political abolitionists, had adopted a temporally narrower and exclusionary understanding of the spirit of 1787–88 that foreclosed the prospect of universal equality. Binding the Constitution back to the historical moment of its creation and imbuing it with the racial values prevalent at that time, the opponents of abolition were moving the recognition of slavery from a sociological fact to a constitutional guarantee. Even those political abolitionists that resisted this tendency nevertheless paid fealty to the idea of an originary constitutional spirit, positing their own version of the spirit of 1787–88 in which antislavery, not slavery, was the essence of the age.

Constitutional spirit offered a response to the core constitutional question of the personhood of the enslaved. The ambiguity of the three-fifths clause had written an elusion of the issue into the constitutional text, presenting slaves as both persons and property. The free black turn to spirit in the 1820s reflected an initial attempt to resolve the broader question of black citizenship in favor of

[1] National Archives, "Thomas Jefferson to 'Henry Tompkinson' (Samuel Kercheval), 12th July 1816," Founders Online, accessed March 27, 2018, http://founders.archives.gov/documents/Jefferson/03-10-02-0128-0002.

freedom. By calling upon the Declaration of Independence, free blacks sought recognition of their American citizenship through a constitutional politics grounded in the truth that "all men are created equal." Marshaling America's ideological nationalism in the service of their claims, they took as real the Constitution's commitment to a "more perfect union." This strand of constitutional spirit remained alive in the attempts of the political abolitionists of the 1840s to explain the founding of 1787–88 as a limited accommodation with slavery that looked to an eventual end to the institution. But they were opposed by a mainstream of American constitutional and political thought that saw in the accommodations of 1787–88 an acceptance of slavery. At the end of the period in question, constitutional spirit – rendered now in terms of recognition or intention – served to resolve the constitutional ambiguity over the personhood of the enslaved against their humanity and to see them only as property. Constitutional spirit, whatever may have been the hopes of free black writers and political abolitionists, had become both more central to constitutional discourse and more conservative in its effects.

This book has demonstrated the important role that the District of Columbia played in this transformation. The District represented a space in which the competing claims over the content of American national identity played out. On one hand, abolitionists saw the nation's capital both as ten miles square of sin and as a territory of exclusive congressional control. The latter served to emphasize the degree to which the nation as a whole was implicated in slavery, but it also offered a mechanism by which the country could act against slavery as a national institution. Decisive action therein could go some way to addressing the criticisms of Daniel O'Connell and others that Americans were "traitors to the cause of human liberty."[2] On the other hand, defenders of slavery saw in the District a threshold battle to protect a racial hierarchy that they believed would allow American republicanism to weather the coming storm of mass industrialization – and, not incidentally, to protect white ownership of the extensive capital contained within the very bodies of enslaved Americans. That the constitutional power of Congress in this regard seemed textually unambiguous meant that the significant obstacle to abolition in the District lay in resolving the enduring ambiguity over the status of enslaved peoples. For abolitionists and their sympathizers, the self-evident truth of universal humanity necessitated understanding congressional power within the District – an "exclusive Legislation in all Cases whatsoever" – as enabling abolition therein. For those opposed to abolition, the very clarity of the constitutional text with regard to congressional power in the District of Columbia brought to the fore the idea of spirit as a counter to the constitutional text. In the mid-1830s, in Congress and in the presidential campaign of Martin Van Buren, the issue of slavery in the District of

---

[2] Quoted in Julius Rubens Ames, *Liberty* (New York, NY: American Anti-Slavery Society, 1837), 172.

Columbia provided the site for the development and reification of a constitutional doctrine of spirit that sought to "clarify" the constitutional text in favor of the continuation of slavery. Often overlooked as a way-marker on the road to the Civil War, the 1830s debates over slavery in the District of Columbia gave rise to a conception of constitutional government, the life of which has greatly outlived those debates.

In such a conception, political life is the product of, and constrained by, a specific historical act of exceptional sovereign intervention. Constitutional politics, as understood within liberal democratic frameworks, has been characterized by a duality of the sovereign people and their government in which the former authorizes and delimits the power of the latter. The constitution, be it written or unwritten, provides an expression of the sovereign's will, against which the actions and powers of the government of the day can be assessed. Although not yet formalized within the mechanism of judicial review, such an understanding of constitutional politics existed and was practiced before the 1830s.[3] However, the centering of constitutional politics upon a duality of sovereign and government does not rely upon a historicized understanding of a moment of sovereign exception. To be sure, the US Constitution was understood to have been given authority through the act of Ratification in 1787–88. But there was no conceptual reason that the sovereign could not reemerge after that historic moment – indeed the very notion of subsequent constitutional amendment was predicated upon such a reemergence. In the debates surrounding the contested presidential election of 1800, the idea of the sovereign people intervening to adjudicate a constitutional impasse was articulated in Democratic–Republican arguments on behalf of Jefferson's claim.[4] The sovereign was not assumed to be a historical figure but rather an ever-present potentiality.[5]

A key facet of the constitutional developments around slavery in the 1830s was the growing consensus that conceived of sovereignty as enacted in a prior and specific historical moment. It was a shift from thinking of 1787–88 as a juncture within a political process in which the popular sovereign had authorized the Constitution, to reconceiving of 1787–88 as the historical origin of the political nation and the encapsulation of the latter's political

---

[3] See variously Sylvia Snowiss, *Judicial Review and the Law of the Constitution* (New Haven: Yale University Press, 1990); Richard Tuck, *The Sleeping Sovereign: The Invention of Modern Democracy* (Cambridge, UK: Cambridge University Press, 2016); Bruce Ackerman, *We the People: Foundations* (London: The Belknap Press of Harvard University Press, 1991); Stephen Holmes, *Passions and Constraint: On the Theory of Liberal Democracy* (Chicago: The University of Chicago Press, 1995).

[4] See, for instance, "On the Election of President No. 3," *National Intelligencer and Washington Advertiser*, January 7, 1801.

[5] On the tensions over the meaning of popular sovereignty and constitution government that this gave rise to in the early Republic, cf. Jason Frank, *Constituent Moments: Enacting the People in Postrevolutionary America* (Durham: Duke University Press, 2010), 139–42.

values. Put another way, the change reconfigured the ever-potentially present
sovereign people of 1787–88 into something more akin to the Lawgiver
discussed by Rousseau – the "great and powerful genius which lies behind all
lasting things" who leaves, never to reappear again.[6] Viewing the founding
moment as irrevocably inflected by the historically concrete identities of the
actors who comprised the sovereign provided mechanisms for understanding
the Constitution as the textual record of that founding moment, which went
beyond the text itself. To be sure, Chief Justice Marshall and others had sought
to address the gaps and ambiguities within the constitutional text through
appeals to intent, plain meaning, and modes of inference, but these efforts had
groped for a "spirit" of the text which, as Marshall said, was to "be collected
chiefly from its words."[7]

The move toward the conception of constitutional government as one in
which contemporary politics is understood to operate within a framework
created by a historic moment of exceptional sovereign intervention had
important repercussions for American political life. Most directly, as noted in
Chapter 9, it made for a constitutional politics tilted toward conservatism and
the preservation of the past. Interpreting the Constitution through the
animating spirit of 1787–88 – whatever the actual content that was ascribed
to that spirit – had the effect of binding constitutional interpretation to
historical exposition. The development of rival pantheons of founders (Jay,
Franklin, Rush, and Hamilton as antislavery, Washington and the Virginians
as proslavery) serves to indicate the degree to which the debate over the
Constitution's relationship to slavery became a debate over the history of the
founding, and perhaps more crucially the founders themselves, from the 1840s
onward. Beyond Spooner and later Frederick Douglass, few sought to debate
constitutional slavery without an appeal to the practices of the past. With fealty
to the founding an overriding consideration, the most radical constitutional
innovations were presented as acts of preservation and continuity. Even as the
Southern Confederacy shattered the constitutional order in 1861, its ideologue
felt the need to reassure his listeners that "[a]ll the essentials of the old
constitution ... have been preserved and perpetuated."[8] As all acts of
preservation are essentially efforts to maintain or repair to an earlier political
settlement, this rendered any radical constitutionalism that could not draw
upon 1787–88 illegitimate. The conservative utilization of historical spirit to
navigate the issue of slavery within the constitutional text worked more widely
to establish an understanding of the Constitution – and constitutions more

---

[6] Jean-Jacques Rousseau, *The Social Contract*, trans. Maurice Cranston (London: Penguin Books, 1968), 88.

[7] *Sturges* v. *Crowninshield* (1819). On Marshall's method of "establishing the meaning of the Constitution from its words and subordinating spirit to text," see Sylvia Snowiss, "From Fundamental Law to the Supreme Law of the Land: A Reinterpretation of the Origin of Judicial Review," *Studies in American Political Development* 2 (1987): 45.

[8] Alexander H. Stephens, "Cornerstone Speech" (Savannah, GA, March 21, 1861).

generally – in which they represent the dead hand of a precise and substantive historical moment upon the present.

The legacy of conceiving of constitutions as authored and given meaning by particular historical actors at a particular historical time can be seen transparently and with serious consequences in contemporary American politics. The founders as political touchstones, while looming large in political and cultural life, are subjected to increased criticism for their attitudes with regard to race, gender, and class. But as framers, their power over us is scarcely diminishing with time. The rise of originalism as a judicial project, in a variety of guises, has only served to heighten constitutional debates that take as their premise the authority of 1787–88. As discussed in the Introduction to this book, attempts to counter originalism with a living constitutionalism tied to constitutional spirit do little to disturb the hold of the historical moment of 1787–88. Understanding the content of constitutional spirit very differently from Martin Van Buren, the advocates of contemporary constitutional spirit are nevertheless treading a similar path in offering ascribed historical attitudes as a basis upon which to push back against unwelcome textual interpretations.[9] A constitutional spirit that relies upon the historical founding for legitimation is unlikely to ever fully escape the gravitational pull that the values present at the founding exert upon the constitution it created. Spirit, understood as an historical artifact, only serves to position us as the ongoing successors to, and servants of, the generation that gave rise to it.

PAINE, JEFFERSON, AND THE CONSTITUTIONAL POLITICS OF THE ETERNAL NOW

A constitutional politics tied back to a moment of founding is not the only available model, however. The views of the Democratic-Republicans of 1800 suggest the possibility of a constitutionalism free from the dead hand of the past, and open to more readily democratic understandings of the relationship between the constitution and the sovereign. Placing the contemporaneous incarnation of the people at the center of a forward-looking understanding of democratic constitutional politics, the Democratic-Republicans hint at a path away from the constrained constitutional politics we have inherited from the

---

[9] Originalism is undoubtedly itself a project which overtly commits to a return to the attitudes and beliefs of founding generations. A central example of the ways in which constitutional interpretation has come to be constrained by an appeal to a past historical moment is offered in *District of Columbia v. Heller*. In the process of finding an individual right to bear arms in the Second Amendment, the Supreme Court split on the intention for the Amendment, using the text as record by which to derive that intent. In the case, the Court engaged in an "extensive debate on the role of original meaning in constitutional interpretation," with both sides marshaling different originalist frames. Lawrence B. Solum, "District of Columbia v. Heller and Originalism," *Northwestern University Law Review* 103, no. 2 (2009): 924; *District of Columbia v. Heller* (2008).

1830s debates over slavery. To more fully explore this possibility, I briefly turn now to Thomas Paine and Thomas Jefferson to begin to elucidate and develop their ideas regarding an alternative mode of constitutional government that prizes the present popular sovereign and not the past generation of founders.

Paine's initial writings during the American Revolution are suggestive of a relationship between constitutions and government that is framed against the passage of chronological time. Among the famous images *Common Sense* provided the world are two vivid depictions of the creation of government that suggest an origin in an initial act of the people. The first is the depiction of self-government emerging beneath "some convenient tree ... under the branches of which, the whole colony may assemble to deliberate on public matters," before growth and inconvenience render that self-government government via representation.[10] The second is his portrayal of the creation of a constitution as the solemn crowning of a charter.[11] Such a continental charter would be drafted in conference and then proclaimed on a day "solemnly set apart," which would see the symbolic destruction of the crown used in the ceremony.[12] Coupled with the reflections upon the passage of and location within time contained in *The Crisis*, and the general sense of being in a historically significant moment ("THESE are the times that try men's souls"), Paine's American revolutionary writings have the effect of emphasizing the claim made in "Common Sense," that the "present moment ... is that particular time, which never happens to a nation but once, *viz.* the time of forming itself into a government."[13] Cleaving close to an understanding of constitutions and constitution-making as initial, originary moments of popular sovereignty, these writings point to a role for the people as the originators of government, who then, like the colonists under the tree, pass responsibility for politics to their representatives.

However, after the conclusion of the American revolutionary wars and the ratification of the US Constitution, Paine moved to offer an extended consideration of constitutions in the second part of his *Rights of Man* which signaled a more complex relation between time and sovereign enactment. Here Paine links alteration of the constitution to the improvement of societal

---

[10] Thomas Paine, "Common Sense: Addressed to the Inhabitants of America, on the Following Interesting Subjects," in *Selected Writings of Thomas Paine*, ed. Ian Shapiro and Jane E. Calvert (New Haven: Yale University Press, 2014), 9.

[11] Paine, "Common Sense," 31.   [12] Paine, "Common Sense," 31.

[13] Paine, "Common Sense," 38; Thomas Paine, "The Crisis: In Thirteen Numbers. Written during the Late War," in *Selected Writings of Thomas Paine*, ed. Ian Shapiro and Jane E. Calvert (New Haven: Yale University Press, 2014), 53. Regarding the references to time in "The Crisis," cf. "But it is pleasant, and sometimes useful, to look back, even in the first periods of infancy, and trace the turns and windings through which have passed" ("The Crisis: Number 3"); "a too great inattention to past occurrences retards and bewilders our judgment in every thing ... by comparing what is past with what is present, we frequently hit on the true character of both" ("The Crisis: Number 3"); "let us look back on the scenes we have passed, and learn from experience what is yet to be done" ("The Crisis: Number 13"). Paine, "The Crisis," 73, 74, 119.

knowledge in a manner that indicates an ongoing resonance between experience and the constitution. While the nation has a right to establish a constitution, there is no guarantee that the established constitution will be "judicious" – only through "continuing" to exercise its judgment can a people hope to explode all the errors within it.[14] Moreover, as the knowledge of politics is ever advancing, the best constitution currently devised "may be far short of that excellence which a few years may afford."[15] Fitting in with his broader rejection of precedent as a source of authority, Paine supposes the nation to be in advance of the government in this regard.[16] Assuming such rapid evolution of the science of politics and the people as the carriers of it, the maximization of their happiness would require almost continuous intervention to set the government on the correct forward-looking course.

Paine's contribution to the debates surrounding the creation of a new French constitution in the mid-1790s, his *Dissertation on the First-Principles of Government* (1795), further developed the ideas offered in the *Rights of Man*. Paine argued robustly in favor of a system of government grounded on the people's sovereign authority and one that crucially located the present moment as the timeframe for enactments of such sovereignty. Taking aim at hereditary orders and claims of custom that supported them, Paine argued that "time has no more connection with, or influence upon principle, than principle has upon time."[17] This reasoning worked to deny the authority that hereditary orders claimed through dint of prolonged existence, but it also positioned the questions of justice and legitimacy of a principle in the immediate moment. Locating the appropriate timeframe for considerations of justice as firmly in the immediate moment, Paine stated, "Time with respect to principles is an eternal NOW."[18] Whenever one discovered or experienced a wrong, it was at that point that it became appropriate to resist it. A history of resistance or, more significantly, the absence of such a history had no bearing upon the legitimacy of opposition to any principle.

Paine linked the conception of an "eternal now" to generational sovereignty. Pointing to the continual movement of individuals in and out of the nation through birth and death, Paine noted that the "nation, though continually existing, is continually in a state of renewal and succession."[19] Without a way to assign heightened authority to any particular moment in time, Paine denied that in "this ever running flood of generations," one was "superior in authority to another."[20] Making recourse, as Jefferson would, to the metaphor of ownership of land, Paine

---

[14] Paine, "Rights of Man," 300.　[15] Paine, "Rights of Man," 308.
[16] England offered the "curious phaenomenon" of nation looking forward while its government looked backward. Paine, "Rights of Man," 299.
[17] Thomas Paine, "Dissertation on First-Principles of Government," in *Selected Writings of Thomas Paine*, ed. Ian Shapiro and Jane E. Calvert (New Haven: Yale University Press, 2014), 506.
[18] Paine, "Dissertation on First-Principles of Government."
[19] Paine, "Dissertation on First-Principles of Government," 507.
[20] Paine, "Dissertation on First-Principles of Government."

suggested "our ancestors, like ourselves, were but tenants for life in the great freehold of rights."[21] To be bound by them would be to be "slaves" and to likewise attempt to bind future generations would be to be "as tyrants."[22] Treating each generation as equally capable of judgment and unencumbered by the past, Paine looked to the present moment – the "eternal now" – for the legitimization of any government.

Although Paine gave thought to how such a presence could be maintained, the elaboration of such mechanisms in his writing was quite limited and often constrained to electoral politics. Upon his return to the United States at the beginning of the nineteenth century, Paine saw the incoming Jeffersonian administration as one instance of popular mobilization against a corrupt and corrupting government. Much as Jefferson himself would see the election of 1800 as a revolution akin to 1776, Paine understood it in terms of a decisive intervention of the body of the people.[23] But even while arguing for an expansive role of the people in political life to ensuring the sovereignty of the existing citizenry, he still saw elections as the mechanism by which this was to be achieved and ultimately trusted elected representatives to implement any necessary revision.[24]

THE PEOPLE IN MASS: THOMAS JEFFERSON'S WARD REPUBLICS AS POPULAR PRESENCE

Jefferson famously advanced a conception of generational sovereignty in which "the earth belongs ... to the living." Alongside his 1787 claim that the "tree of liberty must be refreshed from time to time with the blood of patriots and tyrants" and apparent acceptance of extensive violence in the French pursuit of liberty, Jefferson's opposition to perpetual constitutions has allowed for a depiction of the third president as a radical but somewhat impractical democrat.[25] Following Hannah Arendt, commentators have reframed Jefferson's democratic radicalism as the expression of a revolutionary ethos rather than a substantive commitment, drawing upon his system of ward

---

[21] Paine, "Dissertation on First-Principles of Government."
[22] Paine, "Dissertation on First-Principles of Government."
[23] Thomas Paine, "To the Citizens of the United States: Letter I," *The National Intelligencer*, November 15, 1802.
[24] In 1805, Paine even came to the point of suggesting popular control over all "extraordinary legislation" via intervening elections, with the effect that "the mind of the country" will be brought to bear upon "any important proposed bill: and thus the whole State will be its own Council of Revision." Thomas Paine, *Constitutions, Governments, and Charters*, 1805.
[25] National Archives, "Thomas Jefferson to William Stephens Smith, 13th November 1787," Founders Online, accessed March 23, 2018, https://founders.archives.gov/documents/Jefferson/01-12-02-0282. On Jefferson's radical views of the French Revolution, cf. Carson Holloway, *Hamilton versus Jefferson in the Washington Administration: Completing the Founding or Betraying the Founding?* (Cambridge, UK: Cambridge University Press, 2015), 219–21.

republics to present him as more republican than democrat.[26] Such well-meant dismissal of Jefferson's democratic excesses nevertheless overlooks his very real commitment: the retaining of the voice of the people within constitutional politics. In line with his own framing of his election in 1800 as an instance of democratic revolution in which the people reformed the principles of government just as they had the form in 1776, Jefferson's sense of democracy was predicated on the presence of the people within the sphere of political life.[27] Rereading his commentary on constitutional politics, generational sovereignty, and the ward republics with an eye to this commitment, one can see Jefferson seeking to incorporate the "people in mass" within a system of constitutional politics. Jefferson's conception of the people was undoubtedly white, primarily male, and dedicated to the preservation of the political unity Jefferson uncritically ascribed to the "patriotic" people.[28] But it can be read with an expansive conception of the people in mind – one more in tune with our contemporary understandings – to the end of predicating constitutional politics on a democratic foundation. Thinking of the people not merely as an absent landlord for the representative form of government created under their authority, Jefferson seeks to develop a model of constitutionalism in which the present people are an existing entity whose power and sovereignty can be felt within day-to-day politics and remains a potential agent of sovereign intervention.

Thomas Jefferson's conception of generational sovereignty was most famously spelt out in a letter to James Madison in September 1789.[29] In this

[26] Hannah Arendt, *On Revolution* (New York: Penguin Books, 1990), 248–55. Arendt believed that Jefferson's ward republics were an idealistic afterthought, designed to enable a degree of individual public participation in order to stave off the threat of political corruption from the many. Nonetheless, Richard K. Matthews believes Arendt's treatment of the ward republics "shows the radical democratic nature behind [Jefferson's] theory." Richard K. Matthews, *The Radical Politics of Thomas Jefferson: A Revisionist View* (Lawrence: University of Kansas Press, 1984), 16.

[27] National Archives, "Thomas Jefferson to Spencer Roane, 6th September 1819," Founders Online, accessed March 23, 2018, http://founders.archives.gov/documents/Jefferson/98-01-02-0734.

[28] Jefferson undoubtedly defined the concept of the people in exclusionary terms with the "nation" envisioned as racially white. Peter S. Onuf, "'To Declare Them a Free and Independent People': Race, Slavery, and National Identity in Jefferson's Thought," *Journal of the Early Republic* 18, no. 1 (1998): 1–46; Armin Mattes, *Citizens of a Common Intellectual Homeland: The Transatlantic Origins of American Democracy and Nationhood* (Charlottesville: University of Virginia Press, 2015), 150–51, 167–68; Annette Gordon-Reed and Peter S. Onuf, *"Most Blessed of the Patriarchs": Thomas Jefferson and the Empire of the Imagination* (New York, NY: Liveright Publishing Corporation, 2016), 176. On the complex relationship of women to the "generation" that Jefferson saw as sovereign, see Gordon-Reed and Onuf, 183–84. On the anticipation of national unity and its link to the people see Gordon-Reed and Onuf, 200–206. On the importance of recognizing the constrained form of democracy practiced in the era of founding for contemporary constitutional theory, cf. Jack Jackson, "Unmapped Politics," *Harvard Civil Rights-Civil Liberties Review*, 2012.

[29] For a reading of this letter as offering "important resources for reimagining a politics of founding and refounding as democratic self-constitution," see Angélica Maria Bernal, *Beyond Origins: Rethinking Founding in a Time of Constitutional Democracy* (New York: Oxford University

letter, the distinction between generations and the requirement of consent to one's government resulted in a basic system of generational sovereignty that Jefferson would adhere to. Jefferson contemplates the question of whether "one generation of men has a right to bind another," and comes to the conclusion, that as the "earth belongs always to the living generation," no society can make a "perpetual constitution."[30] Offering his famous calculation of nineteen years as the span of a generation's authority, Jefferson supposed that this interval represented the period after which a majority of the citizenry that had enacted any statute or constitution would no longer be alive. On this basis, the people after nineteen years would be so constituted as to be under no obligation to those at the beginning of such a period. Jefferson suggested on that basis that constitutions and laws ought to expire after nineteen years of operation: "Every constitution then, and every law, naturally expires at the end of 19 years. If it be enforced longer, it is an act of force, and not of right."[31] As each "generation is to another as one independent nation to another," the constitution of any particular generation could not be regarded as binding upon any other.[32]

In the context of early America and Jefferson's faith in democracy, this commitment called for a conception of the people as more than a legitimizing myth. An approach such as Jefferson's that emphasized generational and popular sovereignty only made sense while the people remained a potentially present sovereign, able to intervene to renew or reform constitutions and statutes. Just as his 1819 letter to Spencer Roane, in which he outlined the revolution of 1800, would emphasize that power could only be trusted in the "people in mass," so in the 1789 letter to Madison, Jefferson assumed that the people were an existing and potentially present entity whose consent could be elicited. Expected to be capable of forming themselves into a body for the purposes of constitutional intervention as necessary, the "people in mass" were to be more than a fiction. In 1816, while writing to John Taylor, Jefferson would make recourse to the idea

---

Press, 2017), chap. 6. With a different political theoretical agenda, Stephen Holmes reads the letter (and Paine's similar approach) as evidence that Jefferson and Paine were anticonstitutionalists. Holmes, *Passions and Constraint*, 140–44. For a reading of the letter as a radical reconception of property rights, see Matthews, *The Radical Politics of Thomas Jefferson*, 19–29.

[30] National Archives, "Thomas Jefferson to James Madison, 6th September 1789," Founders Online, accessed March 22, 2018, http://founders.archives.gov/documents/Madison/01–12-02–0248.

[31] National Archives.

[32] Writing the letter in Paris, Jefferson only forwarded his ideas to Madison upon his return to the United States of America in 1790. Madison's response foreshadowed later commentators in offering an endorsement of the idea that politicians ought to be conscious of the burdens they placed upon future generations while gently suggesting the impracticality and even undesirability of the application of Jefferson's ideas in practice. National Archives, "Thomas Jefferson to James Madison, 9th January 1790," Founders Online, accessed March 22, 2018, https://founders.archives.gov/documents/Madison/01–12-02–0311; National Archives, "James Madison to Thomas Jefferson, 4th February 1790," Founders Online, accessed March 22, 2018, http://founders.archives.gov/documents/Madison/01–13-02–0020.

that the people existed in "mass." Indeed, for Jefferson, the very definition of a republic was a government "by it's [*sic*] citizens, in mass, acting directly and personally."[33] Conceding that such a form of government could likely exist on only a small scale, Jefferson looked to representatives held to short terms or for specific purposes as mechanisms for keeping such representatives tied to the will of their electors. But, as the definition offered suggests, representation was only a necessary innovation to ensure that the government by the mass of the people could be scaled and stabilized; to the extent that the Virginian and the federal governments with their life appointments and limited rotation of office had limited the avenues for direct action on the part of the people, they contained "much less of republicanism, than ought to have been expected."[34] Reflecting his deep faith that the "mass of the citizens" were the safest depository of their own rights, Jefferson combined his belief that each generation were but "tenants for life" of the earth with the view that the state is constituted by men, not institutions, in arguing for a government drawn closer to the people and thus readily engaged with the people as an existing entity.[35]

Against this backdrop, Jefferson's much-vaunted system of ward republics can be seen less a commitment to a federal system of representation and more a mechanism for enabling the existence of an ever-present "people in mass" within a coherent political structure. In early 1816, Jefferson had laid out the basic contours of his now-famous system of republics growing out of "elementary" ward republics:

The elementary republics of the wards, the county republics, the State republics, and the republic of the Union, would form a gradation of authorities, standing each on the basis of laws, holding every one its delegated share of powers, and constituting truly a system of fundamental balances and checks for the government.[36]

As well as enabling the people to govern directly at the ward level, Jefferson saw in the wards the potential for a popular presence at higher levels of government: "a general call of ward-meetings by their Wardens on the same day thro' the state would at any time produce the genuine sense of the people on any required point, and would enable the state to act in mass."[37]

Writing a month and a half after he addressed John Taylor, Jefferson developed his understanding of the ward republics as a mechanism for institutionalizing the presence of the people. Writing to Samuel Kercheval in July 1816 in response to a request for an opinion on the calling of a state convention, Jefferson once again articulated an understanding of

---

[33] National Archives, "Thomas Jefferson to John Taylor, 28th May 1816," Founders Online, accessed March 26, 2018, http://founders.archives.gov/documents/Jefferson/03–10-02–0053.

[34] National Archives.   [35] National Archives.

[36] National Archives, "Thomas Jefferson to Joseph C. Cabell, 2nd February 1816," Founders Online, accessed March 27, 2018, http://founders.archives.gov/documents/Jefferson/03–09-02–0286.

[37] National Archives, "Thomas Jefferson to John Adams, 28th October 1813," Founders Online, accessed March 27, 2018, http://founders.archives.gov/documents/Jefferson/03–06-02–0446.

republicanism as the embodiment of the will of people.[38] In the letter, Jefferson distanced himself from the existing Virginia constitution insofar as it had predated the understanding of "the mother-principle" that "governments are republican only in proportion as they embody the will of the people."[39] Marrying this observation to an overview of his proposed ward system, Jefferson offered a more extensive theoretical consideration of his ward system than offered elsewhere. In this set of proposals, the idea that there is "a spirit of the people" is placed at the center of the unified discussion of republicanism and ward republics. Given the imperfect understanding of the "mother-principle" of republicanism, this spirit has survived despite, rather than because of, the constitutional form. Reforms in line with the ward system would reverse that relationship, enabling the constitutional form to "nourish and perpetuate that spirit" through self-government. By dividing the county administrations such that every citizen can attend when needed and "act in person," the constitution could be made to conform to the spirit, tapping into the capacity for each individual and community to administer in their own best interest matters "relating to themselves exclusively."[40]

The invocation of the spirit of the people as the basis of the ward republics points to the desirability of making present the people as a whole within the political system. In the September letter, Jefferson spells this conception out more directly by claiming, with regard to the wards

these will be pure & elementary republics, the sum of all which, taken together, composes the state, & will make of the whole a true democracy as to the business of the Wards, which is that of nearest and daily concern.[41]

Conceding the need for representation at levels of government above the wards, Jefferson nevertheless sees the wards as institutions by which the people can be called into being at those higher levels when needed. Should representatives become corrupted "the division into wards, constituting the people, in their wards, a regularly organised power, enables them, by that organisation, to crush, regularly and peaceably, the usurpations of their unfaithful agents."[42] It was, said Jefferson, "in this way [that] we shall be as republican as a large society can be; and secure the continuance of purity in our government by the salutary, peaceable, and regular controul of the people." The wards not only enabled the cultivation of self-government at the local level – they also provided the capacity for the mass of the people to

---

[38] National Archives, "Thomas Jefferson to 'Henry Tompkinson' (Samuel Kercheval), 12th July 1816."

[39] National Archives.   [40] National Archives.

[41] National Archives, "Thomas Jefferson to Samuel Kercheval, 5th September 1816," Founders Online, accessed March 27, 2018, http://founders.archives.gov/documents/Jefferson/03-10-02-0255.

[42] National Archives.

intervene at higher levels of government, thus ensuring the whole was made "a true democracy."[43]

Between the theoretical work of Paine and the practical system of Jefferson, we have then a route toward a constitutional politics freed from the moment of sovereignty. Paine's latter formulation of the "eternal now" opens up a possibility for asserting constitutional authority without regard to secular time. Jefferson's ward republics illustrate the potential for the sovereign people's presence within constitutional politics beyond episodic grants of power and retroactive assent to textual reinterpretation. A system of ward republics in which self-governing communities assemble to form a people in mass and voice constitutional concerns and remedies offers a vision of a radically democratic and radically continuous constitutionalism. Crucially, it need not be the case that such a constitutional system foregoes the benefits of a written constitution – for both Paine and Jefferson seem to hold the textual nature of constitutions as central to the conceptual division of sovereign and government. But the written constitution is reconceptualized here. It is no longer the evidentiary record of a moment of sovereignty. Instead, it becomes the basis for constitutional deliberation, the draft upon which the community is ever working. Positioned as authors continually writing and rewriting their own story, the people become not the grantees of constitutional authority but its very embodiment. The reconceived constitutional politics here offers the prospect of an enhanced democratic agency. In reclaiming the Constitution from the past, Paine and Jefferson offer us a way to overcome the grip of a founding moment and to render the popular sovereign present. They offer us a glimpse of the democratic constitution that time and history have made elusive.

---

[43] Matthews sees the ward republics as "a way to keep alive the revolutionary ardor of the founding era, and a mechanism to allow the citizens truly to govern themselves." Matthews, *The Radical Politics of Thomas Jefferson*, 87. Alternatively, Gordon-Reed and Onuf offer a more individualistic sense of the ward republics as a basis for a "Jeffersonian democracy … grounded in the sovereignty of the individual, secure in his rights." Gordon-Reed and Onuf, "*Most Blessed of the Patriarchs*", 294.

Bibliography

Ackerman, Bruce. *We the People: Foundations.* London: The Belknap Press of Harvard University Press, 1991.

Adair, Douglass. "Fame and the Founding Fathers." In *Fame and the Founding Fathers: Essays by Douglass Adair,* edited by Trevor Colbourn, 3–26. New York: W. W. Norton & Company, 1974.

Adams, John. "John Adams to Benjamin Rush, April 4, 1790." In *Old Family Letters, Series A,* edited by Alexander Biddle, 55–58. Philadelphia: J. B. Lippincott Company, 1892.

Albanese, Catherine L. *Sons of the Fathers: The Civil Religion of the American Revolution.* Philadelphia: Temple University Press, 1976.

Appleby, Joyce. *Inheriting the Revolution: The First Generation of Americans.* Boston: The Belknap Press of Harvard University Press, 2000.

"The American Heritage: The Heirs and the Disinherited." In *A Restless Past: History and the American Public,* edited by Joyce Appleby, 71–90. Lanham: Rowman & Littlefield Publishers, Inc., 2005.

Arendt, Hannah. *On Revolution.* New York: Penguin Books, 1990.

Ashworth, John. *Slavery, Capitalism, and Politics in the Antebellum Republic: Volume 1: Commerce and Compromise, 1820–1850.* Cambridge, UK: Cambridge University Press, 1995.

Atta, John R. Van. *Wolf by the Ears: The Missouri Crisis, 1819–1821.* Baltimore, MD: Johns Hopkins University Press, 2015.

Bacon, Jacqueline. *Freedom's Journal: The First African-American Newspaper.* Lanham: Lexington Books, 2007.

"The History of Freedom's Journal: A Study in Empowerment and Community." *The Journal of African American History* 88, no. 1 (2003): 1–20.

Baker, H. Robert. *Prigg v. Pennsylvania: Slavery, the Supreme Court, and the Ambivalent Constitution.* Lawrence: University of Kansas Press, 2012.

"The Fugitive Slave Clause and the Antebellum Constitution." *Law and History Review* 30, no. 4 (2012): 1133–74.

Balkin, Jack M. *Living Originalism.* Cambridge, MA: The Belknap Press of Harvard University Press, 2011.

Baptist, Edward E. *The Half Has Never Been Told: Slavery and the Making of American Capitalism.* New York: Basic Books, 2014.

Barnett, Randy E. "Originalism for Nonoriginalists." *Loyola Law Review* 45, no. 4 (1999): 611–54.

Restoring the Lost Constitution: The Presumption of Liberty. Princeton: Princeton University Press, 2003.

"Whence Comes Section One? The Abolitionist Origins of the Fourteenth Amendment." *Journal of Legal Analysis* 3, no. 1 (2011): 165–263.

Bay, Mia. "See Your Declaration Americans!!: Abolitionism, Americanism, and the Revolutionary Tradition in Free Black Politics." In *Americanism: New Perspectives on the History of an Ideal,* edited by Michael Kazin and Joseph A. McCartin, 25–52. Chapel Hill: The University of North Carolina Press, 2006.

Beckert, Sven and Seth Rockman. "Introduction: Slavery's Capitalism." In *Slavery's Capitalism: A New History of American Economic Development,* edited by Sven Beckert and Seth Rockman, 1–27. Philadelphia: University of Pennsylvania Press, 2016.

Bercovitch, Sacvan. *The Rites of Assent: Transformations in the Symbolic Construction of America.* New York: Routledge, 1993.

Bernal, Angélica Maria. *Beyond Origins: Rethinking Founding in a Time of Constitutional Democracy.* New York: Oxford University Press, 2017.

Bernstein, R. B. *The Founding Fathers Reconsidered.* Oxford: Oxford University Press, 2009.

Blue, Frederick J. *No Taint of Compromise: Crusaders in Antislavery Politics.* Baton Rouge: Louisiana State University Press, 2005.

Bonner, Robert E. *Mastering America: Southern Slaveholders and the Crisis of American Nationhood.* New York: Cambridge University Press, 2009.

Bourne, Jenny. "Dred, Panic, War: How A Slave Case Triggered Financial Crisis and Civil Disunion." In *Congress and the Crisis of the 1850s,* edited by Paul Finkelman and Don Kennan, 159–202. Athens, OH: Ohio University Press, 2012.

Bouton, Terry. *Taming Democracy: "The People," the Founders, and the Troubled Ending of the American Revolution.* New York: Oxford University Press, 2007.

Brewer Stewart, James. "The Emergence of Racial Modernity and the Rise of the White North, 1790–1840." *Journal of the Early Republic* 18, no. 2 (1998): 181–217.

Brophy, Alfred L. "The Market, Utility, and Slavery in Southern Legal Thought." In *Slavery's Capitalism: A New History of American Economic Development,* edited by Sven Beckert and Seth Rockman, 262–76. Philadelphia: University of Pennsylvania Press, 2016.

Burstein, Andrew. *America's Jubilee.* New York, NY: Alfred A. Knopf, 2011.

Sentimental Democracy: The Evolution of America's Romantic Self-Image. New York: Hill and Wang, 1999.

Carpenter, Daniel P. *The Forging of Bureaucratic Autonomy: Reputations, Networks, and Policy Innovation in Executive Agencies, 1862–1928.* Princeton: Princeton University Press, 2001.

Carrese, Paul O. "Restoring the Lost Constitution: The Presumption of Liberty." *First Things,* August 2004. www.firstthings.com/article/2004/08/restoring-the-lost-constitution-the-presumption-of-liberty

Channing, William E. *Slavery.* Boston, MA: James Munroe and Company, 1835.

Childers, Christopher. *The Failure of Popular Sovereignty: Slavery, Manifest Destiny, and the Radicalization of Southern Politics*. Lawrence: University of Kansas Press, 2012.

"The Old Republican Constitutional Primer: States Rights after the Missouri Controversy and the Onset of the Politics of Slavery." In *The Enigmatic South: Toward Civil War and Its Legacies*, edited by Samuel C. Hyde, 12–29. Baton Rouge: Louisiana State University Press, 2014.

Clephane, Walter C. "The Local Aspects of Slavery in the District of Columbia." *Records of the Columbia Historical Society, Washington, D.C.* 3 (1900): 224–56.

Cleve, George William Van. *A Slaveholders' Union: Slavery, Politics, and the Constitution in the Early American Republic*. Chicago: University of Chicago Press, 2010.

Cole, Donald B. *Martin Van Buren and the American Political System*. Princeton: Princeton University Press, 1984.

Conlin, Michael F. *The Constitutional Origins of the American Civil War*. Cambridge, UK: Cambridge University Press, 2019.

Considerations on the Impropreity and Inexpediency of Renewing the Missouri Question. By A Pennsylvanian. Philadelphia: M. Carey & Son, 1820.

Cooper, Frederick. "Elevating the Race: The Social Thought of Black Leaders, 1827–50." *American Quarterly* 24, no. 5 (1972): 604–25.

Cooper, William J. *The South and the Politics of Slavery 1828–1856*. Baton Rouge: Louisiana State University Press, 1978.

Cornell, Saul. "Meaning and Understanding in the History of Constitutional Ideas: The Intellectual History Alternative to Originalism." *Fordham Law Review* 82 (2013): 721–55.

Corrigan, Mary Beth. "Imaginary Cruelties? A History of the Slave Trade in Washington, D.C." *Washington History* 13, no. 2 (2001): 4–27.

Corwin, Edward. "The Worship of the Constitution." In *Corwin on the Constitution: Volume One, The Foundations of American Constitutional and Political Thought, the Powers of Congress, and the President's Power of Removal*, edited by Richard Loss, 47–55. Ithaca: Cornell University Press, 1981.

Cover, Robert M. *Justice Accused: Antislavery and the Judicial Process*. New Haven: Yale University Press, 1975.

Crothers, A. Glenn. "The 1846 Retrocession of Alexandria: Protecting Slavery and the Slave Trade in the District of Columbia." In *In the Shadow of Freedom: The Politics of Slavery in the National Capital*, edited by Paul Finkelman and Donald R. Kennon, 141–68. Athens, OH: Ohio University Press, 2010.

Currie, David P. *The Constitution in Congress*. Chicago: The University of Chicago Press, 2005.

The Constitution in the Supreme Court: The First Hundred Years 1789–1888. Chicago: University of California Press, 1985.

Curtis, Christopher Michael. *Jefferson's Freeholders and the Politics of Ownership in the Old Dominion*. New York: Cambridge University Press, 2012.

Davis, David Brion. "The Emergence of Immediatism in British and American Antislavery Thought." *The Mississippi Valley Historical Review* 49, no. 2 (1962): 209–30.

The Problem of Slavery in the Age of Emancipation. New York: Alfred A. Knopf, 2014.

Detweiler, Philip F. "Congressional Debate on Slavery and the Declaration of Independence, 1819–1821." *The American Historical Review* 63, no. 3 (1958): 598–616.

Diemer, Andrew K. *The Politics of Black Citizenship: Free African Americans in the Mid-Atlantic Borderland, 1817–1863.* Athens, GA: The University of Georgia Press, 2016.

Dworkin, Ronald. *Freedom's Law: The Moral Reading of the American Constitution.* Cambridge, MA: Harvard University Press, 1997.

Earle, Jonathan H. *Jacksonian Antislavery & the Politics of Free Soil, 1824–1854.* Chapel Hill: The University of North Carolina Press, 2004.

Ericson, David F. *The Debate over Slavery: Antislavery and Proslavery Liberalism in Antebellum America.* New York: New York University Press, 2000.

Fanuzzi, Robert. *Abolition's Public Sphere.* Minneapolis, MN: University of Minnesota, 2003.

Fehrenbacher, Don. E. "Slavery, the Framers, and the Living Constitution." In *Slavery and Its Consequences: The Constitution, Race, and Equality*, edited by Robert A. Goldwin and Art Kaufman, 1–22. Washington, DC: American Enterprise Institute, 1988.

Fehrenbacher, Don E. and Ward M. McAfee. *The Slaveholding Republic: An Account of the United States Government's Relations to Slavery.* Oxford: Oxford University Press, 2001.

Finkelman, Paul. "Garrison's Constitution: The Covenant with Death and How It Was Made." *Prologue* 32, no. 4 (2000): 230–245.

Slavery and the Founders: Race and Liberty in the Age of Jefferson. New York: Routledge, 2015.

"Slavery in the Shadow of Liberty: The Problem of Slavery in Congress and the Nation's Capital." In *In the Shadow of Freedom: The Politics of Slavery in the National Capital*, edited by Paul Finkelman and Donald R. Kennon, 3–15. Athens, OH: Ohio University Press, 2010.

"Story Telling on the Supreme Court: Prigg v Pennsylvania and Justice Joseph Story's Judicial Nationalism." *The Supreme Court Review* 1994 (1994): 247–94.

Supreme Injustice: Slavery in the Nation's Highest Court. Cambridge, MA: Harvard University Press, 2018.

"The Significance and Persistence of Proslavery Thought." In *The Problem of Evil: Slavery, Freedom, and the Ambiguities of American Reform*, edited by Steve Mintz and John Stauffer, 95–114. Amherst: University of Massachusetts Press, 2007.

Fisher, Sydney G. "The Legendary and Myth-Making Process in Histories of the American Revolution." *Proceedings of the American Philosophical Society* 51, no. 204 (1912): 53–75.

Flaherty, Martin S. "Historians and the New Originalism: Contextualism, Historicism, and Constitutional Meaning." *Fordham Law Review* 84, no. 3 (2015): 905–14.

"History 'Lite' in Modern American Constitutionalism." *Columbia Law Review* 95, no. 3 (1995): 523–90.

Foletta, Marshall. *Coming to Terms with Democracy: Federalist Intellectuals and the Shaping of an American Culture.* Charlottesville: University Press of Virginia, 2001.

Foner, Eric. *Free Soil, Free Labor, Free Men: The Ideology of the Republican Party Before the Civil War.* Oxford: Oxford University Press, 1995.

Forbes, Robert Pierce. *The Missouri Compromise and Its Aftermath: Slavery and the Meaning of America*. Chapel Hill: The University of North Carolina Press, 2007.

Ford, Lacy K. *Deliver Us from Evil: The Slavery Question in the Old South*. New York: Oxford University Press, 2009.

Fox-Genovese, Elizabeth, and Eugene D. Genovese. *The Mind of the Master Class: History and Faith in the Southern Slaveholders' Worldview*. New York: Cambridge University Press, 2005.

Frank, Jason. *Constituent Moments: Enacting the People in Postrevolutionary America*. Durham: Duke University Press, 2010.

Fraser, Gordon. "Emancipatory Cosmology: Freedom's Journal, The Rights of All, and the Revolutionary Movements of Black Print Culture." *American Quarterly* 68, no. 2 (2016): 263–86.

Freehling, Alison Goodyear. *Drift Toward Dissolution: The Virginia Slavery Debate of 1831–1832*. Baton Rouge: Louisiana State University Press, 1982.

Freehling, William W. *The Road to Disunion: Volume 1, Secessionists at Bay 1776–1854*. New York: Oxford University Press, 1990.

Friedman, Barry. *The Will of the People: How Public Opinion Has Influenced the Supreme Court and Shaped the Meaning of the Constitution*. New York: Farrar, Straus and Giroux, 2010.

Friedman Goldstein, Leslie. "A 'Triumph of Freedom' After All? Prigg v. Pennsylvania Re-Examined." *Law and History Review* 29, no. 3 (2011): 763–96.

Friedman, Lawrence J. *Gregarious Saints: Self and Community in American Abolitionism, 1830–1870*. Cambridge, UK: Cambridge University Press, 1982.

Fritz, Christian G. *American Sovereigns: The People and America's Constitutional Tradition before the Civil War*. New York: Cambridge University Press, 2008.

Furstenberg, François. *In the Name of the Father: Washington's Legacy, Slavery, and the Making of a Nation*. New York: Penguin Books, 2007.

Genovese, Eugene D. *The Slaveholders' Dilemma: Freedom and Progress in Southern Conservative Thought, 1820–1860*. Columbia: University of South Carolina, 1992.

Goldstone, Lawrence. *Dark Bargain: Slavery, Profits, and the Struggle for the Constitution*. New York: Walker & Company, 2005.

Goodman, Paul. *Of One Blood: Abolitionism and the Origins of Racial Equality*. Berkeley: University of California Press, 1998.

Gordon-Reed, Annette, and Peter S. Onuf. *"Most Blessed of the Patriarchs": Thomas Jefferson and the Empire of the Imagination*. New York: Liveright Publishing Corporation, 2016.

Graber, Mark A. *Dred Scott and the Problem of Constitutional Evil*. Cambridge, UK: Cambridge University Press, 2006.

Gudmestad, Robert H. *A Troublesome Commerce: The Transformation of the Interstate Slave Trade*. Baton Rouge: Louisiana State University Press, 2003.

Habermas, Jürgen, and William Regh. "Constitutional Democracy: A Paradoxical Union of Contradictory Principles ?" *Political Theory* 29, no. 6 (2001): 766–81.

Harrold, Stanley. *Subversives: Antislavery Community in Washington, D.C., 1828–1865*. Baton Rouge: Louisiana State University Press, 2003.

Hinks, Peter P. *To Awaken My Afflicted Brethren: David Walker and the Problem of Antebellum Slave Resistance*. University Park: The Pennsylvania State University Press, 1997.

Holden-Smith, Barbara. "Lords of Lash, Loom, and Law: Story, Slavery, and Prigg v. Pennsylvania." *Cornell Law Review* 78 (1993): 1086–1151.

Holloway, Carson. *Hamilton versus Jefferson in the Washington Administration: Completing the Founding or Betraying the Founding?* Cambridge, UK: Cambridge University Press, 2015.

Holmes, Stephen. *Passions and Constraint: On the Theory of Liberal Democracy.* Chicago: The University of Chicago Press, 1995.

Holton, Woody. *Unruly Americans and the Origins of the Constitution.* New York: Hill and Wang, 2007.

Honig, Bonnie. "Between Decision and Deliberation: Political Paradox in Democratic Theory." *American Political Science Review* 101, no. 01 (2007): 1–17.

Hyman, Harold M., and William M. Wiecek. *Equal Justice Under Law: Constitutional Development 1835–1875.* New York: Harper & Row, 1982.

Jackson, Jack. "Unmapped Politics." *Harvard Civil Rights-Civil Liberties Review*, 2012.

Jonathan Gienapp. "Historicism and Holism: Failures of Originalist Translation." *Fordham Law Review* 84 (2015): 935–56.

   The Second Creation: Fixing the American Constitution in the Founding Era. Cambridge, MA: The Belknap Press of Harvard University Press, 2018.

Jones, Martha S. *Birthright Citizens: A History of Race and Rights in Antebellum America.* Cambridge, UK: Cambridge University Press, 2018.

Kammen, Michael. *A Machine That Would Go of Itself: The Constitution in American Culture.* New York: First Vintage Books, 1987.

Karp, Matthew. *This Vast Southern Empire: Slaveholders at the Helm of American Foreign Policy.* Cambridge, MA: Harvard University Press, 2016.

Knowles, Helen J. "Seeing the Light: Lysander Spooner's Increasingly Popular Constitutionalism." *Law and History Review* 31, no. 3 (2013): 531–58.

   "The Constitution and Slavery: A Special Relationship." *Slavery & Abolition* 28, no. 3 (2007): 309–28.

Knupfer, Peter B. *The Union As It Is: Constitutional Unionism and Sectional Compromise, 1787–1861.* Chapel Hill: The University of North Carolina Press, 1991.

Kramer, Larry D. *The People Themselves: Popular Constitutionalism and Judicial Review.* Oxford, UK: Oxford University Press, 2004.

Lamb-Books, Benjamin. *Angry Abolitionists and the Rhetoric of Slavery: Moral Emotions in Social Movements.* New York: Palgrave Macmillan, 2016.

Leonard, Gerald. "Law and Politics Reconsidered: A New Constitutional History of Dred Scott." *Law & Social Inquiry* 34, no. 3 (2009): 747–85.

Leonard, Gerald, and Saul Cornell. *The Partisan Republic: Democracy, Exclusion, and the Fall of the Founder's Constitution, 1780s-1830s.* Cambridge, UK: Cambridge University Press, 2019.

Levin, Daniel. "Federalists in the Attic: Original Intent, the Heritage Movement, and Democratic Theory." *Law & Social Inquiry* 29, no. 1 (2004): 105–26.

Liu, Goodwin, Pamela S. Karlan, and Christopher H. Schroeder. *Keeping Faith with the Constitution.* Oxford: Oxford University Press, 2010.

Longmore, Paul K. *The Invention of George Washington.* Berkeley: University of California Press, 1988.

Lowenthal, David. *The Heritage Crusade and the Spoils of History.* Cambridge, UK: Cambridge University Press, 1998.

Lucas, M. Philip. "Martin Van Buren as Party Leader and at Andrew Jackson's Right Hand." In *A Companion to the Antebellum Presidents 1837–1861*, edited by Joel H. Silbey, 109–29. Malden, MA: Wiley-Blackwell, 2014.

Ludlum, Robert P. "The Antislavery 'Gag-Rule': History and Argument." *The Journal of Negro History* 26, no. 2 (1941): 203–43.

Maier, Pauline. *American Scripture: Making the Declaration of Independence.* New York: Alfred A. Knopf, 1997.

Ratification: The People Debate the Constitution, 1787–1788. New York: Simon & Schuster, 2011.

Mason, Matthew. "A Missed Opportunity? The Founding, Postcolonial Realities, and the Abolition of Slavery." *Slavery & Abolition* 35, no. 2 (2014): 199–213.

Slavery & Politics in the Early American Republic. Chapel Hill: The University of North Carolina Press, 2006.

"The Maine and Missouri Crisis: Competing Priorities and Northern Slavery Politics in the Early Republic." *Journal of the Early Republic* 33 (2013): 675–700.

Mattes, Armin. *Citizens of a Common Intellectual Homeland: The Transatlantic Origins of American Democracy and Nationhood.* Charlottesville: University of Virginia Press, 2015.

Matthews, Richard K. *The Radical Politics of Thomas Jefferson: A Revisionist View.* Lawrence: University of Kansas Press, 1984.

McCarthy, Timothy Patrick. "'To Plead Our Own Cause': Black Print Culture and the Origins of American Abolitionism." In *Prophets of Protest: Reconsidering the History of American Abolitionism*, edited by Timothy Patrick McCarthy and John Stauffer, 114–44. New York: The New Press, 2006.

McDaniel, W. Caleb. *The Problem of Democracy in the Age of Slavery: Garrisonian Abolitionists & Transatlantic Reform.* Baton Rouge: Louisiana State University Press, 2013.

McGlone, Robert E. "Deciphering Memory: John Adams and the Authorship of the Declaration of Independence." *Journal of American History* 85, no. 2 (1998): 411–38.

McHenry, Elizabeth. *Forgotten Readers: Recovering the Lost History of African American Literacy Societies.* Durham: Duke University Press, 2002.

McInerney, Daniel John. *The Fortunate Heirs of Freedom: Abolition & Republican Thought.* Lincoln: University of Nebraska Press, 1994.

McLaughlin Green, Constance. *The Secret City: A History of Race Relations in the Nation's Capital.* Princeton: Princeton University Press, 1967.

Meinke, Scott R. "Slavery, Partisanship, and Procedure in the U.S. House: The Gag Rule, 1836–1845." *Legislative Studies Quarterly* 32, no. 1 (2007): 33–57.

Mercieca, Jennifer R. *Founding Fictions.* Tuscaloosa: The University of Alabama Press, 2010.

"The Culture of Honor: How Slaveholders Responded to the Abolitionist Mail Crisis." *Rhetoric & Public Affairs* 10, no. 1 (2007): 51–76.

Merritt, Keri Leigh. *Masterless Men: Poor Whites and Slavery in the Antebellum South.* Cambridge, UK: Cambridge University Press, 2017.

Messer, Peter C. *Stories of Independence: Identity, Ideology, and History in Eighteenth-Century America.* DeKalb: Northern Illinois University Press, 2005.

Meyler, Bernadette. "Towards a Common Law Originalism." *Stanford Law Review* 59, no. 3 (2006): 551–600.

Miller, Perry. *The Life of the Mind in America: From Revolution to the Civil War.* New York: Harcourt, Brace & World Inc., 1965.

Miller, William Lee. *Arguing About Slavery: John Quincy Adams and the Great Battle in the United States Congress.* New York: Alfred A. Knopf, 1996.

Mintz, Steven. "Introduction." In *The Problem of Evil: Slavery, Freedom, and the Ambiguities of American Reform*, edited by Steven Mintz and John Stauffer, 127–37. Amherst: University of Massachusetts Press, 2007.

Myers Asch, Chris, and George Derek Musgrove. *Chocolate City: A History of Race and Democracy in the Nation's Capital.* Chapel Hill: The University of North Carolina Press, 2017.

Newman, Richard S. *The Transformation of American Abolitionism: Fighting Slavery in the Early Republic.* Chapel Hill: The University of North Carolina Press, 2002.

Norton, Anne. "Transubstantiation: The Dialectic of Constitutional Authority." *The University of Chicago Law Review* 55, no. 2 (1988): 458–72.

Novak, William J. *The People's Welfare: Law & Regulation in Nineteenth-Century America.* Chapel Hill: University of North Carolina Press, 1996.

O'Brien, Michael. *Conjectures of Order: Intellectual Life and the American South, 1810–1860.* Chapel Hill: The University of North Carolina Press, 2004.

Oakes, James. *Slavery and Freedom: An Interpretation of the Old South.* New York: Alfred A. Knopf, 1990.

The Ruling Race: A History of American Slaveholders. New York: Alfred A. Knopf, 1982.

The Scorpion's Sting: Antislavery and the Coming of the Civil War. New York: W. W. Norton & Company, 2014.

Onuf, Peter S. "'To Declare Them a Free and Independent People': Race, Slavery, and National Identity in Jefferson's Thought." *Journal of the Early Republic* 18, no. 1 (1998): 1–46.

Paine, Thomas. "Common Sense: Addressed to the Inhabitants of America, on the Following Interesting Subjects." In *Selected Writings of Thomas Paine*, edited by Ian Shapiro and Jane E. Calvert, 6–52. New Haven: Yale University Press, 2014.

Constitutions, Governments, and Charters, 1805.

"Dissertation on First-Principles of Government." In *Selected Writings of Thomas Paine*, edited by Ian Shapiro and Jane E. Calvert, 503–20. New Haven: Yale University Press, 2014.

"Rights of Man. Part the Second. Combing Principle and Practice." In *Selected Writings of Thomas Paine*, edited by Ian Shapiro and Jane E. Calvert, 262–365. New Haven: Yale University Press, 2014.

"The Crisis: In Thirteen Numbers. Written During the Late War." In *Selected Writings of Thomas Paine*, edited by Ian Shapiro and Jane E. Calvert, 53–123. New Haven: Yale University Press, 2014.

"To the Citizens of the United States: Letter I." *The National Intelligencer.* November 15, 1802.

Pasley, Jeffrey L. *"The Tyranny of Printers": Newspaper Politics in the Early American Republic.* Charlottesville: University Press of Virginia, 2002.

Patterson, Orlando. *Slavery and Social Death: A Comparative Study.* Cambridge, MA: Harvard University Press, 1982.

Paulus, Carl Lawrence. *The Slaveholding Crisis: Fear of Insurrection and the Coming of the Civil War.* Baton Rouge: Louisiana State University Press, 2017.

Pease, William H., and Jane H. Pease. "Introduction." In *The Antislavery Argument*, xxii–lxxxiv. Indianapolis, IN: The Bobbs-Merrill Company, Inc., 1965.

Peters, Gerhard, and John T. Woolley. "Election of 1836." The American Presidency Project. Accessed July 13, 2018. www.presidency.ucsb.edu/showelection.php? year=1836.

Piketty, Thomas, and Gabriel Zucman. "Capital Is Back: Wealth-Income Ratios in Rich Countries 1700–2010." *The Quarterly Journal of Economics* 129, no. 3 (2014): 1255–1310.

Polgar, Paul J. "'To Raise Them to an Equal Participation': Early National Abolitionism, Gradual Emancipation, and the Promise of African American Citizenship." *Journal of the Early Republic* 31, no. 2 (2011): 229–58.

Quarles, Benjamin. *Black Abolitionists*. New York, NY: Oxford University Press, 1969.

Rable, George C. "Slavery, Politics, and the South: The Gag Rule as a Case Study." *Capitol Studies* 3, Fall (1975): 69–87.

Ratcliffe, Donald J. "The Decline of Antislavery Politics, 1815–1840." In *Contesting Slavery: The Politics of Bondage and Freedom in the New American Nation*, edited by John Craig Hammond and Matthew Mason, 267–90. Charlottesville: University of Virginia Press, 2011.

Richards, Leonard L. *The Slave Power: The Free North and Southern Domination*. Baton Rouge: Louisiana State University Press, 2000.

Richards, Mark David. "The Debates over the Retrocession of the District of Columbia, 1801–2004." *Washington History* 16, no. 1 (2004): 55–82.

Richardson, Charles Francis, and Elizabeth Miner Richardson. *Charles Miner: A Pennsylvania Pioneer*. Wilkes-Barre, PA, 1916.

Riley, Padraig. *Slavery and the Democratic Conscience: Political Life in Jeffersonian America*. Philadelphia: University of Pennsylvania Press, 2016.

Ripley, C. Peter, ed. "Constitution of the Colored Anti-Slavery Society of Newark." In *The Black Abolitionist Papers: Volume III: The United States, 1830–1846*, 132–35. Chapel Hill: The University of North Carolina Press, 1991.

"Introduction to the American Series: Black Abolitionists in the United States, 1830–1865." In *The Black Abolitionist Papers: Volume III: The United States, 1830–1846*, 3–69. Chapel Hill: The University of North Carolina Press, 1991.

ed. "Speech by Charles Lenox Remond, Delivered at Marlboro Chapel, Boston, Massachusetts, 29 May 1844." In *The Black Abolitionist Papers: Volume III: The United States, 1830–1846*, 442–45. Chapel Hill: The University of North Carolina Press, 1991.

Roberts-Miller, Patricia. *Fanatical Schemes: Proslavery Rhetoric and the Tragedy of Consensus*. Tuscaloosa: The University of Alabama Press, 2009.

Rockman, Seth. *Scraping By: Wage Labor, Slavery, and Survival in Early Baltimore*. Baltimore: The Johns Hopkins University Press, 2009.

Rogers, Melvin L. "David Walker and the Political Power of the Appeal." *Political Theory* 43, no. 2 (2015): 208–33.

Root, Erik S. *All Honor to Jefferson?: The Virginia Slavery Debates and the Positive Good Thesis*. Lanham: Lexington Books, 2008.

"Introduction." In *Sons of the Fathers: The Virginia Slavery Debates of 1831–1832*, edited by Erik S. Root, 1–23. Lanham: Lexington Books, 2010.

ed. *Sons of the Fathers: The Virginia Slavery Debates of 1831–1832*. Lanham: Lexington Books, 2010.

Rosenthal, Caitlin. *Accounting for Slavery*. Cambridge, MA: Harvard University Press, 2018.

Ross, Dorothy. "Historical Consciousness in Nineteenth-Century America." *The American Historical Review* 89, no. 4 (1984): 909–28.

Rousseau, Jean-Jacques. *The Social Contract*. Translated by Maurice Cranston. London: Penguin Books, 1968.

Scalia, Antonin. *A Matter of Interpretation: Federal Courts and the Law*. Princeton: Princeton University Press, 1997.

Schermerhorn, Calvin. *Unrequited Toil: A History of United States Slavery*. Cambridge, UK: Cambridge University Press, 2018.

Schocket, Andrew M. *Fighting over the Founders: How We Remember the American Revolution*. New York: New York University Press, 2015.

Schoen, Brian. "Positive Goods and Necessary Evils: Commerce, Security, and Slavery in the Lower South, 1787–1837." In *Contesting Slavery: The Politics of Bondage and Freedom in the New American Nation*, edited by John Craig Hammond and Matthew Mason, 161–82. Charlottesville: University of Virginia Press, 2011.

Sehat, David. *The Jefferson Rule: How the Founding Fathers Became Infallible and Our Politics Inflexible*. New York: Simon & Schuster, 2015.

Shade, William G. "'The Most Delicate and Exciting Topics': Martin Van Buren, Slavery, and the Election of 1836." *Journal of the Early Republic* 18, no. 3 (1998): 459–84.

Shaffer, Arthur H. *The Politics of History: Writing the History of the American Revolution 1783–1815*. Chicago: Precedent Publishing, 1975.

Shalev, Eran. *Rome Reborn on Western Shores: Historical Imagination and the Creation of the American Republic*. Charlottesville: University of Virginia Press, 2009.

Silbey, Joel H. *Martin Van Buren and the Emergence of American Popular Politics*. New York: Rowman & Littlefield Publishers, Inc., 2002.

Singh Grewal, David, and Jedediah Purdy. "The Original Theory of Constitutionalism." *Yale Law Journal* 127, no. 3 (2018): 664–705.

Sinha, Manisha. "Did the Abolitionists Cause the Civil War?" In *The Abolitionist Imagination*, edited by Andrew Delbanco, 81–108. Cambridge, MA: Harvard University Press, 2012.

The Counterrevolution of Slavery: Politics and Ideology in Antebellum South Carolina. Chapel Hill: The University of North Carolina Press, 2000.

The Slave's Cause: A History of Abolition. New Haven: Yale University Press, 2016.

Smith, Rogers M. "Beyond Tocqueville, Myrdal, and Hartz: The Multiple Traditions in America." *American Political Science Review* 87, no. 3 (1993): 549–66.

Civic Ideals: Conflicting Visions of Citizenship in U.S. History. New Haven: Yale University Press, 1997.

Snethen, Worthington G. "The Black Code of the District of Columbia, in Force September 1st, 1848." In *Statutes on Slavery: The Pamphlet Literature, Series VII, Volume 2*, edited by Paul Finkelman, 177–239. New York: Garland Publishing, Inc., 1988.

Snowiss, Sylvia. "From Fundamental Law to the Supreme Law of the Land: A Reinterpretation of the Origin of Judicial Review." *Studies in American Political Development* 2 (1987): 1–67.

Judicial Review and the Law of the Constitution. New Haven: Yale University Press, 1990.

Solum, Lawrence B. "District of Columbia v. Heller and Originalism." *Northwestern University Law Review* 103, no. 2 (2009): 923–81.

Stauffer, John. "Fighting the Devil with His Own Fire." In *The Abolitionist Imagination*, 57–79. Cambridge, MA: Harvard University Press, 2012.

Strauss, David A. *The Living Constitution*. Oxford: Oxford University Press, 2010.

Swisher, Carl Brent. *Roger B. Taney*. New York: The Macmillan Company, 1935.

Tadman, Michael. *Speculators and Slaves: Masters, Traders, and Slaves in the Old South*. Madison: The University of Wisconsin Press, 1989.

Tang, Edward. "Writing the American Revolution: War Veterans in the Nineteenth-Century Cultural Memory." *Journal of American Studies* 32, no. 1 (1988): 63–80.

Tassel, David D. Van. *Recording America's Past: An Interpretation of the Development of Historical Studies in America, 1607–1884*. Chicago: The University of Chicago Press, 1960.

Tate, Gayle T. "Free Black Resistance in the Antebellum Era, 1830 to 1860." *Journal of Black Studies* 28, no. 6 (1998): 764–82.

tenBroek, Jacobus. *Equal under Law*. New York: First Collier Books, 1965.

Thorton, J. Mills. *Politics and Power in a Slave Society: Alabama, 1800–1860*. Baton Rouge: Louisiana State University Press, 1978.

Tomlins, Christopher. *Freedom Bound: Law, Labor, and Civic Identity in Colonizing English America, 1580–1865*. Cambridge, UK: Cambridge University Press, 2010.

Tremain, Mary. *Slavery in the District of Columbia: The Policy of Congress and the Struggle for Abolition*. New York: G. P. Putnam, 1892.

Tuck, Richard. *The Sleeping Sovereign: The Invention of Modern Democracy*. Cambridge, UK: Cambridge University Press, 2016.

Urofsky, Melvin I. *Supreme Decisions: Great Constitutional Cases and Their Impact*. Boulder: Westview Press, 2012.

Varon, Elizabeth R. *Disunion! The Coming of the American Civil War, 1789–1859*. Chapel Hill: The University of North Carolina Press, 2008.

Waldstreicher, David. *In the Midst of Perpetual Fetes: The Making of American Nationalism, 1776–1820*. Chapel Hill: The University of North Carolina Press, 1997.

Slavery's Constitution: From Revolution to Ratification. New York: Hill and Wang, 2009.

Warner, Michael. *The Letters of the Republic: Publication and the Public Sphere in Eighteenth-Century America*. Cambridge, MA: Harvard University Press, 1990.

White, Lawrence H. "Forward." In *Democratick Editorials: Essays in Jacksonian Political Economy*, edited by Lawrence H. White, xi–xix. Indianapolis: Liberty Fund, 1984.

Whittington, Keith E. "The New Originalism." *Georgetown Journal of Law & Public Policy* 22 (2004): 599–613.

Constitutional Interpretation: Textual Meaning, Original Intent, and Judicial Review. Lawrence: University of Kansas Press, 1999.

Wiecek, William M. "'The Blessings of Liberty': Slavery in the American Constitutional Order." In *Slavery and Its Consequences: The Constitution, Race, and Equality*, edited by Robert A. Goldwin and Art Kaufman, 23–44. Washington, DC: American Enterprise Institute, 1988.

The Sources of Antislavery Constitutionalism in America, 1760–1848. Ithaca: Cornell University Press, 1977.

Wilentz, Sean. "Jeffersonian Democracy and the Origins of Political Antislavery in the United States: The Missouri Crisis Revisited." *The Journal of the Historical Society* 4, no. 4 (2004): 375–401.

No Property in Man: Slavery and Antislavery at the Nation's Founding. Cambridge, MA: Harvard University Press, 2018.

Wilson, Clyde N., "Introduction." In *The Papers of John C. Calhoun: Volume XIV, 1837–1839*, edited by Clyde N. Wilson, xi–xxxiii. Columbia: University of South Carolina Press, 1981.

Winch, Julie. "The Making and Meaning of James Forten's 'Letters from a Man of Colour.'" *William & Mary Quarterly* 64, no. 1 (2007): 129–38.

Wirls, Daniel. "'The Only Mode of Avoiding Everlasting Debate': The Overlooked Senate Gag Rule for Antislavery Petitions." *Journal of the Early Republic* 27, no. 1 (2007): 115–38.

Wood, Gordon S. *Revolutionary Characters: What Made the Founders Different*. New York: The Penguin Press, 2006.

Woods Brown, Letitia. *Free Negroes in the District of Columbia 1790–1846*. New York: Oxford University Press, 1972.

Yingling, Charlton W. "No One Who Reads the History of Hayti Can Doubt the Capacity of Colored Men: Racial Formation and Atlantic Rehabilitation in New York City's Early Black Press, 1827–1841." *Early American Studies* 11, no. 2 (2013): 314–48.

Zaeske, Susan. *Signatures of Citizenship: Petitioning, Antislavery, & Women's Political Identity*. Chapel Hill: The University of North Carolina Press, 2003.

Zeitz, Joshua Michael. "The Missouri Compromise Reconsidered: Antislavery Rhetoric and the Emergence of the Free Labor Synthesis." *Journal of the Early Republic* 20, no. 3 (2000): 447–85.

Index

CPSIA information can be obtained
at www.ICGtesting.com
Printed in the USA
BVHW031744050422
633465BV00002B/31